# Party Position Change in American Politics
## Coalition Management

America's two-party system is highly stable, but its parties' issue positions are not. Democrats and Republicans have changed sides on many subjects, including trade, civil rights, defense spending, and fiscal policy and have polarized on newer issues like abortion and gun control. Yet party position change remains poorly understood. In this book David Karol views parties as coalitions of groups with intense preferences on particular issues managed by politicians. He explains important variations in party position change: the speed of shifts, the stability of new positions, and the extent to which change occurs via adaptation by incumbents. Karol shows that the key question is whether parties are reacting to changed preferences of coalition components, incorporating new constituencies, or experimenting on "groupless" issues. He reveals that adaptation by incumbents is a far greater source of change than was previously recognized. This study enhances our understanding of parties, interest groups, and representation.

David Karol is Assistant Professor of Political Science in the Charles and Louise Travers Department of Political Science at the University of California, Berkeley. He was formerly a visiting scholar at the Center for the Study of Democratic Politics at Princeton University. He is coauthor of *The Party Decides: Presidential Nominations before and after Reform* and coeditor of *Nominating the President: Evolution and Revolution in 2008 and Beyond*. His work has appeared in the *Journal of Politics, Studies in American Political Development, International Organization, Brookings Review,* and *The Forum*.

# Party Position Change in American Politics

## Coalition Management

**DAVID KAROL**
*University of California, Berkeley*

**CAMBRIDGE**
UNIVERSITY PRESS

CAMBRIDGE UNIVERSITY PRESS
Cambridge, New York, Melbourne, Madrid, Cape Town, Singapore,
São Paulo, Delhi, Dubai, Tokyo

Cambridge University Press
32 Avenue of the Americas, New York, NY 10013-2473, USA

www.cambridge.org
Information on this title: www.cambridge.org/9780521738194

First published 2009

Printed in the United States of America

*A catalog record for this publication is available from the British Library.*

*Library of Congress Cataloging in Publication Data*
Karol, David, 1969–
  Party position change in American politics : coalition management / David Karol.
    p.  cm.
  Includes bibliographical references and index.
  ISBN 978-0-521-51716-4 (hardback) – ISBN 978-0-521-73819-4 (pbk.)
  1. Political parties – United States.   2. Coalitions – United States.   3. Political
  planning – United States.   4. United States – Politics and government – 21st
  century.   I. Title.
  JK2265.K37   2009
  324.273–dc22        2009005016

ISBN 978-0-521-51716-4 Hardback
ISBN 978-0-521-73819-4 Paperback

*To my parents, Nathaniel H. and Liliane Karol, the only people happier than me to see this book in print*

# Contents

# List of Figures

# List of Tables

# Acknowledgments

This book began as a dissertation at UCLA supervised by Karen Orren and John Zaller. These two scholars differ in many respects, but they share a fierce and uncompromising integrity. Beyond my intellectual debt to both of them, which will be evident to readers, I have benefited enormously over the years from their friendship and wise counsel.

I thank my other friends and teachers from my UCLA days who took the time to read early versions of this project; these include Ben Bishin, Jorge Bravo, Scott Desposato, Joy Farmer, Paul Frymer, Scott James, Mark Kayser, Danise Kimball, Brian Lawson, John Londregan, Tom Schwartz, Barbara Sinclair, and the members of the Political Parties Reading Group, a group that sociologists or intellectual historians might one day note overlaps to a great extent with the Klugies. I also benefited from suggestions offered by readers beyond Westwood, including Larry Bartels, Fred Greenstein, Nathaniel H. Karol, and Eric Plutzer. Tim Nokken was a discussant for a conference paper that was much too long – and that he presciently said was the basis of a book.

More recently, this book has been enormously improved by the insightful suggestions offered by several Berkeley colleagues, including Jack Citrin, Jacob Hacker, Paul Pierson, Eric Schickler, Laura Stoker, Rob Van Houweling, and Ray Wolfinger. I owe special thanks to Eric for organizing a book conference and bringing John Aldrich, Ben Highton, and Byron Shafer to IGS to give me the benefit of their wisdom along with that of other Berkeley colleagues who attended, including Henry Brady, Bob Kagan, Taeku Lee, and David Vogel. This conference was also greatly enlivened and enriched by the participation of Jane Green and Rob Mickey, who were visiting Berkeley at the time.

The enthusiasm of Nelson Polsby for this project was a tremendous source of encouragement to me, and I very much regret that he is not here to see it in print. It was an honor to have been his colleague all too briefly.

I also want to acknowledge Bob Grey of Grinnell College, who is more responsible than any other teacher for my becoming a political scientist. Finally, thanks to Lew Bateman are in order for believing in this project and finding thoughtful, if demanding, reviewers who made this a better book.

# Introduction

When Robert C. Byrd of West Virginia reached the U.S. Senate in 1959, Democrats supported high levels of defense spending and favored tax cuts to stimulate the economy, even at the risk of deficits. Byrd's party was deeply divided over matters of race and on balance less supportive of civil rights than the Republicans. Democrats also retained an inclination toward freer trade that dated back to the antebellum period. Although party positions were evident on these and other topics, issues that now polarize the parties like abortion and gun control were not on the political agenda.

Five decades later Byrd remains in the Senate and very much a Democrat. Yet in many other respects the identities of the two parties have changed radically. By the latter part of Byrd's tenure, his party was associated with opposition to high levels of defense spending, willingness to raise taxes to balance the budget, and support for civil rights. Support for freer trade had become a Republican cause. Meanwhile, new issues, including abortion and gun control, had arisen and become increasingly partisan.

These shifts occurred over decades during which many politicians came and went. None of the senators with whom Byrd served in 1959 remain in office. Thus many reasonably assume that elite replacement must underlie the changes in party policies that have occurred. Yet this view is largely mistaken. To a great extent, adaptation at the microlevel of individuals has driven change at the macrolevel of parties. Senator Byrd himself has not survived without adapting. Although often seen as an independent-minded relic of a bygone age, close study reveals that on issue after issue, as his party changed, Byrd did as well. In this respect he was typical of leading politicians in both parties.

In this book I seek to explain why and how such changes occur. The dynamics of party position change are well worth exploring. Some may simply be interested in why it is that Democrats and Republicans shifted positions on a particular issue. Many readers may be surprised to learn how recent parties' associations with issue positions that now seem central to their identity really are. More broadly, students of politics may seek to understand what logic underlies the ever-changing combinations of policies the parties offer voters.

Beyond its intrinsic interest, even gaining a better understanding of party position change is important for those chiefly concerned with other aspects of politics. Parties' relative positions on issues as well as their absolute ones influence voter choice. This is even true to an extent when candidates break from their party; voters use parties' issue reputations to infer individual candidates' stands. For students of public opinion, party positioning on issues also matters a great deal. Given the well-documented tendency of voters to adopt stands espoused by their party's leaders, shifts in parties' positioning also affect public opinion.

The chapters that follow include much historical detail, many simple quantitative analyses, and extensive engagement both with previous scholarship on the phenomenon of party position change generally and with prior studies of the development of particular issues. Yet amid all this complexity, four simple claims, each of which contrasts in important ways with prevailing theories, emerge in this book.

First, the best way to understand the dynamics of party position change is to model parties as coalitions of groups with intense preferences on particular issues managed by politicians. This understanding is not the only possible view of parties; they have also been seen as groupings of individuals united by shared values, or, rather more plausibly, as entities designed to serve candidates and officeholders. The coalitional view I develop inclines us to expect different dynamics of party position change in issue areas in which groups are prominent compared to those in which they are weak or absent. Similarly, this view implies that development of parties' positioning will differ notably, depending on whether groups are focused on an issue.

Second, I show that parties' repositioning on policies, be it a polarization on a previously cross-cutting issue or a reversal of the parties' previous relative positions, occurs chiefly via adaptation on the part of incumbents. Conversion or "flip-flopping" is pervasive both among politicians who seek positions of national leadership and among more obscure members of Congress as well. It drives party position change. This means that even in an era of incumbency advantage and low turnover in Congress parties can realign on issues rapidly.

Third, since parties' positions on issues change over time while very few politicians change parties, a reinterpretation of the stability in the "spatial" positions of members of Congress revealed by various roll-call scaling or "ideal point" estimation techniques is in order. This stability in the spatial positioning of legislators has often been attributed to their reputational concerns; fear of being branded an unreliable flip-flopper is said to inhibit position changing.

Yet, as I show, the only way a politician can maintain a reputation as a loyal Democrat or Republican over time is by adopting the new party line when it changes. I demonstrate that the most successful politicians in both parties have repeatedly demonstrated this sort of flexibility. Seen this way, flip-flopping is the key to ideological consistency and party loyalty; the stability in politicians' spatial positions is a result of perpetual adaptation on particular issues. This understanding casts a new light on studies focused on "polarization," emphasizing that the ideological poles themselves have changed greatly over time. What it meant to be a liberal in 1963 was different in several ways from what it implied in 1983, and such changes cannot be usefully understood by viewing politics in a unidimensional way. In some cases parties took up entirely new issues. In other cases they traded places, with each party taking up the side of the argument they had previously opposed. These changes occurred while the relative positions of two major parties remained stable in many other issue areas.

Finally, building on my coalitional view of parties, I develop models that explain variation in the process of party position change along several dimensions. There is much variation to explain. Some party position changes are rapid while others are gradual. Some party positions are durable while others are reversed repeatedly. Although conversion or "flip-flopping" by leading politicians is always a key mechanism producing party position change, its importance varies across issues as well. In some cases the role of adaptation by existing elites is overwhelming, yet in other instances conversion combines with elite turnover to reposition parties on issues.

Although this process may appear messy, an understanding of parties as coalitions of groups with intense preferences managed by office-seeking politicians reveals an underlying logic. Identifying the impetus for a party position change enables us to predict its speed, its durability, and the extent to which it occurs via adaptation by existing elites or their replacement by new ones. Politicians' electoral concerns underlie their actions in all cases, but the development of parties' positions on issues will vary systematically depending on the impetus for change.

In some cases elected officials react to new preferences expressed by long-standing party coalition components. If keeping old friends requires new policies, most politicians are happy to oblige. When a party elite is responding to new demands by an existing coalition, component change is rapid and occurs primarily through adaptation or position switching by incumbents. The new position should be stable since the party coalition component will compel party leaders to maintain it.

Yet politicians are also proactive, recruiting new components to their coalitions and experimenting with policies that are not important for narrow groups but may attract broad-based support for their party and themselves. Change stemming from politicians' incorporation of a new group in their coalition will be more gradual. Some elected officials will adapt in order to stay in the good graces of the new entrant into their party's coalition.

However, elite replacement also plays an important role in such cases because entrenched incumbents can often win reelection without courting new groups. By contrast, the next generation of aspirants to office within a party will have a strong incentive to adopt stances popular with party-linked groups. So there is more inertia in parties' stands in these cases.

Such inertia also exists at the mass level. Voters' party identification and the initial deference of many incumbents to local opinion mean that new groups' entry into party coalitions and the related reorientation of parties' issue positions is a gradual process. Yet once a group is ensconced in a party the new position should be stable.

Finally, in some cases party politicians experiment with new positions that they hope will prove broadly popular, but that are not of special concern to a particular group of voters and activists. Since such changes are not dependent on the movement of voters into party coalitions they can be rapid and will occur chiefly via adaptation among incumbents rather than elite replacement. Yet because these positions are not anchored by components of parties' coalitions, they are apt to prove unstable over time.

PLAN OF THE BOOK

The book proceeds as follows. In Chapter 1, after examining existing work on party position change, which is mostly found in the "realignment" and "issue evolution" literatures, I define key terms and lay out my perspective on party position change, stressing a view of parties as coalitions of groups with intense preferences on different issues in a multidimensional political setting. I also discuss issues of measurement.

In the subsequent chapters I present three different models of change and examine several issues in light of them. In Chapter 2 I focus on the process of coalition maintenance via a case study of the evolution of party positions on trade policy. Chapter 3 includes elaboration of coalition group incorporation with close studies of the parties' polarization on the issues of abortion and gun control. I also more briefly discuss other issues that this model may illuminate, including support for private schools and tort reform.

In Chapter 4 I focus on the case of civil rights or racial politics. This case, so important in the literature and American politics, is worthy of special attention. It is also distinctive in that key aspects of its development are captured by both the coalition maintenance and group incorporation models I present in previous chapters. I briefly note that this was also true of other issues including women's rights.

In Chapter 5 I explore two "groupless" issues: defense spending and fiscal policy. In both cases parties adopted stands trying to expand their support, but not targeting or incorporating an organized group that would subsequently constrain them. As a result, both issues developed in a different manner from cases in which parties are appeasing allies or incorporating new groups. I note that some other issues, including support for the space program, also seem to fit in this category. In Chapter 6 I conclude with a summary of my findings, discussion of their implications, and review of directions for future study.

I

# Explaining Party Position Change

## Theory and Method

> The Right Honourable Gentleman caught the Whigs bathing and walked away with their clothes. He has left them in the full enjoyment of their liberal position, and he is himself a strict conservative of their garments.
>
> Benjamin Disraeli on Lord Peel's support for the repeal of the Corn Laws, speech in the House of Commons, 1845

In this book I seek to explain party position change in American politics. Although every issue is unique, my contention is that we can generalize about the process of parties' development of positions to a great extent. Close inspection reveals that similar dynamics are evident in very different issue areas. The argument I make is about the interaction of parties, issues, and groups. It is also focused on parties' *relative* positions on issues. All these terms can be used in different ways for diverse purposes. So before proceeding to an elaboration of theory, cases, and evidence, I define the key concepts I employ. I also explain my focus on parties' *relative* positions on issues.

### WHAT IS A PARTY?

American political parties are notoriously poorly bounded institutions. Unlike parties in most democracies, they have no formal membership. Party registration exists only in some states and is managed by state governments. The parties themselves do not admit and expel members, unlike any true membership organization.

As a result of these fuzzy boundaries, scholars have long disagreed over basic questions such as "what is a party?" and "who runs parties?" Two pioneering students of American parties, V. O. Key and

E. E. Schattschneider, differed over whether voters, even those who supported a party's candidates, registered under its name, and voted in its primaries, could usefully be seen as part of the party. Key (1958, 181) wrote of the "party in the electorate" referring to "groups who regard themselves as party members," yet Schattschneider (1942, 53) insisted that "whatever else the parties may be, they are not associations of the voters who support the party candidates."

For purposes of this book I define parties as coalitions of groups with intense preferences on issues managed by politicians. This may not seem like a controversial view, but other conceptions of parties have been quite prominent in the scholarly literature. Influential accounts model modern American parties as groupings dominated by candidates (Downs 1957; Schlesinger 1991) motivated by the desire for office.

Scholars have not always looked at parties from the candidate perspective. They have often acknowledged – sometimes ruefully – the importance of party activists who do not seek office for themselves and are motivated by policy concerns. Wilson (1962) and Wildavsky (1965) are two early studies in this vein. A recent example is Bawn et al. (2006).

Some scholars have combined these perspectives. In an influential study Aldrich (1995) offers a primarily candidate-centered account but makes room for the role of policy-oriented activists, especially in recent decades when patronage has declined as a motivation for party work.

The view of parties as coalitions of groups with intense preferences on particular policies managed by politicians that I develop has certain advantages. Unlike models of parties as "top-down" candidate-dominated institutions or "bottom-up" groupings controlled by activists with broad ideological concerns, it leads us to expect different dynamics of party position change on issues in which parties incorporate groups with intense preferences in contrast to those evident in policy areas in which such groups are largely absent. I show that the autonomy of party politicians varies systematically across issues depending on the composition of their coalitions.

Although my focus is on group–party interaction, I recognize that some voters support a party without identifying with any component group and others are active in it because they are attracted to its platform across a range of issues. A successful party will attract many such people, and they are worthy of study. They are not, however, my focus in this book because I contend that they are seldom the source of party position change. Specific policy reorientations usually have specific causes and focused advocates. It is precisely the intense focus of these groups that gives them power and compels politicians to be responsive to them.

In this book I also largely ignore the formal structure of committees that is an important part of the textbook party, agreeing with Schlesinger (1984, 379) that in the case of American parties, "the formal structure is obviously not the real organization." Although the formal party organizations play an important role in campaigns, they do not determine the policy positions of elected officials that define the party in the minds of voters and that are my focus here.

## WHAT IS AN ISSUE?

It seems clear enough what a roll call is and who is an MC (member of Congress). With a bit more controversy we can define parties as well. Yet delineating "issues" is less straightforward. The conception of "issue" that I employ is broader than some and narrower than others. For purposes of this book, issues are distinct areas of public policy characterized by ongoing controversy.

American political history is replete with issues, the contours of which were agreed on even by individuals who differed greatly on policy. In earlier eras observers tended to speak of "questions": "The Tariff Question," "The Negro Question," and "The Liquor Question" are a few of the most prominent examples. My delineation of issues is based on my understanding of how political actors perceived them at the time.

I focus on durable policy controversies, not disputes over procedure or institutional prerogatives: for example, the filibuster, "judicial activism," "federalism," "independent counsels," or "executive privilege." Richard Piper (1997) shows that parties are quite opportunistic and inconsistent in these matters. Where they stand depends on where they sit at the moment. Thus I do not explore such cases because they do not speak to this book's core theoretical concerns about how partisan coalitions and issue alignments develop.

Instead, I focus on the relative positions of the two parties in controversial policy areas. My cases are trade, abortion, gun control, race, national defense, and fiscal policy. I examine these issues both because of their importance in American politics in the last five decades and because of their prominence in the existing literature, which fails to capture important aspects of their development. Since this is a study of long-term change, I explore parties' basic orientations in policy areas, not on episodic controversies within them. Thus I examine the parties' stands on defense spending, not the MX missile or the B-2 bomber, and trade policy, not the Smoot-Hawley tariff or NAFTA. Although I focus on six issue areas, in each chapter I discuss other examples of party position change that seem to be marked by the same dynamics as the cases under examination.

## WHAT ARE GROUPS?

I argue that parties' changing positions on issues can usually be attributed to shifts in preferences among groups already in their coalition or party elites' attempts to attract a new group to their side. It is important, then, to clarify what I mean by "group." I distinguish between groups and organizations. A group is a self-aware collection of individuals who share intense concerns about a particular policy area. Such a group may support numerous organizations, without being reducible to any one of them.

For example, the "religious right" is a group that has been prominent in American politics since the late 1970s, during which time organizations such as the Moral Majority, the Christian Coalition, and Focus on the Family have waxed and waned. Similarly, the labor movement has been aligned with the Democratic Party since the New Deal, while the AFL competed against and then merged with the upstart CIO, and several unions have entered and left the resulting federation. Such organizations may also be active outside of politics – as unions, firms, and churches all are – but need not be – for example, the League of Conservation Voters.

Party leaders adopt policies that appeal to groups because they believe that doing so, rather than taking stands consistent with the majority preferences revealed by polling, will produce the most electoral benefits. Organizations within groups also control resources such as funds and activist networks that can aid parties in campaigns. In an era in which patronage armies are no more, the resources groups can mobilize as party "subcontractors" (Skinner 2007, 9) are prized by candidates.[1] Yet it is wrong to view these entities as mere business partners whom politicians can easily contract and disengage. Over time groups become entrenched components of party coalitions and influence critical decisions such as the nomination of candidates. Most of the time politicians take the group composition of their party as largely fixed and adapt themselves to it.

---

[1] Not all groups are equally partisan in their orientation. Groups that are in conflict with other groups over policy rather than merely seeking distributive benefits at public expense are most likely to be drawn into parties (Hansen 1991).

WHY DO PARTIES' RELATIVE POSITIONS MATTER?

In this book I seek to explain changes in the parties' relative positions on issues, rather than the emergence of specific or absolute policy stands. In this sense there are several possible changes to explain. An issue may emerge from obscurity. A topic that has cut across party lines may come to separate the two camps. A formerly divisive issue can disappear. Most dramatically, the parties may "trade places," as the Democrats adopt a position once associated with Republicans and the GOP takes up a traditionally Democratic theme.

An effort to understand parties' changing issue positioning might seem more intuitively approached by asking why Democratic or Republican leaders adopted specific or absolute stands rather than relative positions, and many scholars have indeed explored such questions. Why did Nixon turn to wage and price controls (Matusow 1998)? Why did the Clinton administration embrace "managed competition" as the centerpiece of its ill-fated health care plan (Hacker 1997)?

Yet as important as explaining the precise policies enacted and advocated is, the relative positions of parties matter greatly as well.[2] Politicians do not adopt stances in a vacuum. They care greatly about where a stand situates them vis-à-vis the other party. They have reason to do so. Major research programs in political science suggest that the parties' relative positions on issues have important consequences. These traditions, however, are more focused on the results of party positions than their causes.

In the tradition of "spatial modeling" associated with Downs (1957) and his many heirs, voters support the party closest to them on issues. Parties' relative proximity to voters is key, not their absolute distance from them. In some variants the parties' absolute distance matters as well, because a party may suffer from abstentions if it moves too far away from "its" voters. Yet even in this case the parties' relative positions still matter.

One limitation of the spatial approach is that the substantive meaning of the ideological continuum is generally taken for granted. Yet the

---

[2] There is no necessary connection between movement of the debate on an issue and change in the parties' relative positions. For example, when the Cold War ended both parties favored reduced defense budgets, but Republicans remained relatively more supportive of military spending than Democrats. Parties can also move in the same direction at different rates, altering their relative positions. Rochon (1998, 88) notes that when the GOP became the more conservative party on race in the 1960s it was still more supportive of racial equality in an absolute sense than either party had been for most of U.S. history.

bundle of positions that constitute conservative or Republican orthodoxy and its liberal and Democratic opposite is not stable. Instead, it evolves over time in ways that spatial theorists seldom explain.

Party positions also figure prominently in studies outside of the Downsian tradition. Students of political psychology show that voters use "party images" as heuristics to infer candidates' issue stands from their party affiliations (Conover and Feldman 1983; Popkin 1991; Rahn 1993; Koch 2001). Work in this vein focuses on how stable party images affect voter behavior, not how they emerge in the first place.

Other scholars explore the role of parties' issue-specific reputations in campaigns (Norpoth and Buchanan 1992; Ansolabehere and Iyengar 1994; Sellers 1998; Koch 2001; Simon 2002; Holian 2004; Kaufmann 2004; Sigelman and Buell 2004). Petrocik (1996) holds that candidates stress issues their party "owns" and downplay others. Yet issue ownership theory does not explain change in parties' stands. Petrocik (1996, 826–828) notes that parties' reputations "probably change slowly, when they change at all" because they stem from "recursive" relationships: groups support parties that represent their interests while party elites take stands that benefit their backers.

Moreover, scholars hold that party elites' issue positioning matters because it shapes public opinion. Zaller (1992) shows that voters take cues on issues from party elites. If Democratic voters learn that leading Democrats favor less defense spending than Republicans, then they will tend to adopt this view. Campbell et al.'s (1960) view of party identification as the "unmoved mover" that shapes voters' preferences and views more than it is shaped by them still finds much empirical support (Bartels 2002; Goren 2005).

## EARLIER APPROACHES

Thus, for many reasons, it is important to understand the development of party positions on issues. In fact, scholars have long studied this process. The two leading approaches are found in the realignment and issue evolution literatures.

Realignment theory was long the dominant approach to explaining changes in the policies, identities, and fortunes of American parties.[3] In the leading formulation, parties' issue positions were said to shift along

---

[3] An incomplete list of major statements in this research tradition includes Key (1955, 1959), Schattschneider (1960), Pomper (1967), Andersen (1979), Clubb, Flanigan, and

with voters' behavior every few decades. A periodization of U.S. political history into five "party systems" won wide acceptance (Burnham 1970).

Yet discontent with the realignment literature has mounted (Ladd 1990; Silbey 1991; Mayhew 2002; Ware 2006). Explanations of regularly occurring realignments, such as a periodic build-up of societal pressure that overthrows "politics as usual" (Burnham 1970) or generational change among voters (Beck 1974), ultimately failed to convince.

Consensus over periodization has also collapsed. Since the 1960s scholars have argued about what, if anything, replaced the Fifth or "New Deal" party system. In various ways many scholars found the traditional concept of realignment unhelpful in illuminating recent developments. The rise in ticket splitting and resulting stretches of divided government led to claims that the system itself was "dealigning" (Beck 1977; Ladd 1981), that the modern fiscal state made parties less relevant and undermined the potential for realignment (Coleman 1996), and that each party represented a majority coalition, albeit on different issues (Shafer 2003). While arguing strongly for the continued relevance of parties and even embracing the notion of "critical eras," Aldrich (1995, 279) argues that the changes parties undergo can only sometimes be understood as realignments in the traditional sense. In other cases, he contends, it is the institutional form of the parties that evolves more than their coalitions. Bartels (1998) and Mayhew (2002) doubt whether the "System of 1896" marked a true break from the post–Civil War alignment, further challenging the descriptive utility of the "party system" approach.

A final flaw of the realignment approach is that it implies a direct linkage between issues. Policies are seen as bundled and going in and out of fashion with the rise and fall of political alignments.[4] In fact, parties' policies and coalitions are always evolving, but not on one track; stasis may reign in one issue area while parties' stands and coalitions evolve in another. The development of parties' stands on issues is more akin to Orren and Skowronek's (2004) "multiple orders" than to any all-encompassing party system.

---

Zingale (1980), Petrocik (1981) Sundquist (1983), Brady (1988), Gamm (1989), and Plotke (1996.)

[4] In an intriguing formal model of realignment Miller and Schofield (2003) depict parties maneuvering in a two-dimensional space with axes representing "economic" and "social" issues. Despite their move toward realism, these authors, like earlier theorists, assume that issues are bundled and parties' positions on them evolve simultaneously. Yet politicians target groups with particular concerns. They do not court gun owners by opposing abortion or cater to labor unions by defending wilderness.

One promising alternative to the search for realignments is exploring the effect of particular issues on parties. This "issue evolution" approach dates from Carmines and Stimson's (1989) pioneering study of race and party politics. More recent examples include Berkman (1993) and Burns (1997) on taxes, Adams (1997) on abortion, Fordham (2007a) on defense, Sanbonmatsu (2002) on "gender issues," Shoch (2001) on trade, and Wolbrecht (2000) on "women's rights."

The issue evolution studies, while valuable, are seldom comparative and yield few generalizations. Beyond the focus on individual issues, two ideas predominate in this literature. The first is a "top-down" view of change in which party elites adopt positions before their voters do. I present new evidence from some cases supporting this claim. Yet I show that party elites also respond to groups who can determine their own interests.

The second common claim is that parties' policies evolve via elite replacement. In this view politicians do not change their positions. Thus an older generation of leaders must pass the torch to their successors for parties to alter their positions on an issue. When explained, this premise is based on voters' alleged mistrust of inconsistency; fear of being stigmatized as a flip-flopper locks incumbents into positions. A key implication of this claim is that in a system marked by a slow rate of turnover, such as the contemporary Congress, change in parties' issue positioning must be very gradual.

I show that this claim is largely false. Some party position change occurs rapidly, with replacement playing a minimal role. Yet even when change is gradual, it may not stem from elite turnover. Moreover, the single-issue case studies that dominate the issue evolution literature do not explain variation in the speed at which parties adjust their positions on issues, the stability of those new stands, or the degree to which elite conversion explains change.

Faced with the messiness of history, some scholars seek a moratorium on theory. Gerring (1998) finds several monocausal theories wanting and concludes, "Party ideological change resists generalizable causal analysis." He insists that we must resign ourselves to complexity: "The argument that 'lots of things' drive issue evolution is critical to the understanding of American party politics" (275).

Although it is wrong to force all of history onto the procrustean bed of one model, the appropriate response to complexity is not to abandon attempts to generalize in favor of a descriptive approach. I contend that a focus on changes in party coalitions and shifts in preferences among elements of them illuminates most party position change.

Moreover, in the minority of cases in which politicians act independently of groups the dynamics of party position change differ from group-inspired adaptation in predictable ways. Thus it is important to determine the extent to which politicians are constrained or autonomous in determining their party's policy. Philip Converse (1964, 257) addressed the way elites process new issues:

> In politics new issues are constantly arising that are difficult before the fact to relate to such a (liberal-conservative) yardstick.... Some of these intrinsically "orthogonal" issues may remain unrelated to the dimension, and if they become of intense importance, they can split existing parties and redefine alignments. More typically, however, elites that are known on some other grounds to be "liberal" or "conservative" ferret out some limited aspect of an issue for which they can argue some liberal-conservative relevance and begin to drift to one of the alternative positions in disproportionate numbers. Then, either because of the aspect highlighted or because of simple pressures toward party competition, their adversaries drift toward the opposing position. These positions come to be perceived as "liberal" or "conservative" even though such alignments would have been scarcely predictable on logical grounds.

Converse highlights a key difference among issues: some are more explosive than others. I argue that the constraints on party politicians vary according to the composition of their coalitions and the degree to which their components are focused on an issue. On issues that link a self-aware and organized group to a party the dynamics of change differ greatly from what I term "groupless issues" on which politicians are freer to "make it up as they go along" and carry their supporters with them. This is a fundamental distinction among issues that has received little attention from scholars.[5] The ability to explore its implications is a major advantage of the comparative approach I employ in this book.

### IDEOLOGY: A CAUSE OR AN EFFECT?

"Ideology" is one explanation for the divergence of parties on issues, especially when there is no obvious basis for the division in party coalitions. This is not implausible. Although the assumption that officials have only careerist motivations explains much (Downs 1957; Mayhew 1974), politicians do act on their notions of the public good.

---

[5] For example, Aldrich (1995, ch. 6) discusses the role of party activists in leading their parties' nominees to diverge somewhat from the median voter. Yet he does not differentiate among issues in this sense because he is focused on ideological activists with preferences on a range of topics.

Yet reliance on ideology among politicians as an explanation for party position change is problematic. It can explain too much. To use ideology as an independent variable we must determine its origins and measure it independently of the result to be explained. Yet although politicians' constituency characteristics and party affiliation can be measured, ideology is not directly observable.

We have also long known that the bundle of beliefs often called ideology is far less pervasive among voters than it is among political elites (Campbell et al. 1960; Converse 1964). For example, despite decades of signals from politicians that views on social issues "go with" opinions about the welfare state, recent studies (Layman 2001, 34; Stimson 2004, 78) still reveal little connection between survey respondents' views on abortion and their attitudes on economic issues. These findings strongly suggest that the bundling of issues evident among politicians is less a straightforward reflection of voters' values than a contingent result of coalition politics.

Moreover, any ideology that is more than a single-sentence *directive*, for example, "reduce the size of government," will be open to interpretation in its application. Multiple values are often implicated, and trade-offs are not clearly specified. Often one value wins out as a liberal or conservative position crystallizes. Yet it remains necessary to explain *how* elites decide that a certain policy is the best expression of conservative or liberal values and especially why they come to see a change is necessary.

Trade policy, one of my cases, illustrates the complexity. Should "liberals" view free trade as a policy promoting cooperation among nations and providing jobs for workers in developing countries while freeing consumers from the regressive tax of tariffs? This is, in fact, the traditional "liberal" view.

Or should free trade be seen as a policy that undercuts unions and decimates the "Rustbelt" and textile towns while leading to sweatshops and pollution in poor countries? *Both* those descriptions capture something of the truth, and it is unclear why one has come to trump the other if we remain in the realm of ideas.

Even when the values that inform decision making are shared, causal understandings are crucial and malleable. People with the same goals can differ over empirical questions. Can guns be combined with butter without damaging the economy? Do deficits cause inflation? The frequent emergence of consensus as to the "correct" position in each partisan camp should not lead us to accept the circular claim that every shift was the inevitable fruit of shared if unobserved values. Yet policies fall in and out of fashion among party elites. Below I explain how such shifts occur.

## EXPLAINING PARTY POSITION CHANGE: PREMISES AND THREE MODELS

In discussing shifts in parties' positions on issues, scholars differ regarding several dimensions of change. One key dispute concerns the role of elites. Carmines and Stimson (1989), Zaller (1992), and others emphasize the role of leading politicians in producing party position change in what has been termed a "top-down" approach. By contrast, Lee (2002) stresses the "bottom-up" role of social movements. Scholars also differ over the speed at which parties change. Burnham (1970) discusses rapid "critical" realignments, while Key (1955, 1959) also saw the possibility of gradual "secular" realignments. Carmines and Stimson (1989, 143) argue that "issue evolutions" feature a "punctuated equilibrium" in which a burst of change is followed by a long period of accretion.

To make progress we must move beyond these "either or" debates. Instead of insisting that leaders are proactive or reactive, constrained or unconstrained, that issue shifts are necessarily rapid or slow, or that they occur via elite replacement or conversion, we should recognize and seek to explain the variation evident on all these dimensions.

Politicians in interaction with groups that have intense preferences on particular issues are continually reinventing parties. When seeking to understand the development of an issue the two key questions are these: (1) Are politicians adapting in order to please a particular group and (2) Is this group already in their coalition at the beginning of the process? The answers to these questions determine the pattern of the resulting change.

Although many cases of party position change stem from the changing preferences or alignment of a group, there are also instances in which parties revise their stand on "groupless" issues. Some scholars might argue that issues that do not alter the group composition of party coalitions are not "realigning issues" or cases of issue evolution. Yet even if an issue does not alter the group basis of parties, it may still affect their electoral fortunes by adding or subtracting from their strength across the board.

For example, although I show that the parties' changing positions on defense spending do *not* derive from the presence of groups in their coalitions, such stands may still have electoral consequences. Several authors (Abramowitz 1994; Miller and Shanks 1996; Petrocik 1996; but see Mayer 1993) contend that this issue helped GOP presidential candidates during the 1980s.

Moreover, the process of party position change is interesting in its own right, even if in a given case it may have few immediately identifiable electoral consequences. If we seek to understand parties' behavior, it is useful to study shifts on issues even when they are not associated with the realignment of voting blocs, while recognizing that the dynamics of such changes may differ from cases in which the group composition of a party evolves.

## PREMISES AND MODELS OF PARTY POSITION CHANGE

Below I present three models of party position change, each of which is an aspect of *coalition management*. I explain their differing consequences for the speed of change, the role of conversion versus replacement among elites, and the stability of the new position. I group cases according to which model best captures their development. In creating these models I build on simple and mostly intuitive premises:

1. *Issues vary in the extent to which they are characterized by active interest groups focused on the topic.* Some issues are groupless, whereas others are characterized by a tug of war between groups focused on the topic who dominate the policy debate.
2. *Groups vary in the extent to which they are included in party coalitions;* for example, environmentalists and pro-life activists are at present far more closely tied to parties than are advocates for veterans or farmers.
3. Groups present in party coalitions constrain their party to be "better" than its rival on their issue, that is, to take a position relatively closer to the group in question. This is simply the claim that each party's core constituent groups are, at a minimum, able to force party elites to promote more favorable policies than the other party offers on its core issue.
4. It takes time for a group to change its position in the party system, whether it moves from one party coalition to another or along the continuum from nonpartisanship to partisanship. This premise is supported by decades of research on the stickiness of party identification. Voters' identities are multifaceted, and their identification with a single group is seldom total. To the extent that a group's power stems from its ability to sway voters as opposed to providing funds, changes in its alignment vis-à-vis the party system will be especially gradual.
5. *Politicians have more difficulty making connections with new groups than in adapting in response to old allies.* This is the least

intuitive premise. Certainly, elected officials modify their stands in order to win new friends. Indeed, one of my chief claims in this book is that "flip-flopping" is more common than scholars say. I merely contend that making new friends is harder than adapting to please old ones. This premise is supported by Fenno's work on the phases of congressional careers. Fenno (1978, 210) identifies a "protectionist" phase in which "established practices – and particularly their associated patterns of access – become constraining; and home styles tend to be resistant to change." Incumbency advantage lets legislators survive for a time without forging new ties.

A few conclusions flow from these plausible premises. Position changes linked to movement of groups into party coalitions should be slower than those stemming from shifts in the preferences of old allies, and slower than repositioning by parties on issues on which groups are not influential. Party position changes based on the incorporation of groups should be more dependent on elite replacement. By contrast, party position changes based on group activity, be it the shift in preferences of an existing party ally or the entry of a new one, should be more stable than those not connected to groups. We can now identify three models of party position change. I summarize them in Table 1-1.

In the case of *coalition maintenance,* elected officials respond to new demands by groups already ensconced within their party coalition. Typically, social or economic changes will convince a group's leadership that traditional policies no longer serve their interests. The group in question can articulate its own interests and give cues to party leaders, a fact that limits the autonomy of politicians. Party leaders may not accede to all of a group's demands, but they will be constrained to maintain a sufficient differential between themselves and the opposition on the issue to motivate the group in question to remain loyal.

When a shift stems from changing preferences on the part of a party coalition component it should be rapid, because it does not require politicians to forge ties to new groups, or voters to alter their loyalties, processes characterized by inertia on both sides. The new stand should be stable as well, so long as the conditions that caused the party-linked groups' preferences to shift persist. Elite replacement should not be an important factor because incumbents will have strong ties with the group seeking the new policy. I argue that the reversals in the parties' relative positions on trade policy and race (chiefly among Northern politicians and voters) can be understood as instances of this process.

TABLE 1-1. *Models of Party Position Change*

| | Coalition Maintenance | Coalition Group Incorporation | Coalition Expansion |
|---|---|---|---|
| Initiators of change | Party-linked group | Party politicians | Party politicians |
| Autonomy of party elites | Limited throughout | Initially great, but declining over time | Great throughout |
| Role of elite turnover | Minor | Significant | Minor |
| Speed of process | Rapid | Gradual | Rapid |
| Stability of new position | Stable | Most stable | Unstable |
| Cases | Trade policy, race (in the North) | Abortion, gun control, race (in the South) | Defense spending, tax/fiscal policy |

In the second process: *coalition group incorporation*, party leaders shift positions to attract a particular constituency. A formerly cross-cutting issue becomes increasingly partisan. Parties change positions more slowly in such cases than in instances of coalition maintenance (or coalition expansion described below), and elite replacement may matter more than in the other processes. This process bears a resemblance to V. O. Key's "secular realignment" model of change.

The slower pace of change and greater role of elite replacement in such cases stem from the fact that these issues require politicians to redefine their coalitions along with their policies. When new issues arise outside the party system, entrenched incumbents respond initially to localized cues and seek to reflect majority sentiment in what Fenno (1978) terms their "geographical constituency." At first the "subconstituencies" of politicians of both parties in a state or district, that is, the primary voters and activists to whom officials are closest, might differ little on a new issue. Division among a party's officials leaves the party's image fuzzy and discourages the realignment of groups. Party identification also initially holds back some members of a group, especially while many elected officials defer to local sentiment on the issue. The slowness of the group's entry into a party coalition further delays the parties' crystallization of new stands.

Yet as a new group enters a party, it gains leverage over the party's elected officials, leading them to increasingly reflect the group's preferences rather than overall sentiment in a state or district. This shift in turn further stimulates group members to support the party. This process is iterative and may occur over many years. As in the case of coalition maintenance, once inside the party, the group in question ensures that the new stand is maintained. If it is not, the group can support challengers in primaries or – in extremis – disrupt the coalition in the general election. Thus politicians' autonomy declines over time on such issues. The cases of abortion, gun control, and race (chiefly in the South) fit this model.

Finally, in the third process, *coalition expansion*, party leaders adopt a new position to improve their standing with the public generally. These issues can be seen as groupless because the shift is prompted by neither the demands of a party's current or prospective organized constituency. In such cases leaders are freer to craft new positions and explain how they are consistent with the interests of their supporters.

Such change is rapid because it is initiated by party elites and district-based cues do not cross-pressure elected officials. Nor is the gradual readjustment of voters' party identification a prerequisite for change. In this respect such movement is more similar to coalition maintenance than coalition group incorporation. Both of the former are closer to the "critical" realignment model than the "secular realignment" one that seems to capture the dynamics of coalition group incorporation.

Yet since no organized group constrains party leaders, the new issue position that has been rapidly adopted is less stable than stands resulting from coalition maintenance or coalition group incorporation. Having shifted, leaders retain autonomy and are free to reverse themselves again. Tax and defense politics offer examples of this dynamic.

When groups linked to parties are focused on an issue, the persistence of divergent party policies is no surprise. Downs himself argued that total convergence would occur only under certain highly unrealistic conditions. To the extent that a group is bound to a party on the basis of an issue, politicians are compelled to maintain some differential between their position and that of the opposing party, both to motivate the support of the group in question in general elections and to secure renomination given group influence in the nomination process.

It might seem, though, that in issue areas in which groups are absent, party elites' greater latitude should produce convergence. Indeed, in many policy areas little controversy exists. Parties pick their battles, differentiating themselves on issues selectively. Yet the absence of groups focused on an issue area does not always result in parties converging on policy. Instead I show that in some important cases the lack of constraining groups allows for repeated reversals in the parties' positions. Several explanations exist.

One explanation is sincere ideological disagreement by politicians. Another factor enjoying considerable prominence in the literature is credibility based on reputation. A frequent claim runs that even if politicians are opportunists, they are inhibited from changing their stands for fear that voters will consider them too unpredictable. However, I show that there is much contrary evidence at the level of individual issues.

It is true that on one level there is much stability. Politicians seldom change parties, and their basic ideological orientations or "spatial positions" (as party stalwart or moderate) are also generally stable, as Poole and Rosenthal (1997) show. Yet politicians and parties have changed positions on individual issues far more often. Reputational concerns may help explain inertia, but their importance has been greatly overemphasized.

I offer two different explanations for the persistence of party policy differences on groupless issues. One factor is uncertainty as to the most advantageous position. Interpretation of electoral outcomes is not an exact science. It is difficult to isolate the effect of a particular policy stand. Downs (1957, 101) discusses uncertainty as a cause of ideological differentiation among even parties that care solely about winning office:

> Thus each party can ideologically woo only a limited number of social groups, since its appeal to one implicitly antagonizes others. But because of uncertainty it is not obvious which combination of groups yields the greatest number of votes. Furthermore, society is dynamic; hence the right combination in one election may turn out to be the wrong one in the next. Therefore it is quite possible for parties to disagree about what social groups to appeal to. This fact, combined with their inherent desire to differentiate their products, means that parties in our model may design widely varying ideologies in spite of their identical objectives.

The politicians' uncertainty described by Downs concerns which groups to target. If uncertainty can persist even when politicians know roughly the size of various groups and their preferences, it should be even more prevalent for issues that lack clear group referents, such as budget balancing and defense spending, as I discuss below.

Some argue that the rise of polling has reduced politicians' uncertainty about the state of public opinion, and greater fidelity to the view of the median voter on "salient" issues should follow.[6] Yet polls cannot answer candidates' key question, which is *not* "What do voters

---

[6] Examples include Geer (1996), Gerring (1998), and Quirk and Hinchliffe (1998). By contrast Karol (2007b) shows that senators were about as responsive to public opinion in their states during the interwar period before the rise of scientific surveys as they are today.

think now?" but rather "What stand will win the most votes at the next election?" This factor, which Key (1961) termed "latent opinion," is easier to theorize about than to measure. Even after an election result is known, its causes remain debated, exit polls notwithstanding. Political actors promote explanations that further their interests (Hershey 1992). Uncertainty reigns. Did President Bush's opposition to same-sex marriage help him in 2004? Should Democrats push for gun control, which polls well? Or should they retreat in the face of the seemingly asymmetric mobilizing power of gun rights organizations?[7]

Scholars cannot reach consensus on such questions. It is reasonable then to expect that politicians can disagree too, and absent a clear target group outside the coalition or pressure from one ensconced in it, they may maintain the same policy through inertia. They may experiment on occasion, leading to reversals in the parties' relative positions, but we should not always expect them to converge, even when they are not constrained by reputational concerns, their own principles, or group pressures.[8]

The second factor inhibiting convergence, even absent group constraints, is perceived interconnection between policies. For example, Democrats who believe that Republicans profited from the public's view of them as advocates of a strong military might be tempted to match or even outbid the GOP in this area. Yet Democrats might believe that doing so credibly would require them to support increased taxes or reduced social spending or tolerate a larger deficit. To the extent that they believe that these trade-offs exist and that these consequences outweigh the political benefits of a pro-defense stand, they may choose to retain their traditional position on the issue.

The way in which parties weigh consequences may stem partially from their coalitions, but it does not follow that these issues are therefore group dominated. Party elites enjoy much autonomy in such cases, and the constraints that exist are often in their own minds and based on assessments that can change. As a result, parties' positioning on such issues is far more volatile than it is on topics that bind groups to party coalitions.

The three models of party position change I present are ideal types. Although the development of parties' positions on some issues is marked overwhelmingly by one dynamic, multiple processes are often at work in a given case. For example, Wolbrecht (2000, 9) ascribes the

---

[7] Compare "Shooting Blanks," *New Republic*, May 19, 2003, with "Democrat Killer?" *The Nation*, April 18, 2005, for diametrically opposed analyses.

[8] Grofman (2004) lists several reasons why convergence is seldom observed in practice. Aldrich (1995, ch. 6) stresses the role of activists in producing parties that fail to converge to the median voter's position, despite the presence of careerist politicians.

parties' polarization on women's rights to both the incorporation of social conservatives and feminists in their coalitions *and* Democratic-leaning unions' abandonment of their opposition to the Equal Rights Amendment. Both the parties' incorporation of new constituencies and their maintenance of old ones combined to produce their polarization on the issue of women's rights.

Similarly, as I show, the development of party positions on the civil rights of African Americans, which Carmines and Stimson (1989) term "racial liberalism," is marked by two of the three dynamics. The parties' redefinition on race stemmed not only from the well-known movement of African Americans into the Democratic Party and Southern whites into the GOP, but also from a incompatibility between the desires of the Republicans' traditional business allies and those of blacks. The former led to gradual change in parties' positioning, while the latter produced dramatic shifts.

In addition, the relationship between an issue and political groups is not fixed for all time. A preexisting group may develop an interest in a new topic. New groups also may arise, removing an issue from the group-less category. For example, the recent rise of the "Club for Growth" and Americans for Tax Reform, antitax organizations strongly aligned with the GOP, may mean that the parties' repeated changes of position on fiscal policy will be less likely to recur.

The relationships between groups and issues can be placed along a continuum. At one extreme are policy areas in which groups focused solely on that topic dominate. At the other are issue areas in which significant interest group activity, even by lobbies with other concerns, is absent. The cases I examine vary notably in this respect.

Groups may also care intensely about a policy, but in a way that is – paradoxically – too narrow to influence party deliberations, so that they remain outside the party system. For example, military procurement stimulates very parochial lobbying by contracting firms. No sizeable organization is pro- or antidefense spending in the way the NRA fights gun control or the Sierra Club backs environmental protection. Defense contractors all may favor generous defense budgets. Yet they compete against each other for contracts and to direct scarce resources to the weapons they produce at the expense of others within the overall defense budget. The broader issue of military spending is not the firms' focus. As a result, the defense issue is not one on which group activity shapes party positions, leaving politicians more autonomy to adjust their parties' positioning.

SHIFTS AMONG ELITES: CONVERSION OR REPLACEMENT?

In all the cases in this book I seek to assess the relative importance of conversion or flip-flopping by politicians as opposed to replacement or turnover in producing party position change. In contrast to the prevailing view, I argue that adaptation by elites is a greater source of change than replacement, although the importance of these two mechanisms varies across issues.

This claim is important for multiple reasons. On the most basic level it is necessary to enhance the correspondence of our models with the historical record. Recognition of the centrality of the adaptation mechanism also allows for more rapid change in party positioning than replacement does, given the high rates of incumbent reelection in recent decades. Moreover, it shows how responsive ambitious politicians are to change in their parties' coalitions and how parties structure representation in American politics.

Given the decentralized nature of the U.S. political system, no single individual, even a president, ever wholly defines a party's position. Party positions result from the aggregated behavior of many politicians. A politician may alter her stand because her constituency has changed. This often happens as she moves up the political ladder, whether her constituency expands geographically or because she takes on a leadership role that requires her to represent broader currents of opinion in her party.

A famous example is Lyndon Johnson's evolving position on race as he moved from representing Texas to a leadership role in the Democratic Party, first in the Senate and then as vice president and president. In later chapters I discuss other prominent figures; several recent presidential nominees including Reagan, both Bushes, Gore, and – to a lesser degree – Clinton revised their positions on abortion as they moved onto the national stage.

Cases of this kind are notable for several reasons. They show that prominent politicians have revised their positions on sensitive issues and prospered politically, contrary to claims that reputational concerns deter such reversals. Moreover, they demonstrate that the most visible party leaders were often individuals who had flip-flopped on high-profile issues. These examples suggest that parties *can* credibly alter their positions, even with leaders who have inconsistent records. They also tell us something of the demands of political leadership.

Still, such leading politicians are by definition a small minority even among the office-holding elite. Accordingly, their maneuvering cannot account for most of the change that occurs when there are major shifts in party positioning on issues. Yet because of the movement of groups into party coalitions, even midlevel officials such as members of Congress may find that their constituency has changed, even if they never seek higher office and the demographics of their districts remain unaltered.

Leading scholars of realignment such as Sundquist (1983, 306–310) and Riker (1982) argue that while party leaders tend to be vested in existing polarizations, insurgents use new issues to overthrow the old order and improve their own standings. Yet these authors focus on the most senior party leaders and do not examine the careers of midlevel officials such as MCs. Thus it may be that many of those whom they term "insurgents" are actually established politicians who once toed the line their elders set but later developed a new one.

Others go further and posit wholesale turnover of a party's officialdom as necessary for an issue evolution. "Membership replacement," Carmines and Stimson (1989, 63) claim, is "the principal agent of interparty change over time" in Congress. Voters' party identifications and attitudes shift in response to the elite's new issue alignment. In what these authors term a "punctuated equilibrium," Democratic landslides in 1958 and 1964 reversed the parties' traditional stands on race. Liberal Democrats replaced moderate Republican MCs in the North, empowering conservatives in the GOP and diluting the Southern element among the Democrats. Later elections widened the partisan gap on race. Yet while Carmines and Stimson cite cases in which replacement of an MC seemed to matter, they do not explore the possibility of shifts among veteran MCs.

Adams (1997, 726) applies the issue evolution model to abortion politics, claiming that "retirements and turnover in seats" explain the parties' polarization on the question in Congress. He theorizes that party activists increasingly favored "pro-life" candidates in the GOP and "pro-choice" ones among Democrats. The parties' stands thus "evolved," even though few MCs shifted over the course of their careers. This model echoes neo-Darwinian theory in that populations' attributes evolve via selection of individuals with certain fixed traits.

Other scholars have studied the evolution of issues, sometimes implying that elite replacement plays a key role. Trubowitz (1998) and Shoch (2001) see the shifts in the geographic constituencies of parties as the key to their evolution on trade and national defense issues. Since modern elected officials do not move from state to state, these theories imply that elite turnover was a key mechanism of party policy change.

Even critics of the issue evolution model do not challenge its treatment of elite-level change. Abramowitz (1994) focuses on voters.

Coleman (1996, 189) finds the model an implausible rival to realignment theories given slow turnover in Congress *because* he accepts the premise that MCs' positions are stable. Burns and Taylor (2000) dispute only Berkman's claims about the role of turnover in party policy change on taxes. Wolbrecht (2000, 225) shows that a "change in the behavior of elites" explains the parties' shift on women's rights, yet still asserts, "elite replacement processes represent the most likely mechanism for the realignment of party positions on any issues" (131).

This is a puzzling premise. Most scholars attribute politicians' stands to constituents' preferences (whether those of the median voter, or some party-based "sub-constituency"), the politicians' own values, or some combination of the two. Social or economic change might cause voters to decide that a policy no longer serves their interests or lead principled politicians to see that a policy has ceased to advance their values. In either case one would expect politicians to alter their positions.

So why assume that politicians' positions are fixed? Carmines and Stimson are silent on this point, but Stimson (2004, 65) notes that changing positions is "not costless" because it might make a politician appear "inconsistent" and "unprincipled." Adams (1997, 724) holds that "vacillating on a highly visible and emotional issue such as abortion is politically risky, and one would be hard pressed to come up with the names of more than a half-dozen politicians who did so successfully. George Bush's notoriety for switching attests to the rare and conspicuous nature of publicly changing one's abortion beliefs."

Political economists also have long used the notion of reputation to explain stability in politicians' stands. Downs (1957, 110–111) argued that parties and politicians have electoral incentives to build consistent records. He claimed, "because individual men become identified with certain policies, it is often necessary for a party to shift its leadership before it can shift its platform." Poole and Rosenthal (1997, 85) build on Bernhardt and Ingberman's (1985) claim that voters might see inconsistent officials as "risky," using "the role of reputation" to explain the "spatial" stability they find among MCs. Dougan and Munger (1989), Enelow and Munger (1993), and Hinich and Munger (1994) also argue that ideological reputations constrain politicians.

We must distinguish broadly valid claims about *spatial* or *ideological* stability, that is, that "liberal" MCs generally stay "liberal" while "conservative" ones remain "conservative" from the idea that politicians have stable relative stances on particular issues. The latter underpins the issue evolution model and some political economists' theories, yet is untenable. Since the policy implications of liberalism and conservatism are unstable, the two claims are mutually exclusive. Over time, ideological consistency entails substantive inconsistency and vice versa.[9]

Theories of reputational consistency require voters to notice changes in a candidate's stands and as a result fail to support her against a more consistent but otherwise less congenial rival. The notion that a flip-flop might repel some voters is plausible. Yet other factors limit and counteract this effect. Many voters will be unaware of the inconsistency or still unwilling to support a less appealing opponent. Politicians and parties that shift on an issue may maintain many other positions and thus still seem fairly consistent. In this way a party or politician could gradually change its positions radically, but the shift at any one moment might appear minor. In addition, as I show, organizations focused on the issue may vouch for the politician, enhancing his credibility.

Whether voters' preferences are exogenous or derive from elite cues, one might expect them to penalize politicians who *don't* change when conditions warrant. The question of the magnitude of these competing effects is an empirical one. I argue that flip-flopping has a cost, but one often worth paying, and that adaptation by elites is usually the key mechanism of change.

This is important for two reasons. First, it is useful to have accurate accounts of key transitions in U.S. political history. Second, if adaptation is the chief mechanism producing party position change, then rapid shifts are possible even absent the electoral upheaval and turnover that has been increasingly rare since the "institutionalization" of Congress (Polsby 1968), the emergence of career legislators (Brady, Buckley, and Rivers 1999), and the growth in incumbency advantage during the twentieth century.

## CASE SELECTION, DATA, AND MEASUREMENT

My empirical focus in this book is on six cases: the issues of race, abortion, gun control, trade, defense spending, and fiscal policy. This set of cases allows for a comparative analysis in a research area that has been dominated by single-issue case studies. I chose the issues based on two factors: their prominence in modern American politics and their importance

---

[9] Even on issues where the parties' relative positions have not changed, their absolute ones have. Although Republicans have always been *relatively* hostile to social programs, Nixon's welfare plan, while attacked by liberals as insufficient, was more statist than the bill Clinton signed in 1996.

in the literature. In several instances I provide evidence that suggests a different interpretation of key cases than currently prevails in the literature.

Describing the development of party's positions on these particular issues is worthwhile and justified given their importance both in politics and the literature. Yet the models of coalition management I develop are not only applicable to the six cases in this book, but illuminate others as well. For that reason each chapter includes brief discussion of other issues, the development of which the model in question seems to capture: immigration for coalition maintenance, school vouchers, and tort reform for coalition group incorporation and the space program for coalition group expansion. I devote a chapter to the issue of race, the development of which was characterized by elements of both coalition maintenance and coalition group incorporation, something true of other issues such as women's rights and environmentalism.

Although I focus on cases in which change occurred, there is, of course, much stability in parties' issue positioning and coalitions. I note the long periods parties held the positions they later discarded on race and trade, for example. Beyond that, there are issue areas on which I do not focus, such as labor law, where the relative positions of the parties and the alignment of the groups concerned have changed very little since the New Deal.

Even if we determine which issues are worthy of study, how can we determine the positions of parties? American parties are famously weak and heterogeneous. One possible data source is platforms and leaders' speeches. I do cite these where appropriate, yet they are not my chief data source for several reasons. Platforms and presidential nominees' speeches appear only every four years, and in the intervening period a party may adopt and abandon a position.

Moreover, an emphasis on broad rhetorical themes contained in platforms and speeches may be misleading. In an erudite study of speeches and platforms Gerring (1998, 140) finds that "the Republican Party's long-standing and visceral dislike of big government, therefore had its origins in the 1924 and 1928 campaigns, not in the party's response to the New Deal, as is so often claimed." Yet the significance of this finding is questionable given that in the 1920s Republicans tended to favor the two most visible "big government" policies, the tariff and Prohibition, and supported a larger military than Democrats did. In later years there have been too many exceptions to this alleged "dislike of big government," including corporate subsidies, regulation of labor unions, a "law and order" view of crime, support for a large military, and, increasingly, religiously based regulations to accept claims that antistatism is *the* core value that has inspired Republican policies.

The inadequacy of a focus on broad themes in party rhetoric is not due to some gap between theory and practice unique to contemporary Republicans. Most modern Democrats are "pro-choice" on abortion. Yet they do not rate "choice" as their highest value when it comes to the question of vouchers for parents of school-age children or making participation in Social Security voluntary. The same antebellum Southerners who favored "states' rights" supported provisions in the Fugitive Slave Act that reduced the autonomy of free states. Those searching for a party that is a consistent advocate of limited government, federalism, judicial restraint, or presidential power will not find one. The point is not that politicians and parties have no true beliefs or that ideas do not "matter," but that it is a mistake to take rhetoric as an unproblematic guide as to politicians' and parties' goals.

Even when we consider specific policy pronouncements rather than broad rhetorical themes, platforms and speeches do not always reveal the extent to which a party elite cohered on an issue. At best, divisions can be inferred from the deemphasis or omission of an issue or the use of cautious language. Yet these judgments might easily be mistaken. Deemphasis of an issue may reflect less a divided party elite than one that views their stand as unpopular. Similarly, a moderate wording may be less a straddle than a real reflection of a centrist view that has broad party support.

The data I use to assess party positions are found chiefly in recorded votes in Congress. My empirical focus on Congress is a practical one and does not imply that presidents and even failed presidential nominees are unimportant in the process of party position change. Where appropriate I frequently supplement analysis of roll-call data with the statements of the most visible party spokespersons: presidents, presidential candidates, and congressional leaders.

However, congressional voting records are the best record of the stand party elites take for several reasons. Although presidential campaigns occur only every four years, and only one party has a president at any given time, both parties are always present in Congress where they face issues with greater regularity. Moreover, although a party may duck an issue in its platform or campaign speeches, its legislators are often forced to take a stand on Capitol Hill. Another advantage of studying congressional votes is that they allow us to see party positions as more continuous than dichotomous variables. We can observe how an issue goes from being cross-cutting to one that neatly divides the parties, and we can observe how long it takes to move from one condition to the other.

In addition, since many MCs serve for several terms and have to vote on many issues repeatedly, Congress can serve as a sort of naturally occurring "panel study." This allows us determine the extent to which elite turnover as opposed to conversion produces party position change. There are alternatives, for example, convention delegate studies or surveys of party committee members, but these bodies are marked by massive turnover and do far less to define their parties' images than the candidates they nominate. In addition, such surveys' coverage of the periods and issues I explore is spotty at best.

Having identified key cases in which parties' stands shifted, I employ four different tests. There is no perfect measure, but approaching the problem from multiple angles should increase our confidence in findings that appear in different types of analysis. First, I examine the careers of leading politicians in each party who were active during the period when the parties' positions changed on the issue in question. These leaders are the "face" of the party for many voters, so they merit special attention.

I then systematically assess the relative importance of elite replacement and conversion by comparing MCs whose careers span the realigning period to the Congress as a whole. I do not present "cohort analysis," for example, following the class of 1956 over several Congresses. Since such legislative cohorts undergo attrition, the fact that their voting behavior changes along with that of their party as a whole could stem from the quasi-Darwinian process of "selection" that issue evolution theorists posit in which MCs who happened to start their careers with a position that would later prove convenient are more apt to survive than others who committed to stands that later became liabilities.

Instead of following a shrinking class of legislators I identify a period during which the parties' issue positions changed and then look at the MCs who served throughout this era. As this group's membership is stable, if the relationship between party and position trends in the same direction among them as in the Congress generally, then change must be due to adaptation. These veteran legislators cannot remain in the mainstream of their parties without shifting. Similar correlations between party and issue position among both long-serving MCs and the broader Congress are evidence for the role of conversion or flip-flopping. Conversely, the larger the gap evident between this group and their colleagues, the greater the role turnover must have played in the parties' realignments.

To have a sizeable group of long-serving MCs to observe I focus on representatives rather than senators, except when there are too few recorded votes in the House on the issue in question during the years in which change in parties' positioning occurs.[10] I also highlight the stands of the most visible politicians, presidential candidates, and congressional leaders. In addition I compare the speed at which the shifts occurred and the stability of the new positions in light of the mechanism(s) underlying them. For details on scale construction and data sources, see the appendix.

Determining the importance of elite conversion or flip-flopping as opposed to replacement or turnover is not as straightforward an exercise as it might seem. There are important data limitations and difficulties in interpreting the available evidence as well.

The leading formula for estimating the relative importance of conversion and replacement in accounting for change within a population is Rapoport and Stone's (1994) formula. Herrera (1995) and Wolbrecht (2002) employ variants. They developed this formula to assess the causes of change in the views of Iowa presidential caucus participants from 1984 to 1988. It is

$$T_2 - T_1 = (\beta\alpha)(S_2 - S_1) + \beta(1 - \alpha)(N_2 - D_1) + (1 - \beta)(N_2 - T_1),$$

where

$T_1$ and $T_2$ are the mean values of the variable at the first and second period observed

S is the mean value for the "Stayers," those present at both $T_1$ and $T_2$

$\beta$ is the size of the group at $T_1$ divided by the size of the group at $T_2$

$\alpha$ is the proportion of the population at $T_1$ comprised by Stayers

$D_1$ is the mean value for the "Dropouts" who are present at $T_1$ only

$N_2$ is the mean value for the "Newcomers" who are present at $T_2$ only.

When I report the share of change accounted for by conversion in the cases below I am referring to $\alpha(S_2 - S_1) / T_2 - T_1$.

This is the most straightforward measure available. Yet it is biased in an important way. Rapoport and Stone assume that *all* change among the portion of the population that is replaced from one period to the next is *caused* by turnover. In some instances this assumption is not reasonable.

---

[10] In analyses not reported I found little difference between the behavior of senators and representatives. I also use Senate roll calls in some cases to assess the effect of variables on legislators' votes that are not easy to measure at the district level, e.g., public opinion.

A simple example illustrates the point. Assume that there are 10 members of a legislature. Initially four favor capital punishment while six are opposed. Half of the members retire at the end of a term. The retirees are split two to three against the death penalty. After the election, two of the five continuing members switch from opposition to support of capital punishment while the one early backer maintains her view. The "switchers" shift the balance in this group from two supporters and three opponents to four supporters and one opponent. Meanwhile, the retirees, two of whom had favored capital punishment and three of whom had opposed it, are replaced by a group of four death penalty backers and one opponent.

In this scenario the legislature evolves from a body in which 40 percent of the membership favors capital punishment to one in which 80 percent of the members do. The change occurring among the legislators serving in both sessions matches that evident in the category in which retired members are replaced by new ones.

Given these data, Rapoport and Stone's formula would produce the following result: half of the change in legislators' positions was due to conversion and half to replacement. Yet this is to assume that no retirees would have modified their position, had they been reelected. This premise might be reasonable if turnover in Congress stemmed chiefly from the defeat of MCs who clung rigidly to particular issue positions.

However, most departures from Congress stem from retirement, not defeat (Cooper and West 1981; Hibbing 1982; Jacobson 2004),[11] and even incumbents' losses are rarely attributable to their stands on a single issue. Thus it seems more reasonable to assign to replacement only that increment of change occurring in the turnover category that exceeds the shift occurring among the continuing MCs.

This limitation of Rapoport and Stone's method becomes especially problematic when several years elapse between votes on an issue. During such a period much turnover in Congress inevitably occurs, and the change observed from the first to the second period will seem to stem in some measure from this elite replacement. Thus Rapoport and Stone's technique is biased toward finding turnover as a cause of change. (It also

---

[11] Admittedly, some MCs who anticipate a difficult campaign for themselves or for their party (and thus a future in the minority) suddenly develop a desire to spend time with their families, which scholars term "strategic retirement" (Jacobson and Kernell 1981). Yet even most of these MCs are not impelled to retire by the unpopularity of their stands on a single issue.

does not differentiate between newcomers who have been consistent on an issue and those who adapted over the course of their political careers, albeit before they entered Congress.)

These biases make the Rapoport and Stone formula a conservative test for my purposes. Even so, I still find that in all cases conversion accounted for most of the change in the position of at least one of the two parties. In some instances it was the chief cause of change among legislators of both parties.

Although the use of roll calls to measure parties' positions has many advantages, it has drawbacks as well. In a true panel study, researchers ask respondents the same questions repeatedly over time. Unfortunately, Congress does not arrange votes for scholars' convenience; the exact same bill is seldom brought up for a vote year after year. This might not seem problematic so long as the various votes "scale" and tap into the same policy dimension. Yet the particular mix of votes occurring in a given Congress affects the results of roll-call analyses.

For example, assume that although diversity of opinion on the minimum wage exists within each party, there is no overlap between them; all Democrats favor a higher minimum wage than do all Republicans. The strength of the observed correlation between party affiliation and position on this issue will still depend on the voting agenda. A modest bill to raise the minimum wage $1 might find all the Democrats and even many Republicans voting yes. A measure of the correlation between party affiliation and position on the minimum wage will reveal a significant, but far from deterministic, relationship. If in the next Congress, however, a $2 raise is proposed, this more ambitious bill might still be acceptable to all Democrats, but opposed by even those Republicans who favored a $1 increase. In this case MCs might divide wholly along party lines.

In this scenario a naive review of the record would suggest that the minimum wage issue had become more partisan. Yet this seeming change would not reflect any shift in MCs' positions. Rather it would stem from a more extreme bill that divided Congress in a different way, that is, tapped another "cutpoint" (Poole and Rosenthal 1997, 24).

This issue also emerges in studying individual legislators' behavior over time. When an MC receives a 40 rating one term from the National Right to Life Committee (NRLC) and a 60 in the next Congress, we cannot infer much about her absolute position. She may indeed have become increasingly pro-life. Alternatively, "easier" measures like the "partial-birth" abortion ban or parental notification may comprise a greater share of the votes used by the NRLC to compute their ratings in the second

Congress than they did in the first one. If so, the increase in the MC's rating may reflect no substantive shift.

Scholars have long recognized this problem, but no perfect solution exists. Groseclose, Levitt, and Snyder (1999) propose indexing roll-call scales over time. Their technique, however, is inappropriate here, as it assumes no systematic change in MCs' preferences, when such change is precisely the subject of this book.

I propose two measurement strategies. One is to present results from the Rapoport and Stone formula based on mean-deviation scores. I subtract the chamber mean from each MC's score in a given Congress. Once this is done, the mean for the chamber using the new scores is always zero. This measure is less "noisy" than raw scores would be, but it too is a flawed solution, as it assumes that while individual MCs' preferences may vary over time, that of the House as a whole does not. Yet this is an appropriate trade-off to make because I am interested in the relative positions of parties and politicians, *not* their stands in an absolute sense.

I also present data in another form. Ideally we would like to have a vote on an issue with the same "cutpoint" recurring over time. If the same share of the chamber voted on the same side of the issue and party composition of the legislative body was also unchanged, then concerns about artificial movement in scores due to agenda change would be reduced.

Unfortunately such perfect votes do not exist. However, it is often possible to find votes that come relatively close to satisfying these criteria. Therefore I present simple analyses showing the changing positions of continuing MCs and those of their colleagues by using two votes in the same issue area taken some years apart but sharing a similar cutpoint. I also choose votes that took place in two Congresses in which the party composition is similar. Comparing MCs' voting patterns on two such votes in which the cutpoint and party composition of Congress varies little allows us to have greater confidence that the change we are observing is real and not a mere artifact of the voting agenda.

In the subsequent chapters I turn from issues of theory and measurement to concrete examples of party position change. The cases I examine are interesting and important in their own right given their prominent roles in modern American politics. Taken together, they illustrate the dynamics that continually reshape parties.

2

# Coalition Maintenance

## *The Politics of Trade Policy*

> They tell us that this platform was made to catch votes. We reply to them
> that changing conditions make new issues; that the principles upon which
> rest Democracy are as everlasting as the hills; but that they must be applied
> to new conditions as they arise. Conditions have arisen and we are attempt-
> ing to meet those conditions.
>
> William Jennings Bryan, "Cross of Gold Speech," 1896

Much of politicians' energies are devoted to keeping the groups that support them happy. Usually that means continuing to take the same stands
that they and their supporters have long championed. In the short term
most groups' preferences change little, and as a result neither do the signals they send the politicians aligned with them.

Yet at times social or economic changes prompt old allies to make
new demands of politicians. In such cases politicians may be forced to
choose between their policies and their supporters. We should not be surprised that elected officials frequently are more attached to their allies,
who mobilize voters and contribute to campaigns, than to their old policy positions. Such politicians are engaging in coalition maintenance. In
these instances elected officials can claim consistency of a sort: consistent
attentiveness to the concerns of a particular group.

The case of trade policy offers a clear illustration of the dynamics
of coalition maintenance. Here we see a shift in parties' positions on
an issue stemming from changing preferences by party-linked groups.
The parties' shift on trade issues is complicated, because the contrast
between them is muted in presidential politics and among voters. Yet the
dramatic transformation in congressional voting patterns on trade issues
illustrates one of the main dynamics of party position change, veteran

politicians altering their stands to maintain traditional alliances. (Racial politics was also marked in part by this dynamic. Yet because this is a complicated case not fully captured by a single model – as well as one of central importance in politics and the literature – I consider it separately in Chapter 4.)

Trade policy is the oldest issue in American politics. Trade restrictions fueled colonists' animosity toward the British crown before the Revolution, and a tariff bill was the first proposal Congress considered in 1789. For over a century the political representatives of industry, first the Whig Party and later the Republicans, championed high tariffs. The more agrarian Democrats were – if not always free traders – consistently the less protectionist party. The eternal "tariff question" was often the most prominent policy disagreement between the parties.[1] U.S. trade policy in the era between the Civil War and the Great Depression was generally protectionist, reflecting the dominance of the Republican Party in these years. The most ambitious attempts to reorient trade policy in a more liberal direction, the Gorman tariff of 1894 and the Underwood tariff of 1913, came during the brief periods when the Democrats controlled both Congress and the White House (Stewart and Weingast 1992).

The Democrats' low-tariff position survived the major changes in their electoral base that occurred during the formation of the New Deal coalition. Organized labor, the most important new Democratic constituency, initially had little to say about the party's stand on trade issues. At the time of their incorporation into the Democratic Party in the 1930s unions were both divided on trade policy and far more concerned with other issues. Later, however, organized labor would take a stand that reinforced the party's traditional policy. However, three decades later labor would reverse itself and work to orient Democratic politicians toward protectionism.

The leading union grouping, the American Federation of Labor, had been nonpartisan and tried in the words of its longtime President Samuel Gompers to "reward friends" and "punish their enemies" in both parties (Shefter 1994, 159). Yet the AFL did not find an equal number of friends in both parties and had been broadly supportive of Democrats between 1906 and 1922 (Greene 1998). The impetus for this alliance had little to do with trade policy. Rather, it stemmed from the increasing inability of unions to win a hearing from Republican leaders on labor

---

[1] The leading histories of U.S. trade policy covering the era in which Congress wrote tariffs are Stanwood (1903) and Taussig (1931).

law issues because of the rising influence of the National Association of Manufacturers (NAM) in the GOP. Yet the relationship between labor and the Democrats did not last, and even at its height during the Wilson administration, the union group represented far fewer workers and played a much smaller role in Democratic politics than it would starting in the New Deal era.

Moreover, during this period and even into the 1930s the AFL and its member unions had no common position on trade issues (Leiter 1961). As Robertson (1999, 153) notes, "workers in the steel industry tended to support the argument that tariffs increased wealth and wages, for example, while workers in other industries were more open to the argument that the tariff was the 'mother of trusts.'"

The alliance between the Democrats and labor unraveled in the early 1920s. After an interlude of nonpartisanship interrupted only by the AFL's controversial endorsement of the Progressive Party presidential candidate Senator Robert LaFollette in 1924, labor unions developed strong ties with the Roosevelt administration and, eventually, Democratic MCs. The alliance forged between labor and the Democrats during the New Deal era has endured. Even in their current much reduced state, unions remain the single most important constituent group in the Democratic Party (Dark 2001).

Labor's embrace of the Democrats in the mid-1930s had nothing to do with trade policy. Like their earlier alliance with that party, it was driven by concerns about labor law. Yet after being incorporated into the Democratic coalition on the basis of other issues, unions gradually came to accept and for a time even promote the traditional Democratic position on trade.

After a period of ambivalence, the AFL endorsed reciprocal trade in 1943.[2] The CIO was more enthusiastic and from its founding in 1938 supported the program. In the postwar years American industry was freer from foreign competition than before or since. Sectors that later struggled against imports, such as steel, were exporters during this period. Smaller firms that suffered from imports and lacked export potential were often nonunion. Unions were also well represented in then export-oriented sectors, for example, autos and aerospace (Leiter 1961, 57–58). Thus organized labor had reasons to favor trade liberalization for many years after the end of World War Two. The labor movement's support for

---

[2] "Hail New Support for Trade Pacts: Foreign Traders See Reversal of N.A.M. and A.F.L. Stand as Most Significant." *New York Times*, April 25, 1943, S7.

trade liberalization in the postwar period meant that its incorporation in the Democratic coalition did not initially disturb Democrats' traditional support for lower tariffs.

U.S. trade policy moved in a liberal direction after the high-water mark of protectionism when the Smoot-Hawley tariff was enacted in 1930, but Republicans remained relatively protectionist. Voting in Congress on the adoption of the Reciprocal Trade Agreements Act (RTAA) in 1934 and extensions of it in 1937 and 1940 was highly partisan.

In political discourse the Smoot-Hawley tariff would later come to symbolize the folly of protectionism the way "Munich" has come to stand for the dangers of appeasement (Pastor 1983). Yet it took time for this consensus view of the tariff to emerge. The initial retreat from protectionism that occurred in the 1930s did not stem from any change of heart or lesson learned by high-tariff Republicans. Rather, it resulted from the rise to power of Democrats who exploited their newfound control over Congress and the White House to liberalize trade policy. The Smoot-Hawley supporters who remained in Congress overwhelmingly opposed the passage of the RTAA in 1934 and the renewal of that law in 1937 (Schnietz 2000).

Yet during the 1940s Republican protectionism declined, and the debate over trade policy moved in a liberal direction. Instead of flatly rejecting the principle of reciprocal trade agreements, as they had in the 1930s, increasingly Republicans merely sought to limit the power the president was delegated to reach them (Irwin and Kroszner 1999). GOP MCs' efforts were focused on reducing the length of time during which the president would be granted such authority and promoting "escape clause" and "peril point" provisions that would permit emergency protection for sectors suffering from rapid increases in imports.

The GOP's move toward freer trade in an absolute sense followed the decline in protectionist sentiment among key business lobbies close to that party. The U.S. Chamber of Commerce was a relatively early convert to the cause of freer trade; it supported the reciprocal trade program from 1943 onward.[3]

Yet Republicans' traditional constituencies remained divided on trade in a way that Democrats' were not. The NAM was less enthusiastic about the liberalizing trend of U.S. policy than the Chamber of

---

[3] "Chamber, CIO Back Trade Pact Renewal," *Washington Post,* May 10, 1945, 5; "Chamber of Commerce Asks 3-Year Extension of Reciprocal Trade Act," *Wall Street Journal,* May 10, 1945, 7.

Commerce. The NAM endorsed reciprocal trade as a wartime measure in 1943, but reverted in 1945 to its traditional opposition to the program.[4] Subsequently the group's membership remained divided for many years on trade policy. As a result, the NAM stayed neutral on the issue, while individual firms and sectoral manufacturing associations lobbied on both sides of the question. As late as 1962 the NAM was too divided to take a position on Kennedy's Trade Expansion Act (Bauer, Pool, and Dexter 1972, 334–336).

During this period Democratic MCs, who – outside the South – depended on labor support, heard a unified pro-trade message from the interested groups in their party's coalition. By contrast, their Republican colleagues received much more mixed signals. This may account for the continued gap between the parties' relative positions on trade, even as the whole polity was moving away from protectionism in an absolute sense.

During this period a distinct presidential position emerged on trade policy. While the White House was sometimes more protectionist than Congress earlier in U.S. history, all presidents since Franklin Roosevelt have supported trade liberalization. Yet in Congress the issue remains more partisan (Keech and Pak 1995; Karol 2000, 2007a).[5]

The move of congressional Republicans toward acceptance of the principle of reciprocal trade in the 1940s did not immediately make the issue less partisan. Instead, the entire debate on Capitol Hill shifted away from protectionism in an absolute sense, but the parties retained their relative positions on the trade issue. Although trade politics were far less salient than they had been in the pre–New Deal period when the tariff was still *the* leading economic issue, GOP MCs remained more resistant to lowering trade barriers than Democrats.[6]

For decades, freer trade remained a cause associated with the Democratic Party and with liberals and even radicals. While a later generation of leftists would be fearful of globalization and campus activists would rally against sweatshops in developing countries, the 1962 Port Huron Statement, often termed the founding document of the New Left, included

---

[4] "New Tariff Power Opposed by NAM," *New York Times,* May 12, 1945, 13.

[5] Trade policy is the only one of the six issues I explore in this book for which office trumps party affiliation as a determinant of policy preference. Yet several other issues in American politics have been marked more by interbranch than interparty conflict (Karol 1999).

[6] Mayhew (1966, 160) recalls, "even in the 1950s one could find occasional Pennsylvania Republicans, suggestive of the writhing limbs of a dismembered reptile, who offered higher tariffs as the only solution to the world's ills."

an attack on "tariffs which protect noncompetitive industries with political power and which keep less-favored nations out of the large trade mainstream" (Miller 1994, 339).

Conversely, objections to trade liberalization still emanated largely from Republican ranks in the 1960s. In 1962 the Trade Expansion Act promoted by the Kennedy administration passed over GOP objections. Senator Barry Goldwater (R-AZ), already the conservative standard bearer, had opposed it. Goldwater also ran as a protectionist in 1964 when he was his party's presidential nominee.[7] In 1967 Senate GOP leader Everett Dirksen (R-IL) led the congressional opposition to Lyndon Johnson's tariff reduction plans.[8] As late as 1969 President Nixon won more support for trade liberalization from Democratic MCs than from Republican ones. This alignment was evident even on issues where loyalty to the president of one's party normally exerts a strong pull, for example, the Senate confirmation vote on Nixon's proposed special trade representative, the well-known free-trader Carl Gilbert, whom Democrats were significantly more likely than Republicans to support (Karol 2000, 838).

Yet the picture soon changed. The United States began to run a trade deficit, and unionized industries felt the pressure of imports. These changes in the world economy led to an important development that had major consequences for the politics of trade policy: organized labor turned toward protectionism.

Unions were already becoming concerned about the risk of job losses due to imports at the time of Kennedy's 1962 Trade Expansion Act. Yet the inclusion of provisions concerning "trade adjustment assistance," a program funding retraining for displaced workers and aiding firms found to have suffered from foreign competition, allayed many of their concerns. Trade adjustment assistance was an idea that had long appealed to unions. United Steelworkers president David McDonald had advocated the idea as long ago as 1954 (Bauer, Pool, and Dexter 1972, 43). McDonald served on the Randall Commission, a panel appointed by President Eisenhower charged with studying trade issues. Although committed to trade liberalization, the commission and the Eisenhower administration rejected McDonald's proposal, but the Kennedy administration, which was closer to unions politically, adopted it.

However, as implemented, trade adjustment assistance did not long forestall union skepticism about further trade liberalization. By 1970 not

[7] "Out of Town Fans Join Goldwater," *New York Times,* February 23, 1964, 43.
[8] "Dirksen Defiant on Import Curbs," *New York Times,* November 4, 1967, 1.

only had the pressure from imports increased, but most of organized labor was disillusioned with the operation of the trade adjustment assistance program. Not one claim for assistance brought by unions was accepted until 1969 (Shoch 2001, 307).

The shift of unions toward protectionism had immediate consequences in Congress. Democratic MCs, many of whom were closely aligned with organized labor, were quick to respond. In order to maintain their support coalitions many Democratic MCs adopted a new position. Forced to choose between old friends and old positions they opted for the former.

The new alignment was evident immediately. The same year the AFL-CIO reversed itself the House passed a bill imposing import quotas on textiles, shoes, and several other products. Although lobbying from affected firms was important, observers also credited "the switch of organized labor from the free trade stance it had taken since the nineteen-thirties to a strongly protectionist position this year."[9]

The protectionist push continued the following year. It is notable that Rep. James Burke (D-MA) and Senator Vance Hartke (D-IN), the chief sponsors of the major labor-backed bill limiting imports, the Foreign Trade and Investment Act of 1972 (actually introduced in late 1971), had once been adherents of the traditional pro-trade view long associated with Democrats. Both legislators had backed President Kennedy's 1962 Trade Expansion Act. In 1962 Hartke predicted that the move to freer trade would yield "more jobs, more business and a stronger all-around economy." Yet less than a decade later the Indiana senator distanced himself from "America's old-line free trade policies" and insisted "we can no longer ignore the disastrous effect of our investment and trade policies."[10] The "Burke-Hartke" bill, which included import quotas and tax penalties on U.S. firms moving production abroad, was the most serious protectionist proposal since the Smoot-Hawley tariff.[11]

Burke-Hartke never became law, but it was nevertheless an important turning point. In a historic reversal, a protectionist measure won more support from Democrats than Republicans.[12] This new issue alignment of the parties, based as it was on coalition maintenance, has endured.

[9] "Labor Support a Big Factor in Gain by Trade Bill," *New York Times,* December 23, 1970, 8.

[10] *Congressional Record—Senate,* September 17, 1962, 19591; "Javits, Hartke Debate Trade Bill," *New York Times,* March 28, 1972, 59.

[11] Hughes (1979, 27).

[12] The Burke-Hartke bill was never voted on, but statements and cosponsorship reports reveal the party affiliations of its backers.

The disagreement between business lobbies and organized labor on trade policy that emerged in the early 1970s persists. As a result, nearly four decades later congressional Democrats remain notably more protectionist than their GOP colleagues.

Since the early 1990s another Democratic constituency, environmentalists, has also become skeptical about trade liberalization (Destler 1995, 84). Organizations including the Sierra Club and the League of Conservation Voters are concerned about the environmental effects of trade-related growth in countries with lax regulation and have increasingly lobbied against trade liberalization in Congress. The impact of this development appears limited, however. Although environmentalists now reinforce Democrats' protectionist tendencies, their shift is far too recent to account for the change in the parties' positioning on trade issues that emerged in the early 1970s.

Similar changes in the politics of trade have occurred in other party systems as developments in the world economy have altered the perceived interests of party-linked classes (Rogowski 1989). The British Conservative Party is no longer a force for protectionism. In Canada the Conservative and Liberal parties also traded places, much as the Democrats and Republicans have (Johnston et al. 1992).

If the evidence for the role of interest groups in driving the parties to reposition themselves on trade is strong, the same cannot be said for the role of "experts," ideologues, or policy intellectuals that Zaller (1992), Noel (2007), and others see as leading such ideological transformations. Liberal intellectuals were far more resistant than Democratic politicians to unions' protectionist demands. One way to see this resistance is to examine the chronology of the shift in the position of the Americans for Democratic Action (ADA), the liberal organization that has rated MCs based on their voting records since the 1940s.

The ADA was slower to embrace protectionism than unions or Democratic MCs. As late as December 1970, almost a year after the AFL-CIO's reversal on trade, the ADA still scored a vote against the protectionist "Mills Bill" sought by textile producers as "correct."[13] In 1973 the AFL-CIO counted a vote for a protectionist proposal in legislators' favor. By contrast, that year the ADA chose to ignore trade issues when they calculated their ratings of MCs. The liberal organization, which had often

---

[13] The AFL-CIO by contrast did not score that vote. See "1970 Votes on Which Groups Rated Congress," *Congressional Quarterly Weekly Report*, April 16, 1971, 868. Starting in 1973 the union federation scored protectionist votes as "correct."

used votes on trade policy to compute its congressional ratings in the first two postwar decades – counting a pro-trade position as a liberal one – did not score a trade policy roll call after 1970 until 1986, despite several congressional battles on the issue in the intervening years.

Finally in 1986 the ADA counted a vote for a protectionist bill as the correct liberal position. They would do so repeatedly in later years, opposing NAFTA and permanent normal trade relations with China in the Clinton years and trade promotion authority as well as the Dominican Republic/Central American Free Trade Agreement (DR-CAFTA) during the subsequent Bush administration.[14]

There is evidence beyond the ADA for the view that trade liberalization was still progressive politics in many observers' estimation well after the unions and Democratic legislators began to reject it. As late as 1975, the left-liberal weekly *The Nation* editorialized that the result of the decline of the U.S. auto industry in the face of imports was "a raising of the old protectionist cry which, if answered by Congress, will play havoc with moves toward freer international trade. It's not the answer."[15]

Although *The Nation* eventually became more open to protectionist arguments,[16] as is *The American Prospect* (founded in 1990), other publications long associated with Democrats including the *New Republic* and the *Washington Monthly* as well as prominent Democratic-leaning editorial pages, for example, the *New York Times,* the *Boston Globe,* and the *Washington Post,* have not (Karol 1999). Importantly, most prominent liberal economists consistently opposed protectionism long after many Democratic politicians embraced it. The evidence is overwhelming: ideamongers did not sell Democrats on protectionism, unions did.

Other factors influence MCs' votes on trade and sometimes produce a fair number of defections from party lines. Where economic interests in their states and districts are overwhelmingly supportive of or opposed to a particular trade proposal, MCs will break from their party. Thus Democratic MCs in Silicon Valley are apt to support freer trade, whereas Republican legislators from the textile-producing Carolinas often do not.

Since World War Two MCs have also been more likely to support trade liberalization when a president of their party is in the White House. This is true in part because modern trade legislation includes delegation of

---

[14] http://www.adaction.org/votingrecords.htm and http://www.adaction.org/Key_International_Trade_Votes.htm.

[15] "A Reasonable Little Proposal," *The Nation,* May 17, 1975, 581.

[16] "No to NAFTA," *The Nation,* June 14, 1993, 819.

power to the president to negotiate agreements, and legislators are more
vested in the success of co-partisan chief executives (Karol 2000, 2007a;
Shoch 2001).

This tendency has had the effect of reducing observed partisanship
on trade roll calls when the president from the protectionist party is in
power as he draws votes from among normally protectionist co-partisans
even as he repels some normally pro-trade MCs from the other party.
Conversely, when the relatively pro-trade party controls the presidency,
voting on the issue is more polarized on party lines.

Yet by observing voting patterns over time we can see that MCs'
greater willingness to support trade liberalization when the president is
a co-partisan does *not* outweigh the parties' basic orientation on trade
policy in a given era. Figure 2-1 reflects the difference in support among
House Democrats and Republicans on the 24 trade policy votes in the
House from 1945 to 2005 that *Congressional Quarterly* termed "key
votes." (In the Appendix I list the bills used in this analysis.)

A glance at the figure reveals several key points. First, there is a notable
difference between the support for trade among MCs according to party
in all cases. The figure also shows that the gap between the parties on
trade changed fairly rapidly from positive to negative from the late 1960s
to the early 1970s, the period when organized labor turned protectionist.

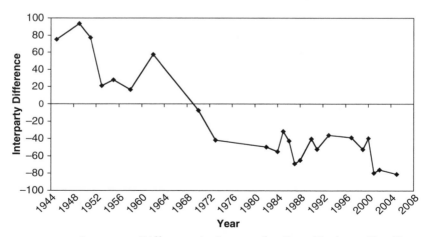

FIGURE 2-1. Interparty Difference in Support for Freer Trade on Key Votes:
House of Representatives (Democratic Support – Republican Support), 79th
through 109th Congresses (1945–2006)

It is also evident the gap between the parties on trade has neither steadily increased or decreased; rather, it has fluctuated and is smallest when presidents from the relatively protectionist party are in office during the Eisenhower administration (1953–1960), the Clinton administration (1993–2000), and at the beginning of the Nixon administration (1969–1970).

Yet although the party affiliation of the president affects the degree of partisan polarization on trade, this co-partisan dynamic remains a secondary factor that does not override the basic orientation MCs get on trade issues from the key elements of their parties' coalition. Thus in all of the key votes from 1945 until 1970 Democratic MCs were more supportive of trade than Republicans. This was true even during the Eisenhower years when there was the most voting across party lines. Eisenhower's liberal trade policies received more support from Democrats than Republicans. From 1970 to 2005 Democrats were consistently more likely than Republicans to cast antitrade votes, even during the Clinton administration, when co-partisanship was cross-pressuring MCs.

Examining the intersection of trade politics with the ideological orientation of members of Congress provides another perspective on the changing politics of trade. The leading indices of congressional voting behavior are Poole and Rosenthal's (1997) Dimension 1 and 2 NOMINATE scores. These scores, often referenced as $D_1$ and $D_2$, measure MCs' positions in a two-dimensional space the authors find by analyzing every recorded vote with at least 5 percent of members on the losing side in a given Congress. They interpret the $D_1$ score, which is highly correlated with party affiliation and captures most of the variance in legislators' voting records, as representing MCs' placement on the left–right continuum, while $D_2$ reflects legislators' positions on the cross-cutting issues that divided parties, including race, Prohibition, immigration, and other topics. Two MCs from the same party may have very different NOMINATE scores, reflecting the ideological diversity that has long been characteristic of American parties.

Figure 2-2 charts the correlation between representatives' votes on the *Congressional Quarterly* key votes on trade policy explored in Figure 1-1 and their $D_1$ and $D_2$ NOMINATE scores. It illustrates a few points. First, votes on trade policy have divided representatives primarily along the first dimension of conflict captured by the $D_1$ score. Put another way, trade politics has been, more or less, a liberal versus conservative issue. With the exception of a procedural vote relating to textile issues in 1970, a time

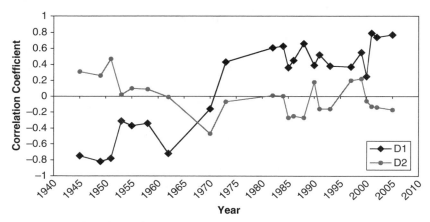

FIGURE 2-2. Correlation between Representatives' Positions on Key Trade Votes and D1 and D2 NOMINATE Scores, House of Representatives, 79th through 109th Congresses (1945–2006)

when the parties were realigning on trade issues, the correlation between representatives' votes and their D2 scores has always been visibly weaker than that between their votes and their D1 scores.

The figure also reveals that the correlation between MCs' D1 NOMINATE scores and their votes on trade policy changes sign. Through 1970 the correlation is negative, meaning that legislators with higher scores, that is, conservatives, are more likely to be found on the protectionist side of the debate. Subsequently, the direction of the relationship reverses, and conservatism becomes associated with support for freer trade. (By contrast, there is no clear pattern in the consistently weaker association between votes on trade policy and the D2 scores.)

These findings are important because the stability of MCs' NOMINATE scores has been widely noted. Poole (2007) views this finding as evidence of "ideological stability," asserting, "people are suspicious of those who change their minds, especially about something as fundamental as what is *good* in politics." He concludes that people may be changing their minds, but they are not in Congress.

Yet given the radical reversal of the polarity of the trade issue in a short period and the other shifts on key issues I document in later chapters, this interpretation of the stability of NOMINATE scores needs to be revised. MCs do tend to remain part of the same political coalition and vote with some politicians and against others throughout their careers. Yet the consistency at work is *not* one of policy preferences or high principle, but rather one of politicians' consistent alignment with particular groups and responsiveness to those groups' concerns.

It seems more apt to say politicians are consistent in their views of "who" is good and deserving of help than "what" is good in terms of policy and principles of governmental action.[17] Republicans have been the party of the business community since Lincoln's day. Initially this meant supporting a strong national government that would promote economic development by subsidizing railroads, promoting public works and land grant colleges, and shielding industry from foreign competition. Later, when New Dealers began to use the national government to redistribute wealth downward instead of upward, Republicans were able to denounce "big government" without being compelled to drop their support for tariffs until changes in the world economy altered the preferences of their supporters in the business community. Similarly, Democrats supported a freer global market while pursuing interventionist policies domestically until labor unions decided that freer trade no longer served their interests.

The parties' shift on trade issues has stimulated interest among scholars. Some students of trade policy have seen this reversal as stemming from the shifts in the geographic bases of the two parties. As the Democrats gained strength in the Industrial Northeast and Midwest, sometimes called the "Rustbelt," and the Republicans became the party of the traditionally Democratic South and West, the so-called "Sunbelt," their positions on trade issues shifted to coincide with the dominant economic interests of those regions.

Trubowitz (1998) and Shoch (2001) both make this argument. Building on Bensel's (1984) claims that "sectional" conflict underpins party competition and issue conflict in Congress, Trubowitz (1998, 200) asserts, "By the 1980s the Republicans, once the party of protection, had become the party of free trade. There is little mystery as to why; as the party was becoming increasingly 'westernized,' the West was becoming increasingly internationalized." Shoch (2001, 68), while conceding that "labor's turn toward protectionism prompted a similar move by Northern Democrats," still holds that "the geographical shift in the parties' bases of support" was a key factor in their role reversal on trade.

---

[17] Of course, even here, inconsistencies emerge as politicians seek to lure new groups into their coalitions, as I discuss in Chapters 3 and 4.

It is important to address such contentions because they have two key implications relevant to this book. First, the theory that the changing geographic constituency of the parties produced their reversal on trade implies that this shift stems less from coalition maintenance than coalition group incorporation. Second, since modern MCs do not move from state to state, these authors imply that the change in Congress on trade issues occurred via replacement rather than adaptation among MCs.

In fact, the explanation based on regional shifts is largely mistaken. It cannot account for most of the change that has occurred in the parties' positions on trade policy. I demonstrate this in two ways below. First, I examine the effect of party affiliation on senators' voting on selected major trade bills over the last several decades. Then I examine the voting behavior of MCs over time.

Table 2-1 includes results that allow for an assessment of the claim that the divergent economies of the parties' regional bases underlie interparty disagreement on trade issues. I report the percentage of votes on the pro-trade side cast by senators from each party in several Congresses in which major trade bills were considered. The roll calls are all of the trade policy votes included in the *Congressional Quarterly* key votes series from its inception in 1945 to the present. Higher scores indicate that a party was relatively more supportive of trade liberalization. By subtracting the parties' mean scores we can observe the extent to which a bill divided Congress along partisan lines. I report the resulting statistic, the interparty difference of means.

I also present the same statistics for the subset of senators from states that elected one senator from each party, often termed "mixed delegations." If party divisions on trade stem from the economic interests of the regions they represent, we should expect to see the gap between Democrats and Republicans vanish or be greatly reduced among the subset of senators elected from the same states. If so, the interparty gap in support on a roll call should be far smaller among the mixed-delegation senators than it is in the Senate as a whole.

Table 2-1 reveals two results bearing directly on the claim that shifts in the parties' geographic bases caused them to change sides on trade issues. First, the interparty difference changes from positive to negative over time as Democrats go from taking a more free-trading stand than Republicans as late as the 1960s to adopting a more protectionist policy than them in later Congresses.

More importantly, comparison of the interparty difference for trade liberalization among senators from mixed delegations with that in the

TABLE 2-1. *Interparty Differences in Support for Freer Trade among All Senators and among Democrats and Republicans from the Same States: Key Votes, 79th through 109th Congresses (1945–2006)*

| Year | Issue | Percentage of Democrats on Pro-Trade Side | Percentage of Republicans on Pro-Trade Side | Interparty Difference of Means for All Senators | Interparty Difference of Means for Mixed-Delegation Senators Only |
|---|---|---|---|---|---|
| 1945 | Reciprocal trade | 81% (N = 52) | 26% (N = 39) | 55% (N = 91) | 40% (N = 20) |
| 1949 | Reciprocal trade | 91% (N = 53) | 0% (N = 42) | 91% (N = 95) | 78% (N = 18) |
| 1955 | Reciprocal trade | 48.8% (N = 45) | 0% (N = 46) | 48.8% (N = 91) | 75% (N = 16) |
| 1958 | Reciprocal trade | 62.5% (N = 48) | 78.3% (N = 46) | −15.8% (N = 94) | −16.7% (N = 24) |
| 1962 | Trade expansion act | 77% (N = 60) | 3% (N = 33) | 74% (N = 93) | 87% (N = 30) |
| 1974 | Trade reform act | 71.2% (N = 52) | 89.7% (N = 39) | −18.5% (N = 91) | 0% (N = 38) |
| 1985 | Textile import quotas | 24% (N = 45) | 53% (N = 53) | −29% (N = 98) | −20% (N = 44) |
| 1987 | Omnibus trade bill | 0% (N = 54) | 58.7% (N = 44) | −58.7% (N = 98) | −50% (N = 44) |
| 1988 | Omnibus trade bill | 3.8% (N = 53) | 77.8% (N = 45) | −74% (N = 98) | −76.2% (N = 44) |
| 1991 | MFN for China | 12.5% (N = 56) | 86% (N = 43) | −73.5% (N = 99) | −81.8% (N = 44) |
| 1993 | NAFTA | 49.1% (N = 55) | 77.3% (N = 44) | −28.2% (N = 99) | −10% (N = 40) |
| 1994 | GATT/WTO | 68.5% (N = 54) | 67.4% (N = 46) | 1.1% (N = 100) | −16.7% (N = 36) |
| 1997 | Fast track | 57.8% (N = 45) | 78.2% (N = 55) | −20.4% (N = 100) | −21.1% (N = 38) |
| 2002 | Trade promotion authority | 49% (N = 49) | 89.1% (N = 46) | −40.1% (N = 95) | −25% (N = 26) |
| 2005 | DR-CAFTA | 25% (N = 45) | 80% (N = 54) | −55% (N = 98) | −46% (N = 26) |

49

Senate as a whole reveals only modest and inconsistent differences. The gap between the parties in mixed-delegation states is usually at least two-thirds of that among senators generally and in half of the cases it is actually *larger* than the interparty difference in the entire Senate. These findings demonstrate that even on trade issues, where local concentrated interests do clearly play a role, differences in geographic constituencies were not the chief source of parties' disagreement. Even in the same states Democratic and Republican senators differed significantly on trade policy throughout the period studied.

### SHIFTS AMONG ELITES

Although informative, the results in Table 2-1 do not allow us to assess the relative importance of elite replacement versus conversion as sources of change in the parties' positions. Although change stemming from regional shifts must occur via turnover, the fact that geographical change in constituencies was not the key factor does not mean that replacement was *not* important. For example, generational change might have been the major source of the parties' reversals on trade if incumbents did not revise their positions.

We know that the parties in Congress realigned on trade issues, but I have not shown how this happened and the extent to which elite turnover or conversion by incumbents was responsible for the change that occurred. To answer that question I turn to longitudinal examination of MCs' voting patterns on trade issues.

Figure 2-3 depicts the changing positions of the parties on trade. One line represents the difference between the mean level of support for trade liberalization among Republican representatives minus the same statistic for the House Democratic caucus. The other depicts the same statistic albeit for only the 94 MCs who served throughout the period surveyed (1961–1974). The votes used to calculate the means are reported in the appendix. I choose this period because, as Figure 2-1 shows, this is when the most important shift in the parties' relative positions on trade occurred.

To the extent that MCs' stands are stable and replacement is the chief mechanism producing party position change, the two lines should diverge over time as the positions of the parties evolve while the relationship between party and vote among the subset of long-serving MCs remains stable.

The chart reveals two points. First, the shift in the parties' position on trade issues occurred rapidly, with a substantial reversal in the alignment

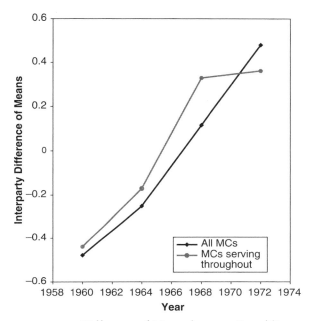

FIGURE 2-3. Difference of Means between Republican and Democratic Support for Trade Liberalization among Representatives (Republican Mean – Democratic Mean), 87th through 93rd Congresses (1961–1974)

of Democrats and Republicans evident in less than a decade. The speed of this process exceeds that of some other cases considered in other chapters in which change stems from the gradual shifts of groups into and out of party coalitions.

Second, the trend among the 94 MCs whose tenures straddled the realignment period was consistently similar to that prevailing in the chamber as a whole. At no time does the relationship between party and trade policy voting differ notably in this subset of long-serving representatives from the pattern among the rest of their colleagues. This suggests that replacement was *not* the chief cause of the party position change on trade policy. Instead MCs heeded signals from party-linked groups and adapted.

Looking at MCs' positions on two trade policy roll calls with similar cutpoints in two Congresses with comparable party compositions offers another angle from which to assess the roles of replacement and conversion among legislators in producing party position change on trade policy.

TABLE 2-2. *Percentage of Long-Serving Representatives (Stayers) and the Rest of House Voting for Freer Trade on Two Trade Policy Votes with Similar Cutpoints: 1962 and 1973*

|  |  | Democrats | Republicans |
|---|---|---|---|
| 87th Congress (1961–1962)[a] | Stayers | 82.0% (N = 102) | 22.2% (N = 36) |
| 93rd Congress (1973–1974)[b] | Stayers | 53% (N = 100) | 86.1% (N = 36) |
| 87th Congress (1961–1962)[a] | Rest of House | 82.7% (N = 156) | 26.5% (N = 136) |
| 93rd Congress (1973–1974)[b] | Rest of House | 36.8% (N = 133) | 83.7% (N = 129) |

[a] 87th Congress (60.7% Democratic), H.R. 11970, June 28, 1962: Motion to recommit Trade Expansion Act (59.6% voting pro-trade)
[b] 93rd Congress (56.2% Democratic), H. Res. 657: Rule for consideration of Trade Reform Act (60.6% voting pro-trade)

Table 2-2 reports the positions of long-serving representatives and the rest of their colleagues on two trade policy votes, one taken in 1962, when Democrats still were the more free-trading party, and another from 1973, when they had moved to the protectionist side of the debate. The partisan composition of Congress and the percentage of legislators voting on the pro-trade side is quite similar in both years, making this comparison especially useful in obviating concerns that the movement evident in Figure 2-3 is due to shifts in party composition of the House or changes in the cutpoint of measures brought up for a vote.

The table reveals that the parties' reversal on trade is quite visible among the long-serving MCs voting on both occasions more than a decade apart, much as it is in the rest of the House, a category including members serving during the first vote but not the second and vice versa. Among long-serving Democratic MCs the shift is slightly less pronounced than in other categories, but still quite substantial.

To supplement this analysis I also provide a more comprehensive statistical look at the role of conversion based on Rapoport and Stone's formula. There are two statistics of interest, the conversion share and the net conversion effect. The conversion share is the fraction of change explained by shifts among continuing MCs of each party calculated according to the Rapoport and Stone formula. To calculate the net conversion effect I multiplied the shift in party means occurring in each Congress by the conversion share. Summing the resulting amounts yields a total that I divide by the change in the mean score from the first Congress observed until the last one. The resulting figure is the net conversion effect.

The results show that 58.6 percent of change in House Democrats' position on trade issues stemmed from conversion, rather than replacement. For the Republicans the percentage is 49 percent. Since most MCs were Democrats throughout this period, most of the change in the chamber as a whole, 53 percent, occurred via conversion.

Recall that the Rapoport and Stone formula is apt to overstate the effect of replacement in that it assumes that had individuals not left the sample, their positions on issues would not have changed at all – unlike those who remained. Even so, this measure still shows conversion accounting for a majority of change in this case.[18] Taking this bias into account, these results imply that while Republicans might have been more recalcitrant than Democrats (or simply more apt to leave office during this period, such as because of the 1964 election), most of the change in *both* the parties' positions stemmed from conversion, with replacement playing a secondary role. One could also argue that there was less change in the absolute position of GOP MCs, but that they were leapfrogged by newly protectionist congressional Democrats.

It is not surprising that many MCs changed their position on trade policy in the early 1970s. Labor unions and business groups that had long-standing relationships with legislators were not shy in pressuring these officials to modify their position on trade policy. Although trade was not the only item on these lobbies' agendas, it was quite salient for them and has remained so in many cases. Scholars have shown (Engel and Jackson 1998; Francia 2001; Jackson and Engel 2003) that MCs who voted the "wrong way" on key trade issues received significantly less financial support from these sectors in the subsequent election, even when they had otherwise consistently sided with the union or business lobbies in question.

There have also been cases of Democratic MCs who voted against the AFL-CIO position on trade policy and were subsequently defeated in primaries. Prominent examples include Rep. Marty Martinez (D-CA) and Rep. Thomas Sawyer (D-OH). Although we cannot assign causality in these cases with certainty, reports suggested that the strong opposition of unions to these incumbents inspired by their support for freer trade was

---

[18] The combined total is simply the percentage of change accounted for by conversion in each party as a fraction of the total change. This statistic gives more weight to the party that has changed more.

a key factor leading to their downfalls.[19] In any case, the mere perception that the unions played this role enhanced their ability to influence other Democratic MCs on trade issues.

Yet partisan divisions on trade among voters have been far less evident among voters than in Congress. Destler (1995) attributes this absence of mass-level polarization on trade to the free-trade consensus reigning among recent presidents from both parties. Linking this claim with Adams's (1997) account of the lag in polarization on abortion among voters discussed in Chapter 3, it seems that presidential campaigns may do at least as much as roll calls to establish parties' reputations on issues. Usually, however, there is little discrepancy between these signals.

OTHER CASES OF COALITION MAINTENANCE

On trade policy MCs changed their positions in order to retain the support of long-standing allies. This was an almost pure case of coalition maintenance. Yet trade policy is not the only issue area in which this dynamic is evident. It was visible in racial politics as well. As I show in Chapter 4, once the demands of the civil rights movement began to impinge on the business community, Republican support for a strong governmental role in ensuring racial equality declined precipitously.

There are still other examples that I do not explore at length here. One case is the politics of immigration. Traditionally this issue has cleaved both party coalitions. Republicans have been torn between nativists and business interests seeking cheaper labor. Democrats have been no less divided. Traditionally the home of immigrant groups, the Democratic Party also won support from unions that long viewed newcomers as a threat to their members' wages. As a result, legislators in both parties were often cross-pressured by different components of their party coalitions and votes on immigration frequently cut across party lines on Capitol Hill.

Tichenor (2002, 255) describes how immigration politics cross-pressured politicians in the 1980s. He notes, "Employer sanctions were originally a liberal cause championed by organized labor and its

---

[19] On Martinez: E. J. Dionne, "Lean Labor's Big Win," *Washington Post,* March 14, 2000, A17; "A Clean Sweep," *American Prospect,* June 19, 2000, 24; "California: Thirty-first District," *Almanac of American Politics 2002.* On Sawyer: "In Ohio, Upset of Sawyer Muddies November Outlook," *Congress Daily,* May 8, 2002, "17th District Rejects 'Import' Tom Sawyer," *Plain Dealer,* May 12, 2002, H1; "Out of Home, House; Redistricting Combines with NAFTA Foes' Long Memory to Pull the Seat Out from under Longtime Incumbent Sawyer," *Plain Dealer,* May 9, 2002, B8.

congressional allies. But once ethnic lobbies and civil rights groups protested that sanctions would produce job discrimination against all who looked and sounded foreign, the question of immigration control hopelessly divided liberal interest groups and Democratic politicians."

Yet the politics of immigration have changed in recent years. Many labor leaders have become convinced that immigration cannot be stopped and that employer sanctions never will be rigorously enforced. Accordingly, unions' best hope for the future is to organize those working in the United States, regardless of their current legal status. Although still critical of "guest worker" programs, in 2000 the AFL-CIO reversed course and embraced a policy of what is variously termed "amnesty" or a "path to citizenship" for millions who immigrated illegally to the United States (Freeman and Birrell 2001, 540).[20] Other components of the labor movement, most notably the new Change to Win (CTW) group including the SEIU – now the nation's largest union – and UNITE-HERE, a union that has many Latino members, go farther than the AFL-CIO and even accept guest-worker programs. These unions supported the failed McCain-Kennedy "comprehensive reform" bill in 2007. More recently, gaps between unions on immigration issues appeared to have narrowed. In 2009 leading unions previously divided over the guest-worker issue embraced a compromise proposal in anticipation of a renewed push for immigration reform.[21]

These shifts by a key coalition component have had visible consequences for parties' positioning on immigration policy. While Republicans in Congress remain divided over immigration between business interests and grassroots nativists, the shifts in the stands of labor unions have reduced cross-pressures and divisions among Democratic elites on the issue.[22] Some disagreement remains among both unions and congressional Democrats on immigration issues, but far less than once existed.

Party position change has multiple sources. The rapid reversals based on preference shifts among existing constituencies I have discussed in this chapter are only one cause. The drive to add new groups to the party or coalition group incorporation is important as well. I turn to it in the next chapter.

[20] See also "Labor Urges Amnesty for Illegal Immigrants," *New York Times*, February 17, 2000, A26.
[21] "Fence-Sitters; Democrats Are Having a Grand Old Time Watching the Republican Rumble over Immigration," *Boston Globe*, April 9, 2006. C1; "Labor Groups Reach an Accord on Immigration," *New York Times*, April 14, 2009, 1.
[22] "GOP Divided on Immigration Policy," *National Public Radio* (Nexis transcript), December 2, 2005.

# 3

# Coalition Group Incorporation

## *The Politics of Abortion and Gun Control*

> If a man does not make new acquaintance as he advances through life, he will soon find himself left alone. A man, Sir, should keep his friendship in constant repair.
>
> Dr. Johnson, quoted in Boswell's *Life of Samuel Johnson*

Although much of politicians' energies are devoted to retaining support from their traditional backers, this is not all they do. Attempts to win over new allies are also important, if less frequent endeavors. One of the major causes of party position change is the attempt by party elites to bring a new group into their coalition. This process differs in some important respects from the dynamics of coalition maintenance discussed in Chapter 2. Two well-known instances I explore in this chapter are the cases of abortion and gun control.

Since the 1970s the abortion issue has become very prominent in national politics. The debate has become increasingly partisan, with Republicans tending ever more toward the "pro-life" side and Democrats to the "pro-choice" one. Many scholars (Abramowitz 1994; Adams 1997; Cook, Jelen, and Wilcox 1998; Layman 2001) have examined the relationship between attitudes on abortion and partisanship and voting behavior. Yet most research is focused on mass responses to cues from political elites such as members of Congress, among whom positions on abortion have increasingly become a function of party affiliation. It remains to be shown how this elite polarization developed.

The dynamics of abortion politics differed from those evident on race or trade policy. While abortion is not a new practice, it has not always been a matter of public controversy the way that trade policy or the status of African Americans have been. When the topic was politicized in the

late 1960s it initially cut across party lines. The parties' gradual polarization on the issue of abortion cannot be explained as the responsiveness to traditional constituencies of coalition maintenance. Democratic
voters were *more* pro-life than Republicans until well into the 1980s, as
Adams (1997) shows. Yet gradually pro-life and pro-groups, encouraged
by political leaders, have become key components of the Democratic and
Republican coalitions, and partisans at the elite and mass levels have
become increasingly polarized on abortion.

This process has been a gradual one along the lines of Key's (1959) "secular realignment" because it has required behavioral shifts on the mass
and elite levels. As groups active on one side or the other of the abortion
issue have become more central to each party, the pressure on politicians
to conform to their demands has increased. Elected officials' greater con-
formity to their camp's dominant position on the issue has in turn sharp-
ened the parties' images on abortion, further encouraging pro-choice and
pro-life voters and activists to find a home in Democratic and Republican
parties, respectively.

Adams (1997) finds that the development of abortion politics fits
the issue evolution model: elites realign via replacement, giving cues to
masses as an issue becomes partisan. Layman and Carsey (1998) show
that some voters and party activists have adjusted their views to conform
to those of elites, while others have switched parties over the issue. Such
attitudinal and partisan conversion may produce more rapid change
than models based on generational replacement at the mass level can
accommodate.

Yet these studies leave key questions unanswered. Whatever combination of generational replacement, partisan conversion, and attitudinal conversion accounts for change among voters, most scholars believe
that elite cues precipitate these shifts. Yet except for Adams, who pos-
its replacement among MCs, the works cited do not explain elite-level
change. Below I show the importance of conversion among the most
prominent cue-giving elites, presidential candidates, and nationally
known politicians, as well as among MCs generally.

Abortion was largely undiscussed in national politics until the early
1970s. The drive to reform and liberalize abortion laws that began in
the 1960s was led by physicians seeking to increase their professional
autonomy and gain the ability to perform abortions without fear of legal
sanction (Luker 1984). These doctors were not making rights-based
claims that would invoke scrutiny by federal courts. Medical practices
were traditionally regulated at the state level. Moreover, reform seemed

achievable as states in different regions of the country liberalized their abortion statutes starting in 1967.

However, there were factors that brought the abortion issue into national politics. Some observers credit the Supreme Court's 1973 *Roe v. Wade* decision. Without this controversial ruling, they argue that the issue might not have become nationalized, and both the legal status of abortion and American politics might have evolved very differently (Rosenberg 1991). Similarly, in the aftermath of *Roe*, Ronald Reagan is often seen as the politician most responsible for the parties' polarization on the abortion (Adams 1997).

Yet even before *Roe*, let alone Reagan's election in 1980, various actors began to import the abortion controversy into national politics. The author of the first proposed federal legislation on abortion was a Republican, Senator Bob Packwood of Oregon. In April 1970 he introduced the "National Abortion Act," a bill designed to secure the "fundamental and constitutional rights" of women. A year later Packwood proposed to liberalize the abortion statute of the District of Columbia (Rosenberg 1991, 183).

More importantly, leadership of the struggle for liberalization of abortion laws passed from doctors to feminists in the early 1970s. These activists were not satisfied with a gradual state-level reform process in which the professional prerogatives of physicians – as opposed to the reproductive rights of women – were expanded. In May 1972 Rep. Bella Abzug (D-NY) introduced a bill to guarantee abortion rights.[1] At the 1972 Democratic Convention feminists forced a floor fight when they sought to add an abortion rights plank to the Democratic platform.

The influence of this group in the Democratic Party was quite limited in 1972 and far less than they would later enjoy. The Democratic presidential nominee that year, Senator George McGovern (D-SD), held to a "states' rights" position on abortion and blocked the feminists' proposed pro-choice plank. Still the episode indicated that the issue was beginning to emerge in party politics at the national level. Despite rejecting the feminists' plank, McGovern was still tarred as the candidate of "acid, amnesty and abortion."[2]

---

[1] "Javits Clears Path for a Conservative," *New York Times*, May 27, 1972, 16.

[2] This phrase has been attributed to Senate minority leader Hugh Scott (R-PA) (Kaufman 2000, 236), but columnist Robert Novak (2007) asserts that the originator of this turn of phrase was Senator Thomas Eagleton, a pro-life Catholic Democrat from Missouri. These not-for-attribution comments, which Novak revealed only after Eagleton's death,

Yet on the Republican side President Nixon saw the abortion issue as a useful tool in his bid to expand his electoral coalition. Nixon was widely seen as an accidental president from the minority party who owed his narrow victory – his 43 percent of the popular vote was the lowest share of any president since Wilson in 1912 – to the turmoil of 1968 and the Vietnam War. During much of Nixon's first term he feared that George Wallace would make another run for the White House as an independent candidate, cutting into his support (Carter 1995, 397).

Recognizing his vulnerability, Nixon actively sought support from groups outside the traditional Republican base. He made some moves designed to appeal to the public broadly, including his détente policy and his largely successful effort to use fiscal and monetary policy to ensure that the economy would be booming when he sought reelection (Matusow 1998). As befitted a president from the minority party who had won only a narrow plurality, Nixon also hewed to a moderate line in domestic policy and acquiesced in many popular policies associated with his opponents, acting as what Skowronek (1993) terms a "third-way" president.[3]

Yet Nixon also sought to expand his support by targeting particular elements of the Democratic coalition. White Catholics were one major candidate for group incorporation. Nixon's chief of staff, H. R. Haldeman, reported in his diary that by January 1970 the president had begun to envision "our own new coalition based on Silent Majority, blue collar Catholic, Poles, Italians, and Irish" since there was "no promise with Jews or Negroes" (Frymer and Skrentny 1998, 151).

White Catholics might have been expected to respond much as other voters did to the improved economy, détente, winding down of the Vietnam War, and Nixon's popular stands on "law and order" and busing. Yet in order to woo them away from Democrats the president also employed two focused appeals. Nixon jettisoned the Republicans' traditional GOP resistance to public aid for church schools, advocating a program of "parochiaid." He also signaled opposition to abortion, entering a debate he could have easily avoided. (Nixon also was open to symbolic appeals and sought to name a Catholic to the Supreme Court.)[4]

---

came just months before McGovern selected Eagleton as his running mate. In any case, the phrase was picked up by Republicans and used against McGovern that year.

[3] See Hoff (1994) for an extensive discussion of Nixon's domestic policies.

[4] In a recorded discussion with his aides Nixon argued, "Politically, we are going to gain a lot more from a Catholic. ... It'll mean more to the Catholics, that's my point, than it will to the Protestants. The Protestants expect to have things. The Catholics don't"

In April 1971 Nixon issued an executive order directing military hospitals to follow the laws of the states in which they were located when deciding whether to perform abortions, even though federal facilities were exempt from such statutes.[5] This move reversed a Defense Department policy adopted a year earlier allowing doctors in military hospitals to perform abortions when the mental or physical health of the mother was in danger, a standard more liberal than that prevailing in many states at the time.

Nixon took more visible steps on abortion during his reelection campaign. On May 5, 1972, the president publicly rejected the report of the Commission on Population Growth that he himself had appointed in 1970. The commission called for states to allow doctors to perform abortions on a woman's request and advised that they make contraceptive and family planning services available to teens. In response, Nixon issued a statement noting abortion was "an unacceptable means of population control" and that he opposed "unrestricted abortion policies." He also rejected the commission's call for state provision of contraception for teens.[6]

Since the chairman of the panel, John D. Rockefeller III, was well known as an advocate of population control before his appointment, the commission's findings were unlikely to have come as a surprise to the Nixon administration.[7] Thus Nixon's rejection of the group's report, along with his reversal in 1971 of the military hospitals' policy he had allowed to go into effect in 1970, suggests a political shift on the president's part.

More dramatic evidence of Nixon's decision to take an unmistakable stand on abortion emerged when he publicly intervened in the abortion controversy in New York state. In 1970 that state had greatly liberalized its abortion statute, a move backed by then-governor Nelson Rockefeller, a Republican (and brother of John D. Rockefeller III). In 1972 Cardinal Terence Cooke of New York City figured prominently in the campaign to repeal his state's new abortion law. Nixon wrote a letter to the cardinal that was promptly leaked. The letter became front-page news

---

(Dean 2001, 73). Absent a compelling candidate who was conservative, well qualified, available, and young, Nixon eventually dropped the idea.

[5] "Statement about Policy on Abortions at Military Base Hospitals in the United States," April 3, 1971, *Public Papers of the Presidents of the United States, Richard Nixon 1971, 1972*, 500, cited in Burelli (2002).

[6] "President Bars Birth Curb Plans," *New York Times*, May 6, 1972, 1.

[7] "Population Student: John Davison Rockefeller 3d," *New York Times*, March 17, 1970, 27.

the day after his rejection of the Rockefeller Commission's report was announced. Nixon wrote that while abortion was a state issue, he wanted to make clear that he supported the cardinal's efforts to repeal the liberal New York statute:

The unrestricted abortion policies now recommended by some Americans, and the liberalized abortion policies in effect in some sections of this country seem to me impossible to reconcile with either our religious traditions or our Western heritage. One of the foundation stones of our society and civilization is the profound belief that human life, all human life, is a precious commodity – not to be taken without the gravest of causes.

Yet in this great and good country of ours in recent years, the right to life of literally hundreds of thousands of unborn children has been destroyed – legally – but in my judgment without anything approaching adequate justification. Surely in the on-going national debate about the particulars of the "quality of life" the preservation of life should be moved to the top of the agenda.

Your decision and that of tens of thousands of Catholics, Protestants, Jews, and men and women of no particular faith, to act in the public forum as defenders of the right to life of the unborn, is truly a noble endeavor. In this calling, you and they have my admiration, sympathy and support.[8]

The release of the letter set off a controversy. Gov. Rockefeller was reportedly "deeply wounded." John Ehrlichman, the president's chief domestic policy aide, claimed that the letter – drafted by Nixon speechwriter Pat Buchanan – was intended to remain private. Ehrlichman conceded that the White House had authorized the archdiocese to release the letter, but contended that this was a result of "sloppy staff work."[9] During the campaign, however, Nixon's campaign used his statements of support for parochial schools and opposition to abortion to appeal to traditionally Democratic Catholic voters.[10]

Having staked out a pro-life position that distinguished him from his opponent, Nixon did little to limit the occurrence of abortions. As Epstein and Kobylka (1992) note, Nixon made no move to restrict the use of Medicaid funds for abortions, although he could have done so without contradicting his stated view that regulation of abortion was generally a matter for the states. Nixon's Justice Department also filed no brief in

---

[8] "President Supports Repeal of State Law on Abortion," *New York Times,* May 7, 1972, 1.
[9] "Nixon Aides Explain Aims of Letter on Abortion Law," *New York Times,* May 11, 1972, 1.
[10] "Nixon Steps up Wooing of the Catholic Ethnics, Traditionally Democrats," *Wall Street Journal,* June 1, 1972, 1.

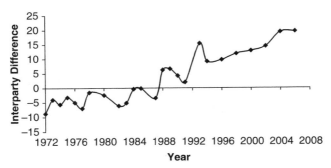

FIGURE 3-1. Interparty Difference in Support for Abortion Rights (Democratic Support – Republican Support), General Social Survey, 1972–2006

*Roe,* and he seems not to have reacted publicly to the decision, in which three of his four Supreme Court appointees voted with the majority.

In taking a pro-life stand Nixon was *not* reflecting majority opinion in his party. Polls taken since the abortion reform movement began in the mid-1960s showed Republicans to be *more* supportive of abortion rights than Democrats. A Gallup poll in June 1972, shortly after Nixon's intervention in the New York debate, found that 68 percent of Republicans, but only 59 percent of Democrats, agreed that "the decision to have an abortion should be left solely to a women and her doctor" (Pomeroy and Landman 1972, 45).

Surveys in later years revealed that GOP identifiers remained at least slightly *more* pro-choice than Democrats until the mid-1980s (Adams 1997). Figure 3-1 tracks the difference between Democratic and Republican identifiers on abortion rights in the General Social Survey from 1972 to 2006. The interparty difference measured here is the average of the gap in support for legal abortion in various circumstances between Democratic and Republican identifiers.[11]

The figure reveals that the polarization of the parties on the mass level was very gradual and that the now familiar pattern of Republicans being more pro-life than Democrats emerges only toward the end of the Reagan

---

[11]  The six cases about which respondents were surveyed are: when the health of the mother is in jeopardy, when she is a rape victim, when she is single, when she wants no more children, when she is poor, and when the child will have birth defects.

administration. Yet although slow to emerge, the gap has continued to grow.

They may be strange to read today, but the poll numbers from 1972 should not be surprising. The Republican Party then drew support chiefly from Northern white Protestants and more affluent and educated voters generally. Many of these voters were from the more theologically liberal "mainline" Protestant denominations that did not unequivocally oppose abortion. The Protestant Christian right tendency so prominent in contemporary American politics had yet to emerge. Many socially conservative Protestants the issue would later mobilize were still Democrats in 1972 or apolitical.

Anti-abortion views were most common among Catholics, Southerners, and less-educated voters. Many black voters were also pro-life. All of these groups were primarily Democratic during this period. Some of them, for example, white Southerners, had in many cases voted for Barry Goldwater and George Wallace but were not yet Republican identifiers and still often favored Democratic candidates in congressional and state elections.

If Nixon was not representing majority sentiment among Republicans on abortion, neither was he catering to an organized pro-life constituency within his party. Yet, importantly, nor was there an organization that could mobilize the pro-choice Republican majority that might have deterred Nixon from taking the stand he did. The leading pro-choice Republican organizations now active, the WISH list, Republicans for Choice, and the Republican Majority for Choice, are small and were not founded until 1989, 1992, and 1999, respectively, well after pro-life forces had gained ascendancy in the GOP.[12] The absence of sizeable groups on *either* side of the issue in the Republican Party of the early 1970s gave Nixon room to maneuver on the question of abortion.

Patrick Buchanan explicitly compared Nixon's use of the abortion issue to Goldwater's focus on race as a way to split the Democratic coalition eight years earlier. "As Sen. Goldwater said, 'you have to go hunting where the ducks are,' and this is where the ducks are," the Nixon aide explained.[13]

Politicians always have to act in an uncertain context. It was not clear that taking any stand on abortion, let alone siding with the pro-life

---

[12] http://www.republicansforchoice.com/annstone.htm, http://www.thewishlist.org/History.htm. On the Republican Pro-Choice Coalition's formation see "Bush Looks Just Darling to GOP Establishment," *Washington Post*, May 5, 1999, A8.

[13] "Nixon Steps Up Wooing of the Catholic Ethnics, Traditionally Democrats," *Wall Street Journal*, June 1, 1972, 1.

forces, would be politically wise for President Nixon. Yet some of his advisors thought it was. An unnamed Nixon aide in the same story in which Buchanan was quoted argued:

The liberal Republican woman in the suburbs who favors abortion won't vote against the President just because he's against it. It isn't as important to her as other issues. And the strong pro-abortionists, the women's-libbers like Gloria Steinem, they aren't going to vote for him anyhow. But the working-class Catholic mother, who thinks abortion is evil, will vote for him just because he's against it.[14]

Nixon was reelected in a landslide, greatly improving on his 1968 showing among white voters generally, including Catholics. Yet many factors were working in Nixon's favor in 1972, so the effectiveness of his use of the abortion issue as a targeted appeal to Catholics remains unclear. Yet it is strategic calculations like the one quoted above that politicians must make, often with limited information.

Nixon's stand was maintained, more or less, by his successor, Gerald Ford, who had to maneuver in a post-*Roe* context in which abortion was becoming more salient and MCs were beginning to cast votes on the issue. The fact that the issue's visibility in politics remained limited, however, is demonstrated by the fact that the word "abortion" does not appear in Ford's presidential papers until 1976. Ford, unlike later GOP presidential nominees or his rival for the Republican presidential nomination, Ronald Reagan, did not even in principle favor a national ban on abortions. Yet he did support an amendment to the Constitution that would overturn *Roe*, which he said "goes too far," and favored returning the issue to the states.[15] Ford also opposed federal funding for abortions.[16]

Ford's opponent in 1976, Jimmy Carter, did not support an amendment overturning *Roe*. Yet, like Ford, he took a more moderate position than subsequent nominees of his party would. Carter coupled his support for the continued legality of abortion with unequivocal statements that the practice was "wrong," and – unlike later Democratic presidential nominees – he opposed federally funded abortions. With this position Carter displeased activists on both sides of the issue (Flint and Porter 2005).

---

[14] Ibid.

[15] "The President's Press Conference of February 8th, 1976," no. 67 at "The American Presidency Project," http://www.presidency.ucsb.edu.

[16] "Veto of the Appropriations Bill for the Departments of Labor and Health, Education, and Welfare," no. 830 at "The American Presidency Project," http://www.presidency.ucsb.edu.

Still, the parties were beginning to differentiate themselves on abortion. The gap between them in 1976 was already sufficient to prompt speculation about whether Carter would lose ground among traditionally Democratic Catholics and Ford would consolidate the gains that Nixon had made among them in 1972. Even so, Ford's position was reportedly "only marginally more acceptable to church leaders" than Carter's.[17] In 1976 the Republican platform was a bit more equivocal than it would be in later years on abortion, but, in part reflecting the efforts of the Reagan forces, it leaned toward the pro-life side:

The question of abortion is one of the most difficult and controversial of our time. It is undoubtedly a moral and personal issue but it also involves complex questions relating to medical science and criminal justice. There are those in our Party who favor complete support for the Supreme Court decision which permits abortion on demand. There are others who share sincere convictions that the Supreme Court's decision must be changed by a constitutional amendment prohibiting all abortions. Others have yet to take a position, or they have assumed a stance somewhere in between polar positions. We protest the Supreme Court's intrusion into the family structure through its denial of the parents' obligation and right to guide their minor children. The Republican Party favors a continuance of the public dialogue on abortion and supports the efforts of those who seek enactment of a constitutional amendment to restore protection of the right to life for unborn children.[18]

However, despite this platform, Ford made it known that he "personally" supported only an amendment returning abortion jurisdiction to the states. It is also notable that in 1976 opposition to abortion was still seen by political reporters – more than three years after *Roe* – as a "Catholic" concern.[19] The Moral Majority was founded only in 1979, and pro-life activism was not yet widespread among conservative Protestants at the time of the contest between Ford and Carter (Harding 2000).

In Congress the polarization on abortion was not yet striking either. The most prominent opponent of abortion, Rep. Henry Hyde (R-IL), was a Catholic Republican, and GOP MCs were already less supportive of abortion rights than Democrats, especially in the House. Yet the issue still cut across party lines to a great extent. For example, when the Senate

---

[17] "Ford Hopes Linked to Catholic Vote," *New York Times,* September 5, 1976, 1.
[18] "1976 Republican Platform," http://www.ford.utexas.edu/library/document/platform/rights.htm.
[19] See "Can Carter Win the Catholic Vote?" *U.S. News & World Report,* September 20, 1976, 15; "The Abortion Issue: Candidates Hear It from All Sides," *U.S. News & World Report,* September 20, 1976, 18; "Courting the Catholics," *Newsweek,* September 20, 1976, 16; "Is Abortion Really an Issue?" *Newsweek,* September 20, 1976, 18.

voted on a motion to table an anti-abortion constitutional amendment on April 28, 1976, Democratic senators split 33 to 23 to kill the pro-life proposal while Republicans voted 20 to 16 against tabling the measure.[20]

In 1980, however, the gap between the parties on abortion widened with the nomination of Ronald Reagan. The former California governor was far more associated with the pro-life cause than Nixon or Ford had been. Moreover, by the time of Reagan's nomination that movement had grown beyond its Catholic origins. Conservative Protestants were increasingly active politically and more opposed to abortion. Many conservative Protestant leaders were disappointed by Jimmy Carter, whose religiosity and studied vagueness on abortion during much of the 1976 campaign had led some of them to believe he was closer to them on social issues than proved to be the case. In 1980 many in this group supported Reagan (Flint and Porter 2005).

The Republican national convention that nominated Reagan in 1980 showed the increased influence of religious conservatives on the GOP. Not only did it strengthen the pro-life language in the platform, but the endorsement of the Equal Rights Amendment that had been included in prior platforms was removed. Reagan's leading rival for the Republican presidential nomination, George H. W. Bush, took a pro-choice stand during the primaries and won six contests, including the Iowa caucuses. Yet Bush abandoned his abortion stance (along with his support for the ERA and his criticisms of "voodoo economics") when he became Reagan's running mate. No pro-choice Republican has ever come as close as Bush did to winning the party's nomination in 1980.

The Democratic Party also became increasingly identified with one pole in the abortion controversy. George Wallace ran in the primaries in 1976 as an opponent of abortion, as did one-issue protest candidate Ellen McCormick. Former Florida governor Reubin Askew also ran as an abortion foe in 1984. None of these candidates enjoyed any success. Meanwhile Democratic presidential candidates have become less equivocal in their stands on abortion, abandoning Carter's opposition to Medicaid funding of abortions for poor women.[21]

---

[20] See ICPSR Study no. 4.

[21] For Mondale's position, see "Where Democratic Candidates Stand: Part 3," *U.S. News & World Report,* May 28, 1984, 55. For Dukakis, see "Both Candidates Project Family Image, but Differences Appear as They Outline Policies," *St. Petersburg Times,* October 21, 1988, 1A. For Clinton, see "Bush, Clinton and Perot: Where They Stand," *Associated Press,* October 18, 1992.

As the religious right gained influence in the GOP, women's groups that favored both the ERA and abortion rights became more prominent in the Democratic Party. There are several indicators of this trend. The first is the increasing role of feminists in general and the National Organization for Women in particular at Democratic national conventions from 1980 onward (Freeman 1988; Hershey 1993).

Further evidence of the sorting of pro-choice and pro-life activism into the two parties emerges when we examine campaign contributions. There are political action committees dedicated to aiding pro-choice women candidates in both parties. Yet the resources of the Republican pro-choice groups pale before those of their Democratic equivalents. By the 1995–1996 cycle the Democratic group EMILY's List was the single biggest PAC in existence, channeling $12,000,000 to pro-choice Democratic female candidates. The GOP equivalent, the WISH List, contributed just over $1,000,000 to pro-choice female Republican candidates in the same period (Day and Hadley 2001, 674).

When we look at the formally nonpartisan lobbies focused on abortion the story is similar. Already by the 1989–1990 campaign cycle, the leading pro-choice groups, the National Abortion Rights Action League (NARAL) and Planned Parenthood, were giving 89 percent and 98 percent of their contributions, respectively, to Democratic congressional candidates, while the National Right to Life Committee sent 85 percent of their donations to Republicans. Since then these groups' contribution patterns have become even more one-sided.[22]

## CHANGE AMONG ELITES

For many years there was a discrepancy between the parties' elites and masses on abortion. As noted above, Republican voters were more pro-choice than Democrats well into the 1980s. Adams (1997) explains this lag, which contrasts with the rapid shift evident at both the elite and mass levels on race in the mid-1960s, by asserting that until 1980 presidential candidates did not differ greatly on abortion. This explanation, arguable in itself, begs the question of stability in the stands of presidential nominees. Adams (1997, 724) sees George H. W. Bush's reversal on abortion as anomalous, calling it "more likely the exception that proves the rule."[23]

[22] http://www.opensecrets.org/industries/contrib.asp?Ind=Q14&Cycle=1990, http://www.opensecrets.org/industries/contrib.asp?Ind=Q15&Cycle=1990.
[23] In contrast, Poole and Rosenthal (1997, 113) concede that some of the increased correlation between their first-dimension NOMINATE score and MCs' abortion stands

Yet Bush's shift was hardly unique. A surprising number of presidential aspirants in both major parties have altered their position on abortion, with the timing of the shift often suggesting that the motive was the politician's desire to reorient himself from a local constituency to a prospective national party one. Bush's evolution drew comment because it coincided with his selection as Ronald Reagan's running mate in 1980. Pressed by journalists during his 1984 vice-presidential debate with Geraldine Ferraro, Bush stated, "Yes, my position's evolved, but I'd like to see the American who faced with 15 million abortions isn't re-thinking his or her position."[24]

Reagan's earlier "evolution" on the issue attracted less notice than Bush's, but was even more consequential. In 1967, six years before *Roe,* Governor Reagan signed what was then one of the nation's most liberal abortion laws (Boyarsky 1981; Cannon 1991). The California law Reagan approved expanded the category of legal abortions from those required to save a woman's life to cases of rape, incest, and pregnancies endangering a mother's physical or mental health.

The politics of abortion when Governor Reagan signed that California statute differed greatly from the alignments that emerged in later years. In 1967 abortion was not part of a "culture war" as it is today. At the time the chief support for reforming the California law came from doctors, not feminists. On the other side of the debate the Catholic Church constituted the main opposition to abortion law reform. Protestants were not mobilized on the issue. Given this set of combatants, the debate was far less partisan than it would later become. Republican legislators in Sacramento were almost as likely as Democrats to favor a liberalization of the state's abortion statute.[25] The bill passed by a narrow margin and could not have survived a Reagan veto.[26] As critics had warned, many

---

"resulted from well-known flip-flops such as the conversion by Richard Gephardt (D-Mo.) to a pro-choice position."

[24] "The Candidates Debate: Transcript of Philadelphia Debate between Bush and Ferraro," *New York Times,* October 12, 1984, B4.

[25] The same pattern of nonpartisan disputes over abortion pitting doctors against Catholics was evident in other states. Groups later prominent in the controversy including feminists and conservative Protestants were relatively inactive in the state-level debates of the late 1960s. Feminists entered the fray after doctors and Catholics. Conservative Protestants were neither as politically active nor as solidly opposed to abortion as they would come to be in the years following *Roe.* See Harding (2000, 190). Even in Georgia opposition to the 1968 reform came primarily from Catholics (Jain and Gooch 1972).

[26] "Senate Passes Bill to Liberalize Abortion Law," *Los Angeles Times,* June 7, 1967, 1; "Assembly OK's Abortion Bill; Reagan Says He Will Sign," *Los Angeles Times,* June 14, 1967, 1.

doctors – helped by favorable court rulings – construed the "mental health" clause broadly, and legal abortions in California increased 2,000 percent by 1971 (Luker 1984, 94).[27]

As late as April 1975, long after the results of the 1967 California reform were apparent, Reagan defended his initial position (which by then seemed relatively strict), including the crucial health exception that had allowed for so many abortions. Yet just months later Reagan reversed himself, terming his earlier stand a mistake. He claimed that in 1967 he had not realized that physicians would abuse the autonomy they had been given. (Why this was not evident by 1975, Reagan did not explain.) Reagan's new position was that abortions not necessary to save the mother's life should be prohibited.[28]

Reagan's reversal was important in shoring up his support among social conservatives who supported his insurgent challenge to Gerald Ford for the GOP's presidential nomination. Although Ford defeated Reagan after a hard-fought series of primaries, the GOP's platform was modified in line with Reagan's new position in an attempt to unify the party. This plank, and the GOP's identification with the pro-life cause, was further strengthened when Reagan finally captured the party's presidential nomination four years later. Adams (1997, 235) notes that "more than anyone, Ronald Reagan helped establish his party's signals on abortion." If so, the clarity of that signal stemmed in part from Reagan's own recent conversion.

Reagan and the elder President Bush were not the only leading Republicans to change their stands on abortion. George W. Bush as president favored a ban on most abortions. Yet in his first race, a failed 1978 House bid before he had become a born-again Christian and his father had changed his own abortion stand, the younger Bush did not.[29]

Democratic presidential candidates have also modified their positions on abortion over the course of their careers. Both Bill Clinton and Al Gore abandoned their initial opposition to the use of public funds and facilities for abortions. Gore's shift seems greater than Clinton's. In 1984 while serving in the House, Gore even voted for an amendment

[27] Some of this massive increase may reflect greater reporting by doctors who were already performing abortions.

[28] "Reagan Writes," *New York Times Magazine,* December 30, 2000, 38; "Reagan Affirms Anti-Abortion Stand," *New York Times,* February 8, 1976, 44. Interview with former U.S. Rep. and State Senator Anthony Beilenson, sponsor of the 1967 California Therapeutic Abortion Act, Los Angeles, February 23, 1999.

[29] "Magazine Drops the Other Flip-Flopping Shoe on Bush," *Washington Post,* June 15, 2000, A9.

"declaring an unborn child a person at conception." Yet he later became sufficiently pro-choice to win NARAL's endorsement for the Democratic presidential nomination in 2000.[30]

Remarkably, until 2008 there was never a presidential race between two major party nominees who had taken consistent positions on abortion throughout their careers.[31] Thus, although much replacement has occurred among presidential nominees, conversion accounts for the most visible partisan contrasts on abortion in national politics.

It is not only presidential nominees who have revised their positions on abortion. Many less successful presidential contenders also shifted. Senator Edward Kennedy (D-MA), a pro-choice stalwart by the time he sought his party's presidential nomination in 1980, earlier compared "abortion on demand" to euthanasia, eugenics, and the killing of the mentally retarded. Senator Henry "Scoop" Jackson (D-WA), a presidential contender in 1972 and 1976, denounced Senator George McGovern (D-SD) as the candidate of "acid, amnesty and abortion" and at first opposed *Roe*. Yet after the issue reached the Senate in 1974, Jackson established a solidly pro-choice record. The Washington senator not only opposed efforts to ban abortion, but backed federal funding for poor women as well.

In 1972 George McGovern actually held that abortion was a state matter and even after *Roe* initially opposed most publicly funded abortions, although he later became unreservedly pro-choice in his last Senate term and his 1984 bid for the Democratic presidential nomination. Senator Edmund Muskie (D-ME) ended his career as an abortion rights supporter. Yet in 1971 Muskie, then the Democrats' presidential front runner, rejected abortion after the first six weeks of pregnancy. Unlike other

---

[30] "Clinton and Gore Shifted on Abortion," *New York Times*, July 20, 1992, 10A; "Drawing a Line in the Shifting Politics of Abortion," *New York Times*, September 8, 1992, 16A; "Abortion Stance Evolved, Gore Says; Vice President Says He No Longer Backs '87 'Taking of a Human Life' Statement," *Washington Post*, January 30, 2000, A14.

[31] Even Senator McCain and Senator Obama showed some inconsistency on the issue, albeit far less than previous nominees. In 1999 McCain did briefly suggest that he did not support the repeal of *Roe*, but under fire he speedily clarified this position. See "Anti-Politician McCain Shows Political Skills," *New York Times*, December 30, 1999, A1. Before and after these statements McCain consistently voted an anti-abortion line over the course of his long career, including support of resolutions condemning *Roe*. Obama voted "present" on abortion-related issues several times while serving in the Illinois Senate, However, this was part of a strategy coordinated with pro-choice activists and was not taken by these groups as a reflection of real ambivalence on Obama's part regarding the issue. "It's Not Just 'Ayes' and 'Nays': Obama's Votes in Illinois Echo," *New York Times*, December 20, 2007, A1.

Democratic presidential contenders, Alabama governor George Wallace went from favoring *Roe* to supporting efforts to overturn it.[32]

The cast of characters in Democratic presidential nomination contests in the 1980s included several candidates who revisited the abortion issue before launching their White House bids. Invariably such shifts were in the pro-choice direction. Rep. Dick Gephardt (D-MO) and Senator Joseph Biden (D-DE) stopped supporting a "human life" constitutional amendment before their 1988 presidential bids. The Rev. Jesse Jackson attended pro-life rallies in the 1970s and endorsed the Hyde Amendment barring federal funding of abortions. Yet in the 1980s candidate Jackson was a fixture at pro-choice gatherings and a staunch defender of reproductive rights. Senator Sam Nunn (D-GA) stopped opposing *Roe* while exploring a presidential bid he later abandoned. By the time Senator Bob Kerrey (D-NE) ran for president in 1992 he was pro-choice. Yet Kerrey had endorsed a ban on abortion during his 1982 gubernatorial race and opposed federal funding for the practice as late as 1989.[33]

Even in recent years, long after the parties have established their reputations on abortion, presidential contenders continue to reinvent themselves on the issue. In many cases the temporal proximity of their shift on the issue and their White House bid suggested that the latter prompted the former. Rep. Dennis Kucinich (D-OH) ran as the candidate of the left-wing purists in his long-shot bid for the Democratic presidential nomination in 2004. Along the way he abandoned a long-standing pro-life position better suited to pleasing his working-class "ethnic" district in Cleveland than to winning over liberal activists.[34]

Kucinich's shift followed criticism of his stand on abortion in otherwise sympathetic articles in left-wing publications. More than one

---

[32] On Kennedy, see Clymer (1999, 170). On Jackson see Kaufman (2000, 216, 236), "Abortion Dispute Is Troubling Bayh," *New York Times*, February 12, 1976, 27, and "Correction," *New York Times*, May 23, 1981, 25. On McGovern see "S. Dakota – Will McGovern Liberalism Be Plowed under?" *Christian Science Monitor*, September 30, 1980, 3. On Muskie see "Nixon and Muskie on Abortion," *New York Times*, April 7, 1971, 43. On Wallace see Carter (2000, 458).

[33] On Gephardt: "After Changing Abortion Stand Gephardt Gains among Women," *Washington Post*, May 3, 1987, A6. On Biden: "Abortion Curbs Endorsed 10–7 by Senate Panel," *New York Times*, March 11, 1982, A1. On Jesse Jackson: "Jackson's Politics of Involvement," *Washington Post*, June 10, 1984, K2, and *A.P. File*, A.M. Cycle, June 16, 1978. On Nunn: "In Shift, Nunn Backs Right to Abortion in Most Cases," *New York Times*, September 5, 1990, A20. On Kerrey: "Kerrey on Abortion: I Changed," *St. Petersburg Times*, January 23, 1992, 1A.

[34] On Kucinich: "Ohio Presidential Hopeful Pivots over to Pro-Choice Camp," *San Francisco Chronicle*, February 23, 2003, A3.

writer suggested that the former Cleveland mayor's pro-life stand was a
key impediment to his consolidation of support on the left fringe of the
Democratic Party. As Katha Pollit, a leading feminist columnist, put it,
"if he plans to run for President, Kucinich will have to change his stance,
and prove it, or kiss the votes of pro-choice women and men goodbye."
In the middle of an otherwise glowing profile Studs Terkel addressed a
"personal note" to Kucinich, "Dennis, there's one thing I'd like to change
*your* mind on – your stand on a woman's right to choose. ... I have faith
in your honesty and in your belief in the dignity of the person that you
will make the right choice: pro."[35] Although Kucinich was in no danger
of being nominated, his adoption of a pro-choice stance did win him
support that otherwise would have eluded him. He eventually received
the endorsement of well-known activists who formed a group called
"Feminists for Kucinich."[36]

The 2008 presidential campaign featured more than one candidate
who has modified his position on abortion. Former Massachusetts governor Mitt Romney abandoned his pro-choice position in preparation for a
bid for the GOP's presidential nomination in 2008. A stand that was useful for campaigns in Massachusetts in 1994 and 2002 became a liability
in a bid for Republican support nationally.[37] Former New York mayor
Rudolph Giuliani, who moved from pro-life to pro-choice during his first
mayoral bid in 1989, also revised his position, albeit far less dramatically
than Romney, displaying new opposition to "partial-birth" abortion.[38]

Comparison of the fates of these two erstwhile Northeastern moderates in the 2008 campaign for the Republican presidential nomination is
instructive. Although Romney was widely criticized for his flip-flops, his
shifts on social issues including abortion and gay rights enabled him to win
far more support from social conservatives at both the elite and mass levels
than Giuliani ever could. Romney's presidential bid ultimately failed. Yet
comparison of his showing – victories in ten states' primaries and caucuses
and second-place finishes in other important contests including Iowa, New

---

[35] "Kucinich Is the One," *The Nation,* April 18, 2002; http://www.thenation.com/
archive; "Regressive Progressive," *The Nation,* May 27, 2002, http://www.thenation.
com/archive.

[36] "Vermont State Poet Backs Dean Rival Kucinich," *The Associated Press State & Local
Wire,* July 11, 2003.

[37] On Romney see "Romney Hints at a Shift on Abortion," *Boston Globe,* May 25, 2005,
B1; "Did Romney Fake Left, Move Right on Abortion?" *Boston Herald,* June 3, 2005,
4.

[38] "Giuliani Shifts Abortion Speech Gently to Right," *New York Times,* February 10,
2007, A1.

Hampshire, and Florida – with the spectacular collapse of Giuliani – who led in early polls yet captured only one delegate – suggests that the former Massachusetts governor would have fared even worse had he not belatedly adopted stances that were acceptable to social conservatives.

Although Romney and Giuliani's recent shifts coincided with their presidential candidacies, some of their rivals seem to have revised their positions earlier in their careers. Former Senator Fred Thompson (R-TN) made several statements in the mid-1990s, both before and after his election to the Senate, suggesting that he both opposed banning abortion and supported *Roe v. Wade*.[39] In 1991 Thompson was even retained as a lobbyist by the National Family Planning and Reproductive Health Association to lobby the first Bush administration to life a restriction known as the "gag rule" that banned counselors at federally funded clinics from discussing abortion with patients.[40]

Thompson later earned high ratings from pro-life lobbies as a senator. Yet for several years he was able to do this without contradicting his earlier statements because the Senate voted only on modest reforms such as bans on federal funding for abortion and the so-called partial-birth procedure rather than overturning *Roe* or banning most abortions. Thompson suggested that a mistaken aide was at fault for his response in a 1994 questionnaire and insisted that he had "always thought *Roe* was a wrong decision,"[41] but these claims were at variance with numerous earlier statements and contemporary reports. Yet the wide publicity given to Thompson's shifts on abortion did not deter the National Right to Life Committee from endorsing him for the presidency in late 2007.[42] Like his rival Romney, Thompson appeared instead to have profited from his revised stand on abortion by winning backing from those most concerned with the issue.

Senator Sam Brownback (R-KA) was more closely identified with social conservatives' agenda than any other 2008 GOP presidential contender

---

[39] "Thompson Edges Closer to GOP Run for Senate," *Commercial Appeal,* July 29, 1993, B1; "Family Issues May Divide GOP," *Commercial Appeal,* August 25, 1993, A7; "Thompson Wants Abortion Debate Downplayed," *Commercial Appeal,* August 7, 1996, A12; "Thompson Defends Abortion Record," *The Tennessean,* June 10, 2007, 1A; "Inconsistencies on Fred Thompson's Abortion Views Raise Questions," *Gannett News Service,* June 11, 2007.

[40] "Group Says It Hired Fred Thompson in Abortion Rights Bid," *New York Times,* July 7, 2007, A9.

[41] "Interview with Fred Thompson," *Fox Hannity & CO – Fox News Network,* June 5, 2007 (Nexis transcript).

[42] "The Nation: Key Antiabortion Group Supports Thompson," *Los Angeles Times,* November 13, 2007, A9.

except perhaps for former Arkansas governor Mike Huckabee. Yet while Brownback has held office since the 1980s, the senator's pro-life position emerged only during his 1994 congressional bid. The executive director of Kansans for Life argued that Brownback "changed his position" that year, and both pro-life activists and moderate Republicans disappointed in Brownback concurred, although the senator disputed the charge.[43]

Some evidence suggests that politicians are no longer even eligible for the vice-presidential nomination unless their stand on abortion conforms to the dominant view within their party. Leading vice-presidential aspirants in both parties (Republicans Alan Simpson in 1988 and Tom Ridge in 2000 and 2008, and Democrat Evan Bayh in 2000) were given serious consideration as running mates, but were eventually rejected, reportedly in part because their abortion stands were deemed unacceptable by key party constituencies.[44] Observing these examples of thwarted ambition must only heighten other politicians' motivations to adhere to the party line on abortion.

It is not only politicians who sought to run on national tickets that changed their positions on abortion. In several cases congressional leaders aligned their positions on abortion with those of the majority of their caucuses. Senator Robert Byrd (D-WV) dropped his support for a ban on most abortions after becoming majority leader, as did Rep. Thomas "Tip" O'Neill (D-MA), while Speaker Rep. Jim Wright (D-TX) and Senator George Mitchell (D-ME) both moved toward the pro-choice side after becoming majority leaders. Rep. Bob Michel's (R-IL) record was mixed (and sometimes more pro-choice than Wright or O'Neill's), until the term before he became House GOP leader.[45] House Democratic whip

[43] "Position on Abortion Misunderstood, Brownback Says," *Kansas City Star,* October 8, 1996, A2.

[44] Celebreeze Changes His Stand on Abortion," *UPI Regional News,* December 3, 1989; "Abortion Issue Dominating New Jersey Gubernatorial Race," *Boston Globe,* August 5, 1989, 3; "Bush Holds Final Session on Ticket; Simpson Bows Out as Running Mate Contender, Gives Support to Sen. Dole," *Los Angeles Times,* August 15, 1988, 1; "Bush Is Reported Set to Name Cheney as Partner on Ticket," *New York Times,* July 25, 2000, 5; "Possible Gore Pick Provokes Protest, Bayh's Abortion Record an Issue," *Baltimore Sun,* June 23, 2000, 1A.

[45] On Byrd: Rubin (1982, 96). On O'Neill: Farrell (2001, 520–521) and "Bishop Won't Attend Scranton Graduation, Cites O'Neill," *Associated Press,* March 14, 1985. On Wright: "Washington Talk: Congress; Positions of the Probable Speaker Can Be Volatile," *New York Times,* December 6, 1986, 33. On Mitchell: "Anti-Abortion Group Alienates Staunch Supporters in Congress," *Washington Post,* June 4, 1981, A1; "FOCA: Pro-Choicers Divided on Strategy and Tactics," *Abortion Report,* February 19, 1993, via Nexis.

David Bonior's (D-MI) support for abortion rights, while still more limited than that of most Democrats, increased markedly when he assumed a leadership position in his party.

Other well-known politicians have shifted positions on abortion even without the stimulus of a presidential campaign or national leadership role. Sometimes the shift has coincided with a move toward a larger, if still subnational, constituency. After being elected to the House in 1974, Paul Simon (D-IL) initially supported the "Hyde Amendment" barring funding of abortion. At the time Simon represented the southernmost district in Illinois, a socially conservative area. Yet before his successful 1984 Senate campaign Simon shifted to a pro-choice position he maintained for the rest of his political career, including a 1988 presidential bid.

Simon's trajectory on the issue of abortion was matched by his successor, Senator Dick Durbin (D-IL). Like Simon, Durbin served for a time as a representative from a socially conservative downstate district before making a successful Senate race. Like Simon, Durbin moved in the pro-choice direction, although in his case the shift was more dramatic. Before his election to the House, Durbin had favored banning abortion.[46]

Reversals on abortion on the part of candidates seeking higher office were hardly limited to Illinois. There were several examples of reversals on abortion among leading politicians in Florida who never sought the presidency or the leadership of their party in Congress. Then Rep. Connie Mack (R-FL) revised his position during his winning 1988 Senate bid, moving from pro-choice to pro-life. His predecessor, Democrat Lawton Chiles, had voted to overturn *Roe*. Yet, pressed by his primary rival (Rep. Bill Nelson, himself a late-blooming pro-choicer), Chiles "evolved" *during* his successful 1990 run for governor. (In 2000 Nelson replaced Mack in the Senate.)[47]

Even if officials' geographic constituency does not change and they merely seek to retain the office they already hold, the changing composition of their party's coalition may result in pressure on them to accommodate the new faction as it makes its weight felt in the local party.[48] Barry Goldwater is a case in point. The Arizona senator's days as a

[46] "Abortion Leads off Issues in Race to fill Simon's Seat," *Chicago Sun-Times*, January 22, 1996, 10.

[47] On Mack: "Surprises Keep Senate Races Sizzling: Mack Reverses Stand on ERA and Abortion," *St. Petersburg Times*, August 26, 1988, 1B. On Chiles: "Issues Heat Up Tepid Debate," *St. Petersburg Times*, June 1, 1990, 1B; "Chiles Declares Pro-Choice Stand," *Associated Press*, October 11, 1990.

[48] Cohen (2005) documents the tensions that often accompanied the incorporation of social conservatives in many local Republican organizations.

presidential candidate were behind him by the time abortion became an issue he had to confront. However, Goldwater still felt pressure to represent the concerns of new entrants to the GOP coalition, and his position on abortion changed twice late in his career. Once the issue arose in national politics he initially opposed both banning and funding abortion. Goldwater began his last Senate bid in 1980 still holding that abortion was a private matter. Yet later during that race the senator won Arizonans for Life's support by endorsing a human life amendment. Goldwater later cosponsored such a proposal after he was reelected.

As retirement loomed, however, Goldwater reverted to his former position, voting to preserve *Roe* when the Senate considered a "human life federalism" constitutional amendment. He was vocally pro-choice and even supportive of gay rights in his last years (Goldberg 1995, 308). Goldwater's positions are often recalled selectively today by observers who contrast his allegedly more libertarian outlook with the social conservatism of the contemporary Republican Party. Yet it is important to recall Goldwater's outspoken criticism of that trend came only after he was no longer seeking reelection and especially when he was retired. Until then Goldwater had adjusted, albeit with little evident enthusiasm, to changes in the composition of the Republican coalition.

Goldwater was not alone. Father Robert Drinan, a politically active Jesuit priest and law professor, was once known as a "leading Roman Catholic opponent of liberalizing abortion laws." Yet Drinan later became a pro-choice representative and one of the "longtime targets of anti-abortion forces."[49] Former New Jersey governor Jim Florio, whose election many linked to his pro-choice stand, once opposed abortion. So did Connecticut governor William O'Neill, a Democrat who later signed a bill protecting abortion rights should *Roe* be overturned. More recently, Florida governor Charlie Crist went from calling himself "pro-choice" to "pro-life" in the years between his failed 1998 Senate bid and his successful gubernatorial campaign in 2006.[50]

Although the lion's share of movement on abortion has been among politicians shifting to remain in step with their polarizing parties,

---

[49] "Strategy on Abortion," *America,* February 4, 1967, 177–179; "A Priest Links Easing of Abortions with Racism," *New York Times,* September 8, 1967, 42; "Foes of Abortion Aim at Hill," *Washington Post,* February 11, 1979, A3.

[50] On Florio: "Abortion Issue Dominating New Jersey Gubernatorial Race," *Boston Globe,* August 5, 1989, 3. On O'Neill: "Connecticut: Gov. Signs – Pro-Choice Bill Becomes Law," *Abortion Report,* May 2, 1990, via Nexis; "On Abortion, Crist's Position Is a Moving Target," *St. Petersburg Times,* June 4, 2006, 4B.

politicians have also moved against the trend where their party's stand is a liability, for example, Republicans in the Northeast. New York and Connecticut governors George Pataki and John Rowland and New York City mayor Giuliani once sought to ban abortions but later favored state funding for them. Massachusetts governor William Weld reversed himself on the funding issue.[51]

Another factor promoting successful "conversions" is that voters and activists who care strongly about abortion may take cues from leaders of organizations focused on the issue. These leaders have an incentive to vouch for the bona fides of "converts" so as to encourage politicians to move in their direction. Thus when Senator Bill Bradley (D-NJ), who had been consistently pro-choice, sought to undermine Al Gore's liberal credentials on abortion during their battle for the Democratic presidential nomination in 2000 by pointing to the pro-life votes the vice president cast in the 1970s and 1980s, leading pro-choice activists defended Gore. NARAL endorsed Gore. Kate Michelman, the president of the pro-choice lobby, contended "the fact that he evolved doesn't make him less pro-choice than a Bradley or anyone else."[52]

It is also still possible for relatively recent converts on the abortion issue to win support from activists. Rep. Patrick Toomey won the support of pro-life groups in his strong challenge to Senator Arlen Specter, a pro-choice Republican, in the GOP Senate primary in Pennsylvania in 2004. Yet Toomey himself had run successfully as a pro-choice candidate in 1998, only changing his position during his first term in Congress.[53]

It may be surprising that so many prominent politicians have changed their position on what Adams (1997) terms such an "emotional" issue as abortion and that the switches may have aided them politically. One factor is that abortion is a highly salient issue for only a minority of the electorate.

[51] On Pataki: "Is Pataki's Career That of Maverick or a Mere Politician?" *New York Times,* October 24, 1994, 4B. On Rowland: "Bid Mellows Connecticut Conservative," *New York Times,* September 26, 1990, 1. On Giuliani: "Giuliani Changes His Stance to Accept Right to Abortion," *New York Times,* August 14, 1989, 3B. On Weld: "Weld Shifts on Issues Frustrate Democrats," *Boston Globe,* October 1, 1993, 29.

[52] "The 2000 Campaign: The Abortion Issue: Shifting Views over Abortion Fog Gore Race," *New York Times,* February 25, 2000, A1.

[53] "Abortion Politics Define PA. Race," *Philadelphia Inquirer,* April 18, 2004, B01; "County Center of Specter vs. Toomey Race," *Intelligencer-Journal* (Lancaster, PA), April 24, 2004, A1, available in *American's Newspapers* (Newsbank).

Although in Gore's case it could be argued that NARAL and Michelman backed the likely winner in order to retain influence, Michelman also defended the pro-choice bona fides of long-shot candidates. Regarding Dennis Kucinich's switch, she argued, "Congressman Kucinich has been at work thinking about a lot of these issues, and his votes reflect a thoughtful journey. ... I do accept and I do welcome, that he believes the right to choose is fundamental."[54]

On the other side of the debate, pro-life leaders have also defended "converts" to their cause. Stumping for Toomey during the 2004 GOP Senate primary in Pennsylvania, Dr. James Dobson, the prominent Christian Right leader and founder of Focus on the Family, defended Toomey from critics who noted that the representative's pro-life stand was a recent development. Dobson noted, "I didn't start out pro-life myself. When I went to school at [University of Southern California], I was under the influence of the pro-choice people."[55]

More recently, pro-life activists, apparently seeing Fred Thompson as their best presidential hope in a flawed 2008 Republican field, minimized the importance of his previous statements about abortion. Family Research Council president Tony Perkins argued that Thompson "has a good record on core social issues ... he made those statements before he was in the Senate."[56]

The politicians cited above (and many others whom I omit for reasons of space) flip-flopped on abortion and prospered politically. Others were subsequently defeated, perhaps in part due to their inelegant repositioning. Anthony Celebreeze, the 1990 Ohio Democratic gubernatorial nominee, and 1989 GOP New Jersey gubernatorial nominee James Courter are oft-cited cases.[57] Further research is needed to systematically assess such shifts' effect on candidates' fortunes. My goal here has been simply to show that many important politicians changed their stands and survived, and that the cumulative effect of such shifts helped polarize the parties on the issue.

---

[54] "Ohio Presidential Hopeful Pivots over to Pro-Choice Camp," *San Francisco Chronicle*, February 23, 2003, A3.

[55] "County Center of Specter vs. Toomey Race," *Intelligencer-Journal* (Lancaster, PA), April 24, 2004, A1.

[56] "Away from the Cameras: The Right Has a Crush on Fred Thompson, but His Own Papers Suggest He Is Less Conservative than They Think," *Newsweek*, June 25, 2007, 33.

[57] See "Celebreeze Changes His Stand on Abortion," UPI Regional News, December 3, 1989; "Abortion Issue Dominating New Jersey Gubernatorial Race," *Boston Globe*, August 5, 1989, 3; "Courter Will Surrender House Seat; Loser of New Jersey Governor's Race Had Switched on Abortion," *Washington Post*, May 3, 1990, A15.

Citing examples, even cases of very prominent political figures, will take us only so far, however. Systematic longitudinal examination of representatives' behavior also demonstrates that many politicians changed positions on abortion and collectively did much to polarize their parties on the issue. Using the same votes that Adams (1997) did, I calculate scores measuring representatives' positions on abortion-related issues in each Congress. These scores permit comparison of MCs' stands over time, relative to each other and the whole House.

By contrast, Adams's scores (726–727) are based on MCs' *career* voting records. He infers consistency from the paucity of middling scores he finds. Yet votes on abortion became increasingly common. Thus if an MC changed positions, her first few votes might have little effect on her lifetime average. I report these results in Figure 3-2.

Figure 3-2 calls into question the role of turnover as an explanation of the increasing partisan voting in the House on abortion issues. Forty-nine representatives served throughout the period Adams surveyed (1973–1994). The figure reveals that the strength of the association between party and abortion stance increases among these long-serving MCs, much as it does throughout the House. This group is consistently more polarized than the whole House over two decades, despite a great increase in polarization across Congress. This case suggests that MCs with fixed views are not "selected" by the parties. Rather, elites shift their positions. As in the case of trade, realignment occurs even without replacement. The process was slower in the case of abortion, however.

As in the previous chapter, it is helpful to supplement the figure charting the difference between the positions of long-serving MCs and the rest of the House with a more focused comparison of legislators' votes on two roll calls on the same issue (federal funding of abortion in this case) separated by time but with relatively similar shares of seats controlled by the same parties and a comparable percentage of MCs on the same side of the issue on both occasions. Table 3-1 reveals that in this instance, as in the case of trade policy, the shift the parties undergo is evident among long-serving legislators. Neither at the beginning of the period surveyed nor at the end are they very different from the rest of the House. For these MCs conversion was not uncommon on abortion.

Although the results displayed here suggest that conversion played the chief role in reorienting the parties, they need to be supplemented by a more comprehensive analysis. Using the Rapoport and Stone formula discussed in Chapter 1, I find that 60 percent of the change in the mean position for

TABLE 3-1. *Percentage of Long-Serving Representatives (Stayers) and the Rest of the House Voting Pro-Choice on Two Abortion Votes with Similar Cutpoints: 1974 and 1994*

|  |  | Democrats | Republicans |
|---|---|---|---|
| 93rd Congress[a] | Stayers | 87.5% (N = 32) | 54% (N = 13) |
| 103rd Congress[b] | Stayers | 100% (N = 32) | 15% (N = 13) |
| 93rd Congress[a] | Rest of House | 70.6% (N = 170) | 59.4% (N = 155) |
| 103rd Congress[b] | Rest of House | 97.2% (N = 214) | 19.9% (N = 156) |

[a] 93rd Congress (55.6% Democratic), H.R. 15580, June 27, 1974: Amendment prohibiting use of funds for abortions, abortion referral services, or abortifacient drugs or devices (66.8% voting pro-choice)

[b] 103rd Congress (59.3% Democratic), H.R. 670, March 25, 1993: Motion to kill motion to reconsider passage of bill funding family planning and removing restrictions on discussion of abortion (the "gag rule") at federally funded clinics (65.9% voting pro-choice)

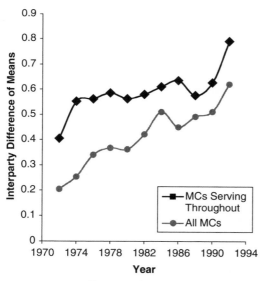

FIGURE 3-2. Difference of Means between Democratic and Republican Support for Abortion Rights among Representatives (Democratic Mean – Republican Mean), 93rd through 103rd Congresses (1973–1994)

the Democratic caucus stemmed from conversion. For the Republicans, however, the net conversion effect was only 28 percent, which suggests that although change among continuing GOP MCs was important, it was a secondary factor in explaining the repositioning of their party on abortion. The combined total effect of conversion, just under 45 percent, is far greater than the literature leads us to expect, and given the conservatism of the Rapoport and Stone measure it suggests that more than half of the change was probably caused by conversion. Yet according to this measure, conversion accounts for less of the change in this case than I find for trade or any of the other issues I study in this book.

Focusing on the House is convenient when we seek to observe a large group of MCs. Yet it has disadvantages as well. Good measures of district-level public opinion with sizeable samples are rare on most issues. So here I turn to the Senate, because estimates of state-level public opinion on abortion are available via the National Election Studies.[58] Figure 3-3 shows the changes in the relative and absolute importance of party and state-level public opinion as independent variables (measured as beta coefficients) in ordinary least squares regression models predicting senators' positions on abortion voting scales.

The figure reveals that at first senators' votes were predicted far better by public opinion in their states than by their party affiliations. Indeed, in the 93rd and 94th Congresses (1974–1976) party was not a significant predictor of a senator's position on abortion. From the late 1970s through the mid-1980s both factors were significant and of comparable magnitude. Since then, party has become a stronger predictor and public opinion a weaker one. The fit of the model improves over time.

Thus despite the abortion issue's increasing salience in American politics since the early 1970s, senators are now marginally *less* responsive to public opinion in their states on the issue than they were at its inception, controlling for party affiliation. The parties' coalitions have changed, and as a result senators are more responsive to the intense preferences of

[58] Matching each Congress with the preceding study allows for possible changes in states' relative positions on abortion over time at the cost of excluding many senators from the analysis due to the small or nonexistent number of NES respondents from many states. Instead, I use the data from the NES Pooled Senate Studies from 1988, 1990, and 1992, since these include many respondents from every state. As comparison of the state public-opinion scores I generated with the 1972 and 2000 studies indicates great continuity over time in states' relative positions, I choose the latter approach. I operationalize state-level public opinion as the mean score of a state's respondents in the pooled study. The results resemble those generated from the smaller groups of states from 1972 through 2000. When both measures are included in the same model for a given Congress, the pooled study-based variable dominates the one generated from the contemporary NES as a predictor. Often it is significant while the other is not.

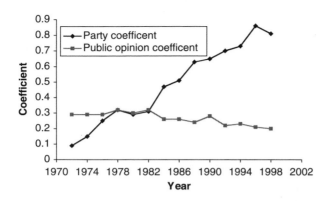

FIGURE 3-3. Effects of Party- and State-Level Public Opinion on Senators' Votes on Abortion, 93rd through 106th Congresses (1973–2000)

factions prominent in their party than to public opinion in their states where abortion is concerned.

It is tempting to see this change as part a larger process of polarization, as classic realignment theory suggests. Yet it is *not* simply the case that legislators' positions on abortion are now more neatly aligned with party affiliation because liberals and conservatives, who always had these positions, now find themselves in different parties. Nor can all change be reduced to the move of white Southerners into the Republican Party, important as that has been.

Figure 3-4, which illustrates this trend, shows the correlation between a senator's position on abortion and his or her placement on the general left–right continuum measured by Poole and Rosenthal's (1997) D1 and D2 NOMINATE scores. It reveals that although abortion used to fall between the two dimensions, now it loads neatly on the first. A greater proportion of liberal senators once opposed abortion rights, and a higher percentage of conservatives once supported them than is now the case. Breaking from one's party on abortion now suffices to earn a senator a reputation as a "moderate."

We can see this shift in rhetoric as well. Initially there was less agreement on what the "liberal" position on abortion was. Many prominent liberal Catholics, who were overwhelmingly Democrats, did not immediately embrace abortion rights. Visible figures including Father Robert Drinan and Senators Kennedy and Muskie made liberal-sounding arguments against the practice, describing it as a step on a slippery slope to

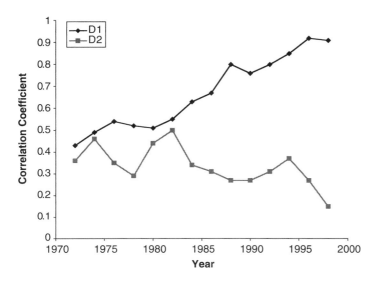

FIGURE 3-4. Correlation between Senators' Positions on Abortion and D1 and D2 NOMINATE Scores, 93rd through 106th Congress (1973–2000)

eugenics, euthanasia, and the killing of the mentally disabled.[59] This rhetoric is almost entirely absent among liberal Catholic politicians today. Instead Catholic Democratic politicians often employ the formulation that they are "personally opposed" to abortion, but cannot legislate their religious beliefs.

Figures 3-1 through 3-4 tell a story of change far more gradual than that evident in the case of trade and more gradual than cases I will discuss in subsequent chapters. There is no critical juncture in the politics of abortion when everything changed. The comparative slowness of the parties' polarization on the issue results from the different mechanism at work in this case. In the cases of the more rapid change on trade and – to a lesser extent – race, party elites maintained their coalition by accommodating existing constituencies that demanded new policies.

By contrast, on abortion the composition and preferences of the parties' bases gradually changed. Via a combination of adaptation and

[59] "Strategy on Abortion," *America,* February 4, 1967, 177–179; "A Priest Links Easing of Abortions with Racism," *New York Times,* September 8, 1967, 42. On Kennedy, see Clymer (1999, 170).

replacement the parties' political elites became more polarized on the issue, a fact that encouraged activists on each side of the controversy to join the appropriate party. Once inside the party they reinforced its new position, producing further polarization and forestalling backsliding. Eventually the activist base and finally the party identifiers in the electorate reflected the parties' new issue positioning. This iterative process of coalition group incorporation is not unique to abortion politics, but is evident in the case of gun control as well.

GUN CONTROL

Like abortion, guns have been present throughout American history, but have not always been the focus of political controversy. However, since the late 1960s gun-related issues have been prominent in American politics. Democrats have become increasingly associated with the gun control cause while Republicans have become identified with the gun rights position and the National Rifle Association (NRA). Observing this trend, Bruce and Wilcox (1998) argue that the case of gun control fits the "issue evolution" model, but they do not systematically investigate shifts among elites and masses.

When gun control emerged as a political issue in the late 1960s it cut across party lines. In 1968 the first federal gun control legislation since the 1930s was enacted in the wake of the assassinations of Martin Luther King, Jr., and Robert Kennedy. Although the bill was promoted by the Johnson administration, congressional Democrats were actually slightly *less* likely than their Republican colleagues to vote for passage of gun control legislation. Yet Democrats were also less supportive on average than Republicans of amendments weakening the bill. As on race, Republican MCs at first clustered around a moderate position, while Democrats in Congress were badly split on a regional basis, with some strongly advocating gun control and others rejecting it entirely.

Figure 3-5 illustrates the existence of the split among Democrats in the 90th Congress (1967–1968) when gun control first reached the political agenda and shows how it had disappeared by the 103rd Congress (1993–1994). The bimodalism evident in the distribution of Democratic MCs' scores in the first period is no longer present in the second.

Already in 1968 Republican MCs were less supportive of gun control than Democrats with region held constant. Yet this tendency was far weaker in 1968 than it is at present. Unlike today, in 1968 in some states a Democratic senator was less supportive of gun control than his

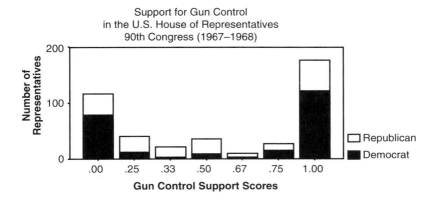

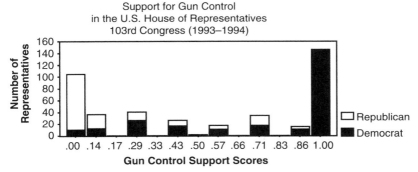

FIGURE 3-5. Support for Gun Control in the House of Representatives, 90th (1967–1968) and 103rd Congresses (1993–1994)

Republican counterpart. Regional differences and the rural and urban split far outweighed party affiliation as predictors of MCs' stands on gun issues. Since Democrats represented many of the most rural areas the difference between the parties on roll calls was not great.

A brief look at the positions of the congressional leaders in 1968 illustrates this point. The two Midwesterners who led House Republicans, Minority leader Gerald Ford (R-MI) and GOP whip Les Arends (R-IL), favored President Johnson's gun control proposal. Their Democratic counterparts were Southerners: Carl Albert, who represented rural Oklahoma and consistently opposed gun control, and Hale Boggs, who represented a Southern, but urban, constituency (New Orleans) and had a mixed record on the issue. In the Senate GOP leader Everett Dirksen of Illinois was less supportive of the bill than Democratic leader Mike Mansfield of Montana. Yet by contrast, the Democratic whip Russell

Long (D-LA) was totally opposed to gun control, while his Republican counterpart, Thomas Kuchel (R-CA), was a strong supporter.

The 1968 presidential campaign saw only narrow differences between the parties on gun issues. During the battle for the parties' presidential nominations, there was diversity in the approaches of contenders in each party and an overlap between the parties that no longer exist. New York governor Nelson Rockefeller, a Republican, was a stronger supporter of gun control than Democratic senator Eugene McCarthy, for example. Rockefeller pushed for stronger measures than the majority Democratic Congress would endorse and criticized Nixon's silence on gun issues, noting, "It is not straight talk to issue resounding statements on crime control, which wholly omit the slightest mention of gun control."[60]

By contrast, McCarthy, the darling of liberal antiwar activists, declared in the summer of 1968 that although he favored gun control in principle, a gun control law should not be passed "under panic conditions."[61] McCarthy also skipped all of the votes on gun control in 1968 and did not announce a position on them. His victory over Senator Robert Kennedy in the Oregon primary that year may have stemmed in part from the latter's clearer stand on gun issues, which sparked opposition in that state.[62] On the only occasion he voted on gun control, in August 1967, McCarthy took the pro-gun side, opposing an amendment offered by Senator Edward Kennedy (D-MA) reducing federal subsidies to the National Board for the Promotion of Rifle Practice. Gun control backers including Senator Joe Tydings (D-MD) and Rep. Herbert Tenzer (D-NY) attacked McCarthy for his refusal to campaign for gun control.[63]

In the fall campaign Nixon mostly avoided discussing gun control and appeared to straddle the issue. He signaled approval of some aspects of the bill Congress eventually passed, especially the provisions banning mail order sale of firearms. At the same time, Nixon did not join his opponent Hubert Humphrey (D-MN) in calling for further steps, such

---

[60] "Rockefeller Scores Talks by Kennedy," *New York Times,* May 25, 1968, 16; "Rockefeller Prods Nixon to Debate," *New York Times,* June 14, 1968, 33; "President Calls for Registering of All Firearms," *New York Times,* June 25, 1968, 1.

[61] "McCarthy Cautions on Gun Law 'Panic,'" *New York Times,* June 17, 1968, 36.

[62] "Kennedy Booed in Oregon Gun Debate," *Los Angeles Times,* May 28, 1968, 6; "Kennedy Heckled in Oregon over Gun Controls: Opposition on Issue Is Called Factor in Primary Today," *New York Times,* May 28, 1968, 10.

[63] "Gun Registration Pushed in Capital," *New York Times,* June 17, 1968, 1.

as federal registration of firearms. For his part, Humphrey denounced Nixon for ducking the gun control issue.[64]

In office Nixon continued to take a middle-of-the-road stance, distancing himself from both supporters and foes of gun regulation. In 1969 the president rejected an honorary membership in the NRA, although earlier chief executives including John F. Kennedy had accepted one in an era when gun control was not on the political agenda.[65] In early 1973 Nixon also noted, "I have never hunted in my life. I am not interested in the National Rifle Association or anything from a personal standpoint." In supporting a ban on cheap, concealable handguns known as "Saturday night specials," Nixon claimed, "most reasonable people, except for the all-out opponents of any kind of legislation in this field – most reasonable people believe it should be controlled."[66]

Yet the Nixon administration did not push for gun control as the White House had done during the Johnson years. Nixon administration officials testified in Congress that they did not believe in federal registration of firearms or licensing of gun owners.[67] Instead the president limited himself to the proposed ban on Saturday night specials. Nixon was still at least nominally more supportive of gun control than many Democratic MCs at this time because the Democratic Congress never enacted such a ban. Yet gun control advocates charged that Nixon's support for even this reform was tepid.

The parties' positions on gun issues were not sharply defined in the early 1970s. Even the ideologically polarized 1972 presidential race saw little debate on gun issues. Nixon and McGovern both opposed Saturday night specials and favored the "right to bear arms."[68] In 1968 McGovern, who represented a rural Western state, had voted repeatedly with the opponents of gun control. He did become more supportive of the policy as a presidential candidate, but he was not strongly associated with the issue.

The issue soon became more partisan, however. This was true both on Capitol Hill and in presidential politics. During the 1976 presidential

[64] "Nixon Urges Congress to Strengthen Gun Bill," *New York Times*, July 10, 1968, 20; "Humphrey Challenges Nixon on Gun Laws," *Los Angeles Times*, September 15, 1968, E2.

[65] "Rifle Unit Membership Is Disavowed by Nixon," *New York Times*, February 23, 1969, 48.

[66] "The President's News Conference of January 23, 1973," *Public Papers of the President*, no. 23, Richard Nixon, 1973.

[67] "Administration Opposes Federal Gun Controls," *Los Angeles Times*, July 25, 1968, 6.

[68] Bruce and Wilcox (1998).

campaign Ford denounced gun registration while Carter supported it tepidly.[69] Carter abandoned his initial policy in the face of congressional resistance at a time when there were large Democratic majorities on Capitol Hill. At this time the parties' positions on gun issues had yet to fully gel. One illustration is the fact that the ranking minority member of the House Judiciary Committee from 1977 to 1982, Robert McClory (R-IL), was a strong supporter of gun control.[70] Allowing a gun control advocate to occupy such a key position would be unthinkable for the GOP today.

Nevertheless, the NRA soon drew closer to the GOP. The gun rights organization endorsed a presidential aspirant for the first time in 1980; its support for Reagan that year marked the entry of the NRA into the Republican coalition. Carter's short-lived support for handgun registration may have prompted this shift. It was also important that Reagan seemed more eager than Nixon to have the group's backing. Analysts also point to the ascendance within the NRA of a politically oriented faction that displaced a nearly apolitical sports-oriented leadership in a 1977 convention known as the "Cincinnati coup" (Spitzer 1995; Carter 1997).

Reagan's record in office did much to cement his party's identification with the gun rights cause. In 1981 he sought to abolish the Bureau of Alcohol, Tobacco, and Firearms at the NRA's behest. This effort failed when the NRA eventually reversed itself, fearing that the Secret Service, which was slated to assume the remnants of the ATF's regulatory role, might prove a more formidable watchdog. In addition, liquor wholesalers helped defend the ATF because they wished to retain the regulations it enforced, which reduced competition in their industry.[71]

Reagan supported the McClure-Volkmer Act of 1986, which weakened restrictions on gun dealers that had been enacted in the aftermath of the assassinations of King and Kennedy in 1968. Even in the mid-1980s gun issues were not yet as partisan as they subsequently became; many Democratic legislators from rural, Southern, and Western constituencies backed McClure-Volkmer, whose sponsors, James McClure and Harold Volkmer, were a Republican senator from Idaho and a Democratic representative from rural Missouri, respectively. Yet compared to the 1968

---

[69] "Transcript of Third Ford-Carter Debate," *Congressional Quarterly Almanac 1976*, 941.

[70] "Profiles of the Illinois Congressional Delegation," *Illinois Issues*, September 1978, http://www.lib.niu.edu/ipo/ii780904.html.

[71] "Firearms Agency Still Alive despite Death Knell," *Associated Press*, AM Cycle (Nexis), April 25, 1982.

debate, party affiliation was already a far better predictor of MCs' votes on gun issues.

When the "Brady Bill," a proposal that included a waiting period and background check before guns could be purchased, was proposed in 1988, Reagan initially voiced support for the concept. However, his remarks were later "clarified" by his spokesman, who asserted that the president believed its provisions might be usefully adopted at the state level but that federal action was not necessary.[72] Reagan endorsed the Brady Bill only in 1991, well after he had left office.[73]

Gun politics became still more partisan during George H. W. Bush's presidency, although his own record on the issue was inconsistent. In Congress Bush, like most Republicans, had voted to weaken, but ultimately backed, the 1968 Gun Control Act. His Democratic opponent Lloyd Bentsen criticized Bush for this during their 1970 Senate contest in Texas (Olien 1982, 222). (Two decades later, Senator Bentsen favored measures that then-president Bush did not to restrict the sale of "assault weapons.")[74] Yet during his 1980 presidential bid Bush repudiated his past position on guns (Parmet 1997, 213). In 1988 he won the NRA's endorsement.

As president George H. W. Bush opposed the Brady Bill unequivocally from 1989 to 1991 and in a murkier way thereafter. Bush's stand on the bill was remarkable as it went against an overwhelming majority of the public, all living ex-presidents, and the editorial stances of most leading Republican papers. It did, however, please an element of the Republican coalition that had long mistrusted him.

After Reagan's endorsement of the Brady Bill, Bush modified his stance. He made it known that he would accept the Brady Bill only if it was incorporated in a crime bill with other features he approved of (and which congressional Democrats were known to oppose). Critics charged that Bush was seeking to find a way to avoid signing or vetoing the Brady Bill.[75] By insisting that the Brady Bill be incorporated in the crime bill, Bush and Republican MCs could then oppose other aspects of that legislation, thus gaining cover for their continued support of the NRA's highly unpopular position.

[72] "Reagan Statement Buoys Opponents of Rifle Group," *New York Times,* July 7, 1988, A20.
[73] "A Surprise from Reagan for the N.R.A.," *New York Times,* March 31, 1991, 9.
[74] "Senate Backs Curbs on Assault Rifles by a Vote of 50–49," *New York Times,* May 24, 1990, A1.
[75] "Brady Bill Keeps Coming Up: Why Does It Then Go Down?" *Minneapolis Star-Tribune,* October 10, 1992, A4.

Bush's refusal to sign the Brady Bill, which majorities in both Houses supported, doomed the measure. The Brady Bill, which had passed both Houses on freestanding votes, was yoked to the larger crime bill, which Republicans filibustered on other grounds and kept from Bush's desk. In his 1992 campaign Bush opposed the Brady Bill and assault weapons ban.[76] Sarah Brady of Handgun Control Inc. (the wife of Reagan's press secretary, James Brady, who was gravely wounded by a would-be presidential assassin in 1981) endorsed Clinton. She blamed Bush, whom she termed "a president fearful of crossing special interest gun lobbies," for her proposal's failure.[77] At the same time, Bush's banning of the importation of some "assault weapons" and mixed signals on the Brady Bill cost him the NRA's endorsement. (The gun rights lobby still called on its supporters to "Clinton-proof Congress," however.)[78] Like Reagan, Bush broke with the NRA after leaving office, taking the occasion of its inflammatory denunciation of ATF agents as "jack-booted thugs" to publicly resign from the group.[79]

George H. W. Bush was far from alone in changing his position on gun issues. His opponents in 1992, Bill Clinton and Al Gore, had also adjusted their positions, albeit in the opposite direction from Bush. Clinton and Gore initially took stands on gun issues that reflected their Southern and rural constituencies more than the preferences of Democrats nationwide. Both Democrats made overtures to gun rights advocates earlier in their careers. Clinton altered his stand in a failed bid for NRA backing in his 1982 gubernatorial race.[80] Gore was an NRA ally during much of his time in Congress and voted in 1985 for the McClure-Volkmer bill that the gun rights organization favored. Yet he and Clinton both modified their positions when they sought leadership roles in the Democratic Party.[81]

As president, Bill Clinton was more supportive of gun control than Reagan or either president Bush. In 1993 and 1994 he successfully pushed

[76] "Clinton's Support of Gun Control May Backfire," *Houston Chronicle*, March 22, 1992, 4; "All 3 Candidates Talking Tough: Gun Control Is Key Area of Difference," *USA Today*, October 26, 1992, 10A; "Crime: Guns, Penalties: The Campaign Debate," *Christian Science Monitor*, September 30, 1992, 8.

[77] "Law Officials, Sarah Brady Back Clinton," *Washington Post*, October 18, 1992, A20.

[78] "NRA Won't Back Presidential Candidate," *Washington Post*, September 25, 1992, A21.

[79] "An Angry Bush Ends His Ties to Rifle Group," *New York Times*, May 11, 1995, A1.

[80] "Campaign 1992: Clinton Has Shifted over the Years on Gun Control, NRA," *Philadelphia Inquirer*, October 7, 1992, A4; "Governor's Camp Feel His Record on Crime Can Stand the Heat," *Washington Post*, October 5, 1992, 5.

[81] "The 2000 Campaign: Gun Control; Bradley Tries to Link Gore to the NRA," *New York Times*, February 11, 2000, A27.

for the enactment of the Brady Bill (unsuccessfully opposing the five-year "sunset" provision on the waiting period for handgun purchases) and won temporary restrictions on assault weapons. In the wake of the 1999 Columbine, Colorado, high school shootings, Clinton advocated stronger gun control measures than the GOP-dominated Congress was prepared to enact.

Congressional leaders during this period also shifted on gun control. Democrats Richard Gephardt and George Mitchell became notably more sympathetic to gun control efforts after becoming leaders while former House minority leader Bob Michel (R-IL) abandoned the support for the policy he had shown in 1968.

All these examples suggest that many prominent leaders who symbolized their parties for voters did modify their positions on gun issues. Yet no assessment of party elite adaptation on the issue can be complete unless it includes a broader assessment that goes beyond the most prominent politicians. Figure 3-6 depicts the trend in voting on gun-related topics among representatives from 1968 to 2000, including the difference of party means for all MCs and for the 24 who served from 1968 to 1994.[82]

The figure reveals a great increase in partisanship on gun issues. The change in part reflects the Democrats' decline in the South and West, but independent of these factors gun issues have become more partisan. The importance of region has declined relative to that of party affiliation as a predictor of legislators' votes. Democrats from any region are now more supportive of gun control than Republicans from any region. By contrast, in 1968 Southern and Western Democrats were less supportive of gun control than were Northeastern and Midwestern Republicans.

When the first votes on gun control in modern times were cast in 1968 the correlation between party and preference was weak. In the 1970s and early 1980s greater differences were evident. In the 1990s the issue became much more partisan. This trend was also visible in the voting patterns of the veteran MCs serving throughout the period. As in the cases of trade and abortion, many veteran MCs realigned vis-à-vis each other as their parties' relative positions on an issue changed.

The increasingly partisan nature of the gun control controversy is not just a symptom of the parties' ideological polarization. It also stems from the increased tendency of liberal and conservative MCs to diverge on gun issues. One might argue that support for "limited government" is central

---

[82] Too few GOP MCs serve throughout the entire period to justify extending this trend line beyond the mid-1990s, so the analysis of veteran MCs stops at 1994.

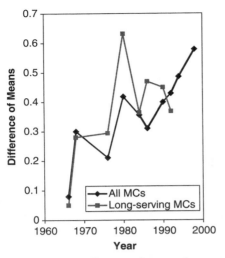

FIGURE 3-6. Difference of Means between Democratic and Republican Support for Gun Control among Representatives (Democratic Mean – Republican Mean), 90th through 106th Congresses (1967–2000)

to modern conservatism and that once the gun control issue was raised support for gun-owners rights would naturally "go with" conservative positions while those supporting a more interventionist role in the economy would favor gun control.

Yet a longitudinal analysis of the correlation between MCs' positions on gun control and their overall voting records does *not* show that the increasingly partisan nature of gun control is merely an aspect of the sorting of liberals and conservatives into the Democratic and Republican parties. Figure 3-7 displays the changing correlation between senators' positions on gun issues and Poole and Rosenthal's first and second dimension NOMINATE scores from 1967 to 2000. The figure reveals that, like abortion, the gun issue initially fell between the two dimensions. Unlike abortion, votes on gun control initially loaded more strongly on the second dimension than the first.[83] After decades of change, however, votes on gun control load almost perfectly on Poole and Rosenthal's first dimension.

---

[83] Both issues differ in this respect from the politics of trade; trade votes almost always loaded primarily on the first dimension, both in the early period when Republicans were the protectionist party and in more recent years when Democrats have become the trade skeptics.

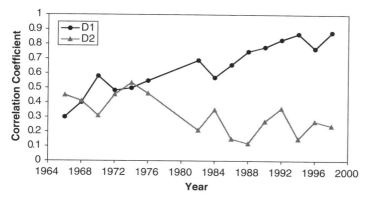

FIGURE 3-7. Correlation between Senators' Positions on Gun Issues and D1 and D2 NOMINATE Scores, 90th through 106th Congresses (1967–2000)

How did this change in the politics of gun control occur? As in the case of abortion, party affiliation has come to guide senators' positions more than views of their constituents. Figure 3-8 shows the results of ordinary least squares regressions estimating the same model for the Senate from the 90th Congress (1967–1968) through the 108th (2003–2004). The dependent variable is senators' positions on a scale based on gun-related roll calls listed in the appendix. The independent variables are a party dummy and the mean response to a gun control survey question among residents of each senator's states. I compute this public opinion measure following Brace et al. (2002), by cumulating respondents to the General Social Survey (GSS) in each state from 1973 to 2002. (I use GSS data because the American National Election Study [ANES] Senate Election Study for the relevant years has no gun control question.)

Figure 3-8 shows that although initially constituent opinion was the stronger predictor of senators' votes on gun issues, it was eventually far out-stripped by party affiliation. With the incorporation of the NRA into the Republican coalition the preferences of gun rights activists were no longer equally salient to senators of both parties. They were part of the Republican base. In states where public opinion was overwhelmingly on one side of the issue senators of either party would still defer to it. Yet in less extreme cases Democrats and Republicans would represent the same states in very different ways on gun issues. Republicans who supported gun control would antagonize a core element of their party coalition, while Democrats taking

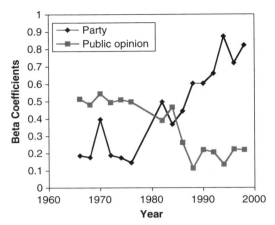

FIGURE 3-8. Effects of Party Affiliation and State Public Opinion on Senators' Positions on Gun Control, 90th through 108th Congresses (1967–2004)

the same stand would not. Thus not only did the predictive power of party affiliation increase, but that of public opinion declined.

The most dramatic change in the relative size of the party and public opinion coefficients occurs between the observation for the 95th Congress (1977–1978) and that for the 98th (1983–1984). Between these two Congresses the NRA endorsed Ronald Reagan for president and became increasingly associated with Republicans generally. The 98th Congress is the first case in which senators' party affiliation's predictive power outweighed that of state-level public opinion, but the gap between the two factors has widened greatly since then.

This decline in the predictive power of public opinion on senators' gun control votes did not have to accompany the growth of the coefficient for the party dummy variable. The fit of the model in the first few Congresses examined was not so good that one coefficient had to increase for the other to decline. To some extent, however, the seeming decline in representation or responsiveness is a result of the fact that over time states with pro-gun electorates have become significantly more likely to elect Republican senators. Public opinion on guns is not only an independent variable that influences senators' behavior, but it affects their party affiliations as well, because Republican candidates should be more likely to win elections in states with pro-gun electorates. I will simply note here that a figure charting only the change in the bivariate relationship between public opinion and senators' voting patterns would show that the decline in the correlation between public opinion on guns and senators' votes, while real, is not as marked as Figure 3-8 suggests.

The analysis of changes in the Senate as a whole does not address the behavior of individual politicians over time and the extent to which party position change on gun issues stemmed from MCs changing their positions. Although there is a great deal of continuity year to year in the composition of the Senate's membership, there is much more turnover throughout the period charted in Figures 3-7 and 3-8. Only four senators served continuously throughout this entire period, and only one was a Republican. To better understand the behavior of individual politicians over time, then we must turn to the House, which offers a larger number of cases to observe.

Table 3-2 shows the results of ordinary least squares regression in which the dependent variable is a scale measuring representatives' support for gun control. I use the same independent variables in modeling MCs' votes on two occasions many years apart: first in 1968, when gun control bills first reached the floor in the modern Congress, and again in 1993–1994, when the issue had become far more partisan. (This is the Congress in which the Brady Bill and the Assault Weapons Ban became law.) I estimated the same models for all representatives in each Congress as well as separate ones for the smaller group (N = 24) whose careers spanned this era and who served in both the 90th and 103rd Congresses.

In their broad outlines the same relationships appear among both the cross sections of the House and the group of veteran MCs in the two Congresses examined. At first the key variable is the one measuring the degree to which the MCs' constituents live in rural areas. MCs from rural areas are less supportive of gun control. Secondarily, regional dummies are important. MCs from the South and West are less likely to support gun control. Republicans are less likely to support gun control than Democrats, controlling for constituency factors, but this is a comparatively small effect. The coefficient for party affiliation is very similar in the two groups, but achieves significance only in the first case because of the far larger number of MCs in that category.

By the 1990s the story is quite different. Party affiliation has greatly increased in predictive power, surpassing the regional dummy variables and even rising to equal importance with rurality. Among the veteran legislators a similar process has occurred. The party coefficient more

TABLE 3-2.  *OLS Regression Models: Support for Gun Control among*
*Representatives: All MCs and Those Serving in Both the 90th and 103rd*
*Congresses (1967–1968 and 1993–1994)*

|  | 90th Congress (1967–1968): All MCs | 90th Congress (1967–1968): MCs Serving throughout the Period | 103rd Congress (1993–1994): All MCs | 103rd Congress (1993–1994): MCs Serving throughout the Period |
|---|---|---|---|---|
| Republican | −.13 (.03)** | −.12 (.2) | −.53 (.03)** | −.32 (.13)* |
| Percentage Rural | −.59 (.05)** | −.73 (.3)* | −.53 (.05)** | −.74 (.19)** |
| South | −.56 (.03)** | −.26 (.18) | −.11 (.03)** | −.10 (.08) |
| West | −.23 (.03)** | −.22 (.21) | −.13 (.03)* | .01 (.13) |
| Adj. $R^2$ | .62 | .44 | .60 | .65 |
| N | 421 | 24 | 423 | 24 |

* p value > 0.05, **p value > 0.01

than doubles and achieves statistical significance, while the regional variables decline considerably in absolute and relative importance. The fact
that the results are similar in the two groups is further evidence that the
parties' polarization on gun issues is not merely a result of the Republican
gains in the gun-friendly South and West. The change is evident among
MCs who do not move across state lines over the course of their long
careers.

The results are not identical for the two groups of MCs. Among the
long-serving MCs party remains less important than rurality, and its
effect appears smaller than in the House as a whole. These results suggest that there may be some inertia in the positions of veteran MCs on
gun issues. Still, among both new and veteran representatives there is a
marked shift away from district-based cues and toward reliance on party
ones. The party coefficient nearly triples for this group of long-serving
MCs and is statistically significant.

A similar impression emerges from Table 3-3 when we observe the
behavior of long-serving representatives and the rest of the House on
two votes, 20 years apart, with similar cutpoints and in Congresses
with very similar party compositions. Here, as in previous cases, we
see that the shift throughout the House is largely mirrored among
long-serving MCs. Much of the change comes from Republicans, who

TABLE 3-3. *Percentage of Long-Serving Representatives (Stayers) and the Rest of the House on Supporting Gun Control on Two Gun Control Votes with Similar Cutpoints: 1968 and 1988*

| Congress | Type of Representative | Democrats | Republicans |
|---|---|---|---|
| 90th Congress (1967–1968)[a] | Stayers | 61.3% (N = 31) | 50% (N = 14) |
| 100th Congress (1987–1989)[b] | Stayers | 64.5% (N = 31) | 21.4% (N=14) |
| 90th Congress (1967–1968)[a] | Rest of House | 51.7% (N = 209) | 37.8% (N = 172) |
| 100th Congress (1987–1988)[b] | Rest of House | 56.7% (N = 215) | 26.7% (N = 158) |

[a] Var. 407, H.R. 17735, July 24, 1968 (57% Democratic): Amendment exempting people, organizations, and institutions engaged in competition and military training from provisions of the Gun Control Act under certain circumstances (53.3% voting pro–gun control)

[b] 100th Congress (59% Democratic), H.R. 5210, September 15, 1988: Amendment to Omnibus Drug Bill removing seven-day waiting period for handgun purchases (Brady Bill) (55.4% voting pro–gun control).

become less supportive of gun control from the late 1960s to the late 1980s.

However, this analysis is based on longitudinal observation of a small number of MCs compared to the rest of the House. A more comprehensive examination is required. Calculations based on the Rapoport and Stone formula using representatives' scores over the more than three decades since Congress began voting on gun control reveal that 59 percent of the change in the parties' mean scores occurred via conversion rather than replacement. This aggregate masks large differences between the parties: 94 percent of change among Democrats occurred via conversion. For the GOP MCs, however, conversion appeared to play a minimal role, accounting for only 9 percent of change.[84]

The parties in the electorate have polarized as well, as Figure 3-9 shows. The figure displays the difference in support for a handgun ban in Gallup polls over a 24-year period among Democratic and Republican identifiers in the electorate. In 1975 Republican identifiers were about as likely

[84] This result is somewhat at odds with the findings in the previous tables. It is possible that it is driven by the high rate of turnover among GOP MCs during this period.

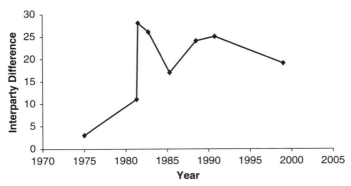

FIGURE 3-9. Interparty Difference in Support for a Handgun Ban (Democratic Support – Republican Support), Gallup Polls, 1975–1999

to support a handgun ban as Democrats. By the 1990s the gap between the parties on gun issues at the mass level had widened considerably and it has remained a divisive issue. Much of the change occurred after the NRA endorsed Ronald Reagan for president in 1980. In this case the parties in the electorate generally appeared to be following more than leading political elites.

As in previous cases, elite conversion was central to the process of party position change on gun issues. Yet the dynamics of the gun control issue are more similar to those of abortion or civil rights in the South than to civil rights (in the North) or trade policy. Gun politics saw important shifts in the constituencies of the parties as the NRA was drawn into the Republican orbit. This lent an increasingly partisan flavor to a debate that had once been primarily regional. Yet it took time for politicians to shift from local cues to party-constituency-based ones, and in some cases this process required elite turnover. Thus, the shift in the parties' positions was gradual.

Although my focus in this chapter has been on two issues, the development of which clearly fit the coalition group incorporation model, they are not the only cases in which such a dynamic has been evident. One more complicated case I discuss in Chapter 4 is the politics of race.

There are other issues that appear to be cases of coalition group incorporation. One is the issue of state support for private education. Historically the Republican Party was associated with support for public education. Private schools, at the primary level at least, were disproportionately Catholic at a time when Catholics were overwhelmingly

Democrats. A major Republican appeal in the late nineteenth century was the effort to end state support for largely Catholic primary schools. The Blaine Amendment was a proposal designed to enshrine a ban on state support for private schools in the Constitution. Its chief sponsor was the leading Republican of the age, James G. Blaine, but President Grant endorsed the amendment as well. The Blaine Amendment failed to receive the necessary votes to go to the states for ratification because senators divided along party lines and Democrats made up more than a third of the Senate (Green 1992).

Although the salience of the issue waned after the failure of the Blaine Amendment at the national level and the adoption of similar provisions in several states, Republican resistance to federal support for private schools was evident as late as the 1960s. In the early postwar years leading Republicans such as Robert Taft cited the First Amendment in rejecting the concept of state support for parochial schools. Such plans would "violate the Constitution and the whole genius of American government," the Ohio senator wrote a Catholic newspaper editor in 1946 (Wunderlin 2003, 121). For years the issue of support for private schools complicated the efforts of those seeking to establish a program of federal aid to education as it was something of a "wedge issue" that could be used to divide Democrats.

However, today the movement for "vouchers" (and, in earlier years, "tuition tax credits" or "parochaid") comes chiefly from the Republican side of the aisle, a trend first evident in the Nixon administration. Corresponding with this shift is the movement of Catholic and Protestant religious conservatives into the GOP coalition and an equally important movement of teachers' unions into Democratic ranks. While the leading teachers' unions, the American Federation of Teachers (AFT) and National Education Association (NEA), are now a significant component of the Democratic coalition, this was not true until the 1970s. The AFT was a very small union until 1961, when it won an election to become the bargaining agent of New York City teachers.[85]

Moreover, the NEA was not a trade union for much of its history (Murphy 1990). For a long time principals and other administrators were included in the group's membership. As a result, the NEA did not represent rank-and-file workers in adversarial relationship with management the way unions typically do. As the NEA evolved into more of a conventional union in the 1970s it began to engage in partisan politics. In 1976,

---

[85] For a useful, if highly tendentious, study, see Lieberman (2000).

for the first time, the NEA endorsed a presidential candidate, Jimmy Carter. Since that time the teachers' union has become a bulwark of the Democratic Party. Thus the issue of school vouchers is another possible case of coalition group incorporation.

Another recent change in party coalitions and policies is evident in the area of the regulation of litigation. Trial lawyers entered politics in the 1970s in order to block "no-fault" auto insurance proposals at both the state and national levels (Burke 2002). At the time the no-fault advocates were primarily liberal and Democratic politicians who presented it as a pro-consumer measure. In the Senate the key sponsors were Warren Magnuson (D-WA) and Phillip Hart (D-MI), two mainstream Democrats. Key Democratic constituencies that are frequently aligned with trial lawyers today, including the AFL-CIO, lobbied for the no-fault measure that the plaintiffs' attorneys sought to block.[86] Meanwhile the Nixon and Ford administrations supported state-level reforms, but opposed federal no-fault legislation. (The insurance industry was divided.)[87] If many individual plaintiffs' attorneys were Democrats, the group was still not a partisan constituency at that time. Their PAC, the Attorneys Congressional Campaign Trust, gave significant contributions to both Republican and Democratic MCs, including the leaders of each party in Congress.[88]

Subsequently, however, the Republican-led, corporate-sponsored campaign to enact "tort reform" limiting plaintiffs' ability to sue and recover damages has led trial lawyers acting chiefly through the Association of Trial Lawyers of America (now known as the American Association for Justice) to ally with Democrats. The trial lawyers have become major donors to Democratic candidates. Perhaps as a result, Democrats generally no longer advocate "no fault" auto insurance. Instead, it is Republicans who have favored a modified version of this policy, termed "auto choice."[89]

The case of the trial lawyers and tort reform may be an especially informative one because this group's incorporation into the Democratic

---

[86] "Labor Unit Says Lawyers Seek to Block No-Fault Law," *New York Times*, February 4, 1973, 49.

[87] "No-Fault Bill Approved by Senate Unit," *Washington Post, Times Herald*, May 25, 1972, A30; "Lawyers Fight No-Fault Idea," *Washington Post, Times-Herald*, June 15, 1972, F4; "Ford Will Oppose No-Fault Standard," *New York Times*, May 6, 1975, 28.

[88] "Trial Lawyers Big Spender against No-Fault Auto Insurance," *Washington Post*, August 30, 1976, A3.

[89] "Senate Bill Offers Auto Policy Alternative," *Journal of Commerce*, June 20, 1996, 8A; "Dole Backs New Options for Auto Insurance," *New York Times*, August 5, 1996, D5.

Party seems to have been quicker than the movement of groups into party coalitions on the gun control or abortion issues. It was also more rapid than the shifts seen in racial politics. I identified two reasons for the comparative slowness of coalition group incorporation as opposed to other forms of party policy change: politicians' difficulty in forging relationships with new constituencies (transaction costs) and the inertia that impedes the shift of a group at the mass level due to party identification.

In the case of the trial lawyers the second factor is much less operative than in other cases. A group made up of a small number of prosperous, highly informed individuals who participate in politics primarily via supplying contributions rather than votes might be able to realign far more quickly than interest groups that have mass followings that are hard to detach from their traditional partisan loyalties.

In the last two chapters I have examined issues marked overwhelmingly by one dynamic; so far party position change has stemmed either from changed preferences of a party-linked group (coalition maintenance) or from the recruitment of new supporters by party politicians (coalition group incorporation). Yet in some cases, the development of an issue is characterized by both these dynamics. In the next chapter I explore such a case.

# 4

## The Politics of Race

### Coalition Maintenance in the North, Coalition Group Incorporation in the South

> When we of the South rise here to speak against ... civil rights proposals we are not speaking against the Negro race.
>> Lyndon Johnson in his maiden Senate speech, "We of the South," 1949
>
> We *shall* overcome!
>> Lyndon Johnson, address to joint session of Congress on voting rights, 1965

No development in postwar American politics has been more dramatic than the reversal of the parties' relative positions on racial issues. This historic shift merits close study for multiple reasons. The parties' reversal on matters of race is the most important change in politics since the rise of the New Deal coalition in the 1930s. Yet beyond the shift's undoubted real-world importance, racial politics has assumed a central role in the theorizing about party position change since Carmines and Stimson (1989) used the issue to illustrate what they intended as a general theory of issue evolution. However, as I show, developments in this issue area are complicated in ways that differ in key respects from the account offered by these and other scholars.

The changes in the politics of race, by which I mean chiefly policies relating to the civil rights of African Americans, are not fully captured by one of the three models I develop in this book. Rather, the changes in parties' positioning on race are best understood as a mix of coalition maintenance and coalition group incorporation. Nor is the race issue unique in being characterized by multiple dynamics. At the end of this chapter I briefly note other issues in which both coalition maintenance and group incorporation are evident, including the politics of women's rights and environmentalism.

In large part the racial realignment in American politics is a case of coalition group incorporation. Most African Americans abandoned the GOP during the New Deal. Thirty years later the remaining black Republicans in the North and the formerly disenfranchised blacks in the South entered the Democratic Party at the same time as racially conservative Southern whites defected to the Republicans. This process is akin to the cases of coalition group incorporation I discussed earlier, abortion and gun control.

This momentous shift, as a result of which the South went from being the most Democratic to the most Republican region, has been described many times (Sundquist 1983; Black and Black 2002; Lublin 2004; Polsby 2005; Shafer and Johnston 2006). These authors stress the gradualism of the process, but disagree about the relative importance of economic and, more recently, culture war or "social" issues opposed to race in transforming Southern politics.

Yet this is not the whole story. Although the shifts in the partisanship of blacks and Southern whites are well known, there is a more obscure aspect of the story that complicates an attempt to place the race issue neatly under the same heading as abortion and gun control. A major factor in the transformation of the parties' positions on race was the collision between civil rights advocates and the business community. When these two groups clashed, Republican officials usually sided with their traditional business allies, even though this meant abandoning their historic role as the "party of Lincoln."

The responsiveness of GOP politicians to their business allies is an example of coalition maintenance comparable to the development of trade politics in which the two parties reversed their historic positions at the behest of their labor and business supporters. Thus race politics is a hybrid case that combines elements of coalition group incorporation with coalition maintenance.

In their influential study Carmines and Stimson (1989) identify 1964 as a turning point in the politics of race. In that year Democratic leaders finally ceased temporizing and endorsed civil rights unequivocally. By contrast, GOP presidential nominee Barry Goldwater opposed the 1964 Civil Rights Act, personifying his party's turn toward the South. The parties' policy images changed radically. In reaction, some voters abandoned their party loyalties. Others adopted their parties' new stances. As a result, the parties in the electorate came to reflect the new elite polarization. How and why did the elites shift? Carmines and Stimson argue for the importance of turnover in Congress, especially in the Democratic landslides of 1958 and 1964. Yet, as I show, the evidence tells a different story.

The combined legacies of the Civil War and the New Deal left the two major parties oddly configured on racial matters. While their presidential nominees (and perhaps the median voters within each party) differed little on the issue from 1936 to 1960, the parties' preference *distributions* were quite distinct. Few Republicans supported Jim Crow, but most did not strongly press for federal action redressing the broader grievances of African Americans either. Most blacks abandoned their GOP allegiances during the 1930s when they were incorporated into the Democrats' New Deal coalition, initially on the basis of economic benefits rather than any strong commitment by Franklin Roosevelt to confronting institutionalized racism (Weiss 1983). Thus the post–New Deal Democratic Party included both segregation's strongest supporters and its most ardent foes.

The shift in voting behavior among African Americans was not instantaneous. One signal development in the movement of blacks into the Democratic Party was the 1934 defeat of the sole African American in Congress, Rep. Oscar DePriest, a Republican from Chicago's south side, by Arthur Mitchell, a black Democrat who had previously been an active Republican.

The timing of shifts in the alignment of black voters in this case is disputed. Gordon (1969) and Nordin (1997) agree that a majority of the district's black voters supported DePriest in 1934 and also backed his failed comeback bid in 1936. Mitchell won his first two terms because of strong support from the South Side's white voters, which, combined with the substantial minority of the black vote he received, gave him an overall majority. Gordon (1969, 601) claims that in 1938 Mitchell finally won a majority of the black vote and did again in 1940. Yet Nordin (1997, 119) contends that, although Mitchell continued to make inroads among blacks, he never won a majority of their votes. Rather, "the pattern of his first victory of 1934 repeated itself three more times; white voters delivered every Mitchell triumph." Mitchell's GOP opponent in 1938, Alderman William Dawson, changed parties in 1939, making his peace with the Democratic Cook County machine. When Mitchell retired in 1942, Dawson succeeded him and served in Congress until 1970.

Scholars agree that a majority of black voters supported Franklin Roosevelt in 1936. While all subsequent Democratic presidential candidates have won majorities among African Americans, no Democratic presidential candidate had come close to doing so before 1936. It is debatable, however, whether blacks were yet part of the Democrats' "base" at that time. Roosevelt's margin of victory among black voters in 1936 may not, contra Weiss (1983, 205), have been greater than that among the public generally.

The timing of the movement of blacks into the Democratic Party seems to have varied significantly from region to region. In some cities, including Philadelphia, Pittsburgh, Detroit, and Cincinnati, Roosevelt's support in black districts indeed exceeded the 60.8 percent of the overall national electorate he won in 1936. Gamm (1989) finds that in Boston Roosevelt received 68 percent of the black vote in 1936, up from 46 percent four years earlier. Yet in Chicago, home of the largest African American community in the North, Roosevelt received only 48.8 percent of the black vote in 1936 and even in 1940 won only a narrow majority. Weiss herself (1983, 207) reports that in 1936 Roosevelt's support in black districts of Cleveland and Knoxville were 60.5 percent and 56.2 percent, respectively, a bit below his national vote share.

If in some areas black movement toward the Democrats was slow, in others it had emerged even before the New Deal. Martin (1971, 93) reports that Roosevelt won majority support among blacks in New York already in 1932. If so, we cannot attribute this early support to any automatic "favorite son" effect because Al Smith, Roosevelt's predecessor as governor of New York, had made only very limited inroads among his state's black voters when he was the Democratic presidential nominee in 1928.

There were other areas in which Democratic gains among blacks were well underway before the New Deal. Mitchell (1968, ch. 8) shows that in Missouri politics Democrats had won over significant numbers of African Americans in the late 1920s and early 1930s. This trend was most pronounced in Kansas City, where "an effective combination of patronage and policies" helped the Pendergast machine "recruit Negroes in ever-increasing numbers" (131). Mitchell finds that Al Smith won notably more votes in the Show Me State's black precincts than previous Democratic presidential nominees and that Roosevelt won a majority among black voters in Missouri already in 1932. Thus there was more gradualism and regional variation in the incorporation of African Americans in the Democratic Party than the conventional account allows.

Although Democratic candidates at all levels were making inroads among African Americans during the New Deal years, Franklin Roosevelt was far more popular among black voters than was his party. To mobilize support among blacks, who remained skeptical of the traditional

Democratic organizations, the Roosevelt campaign established the "Good Neighbor League Colored Committee." This group worked with black ministers and others in the African American community who supported the president. The league was a front funded by the Democratic National Committee, but this was not publicized by Democrats. The league campaigned for Roosevelt's reelection, but not, officially at least, for the Democratic ticket per se. McCoy (1960) and Spencer (1978) credit the league in considerable measure for Roosevelt's strong showing among black voters in 1936.

Yet however we view the political position of African Americans in 1936, there is no disputing that by the end of the decade they had become a base constituency for Roosevelt and increasingly for Democrats generally. The growing importance of black support for Northern Democratic politicians stemmed from two factors: the increasing number of votes Democrats received in Northern black precincts as the African American population swelled via migration and the decline in support for the New Deal among white voters after 1936. As Sitkoff (1984, 1405) notes, "the mass of blacks, despite severe privation, joined the New Deal later than did poor whites, and by 1940 they were far more enthusiastic about the New Deal than other poor Americans."

Focusing only on national party platforms fails to reveal the important coalition changes occurring and the related shift in party positions. Despite the massive black support for Roosevelt already evident in 1944, the Republican platform called explicitly for a permanent Fair Employment Practices Commission (FEPC) that year, and the Democratic one did not. Platforms are the lowest common denominator of parties, and, lacking a large Southern wing, it was possible for Republicans assembled to more forthrightly commit to some federal role in protecting civil rights for African Americans than Democrats could easily do. Yet this simple comparison of platforms obscures as much as it clarifies.

There was, in fact, some early evidence of the parties' shift on race in Congress, although it has been largely overlooked. Northern Democratic MCs, who, unlike Roosevelt, did not have to weigh the concerns of blacks against those of Southern whites, demonstrated increasing support for civil rights in the 1930s and 1940s as blacks were incorporated in Northern Democratic parties across the country.

The history of the antilynching campaign on Capitol Hill illustrates this subtle shift. In the early 1920s the chief sponsor of the antilynching bill was Rep. Leonidas Dyer (R-MO), a white Republican from a St. Louis district in which black voters were numerous (Hixson 1969).

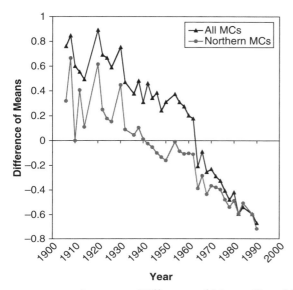

FIGURE 4-1. Interparty Difference of Means (Republican Mean – Democratic Mean) on Support for Racial Liberalism, All MCs and Northern MCs Compared, House of Representatives, 60th through 102nd Congresses (1906–1992)

Dyer's bill passed in the House but died in the Senate in 1922. After this defeat the issue went into abeyance for many years. When an antilynching bill finally reached the floor again in 1934 the chief sponsors were Democrats, Senator Robert Wagner (D-NY), Senator Edward Costigan (D-CO), and Rep. Joseph A. Gavagan (D-NY), a white Tammany Hall politician whose district included Harlem (Zangrando 1965).

During this period congressional voting patterns, far more than presidential campaigns, revealed the unusual distribution of preferences in each party on racial matters. Here I present two analyses. In Figure 4-1 I show the changing interparty difference of means on racial liberalism over most of the twentieth century in the House of Representatives.[1] This chart includes votes from a longer period of time than most studies of this topic cover.

I present interparty difference of means both for all MCs as well as for Northern ones only. It is important to contrast these two statistics to

---

[1] I could find no votes on race from 1900 to 1906, and the pattern changes little after 1992, so Figure 4-1 includes data from the 60th through 102nd Congresses (1906–1992).

assess the degree to which the gap between the parties is a function of the
Democrats' dominance in the South, on the one hand, or represents real
differences independent of regional factors, on the other.

Figure 4-1 reveals three eras in voting on race in the House of
Representatives over the course of the twentieth century. In the first
period, lasting roughly the first four decades of the century, the difference
of means is positive, both among all MCs and, to a lesser degree, among
Northern ones. This indicates that House Republicans were more liberal
than their Democratic colleagues on race during this period. The fact
that difference of means is also positive for Northern legislators demonstrates that the parties' differentiation on race was *not* entirely a function
of their regional composition.

During this era the gap between the parties, throughout the House and
among Northern MCs, fluctuates from Congress to Congress without any
clear trend. The fluctuations are a function of two factors: the shifting
fortunes of the Democratic Party and the stringency or the "cutpoint" of
the civil rights measures considered in a given Congress. The Democrats
nearly monopolized the Southern delegations in good years and bad. Yet
their share of Northern seats varied far more from Congress to Congress.
When the Democrats had done well in the previous election, their share
of Northern seats was relatively large. Since Northern Democrats were
always more liberal on race than their Southern co-partisans, Congresses
in which Democrats held many Northern seats saw a reduced gap between
their party and the GOP on racial issues.

In addition, in those Congresses in which modest civil rights measures opposed only by staunch segregationists were considered, MCs
divided more along sectional lines than partisan ones. For example,
most Northern MCs of both parties backed antilynching bills, even if
Northern Democrats were slightly less likely to do so than the GOP MCs
from their region in the 1920s.

Yet when a stronger measure was considered, for instance, a ban on
interracial marriage in the District of Columbia – a proposal most representatives supported in 1915 – differences between Northern Democratic
and Republican MCs were visible. In such cases Republican MCs emerged
as more liberal on race than even Northern Democrats. Democratic racial
conservatism on race in North and South is evident from the beginning of
the period surveyed in Figure 4-1 until the end of the 1930s.

In the second period, beginning in the early 1940s, a change is evident. The gap between the parties has declined somewhat, although
Republican representatives are still more supportive of racial liberalism

than Democratic ones overall. However, by this time the Republican lead is solely a function of the presence of Southern MCs in the Democratic caucus. If we compare Democrats and Republicans in the North, we find that Democratic MCs are actually *more* liberal on race than their GOP colleagues. Instead of varying trendlessly, but remaining positive, the gap between the parties in the North becomes negative and exhibits a clear downward trajectory during the 1940s.[2]

The shift in congressional voting patterns is consistent with the coalition group incorporation model. These changes parallel the movement of African Americans into the Democratic Party. Riding on Roosevelt's coattails, Northern Democratic MCs began to win support from black voters in the mid-1930s. Unlike the president, they did not have to worry about the attitudes of Southern white voters. Instead they were increasingly sensitive to the concerns of the growing number of blacks casting Democratic ballots in Northern cities.

Another constituency brought into the Democratic Party during the New Deal that pressed for antidiscrimination legislation was the Jewish community. There was open and widespread discrimination against Jews to a degree that is shocking today. A 1941 study found that 32 percent of job listings in the *New York Times* and *New York Herald Tribune* mentioned religion, generally noting that Protestants or gentile applicants were preferred (Reed 1991, 40). The Jewish community was concentrated in states where the other major constituencies backing antidiscrimination legislation (blacks and CIO unions) were also well represented, yet Reed still sees Jews as a very important source of advocacy for the FEPC.

Support from organized labor for civil rights legislation was also very important in orienting Northern Democrats on the issue. While African Americans and Jews were highly concentrated in a handful of cities, labor had a much broader presence throughout the North. This was also an instance of group incorporation. The early labor constituency for civil rights – CIO unions – grew tremendously in the 1930s. Many of these unions' members had not been Democrats before the New Deal or – in some cases – voting at all.

Initially support for civil rights was uneven in the labor movement. Although the new CIO unions were backers, the older, craft-based unions of the AFL were slower to embrace the cause. Although from

---

[2] The one Congress in which the gap between the parties in the North almost disappears is the 84th. This was the term in which the famous "Powell Amendment" banning federal aid to segregated schools was considered.

1935 onward the black-dominated Brotherhood of Sleeping Car Porters was a member of the federation, many AFL unions still explicitly banned African Americans from membership in the 1940s. Even where blacks were not formally excluded they were often marginalized by AFL unions, especially the building trades, some of which became the targets of protracted civil rights litigation in later decades (Frymer 2007). Some of the first targets of the FEPC were AFL-affiliated unions.[3] Starting in 1945, however, the AFL did support an FEPC, although their lobbying effort was initially tepid (Kesselman 1948, 148).

Organized labor's support for civil rights in the 1940s may have influenced Democrats in the large sections of the North where African Americans and Jews were not numerous. Feinstein and Schickler (2008) examine Northern state party platforms over several decades and find Democrats emerging as the more pro–civil rights party in the 1940s. They report preliminary findings suggesting that density of CIO membership was a correlate of Democratic support for civil rights (13).

The upshot of the new pressures from constituencies old and new was that on civil rights matters Northern Democratic MCs increasingly outflanked their GOP colleagues, reversing the positions the parties had held on race since the birth of the Republican Party in 1854. This was generally not visible in roll calls because on most modest measures the more striking divide was between Northerners and Southerners, who were overwhelmingly still Democrats.

The third era, our own, began in 1965. From this year onward the Democrats were more liberal on race than the Republicans in Congress. Although racially conservative Democrats at first dominated congressional delegations elected south of the Mason-Dixon Line, the dramatic change among Northern MCs evident from the 88th to the 89th Congress was seen to reorient the parties.

In fact, changes in the parties' positioning on race were evident well before 1964 on Capitol Hill. In presidential elections this difference was mostly obscured as both parties sought to please their major factions. Yet in Congress a different picture emerges. During the middle of the twentieth century the visible difference in the parties' positions still depended on the stringency of the bill in question. Republicans had a unimodal preference distribution on racial issues and Democrats a bimodal one, as Clausen (1973, 97) shows. Weak civil rights measures, which still

---

[3] "2 Chicago AFL Unions Ordered to Cease Discrimination against Negroes," *Wall Street Journal*, June 15, 1942, 2.

predominated in the 1940s and 1950s, did not fully reveal the distribution of MCs' preferences. Since most Northerners of both parties opposed the poll tax, the subtler differences between Northern Democrats and Republicans on race were seldom visible in Congress.[4] Given this voting agenda, the Democrats' dominance in the South made them appear the more racially conservative party in the aggregate. Yet this comparison is misleading in that it masks the nonlinear relationship between party and racial liberalism during the period.

To observe the preference distributions I describe, we must examine Congresses in which votes on moderate reforms are mingled with roll calls on more ambitious measures. This mixture will allow us to distinguish between segregationists, moderates, and racial liberals. The 78th Congress (1943–1944) and the 81st Congress (1949–1950) offer such tests.

This new alignment is evident in congressional consideration of the FEPC. In response to black union leader A. Philip Randolph's threat to organize a march on Washington, Franklin Roosevelt created the first FEPC by executive order in 1941. The commission was charged with investigating and combating discrimination in defense contracting firms and represented the first serious federal attention to civil rights questions since the end of Reconstruction. Lacking support for the FEPC in Congress, Roosevelt maintained the agency with discretionary funds (Hamby 2004, 485).

Roosevelt's maneuver was only a temporary solution, however. In response, Southern legislators led by Senator Richard Russell of Georgia fought to require that funds could be used for agencies only when specifically appropriated by Congress for that purpose. FEPC supporters then pushed to appropriate funds for the agency, while in March and again in June 1944 Russell offered a series of amendments designed to kill or at least weaken the commission. In most cases voting on these measures broke down broadly along sectional lines. In principle most Republican MCs supported the concept of an FEPC.

---

[4] Republicans *were* more responsive than even Northern Democrats to black concerns until the New Deal. But by the 1950s votes showing this pattern were cases in which Republicans offered amendments barring spending on segregated facilities in federal programs. The prospect that such amendments would sink bills by alienating Southern votes was not unwelcome. Some racially liberal Northern Democrats (including blacks) opposed such amendments because of their support for the underlying bills. See Krehbiel and Rivers (1990).

Yet there was an early exception that revealed the emerging gap between Northern Democrats and Republicans on civil rights. On June 20, 1944, Russell offered an amendment designed to weaken the FEPC's ability to regulate contracting firms by allowing them to appeal adverse findings by the commission to the president (Reed 1991, 159). This amendment passed because in addition to the expected Southern backing it won the votes of a majority of Republican senators, including the minority leader, Wallace White of Maine, and the chief spokesman of the GOP's conservative wing, Robert Taft of Ohio. This roll call is rather obscure, but it was a harbinger of a trend evident in later years: Republicans were less willing than Democrats to support strong enforcement of civil rights when employers were the targets.

As Hamby (2004, 485) notes, "southern Democrats, motivated by the race issue, loathed" the FEPC, whereas "the northern Republicans, motivated by resentment against federal bureaucratic interference in management hiring practices, detested it almost as much." Already in early 1944, Rep. John Taber (R-NY), the ranking minority member of the Appropriations Committee, asserted, "The FEPC hasn't made a very good reputation for itself."[5] Here the coalition of Republicans and Southern Democrats that would be so common on civil rights voting starting in the mid-1960s made an early appearance. Although Republicans were not ready to side fully with Southern Democrats on all civil rights questions, their enthusiasm for a federal role in combating job discrimination, even where contractors were concerned, was minimal.

There was another sign of Republican hostility to the FEPC in 1944 when the House considered an appropriation bill for independent agencies, including funds for the commission. At one point an amendment passed on a "standing vote" that would have cut all proposed funding for the FEPC. Then this decision was overturned by a "teller vote." Unfortunately, there were not recorded votes on these amendments, leaving the precise partisan breakdown on them unknown. Yet we know from contemporary accounts that many Republicans evinced hostility toward the FEPC. Reportedly, "about half of the Republicans present" wound up siding with Southern Democrats "after being challenged by Southerners and one of their own colleagues to evidence the sincerity of their past criticism of New Deal bureaus."[6] The initial vote was 141

---

[5] "See Move to Abolish FEPC," *Chicago Defender*, March 25, 1944, 2.
[6] "House Votes to Restore FEPC Funds: Party Lines Crossed as Move to Withhold Appropriation Fails," *Washington Post*, May 27, 1944, 1.

to 103 in favor of cutting the $500,000 appropriation for the FEPC. Although a move to restore the FEPC funds soon afterward passed by a margin of 123 to 119, the closeness of this unrecorded vote in a chamber in which Southerners made up just over a quarter of the membership suggests that many Republican representatives still opposed funding the FEPC at that time.

When the civil rights controversy revived after the 1944 election Senator Taft emerged as an opponent of all proposals to create an FEPC that had any power. Taft had supported efforts to eliminate lynching and the poll tax, but he was much more attuned to the concerns of the business community than those of blacks. The Ohio senator also evinced skepticism about the ability of Republicans to gain politically from pushing for antidiscrimination policies, noting, "I doubt we can outbid Mrs. Roosevelt" (Patterson 1972, 307).[7] Taft told a delegation of African Americans from his state, "colored people are making a mistake…. I think you are pushing too fast. The colored people are much better off than they were ten years ago" (Reed 1991, 166). When the limits of Taft's support for civil rights became clear he was denounced by NAACP leaders as "a political chameleon, a pre-election friend and a post-election foe of pending legislation to establish a permanent FEPC."[8]

While some other prominent Republicans, including House minority leader Joe Martin of Massachusetts, made more favorable statements about the FEPC, Taft was hardly alone among Republicans in his resistance to proposals to enforce antidiscrimination policies. The *Wall Street Journal* editorialized repeatedly against any governmental enforcement of antidiscrimination at the state or federal levels.[9] When President Truman proposed a permanent Civil Rights Commission and an FEPC, the *Journal* worried about tyranny and claimed, "We shudder to think of what the two commissions might do to the citizen's unalienable right to wipe his nose."[10] In the end the proposals for a permanent FEPC died in the Senate, and the agency shut down in 1946.

Although New York governor Thomas Dewey, the GOP's presidential candidate in 1944 and 1948, did support an FEPC and helped enact the

---

[7] While her husband, Franklin, remained cautious, Eleanor Roosevelt became strongly identified with the struggle against racial discrimination.

[8] "Taft Knifing of Permanent FEPC Splits Republicans in Congress," *Chicago Defender*, February 17, 1945, 3.

[9] "On Job Discrimination Laws," *Wall Street Journal*, February 9, 1945, 6; "'Discrimination' and Law," *Wall Street Journal*, June 7, 1945, 4.

[10] "A Rights-Giving Bureau," *Wall Street Journal*, February 4, 1948, 4.

first state antidiscrimination law, most congressional Republicans in this period were much less interested in taking a strong stand on civil rights. Here the differing electoral incentives for presidential and congressional candidates even within the same party are evident. Just as Roosevelt was not as free as Northern Democratic MCs to ignore the views of Southern whites on race, as a presidential candidate Dewey had to pay some attention to the concerns of African Americans and Jews concentrated in swing states, including his own. By contrast, most Republicans in Congress had few members of these groups in their states and districts.

As a result, Republicans in Congress did very little on civil rights even when they controlled the agenda. In the 80th Congress (1947–1948), the first one under Republican control since the beginning of the Depression, there was not a floor vote in either the House or the Senate on proposals for a revived Fair Employment Practices Commission or any other civil rights legislation except for the poll tax ban that had been considered in two previous Democratic Congresses (Hartmann 1971, 153).[11] The Republicans did not even bring up an antilynching bill. In the only other Congress controlled by their party during this period, the 83rd (1953–1954), Republicans brought up no civil rights legislation whatsoever. In these years it is likely that any civil rights bill would have been the target of a Southern filibuster, but often parties that wish to stake out a position and draw a contrast with their rivals bring up a measure that is unlikely to become law. Certainly GOP leaders could have brought a civil rights measure to a vote in the House had they chosen to do so.

When the Democrats regained control of Congress in 1949 the emerging divide between the parties in the North on race was again evident. The gap between Northern Democrats and Republicans first visible during the controversy over the FEPC in 1944 reemerged in 1950. This Congress saw not only an attack on the poll tax, affecting only the Southern public sector, but a renewed push for an FEPC with enforcement power as well. The bid to create such an agency was supported by the ADA and American Civil Liberties Union, the AFL and CIO, and various ethnic lobbies. By contrast, GOP-oriented lobbies including the National Association of Manufacturers and American Association of Small Business were critical of the measure, especially the proposed enforcement powers.

---

[11] This Congress also debated home-rule for the District of Colombia, which drew opposition from Southerners because of the prospect of empowering what was then the segregated District's large black minority.

There was even some differentiation between the parties on the FEPC issue in presidential politics in the 1952 campaign. In most respects Eisenhower and Stevenson differed little on civil rights. Both candidates were opposed to segregation, but very sensitive to Southern sensibilities. Stevenson was determined to avoid a repeat of the Dixiecrat bolt that cost Truman four Southern states in 1948 and chose a running mate from the deep South, Senator John Sparkman of Alabama. In 1952 Eisenhower did not support "compulsory FEPC legislation" at the federal level (Berman 1970, 221). Initially Stevenson took the same position.

Yet, unlike Eisenhower, the Illinois governor later modified his position on FEPC after coming under intense pressure from civil rights advocates. Stevenson eventually came out in favor of an FEPC bill sponsored by Senators Hubert Humphrey (D-MN) and Irving Ives (R-NY). Stevenson's stand won him praise from the NAACP as the candidate taking "the most forthright" position on civil rights.[12]

Thus outside the South, Democratic and Republican politicians may have read their constituents' concerns on this issue differently, something that did not typically happen on measures like the poll tax and lynching bans, which mobilized little opposition in the North. Most Northerners of both parties nominally favored the creation of an FEPC. The large majority of Republican MCs voted first with Northern Democrats to remove procedural obstacles to the consideration of the bill creating an FEPC in 1950.

However, there were already important differences in the preferences of Northern Republicans and Democrats on racial issues. After voting with Northern Democrats to bring up the FEPC bill on a key amendment, most GOP MCs sided with Southern Democrats to deny the agency enforcement powers, decrying the prospect of federal interference with business.[13] Once that amendment had been adopted – effectively gutting the bill – Republican representatives then again allied with their Northern Democrats colleagues to pass what had become a symbolic measure.

Thus congressional Republicans revealed themselves to be less supportive of a strong federal role in combating racism than their Democratic colleagues in a key respect by 1950 and to a lesser degree even in the 1940s. This chronology clashes with Carmines and Stimson's (1989) account. These authors do not find evidence of Northern Democrats and Republicans differing notably on racial issues at this stage.

---

[12] "Stevenson Hailed for Rights Stand," *New York Times*, September 10, 1952, 15.
[13] Congressional Quarterly Almanac 1950, 382–383.

Figure 4-2 depicting the distribution of racial liberalism scores for MCs in the 81st, 86th, and 92nd Congresses illustrates the parties' complicated positioning on the issue over decades. In the first two Congresses most Republicans have high scores, having supported most, but crucially not all, civil rights measures. Democrats are badly split and predominate at the extremes. The last chart reveals a similar pattern. The key difference vis-à-vis the first two is the skew of the GOP distribution. In the earlier Congresses most Republicans are closer to Northern Democrats than to Southerners, but by the 1970s the opposite is true. On modest proposals, for example, funding for the toothless Civil Rights Commission, opposition still came mostly from Southern Democrats as late as the early 1970s. Yet the more typical votes on the powers of the Equal Employment Opportunity Commission (EEOC) and busing saw most Republicans joining Southern Democrats.

Thus from the 1940s through the early 1970s the correlation between party and racial liberalism depended on the cutpoint. This pattern existed *before, during, and after* Carmines and Stimson's 1958–1964 "punctuation" in the equilibrium. The change in the parties' relative positions stemmed less from replacement via critical elections than from the revelation of latent preferences as the civil rights agenda began to include measures affecting Republican MCs' constituents.[14]

As soon as civil rights measures began to provoke business opposition Republican MCs became less supportive of them. Corporate lobbies sat on the sidelines during the discussion of the 1964 Civil Rights Act (Lytle 1966, 291; Wolfinger and Filvaroff 2000). Although the act did create potential liability for employers, business lobbies did not work against it as they had fought fair employment measures at the state level in the preceding two decades and criticized the Truman administration's FEPC bill in 1950. The absence of any enforcement powers for the EEOC in the final bill may have been a factor in business's neutrality. Wolfinger and Filavroff (2000, 31) also report that business groups were "not too disturbed by the prospects of its passage" because many firms had already adjusted their practices to cope with fair employment statutes that had been enacted in Northern states in the previous two decades. The 1965 Voting Rights Act,

---

[14] Sinclair (1982) has made this argument. Nor did turnover prompt the agenda shift. The Civil Rights Act *preceded* the Democratic landslide in 1964. Its passage irrevocably altered the agenda by ending the Jim Crow controversy (and the easy votes it had allowed Northerners to cast) and nationalized the issue. When Democrats' ranks thinned after 1966 the parties' did not revert to their old relative positions on racial issues.

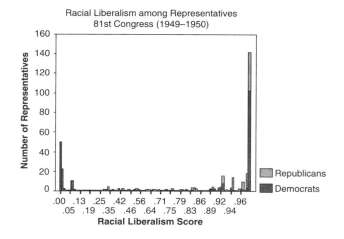

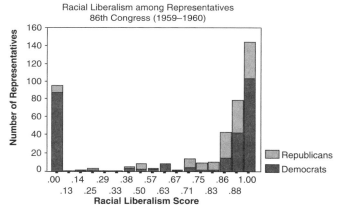

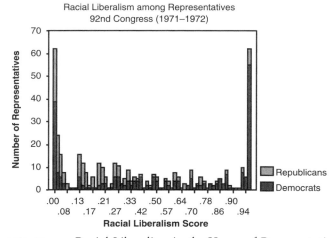

FIGURE 4-2. Racial Liberalism in the House of Representatives by Party, 81st (1949–1950), 86th (1959–1960), and 92nd Congresses (1971–1972)

which did not affect the private sector, was not a focus of business lobbying either and won support from the large majority of GOP MCs.

Yet this neutrality was short lived. The National Association of Real Estate Boards lobbied against President Johnson's "fair housing" proposal in 1966, stimulating opposition to it among most of the Republican MCs who had favored earlier civil rights measures.[15] In later years GOP-leaning business lobbies would oppose proposals to strengthen the enforcement powers of the EEOC in the early 1970s and resisted attempts to make it easier for plaintiffs to win lawsuits claiming discrimination in the early 1990s. The Chamber of Commerce also lobbied against sanctions on apartheid South Africa, which became part of the civil rights agenda in the 1980s.[16]

Thus the GOP's business-inspired resistance to civil rights measures, while usually latent due to the voting agenda in Congress, did not emerge suddenly in 1964 as a result of compositional shifts in the Republican representation on Capitol Hill. Rather, it was evident far earlier, as the FEPC case shows.

More evidence of this pattern is evident at the state level. Norton Long (1951, 195–196) noted, "the entrepreneurs of politics have been faced with the difficult task of reconciling the necessary demagoguery [*sic*] of an era of mass suffrage with the sensitivities of business backers. ... Thus the eager efforts of Republican professionals to regain the Negro vote, a vote that would have elected Dewey, have been uniformly opposed by state manufacturers' associations who stand on principle against the encroachment of FEPC." Erikson (1971) found that Northern states controlled by Democrats were more likely to enact antidiscrimination laws than those under GOP control.

Case studies of developments in particular states also bolster the view that the business community's concerns underlay GOP resistance to civil rights measures long before 1964. Chen's (2006) study of developments in New York State shows that the pattern of Republicans siding with business lobbies in their efforts to forestall enactment of antidiscrimination laws had already emerged in the mid-1940s, two decades before the parties' national reversal on race in the mid-1960s. During the struggle over the passage of the first state antidiscrimination statute, New York's 1945 "Ives-Quinn" Act, this dynamic was visible. Business lobbies opposed

---

[15] Congressional Quarterly Almanac 1966, 457.
[16] "House Due for Showdown Vote this Week on How Much Power to Give Job-Bias Unit," *Wall Street Journal*, September 13, 1971, 4; "GOP Sen. Lugar Ready to Consider Immediate Sanctions on South Africa," *Washington Post*, May 23, 1985, A9.

this bid to enact an enforceable antidiscrimination statute while labor and minority organizations generally favored it.

Although Republicans controlled the New York legislature then, the Ives-Quinn Act passed because unified Democratic support coalesced with some moderate Republicans. Chen notes, "Party leaders like [Gov. Thomas] Dewey and [Irving] Ives – who held or aspired to statewide office – took a liberal stand on fair employment because they needed to compete for minority votes in statewide elections, but most GOP members faced different electoral circumstances." In the end, he reports, "Every single Democratic legislator voted for the bill, but the Republican delegation was divided in both chambers, with the split more pronounced in the Assembly than the Senate" (29). Opposition to the Ives-Quinn Act came largely from GOP legislators who represented rural districts. These Republican elected officials faced virtually no trade-off between black voters and business support, since the former were largely absent from their districts.

What was true in New York was also true in California. In 1946 California civil rights advocates sponsored Proposition 11, which would have created a permanent Fair Employment Practices Commission with enforcement powers. This measure, which was solidly defeated by California voters,[17] was opposed by leading pro-GOP groups including the Chamber of Commerce, the Farm Bureau, and the California Retailers Association.[18] These business lobbies were joined in their opposition by leading Republican papers in the state, including the *Los Angeles Times*, the *San Francisco Chronicle*, and the *San Francisco Examiner*.[19] The partisan division over FEPC in California was again evident during the famous 1950 Senate contest between Democrat Helen Gahagan Douglas, who backed enforcement powers for the FEPC, and Richard Nixon, who did not (Gellman 1999, 327).

California civil rights advocates eventually secured antidiscrimination laws that had eluded them at the beginning of the postwar period. Yet even then resistance from the business community and the Republican Party was evident. Robert Self (2003, 93) notes, "even the relatively modest fair employment and housing laws won in 1959 and 1963 drew enormous

[17] Chen, Mickey, and Van Houweling's (2008) study of precinct-level voting data on the proposition suggests that Republican voters in California strongly opposed the FEPC while Democrats were more divided.

[18] "C. of C. Opposes Proposition 11," *Los Angeles Times*, October 11, 1946, 2; "Farm Bureaus in State Oppose Proposition 11," *Los Angeles Times*, October 29, 1946, 5; "Proposition 11 Hit by Retailers," *Los Angeles Times*, October 17, 1946, 12.

[19] Leonard (1990, 479); "Promotion of Race Prejudice," *Los Angeles Times*, October 27, 1946, 4.

TABLE 4-1. *Interparty Difference of Means on Civil Rights Measures Opposed by Business and on Noneconomic Civil Rights Issues Compared, House of Representatives, Selected Congresses, 1965–1992*

| Congress | Noneconomic Civil Rights Measures | Business-Opposed Civil Rights Measures |
|---|---|---|
| 89th Congress (1965–1966) | .1 | .26 |
| 90th Congress (1967–1968) | .105 | .144 |
| 92nd Congress (1971–1972) | .23 | .52 |
| 96th Congress (1979–1980) | .537 | .515 |
| 101st Congress (1989–1990) | .669 | .781 |
| 102nd Congress (1991–1992) | .616 | .8 |

opposition from the state's Republican Party, lobbyists for employer groups and especially the real estate industry" (see also Casstevens 1967).

At both the state and national levels, Republicans engaged in *coalition maintenance* where the issue of civil rights was concerned. Although the incentives of individual Republican politicians would vary depending on their geographic constituency, in general the party's close ties to business interests and already modest support from blacks meant that when the two groups clashed, Republicans were predisposed to side with the former.

Evidence that the business community contributed to the alignment of the parties on race can be seen in Table 4-1. In this table I present the difference in party mean support for racial liberalism in post-1964 Congresses that included civil rights measures that corporate lobbies opposed, and I contrast it with the same statistic for noneconomic civil rights issues. I do not present scores for Congresses in which only roll calls in one of these categories was considered, and I exclude measures that affected the private sector but about which business lobbies were neutral, for example, the Civil Rights Act of 1964.

This table illustrates two points. In both categories of legislation the gaps increase substantially over time, reflecting the growing partisanship on this issue. Moreover, voting on civil rights measures opposed by the business community was generally more partisan than the alignment on other proposals that did not pit corporate lobbies against civil rights advocates.[20]

The clash between the business community and civil rights advocates is not the entire story of the parties' reversal on race, of course. I highlight

---

[20] The one exception is the 96th Congress, where the gap runs in the other direction, but by a tiny amount.

it because it is less well known than the other factor, the attempt by Republican politicians to win the support of Southern whites by opposing civil rights measures. This was first visible nationally in the Goldwater candidacy of 1964.

During this presidential campaign a clear contrast between the parties emerged on the race issue. This was the most pronounced differentiation on racial issues between major party presidential nominees since the nineteenth century. Goldwater opposed the Civil Rights Act that Johnson championed. This was not a wholly new strategy for the Arizona senator. In *The Conscience of a Conservative,* published in 1960, Goldwater argued at length that the Supreme Court's *Brown* decision outlawing school segregation was unconstitutional (Goldwater 2007 [1960], ch. 4). In 1961 he told fellow Republicans "we're not going to get the Negro vote as a bloc in 1964 or 1968, so we ought to go hunting where the ducks are," in other words, pursue Southern whites (Devries and Bass 1978, 309).

The sharp contrast on civil rights between the two parties' presidential candidates in 1964 cost Republicans lost the limited black support they had retained since the 1930s. Yet Goldwater's Southern strategy had immediate electoral benefits for the GOP as well. The only states he carried outside of his native Arizona were in the Deep South where voters had not favored a GOP presidential candidate since the end of Reconstruction. Yet most Southern whites did not become Republicans overnight. Many continued to identify as Democrats and vote Democratic in local and state races. Not until 1994 would the GOP capture a majority of Southern seats in Congress.

Subsequent GOP presidential nominees would repeat Goldwater's choice of Southern white voters over blacks, but the party's movement was gradual. Nixon was more circumspect and less blatant in his appeal for support in the South in 1968 than Goldwater had been four years earlier. Moreover, for a time after Goldwater's failed candidacy many prominent moderate Republican politicians continued to strongly support civil rights and win substantial numbers of African American voters. Examples included both Nelson Rockefeller and his brother, Arkansas governor Winthrop Rockefeller, Senator Charles Percy of Illinois, Senator Jacob Javits of New York, and New York City mayor John Lindsay (Frymer and Skrentny 1998, 159).[21] Unlike Goldwater, these GOP candidates had not written off black support.

---

[21] Others in this category included Senator Edward Brooke of Massachusetts, the only black member of the U.S. Senate in the 1960s and 1970s, Gov. George Romney of Michigan, and Senator Hugh Scott of Pennsylvania, whose electoral strength Barone,

Similarly, many Southern Democratic politicians remained wedded to traditional constituencies, continuing to focus appeals to their largely white electorates without modifying their positions on race as Lyndon Johnson had done. As a result, the correlation between racial liberalism and party among Southern representatives only gradually came to mirror that in the North. Southern Democrats in Congress remained more conservative on race than Northern Republicans until the mid-1970s.

Over time, however, many incumbent Southern Democratic MCs eventually did modify their positions on race, in reaction to GOP competition and their increasing dependence on black voters (Whitby and Gilliam 1991). This shift eventually ended the extreme bimodalism in voting patterns on civil rights among Democratic MCs depicted in Figure 4-2 and created greater uniformity of the parties on the issue.

Yet these developments among Southern MCs occurred chiefly in the 1970s and 1980s, well *after* the new alignment of the parties on race had emerged in Congress. They reinforced and heightened the shift, but did not cause it in the first instance. Turnover among MCs played more of a role here than in the North. Still, conversion was a major factor in the eventual alliance between white Southern Democratic politicians and newly enfranchised black voters. It is much more an instance of coalition group incorporation than coalition maintenance.

By contrast, the shift in the relative positions of Northern MCs on race stemmed chiefly from politicians reacting rapidly to new demands from old constituencies. Later, when less business-related civil rights issues came up, such as busing, Northern Democratic MCs were cross-pressured by their need to maintain black support while Republicans were freer to court public opinion. However, party position change in the South was driven by the gradual integration of African Americans into the Democratic Party and the defection of whites to the Republicans and was far slower as a consequence.[22]

SHIFTS AMONG ELITES

Carmines and Stimson (1989) claim that "membership replacement" explains the shift of party elites on civil rights. This claim merits close

---

Ujifusa, and Matthews (1972, 679) attributed to a "shrewd cultivation of minority groups, especially blacks and Jews."

[22] Relatedly, Cowden (2001) shows the reversal of the sign of the correlation between racial attitudes and party identification occurred very rapidly among Northern whites but took decades among their Southern counterparts.

scrutiny because these authors used the case of racial politics to develop a model that has influenced subsequent scholarship on numerous issues.

To assess the relative importance of adaptation versus replacement in reshaping the parties on the race issue I turn first to the most visible figures, presidential nominees. Here Lyndon Johnson's realignment vis-à-vis Goldwater and Richard Nixon is crucial.

Goldwater had joined the NAACP and aided the Urban League's desegregation drive in postwar Phoenix as a businessman and city councilman (Goldberg 1995, 123). Johnson had no such ties to the NAACP in the postwar years. In the 85th Congress (1957–1958) Goldwater's support for civil rights, while limited, exceeded Johnson's.[23] This was so even though Johnson had by that time begun to support civil rights. As late as 1960 the two senators' voting records on racial issues were nearly identical.[24]

Yet by 1961 Goldwater was telling his party that its future was in "hunting where the ducks are," the white South. In the same year Johnson chaired the President's Commission on Equal Employment Opportunity, the precursor to the modern EEOC (Dallek 1998, 23). Thus the sharp contrast in the 1964 election that crystallized the parties' images on the race issue owed much to the adaptation of the two nominees, whose stands had been similar in earlier years.

The role reversal between Johnson and his successor Richard Nixon is even more striking. In 1960 Nixon's civil rights record (always stronger than Goldwater's) still generally outshone Kennedy's, not to mention Johnson's. Unlike Nixon, Kennedy and Johnson were not NAACP members. Both Democrats voted to weaken the bill that became the 1957 Civil Rights Act.[25] Until late in 1960 Nixon even had closer ties than Kennedy did to Martin Luther King, Jr. (Ambrose 1987, 414, 596). During the 1960 presidential debates Nixon deplored Johnson's segregationist past (Mayer 2002, 37). Yet by 1968 a reversal had occurred; that year Nixon

[23] Of course, as a majority leader with legendary political skills, Johnson played a much more important role than Goldwater in the passage of the Civil Rights Act of 1957, as Caro (2002) describes at length. Yet his voting record differed little from Goldwater's at this time.

[24] "Senators' Voting Measured against 18-Member 'Southern Bloc,'" *Congressional Quarterly Almanac 1960*, 204. Johnson sided with the Southerners 68 percent of the time while Goldwater did so 67 percent of the time. Admittedly, during these years Johnson was racially liberal for his region and Goldwater racially conservative for his.

[25] Mayer (2002, 16) shows that a black aide had advised Kennedy not to risk joining the group. The one case in which Kennedy had taken the more liberal position than Nixon on race was the 1950 House vote on FEPC enforcement powers already discussed.

deplored Johnson's "dangerous" threats to withdraw federal funds from schools that refused to integrate.[26]

A similar reversal is evident among congressional leaders. Republican Senate and House minority leaders Everett Dirksen and Charles Halleck and House GOP whip Les Arends, Midwesterners all, were all once more racially liberal than Johnson. Yet in 1964 they offered crucial support for the Civil Rights Act only after publicly insisting on concessions in a manner that contrasted with Johnson's pronounced enthusiasm (Whalen and Whalen 1985, ch. 6). This is the sort of positioning that is not fully captured in roll-call analyses. Subsequently these leaders, along with most Republicans, voted to weaken (but again ultimately supported) Johnson's 1965 Voting Rights Act. They then joined with Southern Democrats in 1966 to block Johnson's proposed ban on discrimination in housing.

Democratic congressional leaders "evolved" more dramatically on civil rights. House majority leader Carl Albert of Oklahoma and his whip Hale Boggs of Louisiana entered politics as segregationists. Albert shifted after becoming whip in 1955. Boggs, who replaced Albert as whip in 1961 when the latter became majority leader, changed later, voting against the 1964 Civil Rights Act. But after 1964 both Albert and Boggs were more racially liberal than Halleck, Dirksen, and Arends. For example, the three Republicans initially opposed fair housing legislation the Democratic leaders supported.

A later generation of congressional leaders who had been fairly junior MCs at the time of the civil rights controversy of the mid-1960s also modified their stands on race before rising to the top of their parties. The two GOP congressional leaders in the late 1980s, Bob Dole of Kansas and Bob Michel of Illinois, had supported the 1964 Civil Rights Act. Their Democratic counterparts, Robert Byrd of West Virginia and Jim Wright of Texas, had not. (Byrd entered politics as a Klansman in 1946.)[27] Yet in the 1980s Byrd and Wright were notably more supportive of civil rights than Dole and Michel.

The Democratic congressional leaders I discuss above at first took stands in line with their constituents' views, but moved toward the prevalent view within their party as they rose in it. These leaders went from defending Jim Crow to favoring affirmative action and, in the venerable

---

[26] "Nixon Scores U.S. Method of Enforcing Integration," *New York Times*, September 13, 1968, 1.

[27] See "Robert Byrd's Rules of Order," *Washington Post*, February 11, 1999, C1. On Wright, see "Byrd Endorses Obama," *Charleston Gazette*, May 20, 2008, 4A.

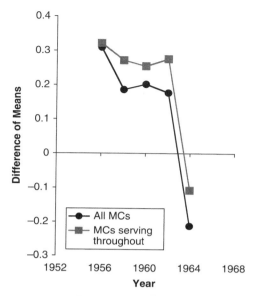

FIGURE 4-3. Interparty Difference between Republican and Democratic Means on Racial Liberalism (Republican Mean – Democratic Mean), All Representatives and Those Serving throughout the Period, House of Representatives, 85th through 89th Congresses (1957–1966)

Byrd's case, even endorsing Barack Obama for the Democratic presidential nomination in 2008. By contrast, the Republicans were more consistent in an absolute sense, supporting attacks on Jim Crow but having reservations on much more far-reaching legislation that affected the private sector. The GOP congressional leaders came to be seen as racial conservatives because the civil rights debate had moved so far during their careers.

Yet for the parties to reposition themselves it is not enough for presidential nominees and congressional leaders to modify their stands. The change must be more widespread. Moving beyond a focus on leaders, I examine voting on racial issues in the House. If replacement drives change, comparison of long-serving MCs with the chamber as whole ought to show increasing divergence between the two. Figure 4-3 shows the changing relationship between party and support for racial liberalism for all representatives and for the 185 serving from the 85th through the 89th Congress (1957–1966). I choose this period because it includes the era in which the two allegedly key elections of 1958 and 1964 said to have reoriented the parties on race occurred.

Figure 4-3 reveals that Republican representatives were more racially liberal on average until the 89th Congress (1965–1966), when a dramatic shift occurred. The same reversal also appears, only a bit less sharply, among the subset of MCs whose tenures in Congress spanned the 1958 and 1964 elections. Since the membership of this latter group is stable, adaptation, not turnover, must be the source of change among them.[28] The combination of coalition maintenance and coalition group incorporation that explain the racial realignment in this subset of MCs were *not* primarily results of elite replacement.

We would like to be certain that apparent party position change is not a product of agenda change in which bills with radically different cutpoints and comparisons of Congresses with very different partisan compositions are compared. For that reason, in Table 4-2 I present evidence based on two votes in the House. One, the vote on the 1964 Civil Rights Act, took place before the parties' overall relative positions on race had reversed. The second vote, concerning Senate amendments strengthening the 1970 extension of the Voting Rights Act, occurred after the parties' reversal on race. However, as the table indicates, both votes took place in Congresses with similar party compositions, and civil rights backers accounted for very similar shares of the House in both cases. The table reveals that change in the parties' positioning on race was gradual, but, as in other cases, it was manifest among long-serving MCs as well as the rest of Congress.

Yet what about MCs more broadly? The long-serving legislators analyzed in the figure and table represent only a minority. Analysis based on Rapoport and Stone's formula reveals that 67 percent of the change among House Republicans occurred via conversion; however, for Democrats the equivalent figure is 38 percent during this period, producing a combined total effect of 55.2 percent in the entire House. In other words, conversion explains a majority of the change in the parties' positioning on race during this period.

Still, differences between the parties are evident. Although conversion played an important role among the Democrats' realignment on race (especially when we recall that Rapoport and Stone's method is biased in favor of finding turnover effects), it appears to have been secondary in importance and is less striking than the result for the Republicans. This is the opposite of what I found on abortion and gun control, issues on which replacement

---

[28] See also Sinclair (1982, 95), who finds that "cohort analysis reveals no significant differences" among Republicans on "civil liberties" issues.

TABLE 4-2. *Comparison of the Positions of Long-Serving Representatives (Stayers) and the Rest of the House on Two Civil Rights Votes with Similar Cutpoints: 1964 and 1970*

| Congress | Type of Representative | Democrats | Republicans |
|---|---|---|---|
| 88th Congress (1963–1964)[a] | Stayers | 67.3% (N = 153) | 80.8% (N = 99) |
| 91st Congress (1969–1970)[b] | Stayers | 73.2% (N = 153) | 62.6% (N = 99) |
| 88th Congress (1963–1964)[a] | Rest of House | 51.5% (N = 97) | 79.2% (N = 77) |
| 91st Congress (1969–1970)[b] | Rest of House | 78.5% (N = 79) | 49.4% (N = 81) |

[a] 88th Congress (59% Democratic), H.R. 7152, February 10, 1964: Passage of the Civil Rights Act (69% voting pro–civil rights)
[b] 91st Congress (55% Democratic), H.R. 4249, June 17, 1970: Agreeing to Senate amendments to Voting Rights Act extension (67% voting pro–civil rights)

played a more important role for Republicans than Democrats. How can we explain this difference between the two parties?

I argue that the difference stems from the way the two parties differently experienced the two dynamics of change at work on racial issues. The change due to coalition maintenance was most strongly felt among Republicans. As business interests with preexisting relationships with GOP MCs came into conflict with the agenda of civil rights groups, Republicans sided with business. As this was a process in which party elites responded to existing allies, it occurred rapidly. Since it did not require MCs to form ties to new constituencies, it was visible among continuing legislators, and replacement was not a prerequisite for change. It is true that Southern Republicans gained support among white voters during this period, but there were few Southern GOP MCs, and the preferences of these newcomers on racial issues were not radically different from those Southern whites already supporting the Republicans.

After 1965 Republicans also increasingly seemed to write off black voters, and the issue became more partisan. Poole and Rosenthal (1997, 232) write, "Race was drawn into the first dimension [of voting] in Congress because race-related issues became, increasingly, redistributional ones – welfare, affirmative action, food stamps and so on."

Yet the parties' repositioning on race cannot be entirely attributed to the redistributive character of civil rights policy. Even on questions that did not pit civil rights organizations against the business community, such as school busing or voting rights, Republican MCs were notably less likely than Northern Democrats and, after the mid-1970s, even Southern Democrats to side with civil rights advocates.

However, the story for the Democrats is different. Almost all Northern Democratic MCs already took a pro–civil rights position at the beginning of the period surveyed. The shift in Democratic voting patterns on racial issues in Congress during this period is primarily a result of changes in the voting patterns of Southern Democrats.

Here the process of coalition group incorporation was at work. Newly enfranchised black voters entered the Southern Democratic Party en masse during this period. Southern Democratic MCs thus faced pressure to respond to new constituencies. Some resisted. Maintaining traditional positions on race often allowed such legislators to retain ties to white voters and forestall significant Republican competition. Where blacks were sufficiently visible to stimulate racial fears among whites, but not numerous enough to dominate Democratic primaries in which many white conservatives still voted, this was a viable strategy for a time. Other Southern Democratic MCs, however, whether because they were philosophically more open to the demands of blacks or because they needed African Americans' votes in the face of strong Republican challenges, did eventually modify their positions on race.

Hood, Kidd, and Morris (1999) suggest that it was the interaction between black enfranchisement and incorporation in the Democratic Party with Republican competition that drove Southern Democratic MCs to moderate their positions on race. In states or districts in which only one of these factors was present, change in Democrats' positioning was much slower. If a Democratic incumbent could avoid a serious challenge by a Republican, he might be able to ignore even those black voters who were enfranchised. This was the case, for example, for the very unreconstructed Senator James Eastland (D-MS), who was reelected twice (in 1966 and 1972) after the passage of the Voting Rights Act and made virtually no concessions to black sensibilities during the balance of his career, despite the enormous growth of the black vote in his state after 1965.

Yet Eastland's colleague John Stennis served another decade, long enough to see not only the enfranchisement of Mississippi's large black community, but the growth of the Republican Party in that state as well. Eastland's successor, elected in 1978, was a Republican, Thad Cochran.

Cochran defeated the Democrats' nominee, Maurice Dantin, a conservative whose campaign was fatally undermined by an independent black candidate who siphoned away African American votes.[29]

Facing a serious Republican challenger in 1982 (Haley Barbour, who later became Republican National Committee chair and governor of Mississippi), and having seen Dantin's fate, Stennis began to "evolve" on racial matters. The octogenarian would never be confused with Malcolm X or even Lyndon Johnson, but he did make some modest gestures toward African American voters that would have been unimaginable earlier in his career. In 1982 for the first time Stennis voted for an extension of the Voting Rights Act. Stennis also endorsed Robert Clark, a black Mississippi state legislator seeking to become his state's first African American congressman since Reconstruction.[30]

In revisiting his positions on race very late in his career, Senator Stennis was not alone. Remarkably, even George Wallace, who, like Stennis faced a serious Republican opponent for the first time in 1982, sought and won black support in his last campaign for governor that year.[31]

The need to adjust to the changing coalition of the Democratic Party in their states and districts was not the only factor that impelled Southern Democratic officials to become more liberal on race. As I have already noted, some Southern Democratic politicians were also prompted to moderate their position in order to gain or retain a leading role in the national party, even when a more progressive view on race was not necessary to secure their reelection or even – as in the case of Hale Boggs, who had more than one narrow electoral escape in the 1960s – an impediment to it.

Beyond the most prominent figures I have discussed there were many other less famous cases of well-timed adaptation that allowed Southern Democrats to retain positions of national responsibility. One such case is Rep. Jamie Whitten, a Mississippi Democrat who was first elected in

[29] "The Candidates and the Issues in Key Senatorial and Gubernatorial Contests," *New York Times*, November 8, 1978, A20.
[30] "Stennis Surveys 35 Years and Decides to Press on," *Washington Post*, September 28, 1982, A1; "Mississippi's Stennis Faces Hardest Race of Long Career," *Christian Science Monitor*, October 14, 1982, 7.
[31] Amazingly, Wallace not only won overwhelming support from African Americans against a very conservative GOP candidate, but he also gained over a third of the black vote in the Democratic primary against an opponent supported by local black political elites. See "Wallace Wins a Third of Black Vote in Capturing Spot in Primary Runoff," *New York Times*, September 9, 1982, B16; "Blacks, Hispanics Show Clout at Polls," *UPI* (via Nexis), November 3, 1982.

1941 and chaired the House Appropriations Committee from 1979 to 1993. Whitten, a onetime segregationist, became considerably more liberal on racial matters (as well as economic issues) in the latter part of his career. Given the composition of his district, Whitten probably could have been reelected until his retirement in 1994 without moderating his stance on racial issues.

Yet it is doubtful whether an "unreconstructed" Whitten could have retained such an important post in Congress. Whitten explained, "A lawyer who doesn't notice when they've changed the judge and jury isn't much for you. I have adjusted to changing conditions" (Barone and Ujifusa 1989, 664). For Whitten, the "jury" included his fellow House Democrats. By the time seniority had made the Mississippi congressman the presumptive chair of the Appropriations Committee in 1979 "reform" had reached Capitol Hill. The Democratic caucus had shown it would overthrow chairs whose deviations from party policies were too great, seniority notwithstanding. Unsurprisingly, Whitten became far more of a "national" Democrat in his positions in this latter phase of his career (Rohde 1991, 76).

Note that the period surveyed above ends in 1992, at a time when most Southern seats in Congress were still held by Democrats. While there had already been significant movement of racially conservative Southern whites into Republican ranks and growth in GOP representation in the South, much of that change was yet to come, as far as congressional elections were concerned. It was only in 1994 that the Republicans finally captured a majority of Southern seats in Congress.

In the cases of abortion and gun control I have shown that MCs were increasingly guided by party affiliation rather than public opinion in their states as these issues became more partisan. This pattern also emerges in the case of racial politics. Figure 4-4 depicts the changing importance of two predictors of senators' votes on racial issues, their party affiliation, and public opinion on racial matters in their states. The values represented are standardized regression coefficients for two variables: a dummy for the party affiliation of the senator and a measure of mean state opinion on racial issues. The latter measure is taken from Brace et al. (2002, 176), who cumulate respondents within a state over time from the General Social Survey of 1974–1998. The GSS is useful because it includes data from far earlier than the 1988–1990–1992 NES Senate Election Study. However, unlike the NES study, which has large samples from all 50 states, the GSS-derived measure includes only 44 states, so senators from Nevada, New Mexico, Hawaii, Idaho, Nebraska, and Maine are excluded from the analysis.

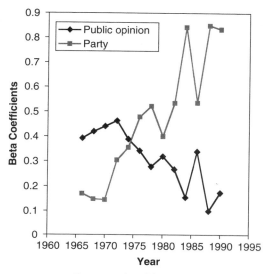

FIGURE 4-4. Party and Public Opinion as Predictors of Senators' Positions on Racial Issues, 90th through 102nd Congresses (1967–1992)

By splitting their data into two half-samples based on the earlier and later waves of the GSS, Brace et al. show that the relative positions of the states on issues are quite stable over time. Thus we can use their measure to predict senators' behavior even for some years before the beginning of the period the GSS studied. I depict Congresses beginning with the 90th (1967–1968) because the GSS includes African American respondents, and that was the first Congress in which all roll calls occurred after the passage of the 1965 Voting Rights Act. Before that point there is little reason to expect Southern senators to take account of the attitudes of disenfranchised African Americans.

The change depicted over time in Figure 4-4 is dramatic. Initially, public opinion was a far stronger predictor of senators' votes on racial issues than party affiliation. In fact, in the first few Congresses shown, the party coefficient fell just short of statistical significance. Yet over time the predictive power of party affiliation increased greatly while that of public opinion declined. By the 95th Congress (1977–1978) party was the stronger predictor. The predictive power of party affiliation on senators' positions later came to dwarf that of public opinion, which declined not only in relative terms, but in absolute ones as well. As in the cases of the abortion and gun control issues, changes in party coalitions meant that legislators eventually gave less weight to public opinion in their state or district and more to party-linked groups. For Democrats this meant reflecting the sentiments of African Americans and other groups that often supported civil rights such as labor unions. Republicans were not aligned with these groups and sometimes faced calls from business allies to oppose civil rights measures.

The parties have traded places on racial issues. The party of Lincoln became the party of the Confederate flag. This was a complicated and very protracted process, with three identifiable stages. First, Democrats gradually incorporated most African Americans into their coalition in the North during the 1930s as a result of black enthusiasm for the New Deal. This process led to the elimination of the traditional voting pattern in Congress in which Republican MCs were more liberal on race than Democratic ones, even in the North. By the early 1940s the Northern Democrats in Congress began to emerge as more liberal on race than their GOP colleagues. For the next two decades the remaining greater support for civil rights by Republicans as a whole was entirely a function of the Southern presence in the Democratic Party.

Two more changes were yet to come. First, the civil rights agenda came afoul of business interests important to the Republican Party. This was evident as early as the 1940s, when "fair employment practices" bills drew business-inspired GOP opposition at the national and state levels at a time when labor unions had begun to lobby Democrats to support such measures. In Congress this factor became increasingly important in the mid-1960s when business groups that had taken no position on antilynching bills, poll tax bans, school desegregation, or even the Civil Rights Act of 1964 objected to fair housing legislation and to attempts to rigorously enforce bans on employment discrimination. The change in elite positions visible through MCs' voting was quite rapid. This contributed to the visible shift in party positioning on race between the 88th and 89th Congresses.

Subsequently, a third shift occurred. Southern blacks became enfranchised and gradually registered to vote. At the same time many Southern whites were leaving their traditional home in the Democratic Party. These two developments occurred over many years along the lines of the coalition group incorporation model. Together they greatly altered the electorate Southern Democratic politicians faced in their bids for nomination. The result was the gradual disappearance of the "Dixiecrat" type from the Democratic caucus and the infusion into the Republican Conference of many Southern GOP MCs who were very conservative on race.

The evidence on the mechanism producing shifts among elites on the race issue is mixed. Many of the leaders in each party clearly altered their positions radically over time. The critical shift from the 88th to the 89th Congress was primarily a result of adaptation among continuing MCs. The longer-term quantitative analyses suggested, however, that although shifts by incumbents (largely in the North) account for most of the change among GOP MCs, conversion was a secondary, if important, factor among Democratic ones, primarily in the South.

The race issue merits special attention given its central role in American political history and the issue evolution literature. As a case, the politics of race reveals that multiple mechanisms can influence the development of parties' issue positions in a given policy area. Yet the race issue is not unique in this latter respect. There are other cases in which the development of parties' positions showed signs of both coalition maintenance and coalition group incorporation.

One example is the issue of "Women's Rights," which Wolbrecht (2000) explores. Traditionally Republicans were more likely than Democrats to favor the Equal Rights Amendment and feminist causes generally, although these issues were barely visible for several decades, but during the 1970s the parties traded places on the issue. Wolbrecht found that this change stemmed in part from the incorporation of new groups into party coalitions: feminists among Democrats and the religious right in the GOP.

However, Wolbrecht also saw evidence of important preference change on the part of traditional party constituencies. Many unions had opposed the Equal Rights Amendment for fear that were it included in the Constitution, "protective" legislation that regulated the treatment of female workers would be struck down. It gradually became clear in the late 1960s that the Equal Pay Act in 1962 and the Civil Rights Act in 1964 made the earlier protective statutes unenforceable. This development obviated many of the unions' concerns about the ERA (Mansbridge 1986, 10). The case of environmental politics might, like my examination of race and women's rights, also reveal a combination of coalition maintenance by Republicans who were responsive to business interests' resistance to regulation and Democrats who incorporated environmentalists in their coalition.

5

## Coalition Expansion

*The Politics of National Defense and Fiscal Policy*

> Now is it to lower the price of corn or isn't it? It is not much matter which
> we say, but mind, we must all say THE SAME.
>
> Lord Melbourne to his Cabinet, circa 1835, reported in Bagehot's *The
> English Constitution*

The cases of party position change I have discussed in previous chapters
have related to partisan constituencies. The preferences of groups and/
or their party affiliations have changed. Yet there are important shifts
in policy areas that shape parties' images that are not attributable to
the movements or targeting of identifiable groups. These issue positions
may affect parties' electoral fortunes by winning (or losing) them support
across the board, even if they do not alter the group basis of the parties.

The politics of these issues is distinctive. Where groups are absent, party
politicians' autonomy is enhanced. They have maximum leeway to take
positions and sell them to their traditional supporters while hoping to win
over other voters in a process I call coalition expansion. Since these positions
are not inspired by party-linked groups, they may be unstable, and since
party position changes in such cases are not linked to the gradual movement
of groups into party coalitions, reversals can be rapid. Two examples are the
politics of defense spending and the politics of fiscal balance and taxes.

Defense spending fits the criteria for a classic issue evolution. Party
elites have changed their stands. The topic has figured prominently in
campaigns. The parties in the electorate have shifted. Yet except for
Fordham's (2007a) recent brief treatment, the issue has yet to be examined in light of this model.[1] I do so here to provide further evidence

---

[1] No consensus exists on the impact of the defense issue on the party system. Sundquist
(1983, 443) minimizes its importance, yet Abramowitz (1994) argues that it played a
significant role.

regarding the dynamics of party position change. I argue that on defense policy parties have been largely unconstrained in altering their positions because of the absence of organized party constituencies active on the topic. There are lobbies active on defense policy, but they are primarily nonpartisan and narrowly focused on "private goods," that is, the concerns of individual firms. Important exceptions to this rule, such as the antiwar and nuclear freeze movements, have been transitory.

Support for a "strong defense" is now widely viewed as a core Republican value. Yet it has not always been this way. From 1933 to 1963 Democrats were usually the strongest supporters of defense spending. Earlier still, in the first third of the twentieth century, Republicans were generally more supportive of the military than Democrats. As Grassmuck (1951) demonstrates, this alignment changed in the 1930s during the first term of Franklin Roosevelt. In the context of discussion of the role of conversion by elites it is worth noting that Roosevelt had criticized the Coolidge administration for planning to build battleships he claimed were unnecessary (Dallek 1981, 17).

From the mid-1930s to the mid-1960s Republicans and conservatives opposed military expenditures on isolationist as well as fiscal grounds. Moderate Republicans such as Dwight Eisenhower rejected isolationism, but warned about the fiscal dangers of excessive defense spending. Eisenhower's "New Look" defense policy, with its threat of "massive retaliation," was a cheaper alternative to Democratic policies based on costly conventional forces. He reportedly feared that if a Democrat succeeded him, the result would be "an orgy of spending on defense and on social programs combined with a tax cut – a prospect he regarded with horror" (Ambrose 1984, 512).

In 1957, however, the parties reversed their positions on defense issues twice. After charging Eisenhower with unwillingness to spend enough on the military during the 1956 campaign the Democrats did a 180-degree turn the following year. This repositioning was part of a broader move toward "economy" by Democrats. As Ambrose (1984, 390) noted, "suddenly, inexplicably, the Democrats joined the Republicans in criticizing Eisenhower for spending too much. Gleefully citing his invitation to find places to save, the Democrats spent the late winter and early spring chipping away.... It was a case of American politics at its worst." George Mahon (D-TX), the chairman of the House Appropriations Subcommittee on Defense, urged his colleagues to " temper slightly the demands of the Pentagon." For Mahon the issue was whether the House would reject "big government" and rein in Pentagon lobbyists. By contrast, House minority leader Joseph Martin (R-MA) insisted, "the poorest place in the world to begin your economy is in the national defense."[2]

Morgan (1990, 85) notes that some leading Democrats justified their reversal in 1957 by arguing that they were opposed only to wasteful spending, not a large military. "[Senator] Stuart Symington, though continuing to urge big Air Force budgets charged that the administration's defense program, notably in missile development, involved 'some unnecessary duplication, and even triplication, always at the taxpayers' expense.'"

Congressional Democrats' turn to support for budget austerity, including but not limited to the Pentagon, did not come in response to either party-linked constituencies or a consensus among "their" policy intellectuals.[3] Morgan (1990, 84) shows that the AFL-CIO, the ADA, and Arthur Schlesinger all denounced this move. The Democrats' abandonment of this posture later in the year appears to have resulted not from these complaints, but from the Russians' launch of *Sputnik* on October 4, 1957. After that event Democrats reverted to their traditional charge that the Eisenhower administration was doing too little in the area of defense, a claim that was now linked to the contention that the United States was lagging dangerously behind in the emerging space race (Morgan, 1990, 91).

The year 1957 proved to be a short-lived exception. In general Democrats during the early postwar years were apt to seek more defense spending than Republicans favored. Political elites' alignment on defense issues during this period is illustrated by the vote on Senator Stuart Symington's 1959 amendment increasing military procurement by 10 percent. Symington (D-MO) was the senator most associated with the charge of a "missile gap" that Kennedy later used against Nixon in the 1960 campaign (Licklider 1970, 603–608). Symington's amendment won support from most Democrats, but Eisenhower and most of his party (including Barry Goldwater) opposed it.

To extent that politicians crossed party lines on the issue, it was GOP liberals who favored defense spending and conservative Democrats who opposed it. The only Republicans supporting Symington's amendment were John Sherman Cooper of Kentucky, later a Vietnam dove, Bill

---

[2] "House G.O.P. Loses Fight to Increase Military Budget," *New York Times,* May 29, 1957, 1.

[3] This is also true of the parties' subsequent reversals in the mid-1960s and in 2000, contrary to the expectation of some scholars (Zaller 1992; Noel 2007) that partisan scribblers and "experts" would develop a new consensus line and their party's politicians would then transmit it to the public.

Langer, a North Dakota "maverick," and Jacob Javits of New York, one of the most liberal Republicans of the postwar era. Democratic opposition to increased defense spending came mostly from Southern conservatives. Southern moderates such as Lyndon Johnson, William Fulbright, and Albert Gore Sr. backed Symington. The earliest Vietnam doves, Senators Ernest Gruening (D-AK) and Wayne Morse (D-OR), who were later the only opponents of the Gulf of Tonkin Resolution, also voted with Symington.

This intraparty split on defense issues existed outside of Congress as well. Nixon's two rivals for the GOP presidential nomination were Goldwater and New York governor Nelson Rockefeller. It was Rockefeller, Nixon's challenger from the left, who pushed the vice president to support several liberal goals of the era, including health insurance for the elderly, civil rights, and increased defense spending. Nixon's agreement resulted in a joint policy statement termed the "Compact of Fifth Avenue." This document reportedly upset Eisenhower. Goldwater, Nixon's conservative rival, publicly called it a "Munich" (Ambrose 1984, 597).

From the standpoint of Converse's (1964) definition of ideology as "what goes with what," it is notable that support for high levels of defense spending was *not* invariably linked to a militaristic outlook during this era. This is evident in the statements of two leading figures of the era, seen as polar opposites, the "dove" Adlai Stevenson and the "hawk" Barry Goldwater.

On many occasions Stevenson combined support for arms control or diplomacy with assertions that the Republicans were too stingy with the Pentagon. Campaigning for Hubert Humphrey in 1954, Stevenson denounced the Eisenhower administration's "saber rattling" but also lamented, "they promised us better, stronger defenses, so they cut our fighting forces."[4] In 1956 Stevenson opposed the draft and criticized Eisenhower for not seeking to control the hydrogen bomb. Yet in the same speech he stated that "we should have stronger, not weaker defenses than we have now" and contended that "Democrats have fought hard to prevent the Administration from putting dollars ahead of defense."[5]

---

[4] "Stevenson States 'Blundering' GOP Weakens Country," *New York Times*, September 26, 1954, 1. Nor was this combination of themes unique to Stevenson. At the same rally, Humphrey, an arms control advocate, insisted, "It is time the security of our country was put above the almighty dollar sign!"

[5] "Stevenson Renews Plea to End 'Wasteful' Draft," *Washington Post & Times-Herald*, September 30, 1956, A1.

The following year Stevenson criticized Eisenhower's response to the Soviets' launch of *Sputnik,* noting, "on the purely military side the proposal is for just a little more money. But the increase doesn't even meet increased costs and it is a smaller proportion of our gross domestic product than any year since 1951."[6] Stevenson's support of *both* arms control and defense spending foreshadowed the Kennedy administration line.

By contrast, in 1962 Goldwater decried Kennedy's laxity in the Cold War struggle, yet denied that the defense budget was too low. In *Why Not Victory?* the senator wrote:

During the Presidential Campaign of 1960 the absurd charge was made by Mr. Kennedy and others that America had become – or was in danger of becoming – a second-rate military power. Any comparison of over-all American strength with overall Soviet strength reveals the United States not only superior but so superior both in present weapons and in the development of new ones that our advantage promises to be a permanent feature of the United States–Soviet relations for the foreseeable future.[7]

Goldwater took this line as late as September 1963 when he voted to cut Kennedy's defense budget. At the same time he and other conservatives opposed the proposed Arms Control and Disarmament Agency and the Atmospheric Test Ban Treaty. These stands may appear incongruous in retrospect.[8] Support for arms control later became linked with calls for cuts in military spending. But this was not the case in 1963. Arms control was seen as more compatible with Democrats' costly "flexible response" strategy than Eisenhower's cheaper approach, which relied on threats of "massive retaliation" premised on U.S. nuclear superiority (Roman 1995, 20–21).

Partisan strife over defense issues abated in 1961 once the Kennedy administration, citing new evidence, conceded that no missile gap existed. The issue degenerated into a dispute over whether Democrats had warned of the gap in good faith or had consciously misled the voters.[9]

Yet the old arguments soon resurfaced. In June 1962 Eisenhower charged that "our current defense budgets reflect unjustified fears" and that Pentagon spending should be "substantially reduced." Later that year

[6] Johnson (1972, 203).

[7] Goldwater (1962, 40).

[8] It confused even some contemporary observers. Schlesinger (1965, 502) notes "Kennedy faced no harder problem of public education than that of convincing Capitol Hill and the Kremlin that his demands for strength and for disarmament, far from being contradictory, were complementary."

[9] Licklider (1970).

the former president asserted that security stemmed from "moral" and "economic" strength as well as military power and that a "hardware" obsession might weaken the U.S. economy.[10] In contrast, Democratic congressional candidates in 1962 reportedly argued that their election would allow Kennedy to "maintain our defense posture." Kennedy responded to Eisenhower's attacks by urging the GOP to adopt "some coordination of policy" as "we seem to be under attack by some Republicans for not doing enough to stand up to the Communists, on the other by those who say we're spending too much on defense."[11]

Actually, although some Republicans may have focused on the Kennedy administration's insufficient anticommunism, while others complained of its excessive defense spending, many made *both* complaints. The two charges were reconciled by assertions, like Goldwater's cited above, that U.S. military power was more than adequate. Instead, the Republicans argued, the real gap was one of leadership: Kennedy was failing to confront communists.

Rep. Melvin Laird (R-WI), then a GOP spokesman on military affairs and later Nixon's defense secretary, wrote in 1962 that the problem was not a "missile gap" but a "strategy gap." Like Goldwater, Laird claimed that the U.S. military edge remained "overwhelming." Nevertheless, communists were on the march because of the Democrats' failure to confront them. The Republicans' midterm policy platform (coordinated by Laird) endorsed nuclear tests and weapons development, but coupled this with a call for "efficiency throughout the defense establishment." Notably absent from the GOP document was any proposal to increase defense spending.[12]

In March 1963, several months after the Cuban Missile Crisis, House Republicans voted to cut Kennedy's defense spending request. During the floor debate, Rep. Laird asserted, "we cannot agree that there is no fat in the defense budget." House minority leader Charles Halleck (R-IN) denied that "there is anything sacrosanct in the defense budget," insisting that "we can find places in this defense budget where savings can

---

[10] "Text of Eisenhower's Address at Republicans' $100-a-Plate Dinner in Washington," *New York Times,* June 23, 1962, 8; "Eisenhower Back, Will Campaign," *New York Times,* August 31, 1962, 3.

[11] "Democrats' Hopes Rising in Midwest," *New York Times,* August 26, 1962, 41; "Transcript of President's News Conference on Foreign and Domestic Affairs," *New York Times,* June 28, 1962, 12.

[12] Laird 1962; "Text of 'A Declaration of Republican Principle and Policy,'" *New York Times,* June 8, 1962, 18.

be had."[13] The 20 House Republicans serving on the Appropriations Committee formed a task force that same month and issued a call for cuts of $10 to $15 billion in Kennedy's budget. Without committing themselves to details, they suggested that defense spending was one possible target. In response Speaker John McCormack (D-MA) insisted that Republicans provide "a bill of particulars" and asked, "Are they going to cut defense several billion? They don't dare do it."[14]

After the House vote, the GOP leadership continued to criticize Kennedy's defense spending on fiscal grounds. At the end of that month Rep. Halleck released a letter he had received from Eisenhower. In the note Eisenhower criticized Kennedy's plan to increase spending and cut taxes and called for a 10 percent reduction in spending, very much including military expenditures. The former president noted that his own final defense budget, which Kennedy exceeded, "provided amply for our security" and asserted that "It is almost incredible to say this program cannot safely be pared." Speaker McCormack rejected this criticism, arguing, "we cannot compromise with [military] expense."[15]

In September 1963 the ranking Republican on the Armed Services Committee, Senator Leverett Saltonstall of Massachusetts, proposed a 1 percent cut in defense procurement funds. Democrats defeated this amendment. Yet it won support not only from Republicans and conservatives (Goldwater included), but in a harbinger of the parties' shift, from some liberal Democrats as well.

Ten early Democratic dissenters from the "cold-war liberal" orthodoxy voted for Saltonstall's proposal, including freshman senator George McGovern (D-SD). McGovern had supported Henry Wallace over Truman in the 1948 presidential election and never was an enthusiastic cold warrior, even writing articles against the Korean War as a young professor. He began calling for defense spending cuts during his unsuccessful 1960 Senate race, at a time when most Democrats were criticizing Eisenhower for spending *too little* on the military and allowing a missile gap to emerge as a result. In June 1963 McGovern made a major speech calling for reduced levels of military expenditures, well before other liberal Democrats reached this position.[16] McGovern, more than anyone

[13] *Congressional Record,* House of Representatives, March 12, 1963, 4003–4010.
[14] "Budget Talk Sharpens," *New York Times,* March 11, 1963, 13.
[15] "Eisenhower Asks Halleck to Seek 10% Budget Cut," *New York Times,* March 30, 1963.
[16] "McGovern Asks Arms Cut to Raise Education Funds," *New York Times,* June 16, 1963, 40.

else, personified Democratic opposition to high levels of defense spending in later years.

Yet despite his radical past, this position was something of a reversal even for McGovern. Like almost all House Democrats, he had voted against Eisenhower's bid to reduce the size of the army as a representative in 1958.[17] After Saltonstall's amendment failed, McGovern proposed a 10 percent cut in the defense budget, but received only two votes. Most Democrats, liberals included, then still opposed *any* cut in defense spending in 1963. In January 1964 McGovern proposed ending funding for a bomber that the administration had not sought, winning support from only 22 senators, a minority of the Democrats. A bid by Senator Gaylord Nelson (D-WI) to cut military spending later that year won no administration backing and only a dozen Democratic votes.[18]

Far more important than the emerging doubts of a rather obscure minority of liberal Democrats was the new tack GOP leaders took in 1964. Pivoting with speed reminiscent of the Democrats' maneuvers in 1957, Republicans turned in 1964 from criticizing Democrats for overspending on defense to condemning them for underspending. Goldwater seems to have pioneered this tactic. Despite his record, throughout 1964 Goldwater attacked Democrats' failure to develop new weapons, charging that Johnson planned "a very drastic cut in defense spending to the point that we will be immediately imperiled." In his acceptance speech at the 1964 Republican national convention, the Arizona senator charged, "it's been during Democratic years that our strength to deter war has stood still and even gone into a planned decline."[19]

While more measured in his criticism, Nelson Rockefeller, Goldwater's chief rival for the GOP presidential nomination, agreed that the Democrats were doing too little on defense. In April he questioned the Johnson administration's decision to reduce production of weapons-grade uranium. "Let's be on the safe side in America," Rockefeller argued, warning that the move "could upset the international balance."[20] Later, the New York governor echoed a theme of Goldwater's and criticized the

[17] Congressional Quarterly Almanac 1958, 386.
[18] "Defense," Congressional Quarterly Almanac 1964, 159.
[19] "GOP Attacks Administration's Weapons Policies," *Congressional Quarterly Almanac 1964*, 445; "Goldwater Lays War Aim to Reds," *New York Times*, October 2, 1964, 21; http://www.washingtonpost.com/wp-srv/politics/daily/may98/goldwaterspeech.htm.
[20] UPI story quoted in conversation between President Johnson and National Security Advisor McGeorge Bundy, April 20, 1964, Conversation no. 3066, at http://millercenter.virginia.edu/scripps/diglibrary/prezrecordings/johnson/1964/04_1964.html.

plan to send a man to the moon as a waste of money that could be better spent by the Pentagon: "I would terminate this, what is, in my opinion, a distorted effort, save two and a half billion a year, and use that money for accelerated effort in advanced weapons technology, which, in my opinion, needs some further support."[21]

Similar arguments were made in 1964 not only by GOP presidential contenders, but on Capitol Hill as well. Congressional Republicans asserted that defense spending was "trimmed down to election year level."[22]

GOP leaders continued to press their attack on defense issues after 1964. In 1965 House Defense Appropriations Subcommittee Republicans led by the same Rep. Laird who had said in 1963 that the United States had "overwhelming superiority" and found "fat" in the defense budget protested that Johnson's proposal fell "far short of what we believe must be done." Johnson was "seeking to achieve a balanced deterrent, rather than insuring a decisive superiority." In June 1966 the Republican Coordinating Committee deplored the Pentagon's lack of "preparedness." Later that year, House minority leader Gerald Ford, who in 1963 had called Defense Secretary Robert McNamara's complaint about congressional defense budget cuts "completely unfounded," charged, "we are behind the Soviet Union." Ford warned that this state of affairs "could become a serious military crisis if we delay much longer." Other leading Republicans including Senator Strom Thurmond (R-SC) and Michigan governor George Romney – then a presidential contender – made similar charges.[23]

Campaigning in 1967, Nixon noted that Kennedy and Johnson had used the missile gap against him in 1960. Now the former vice president deployed an "anti-missile gap" charge against the Democrats, claiming, "this 1960 issue can now be turned on the Administration. It's a deadly boomerang."[24] The next day the Johnson administration reversed itself and voiced support for a "limited" ABM system. Liberal critics

---

[21] "On the Significance of the California Primary: The Kind of America I Want to See," speech by Nelson Rockefeller to the Commonwealth Club of California, San Francisco, May 29, 1964, http://commonwealthclub.org/archive/20thcentury/64–05rockefeller-qa.html.

[22] "Senate Approves Defense Budget," *New York Times*, July 30, 1964, 14.

[23] "Additional Views," *Congressional Quarterly Almanac 1965*, 176; "Republican Leaders Ask a Broad Defense Inquiry," *New York Times*, June 29, 1966, 5; "Arms Fund Bill Voted by House," *New York Times*, June 27, 1963, 1; "Antimissile Funds Seen by Rep. Ford," *New York Times*, December 26, 1966, 10; Halperin (1972, 83).

[24] "Missile Defense Is Urged by Nixon," *New York Times*, September 15, 1967, 9.

and leading journalists charged that the new policy was designed more to deflect GOP criticism than Chinese missiles.[25] Whatever the truth of these claims, they show that by 1967 Democrats no longer "owned" the defense issue. Later in the campaign Nixon broadened his critique of the Johnson administration's defense policies and spoke of a "security gap" and a coming "survival gap."[26]

At the same time liberal Democrats were moving in the other direction on the defense issue. In 1966 George McGovern offered another amendment cutting defense spending, again winning support from only about half of the Northern Democrats and no Republicans. In the same year Senate majority leader Mike Mansfield took up what had been a Republican cause in the Truman years and began his long campaign to reduce U.S. troop strength in Europe.[27] Finally, in April 1968 a majority of Senate Democrats opposed most of their GOP colleagues on a defense vote for the first time in five years. The occasion was a proposal to cut funds for research and development. This time most Senate Democrats favored the cut while their Republican colleagues opposed it. In later years many other roll calls, as well as much campaign rhetoric, would reflect this new partisan alignment on defense issues.

### SHIFTS AMONG ELITES

Politicians whose stands on defense policy did not "evolve" found their ideological reputations transformed. Senator Henry "Scoop" Jackson (D-WA), once seen as a liberal, acquired a different image because of his continued support for the Pentagon budgets long after other Northern Democrats had begun to criticize them (Kaufman 2000). Similarly, the authors of the *Almanac of American Politics* (1972, 50) could write of Senator Clinton Anderson (D-NM): "In his heyday Anderson was considered a flaming liberal. More recently his support for large military and A.E.C. budgets has won him a more middle of the road reputation."

Like Jackson, Anderson had always supported defense spending. By refusing to change, both Western senators forfeited their reputations

---

[25] "The Anti-Republican Missile," *New York Times,* September 22, 1967, 46; "Goodwin, Ex-Johnson Aide, Now One of His Critics," *New York Times,* October 24, 1967, 24.

[26] "The Security Gap," CBS Radio Network, October 24, 1968, in *Major Speeches and Statements by Richard M. Nixon in the Presidential Campaign of 1968* (New York: Nixon-Agnew Campaign Committee, 1968).

[27] Williams (1985, chs. 4–5).

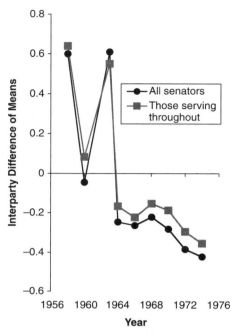

FIGURE 5-1. Interparty Difference of Means on Defense Spending (Democratic Mean – Republican Mean), Senate, 86th through 93rd Congresses (1959–1974)

as liberals. Their ideological inconsistency stemmed from substantive consistency. This prompts the question; how typical were old-fashioned liberals like Anderson and Jackson? To answer that question we need to look at the shifts in voting on defense spending during the period in which the parties changed sides, comparing the entire Senate with the subset of long-serving senators.

Figure 5-1 depicts the changing relationship between party and support for defense spending among all senators and those serving from 1959 through 1974.[28] It reveals that a radical shift occurred during the 88th Congress (1963–1964).

The figure demonstrates that the reversal in the parties' position was very rapid and appeared to occur at virtually identical speed among the subset of long-serving senators and in the Senate as a whole. These results

---

[28] I use Senate votes because there were virtually no contested, recorded votes in the House on defense issues in the mid-1960s. I bifurcate the 88th Congress in Figure 5-1 because the reversal occurred *during* this Congress.

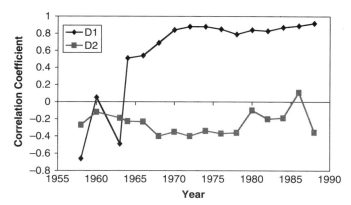

FIGURE 5-2. Correlation between Defense Spending Scores and D1 and D2 NOMINATE Scores: Senate, 86th through 100th Congresses (1959–1988)

indicated that conversion, not replacement, was by far the most important mechanism in producing party position change on the defense issue. The reversal was not total, because Southern Democrats were less likely to abandon support for the Pentagon than their Northern colleagues, but this was not a function of replacement.

Turning to a measure of senators' "spatial" or "ideological" positioning, we can learn two things from Figure 5-2. Defense spending has generally been a "first dimension" issue, that is, MCs' votes in this area are highly correlated with those on other issues within the dominant cleavage. In addition we can see that there were radical reversals in the polarity of the relationship between the NOMINATE scores and senators' votes on defense spending. Consistent with the story told above, the liberal position and the conservative position on this issue have changed greatly over time. In 1960 a liberal senator with a low D1 NOMINATE score supported increased defense spending more than conservatives did. By the mid-1960s the converse was the case.

In Table 5-1 I turn to a focused comparison of two roll calls on defense spending, one from the earlier period when Democrats were more supportive of it, and one from the later period when Republicans were the strongest backers of the Pentagon. These two roll calls occurred in two Congresses a decade apart in which Democrats had similar majorities and the number of senators voting on the pro-defense side of the bill differed little. The results reported in the table show, consistent with Figure 5-1, that continuing senators reversed course on defense spending, much as

TABLE 5-1. *Percentage of Long-Serving Senators (Stayers) and the Rest of the Senate Supporting Defense Spending on Two Votes with Similar Cutpoints: 1959 and 1968*

| Congress | Type of Senator | Democrats | Republicans |
|---|---|---|---|
| 86th Congress (1959–1960)[a] | Stayers | 71.9% (N = 32) | 16.7% (N = 18) |
| 90th Congress (1967–1968)[b] | Stayers | 34.4% (N = 32) | 77.8% (N = 18) |
| 86th Congress (1959–1960)[a] | Rest of Senate | 65.5% (N = 29) | 6.3% (N = 16) |
| 90th Congress (1967–1968)[b] | Rest of Senate | 41.2% (N = 17) | 84.6% (N = 13) |

[a] 86th Congress (Senate 65% Democratic), Var. 32, H.R. 7454, July 13, 1959: Amendment to Defense Department appropriation to increase army procurement funds and designate $453 million of the total for modernizing army combat equipment (48.6% voting pro–defense spending)
[b] 90th Congress (Senate 64% Democratic), Var. 405, S. 3293, April 18, 1968: Amendment to military procurement authorization limiting aggregate authorizations for research and development to $7.366 billion (53.1% voting pro–defense spending)

their parties did. The shift was a radical one and not an artifact of movement in the cutpoint of defense policy roll calls or the changing fortunes of the parties.

For a more systematic estimate of the effect of conversion and replacement on senators' voting on defense issues I report results based on the Rapoport and Stone technique outlined in Chapter 1. It shows that the change in voting on defense issues in both parties stemmed overwhelmingly from conversion among incumbent MCs. Ninety-five percent of the total change stemmed from conversion, with 86 percent among Democratic senators and 102 percent among Republicans. (Conversion can explain more than 100 percent of change if replacement effects run counter to the overall trend of party position change.)

## SUBSEQUENT CHANGES

The party positions on defense policy that emerged in the mid-1960s were quite stable, surviving the end of the Cold War and the declining salience of national security concerns in the 1990s. They were revisited only in the 2000 campaign.

In that election year the Democratic presidential nominee, Vice President Al Gore, promised to spend more than the GOP candidate, Texas governor George W. Bush. Instead of "Guns vs. Butter" the trade-off discussed was "Guns vs. Tax Cuts." Gore argued that Bush's proposed $1.3 billion tax cut would "wreck our good economy and make it impossible to modernize our armed forces, meet our commitment to our veterans and keep them ready for battle."[29]

In the final presidential debate Bush conceded, "If this were a spending contest, I'd come in second. I readily admit, I'm not going to grow the size of the federal government like he is."[30] Bush's implication that defense spending was just part of big government recalled arguments that had not been heard from conservatives for decades. It was an odd campaign, with Gore defending the Clinton administration's stewardship of the military, but insisting that much more funding was needed, and Bush saying that the military had been neglected, but a smaller increase would suffice.

The only visible continuity in the parties' positioning concerned missile defense. In this area Bush was more committed to spending than Gore, reflecting Republicans' long-standing support for such programs untempered by Democrats' concerns about the destabilizing effect of such a technology from the arms control standpoint.[31] Even in the 1950s and early 1960s, when Democrats favored higher defense budgets than Republicans, they were more supportive than the GOP of arms control.

The parties' surprising new alignment on defense issues survived the end of the campaign and the departure of Gore from center stage. The ranking minority member on the House Armed Services Committee, Ike Skelton (D-MO), insisted in early February 2001 that Bush's planned Pentagon funding level was inadequate; "we need an immediate supplemental appropriation right now," Skelton contended.[32]

Democrats increasingly linked the defense issue to tax policy, framing a vote for tax cuts as a vote against military preparedness. In his response to Bush's first address to Congress, Senate minority leader Tom Daschle (D-SD) warned that Bush's tax cut proposal would "consume

---

[29] "Gore Tells VFW of His Support of Military," *Washington Post*, August 23, 2000, A8.
[30] "Election 2000 Presidential Debate," *Federal News Service*, October 17, 2000, via Nexis.
[31] "Bush, Gore Unite on Military Readiness, Divide on Strategies," *Tampa Tribune*, November 3, 2000, 2.
[32] "Bush Defense Funding Decision under Fire," *CNN.com*, February 9, 2001.

nearly all of the budget surplus, at the expense of prescription drug coverage, education, defense and other priorities."[33] Even the staunchest liberals used the defense issue as a wedge against Bush's tax plan. Rep. Charles Rangel (D-NY) – an unlikely Pentagon ally – argued in the Democratic response to Bush's weekly radio address, "His plan will undermine national defense to pay for excessive tax cuts for those in the upper brackets."[34]

To an extent this was a return to the framing of the 1950s when Republicans viewed defense spending as big government, although at that time they objected to military expenditures' inflationary and deficit-causing effect and did not complain that they impeded tax cuts. Yet this surprising shift cannot be traced to a shift in preferences or party allegiance by any social grouping. As in 1957, party-linked activists and intellectuals were critical of their own parties' stands. The arms-control group Council for a Livable World denounced the Democrats' move in an open letter to Democratic MCs:

We are appalled that leading members of the Democratic Party advocate increasing that budget. ... The Democratic Party has traditionally fought for social and domestic programs such as health care, civil rights enforcement and the environment. Those who benefit from, and believe in, these programs are the pillars of the Democratic Party. Committing the party to supporting massive increases in military spending will jeopardize these programs.[35]

Meanwhile leading conservative publications, including both the *National Review* and *Weekly Standard,* ran editorials critical of Bush's plan.[36] These criticisms demonstrate that the repositioning of the parties on the defense issue was not a product of changed sentiments among the intellectuals and idea-mongers associated with the Democrats and Republicans. Rather, it was an initiative of the politicians themselves.

Nonetheless, party elites in Congress continued along this surprising new course. On April 4, 2001, Senator Mary Landrieu (D-LA) offered an amendment increasing spending on defense. It was supported by most of her Democratic colleagues and opposed by most Senate Republicans.

---

[33] "Democrats: Do the Math on Bush's Plan," *CNN.com,* February 27, 2001.

[34] "Partisanship, Doubts within GOP Are Roadblocks to Bush's Tax Plan," *St. Louis Post-Dispatch,* February 18, 2001, A17.

[35] "Council for a Livable World Criticizes Democrats on Defense Budget," *Council for a Livable World Press Release,* February 27, 2001.

[36] "Defense: More, Please," *National Review,* March 5, 2001, http://store.nationalreview. com/archives; "Cheap Hawks: The Bush Administration's Surprisingly Stingy Defense Spending Request," *Weekly Standard,* June 11, 2001, 14.

The Chairman of the Senate Armed Services Committee, Republican John Warner of Virginia, reacted to Landrieu's proposal by arguing that although a long-term increase in military spending might be called for, it should be delayed pending a study of the Pentagon's operations. Landrieu's amendment was defeated on a largely partisan vote, and Warner's proposal for a smaller one-time increase for fiscal year 2002 was approved overwhelmingly.[37]

As in the case of the parties' reversals on defense spending in 1957, this new alignment changed as a result of events, more than any uprising by party-linked constituencies or aggrieved intellectuals. In the wake of the attacks of September 11th, controversy over defense spending largely subsided and has yet to truly reemerge. Even so, there have been episodes in which Democrats have positioned themselves on the pro-spending side. As the Democratic presidential nominee, Senator John Kerry (D-MA) called for an increase in the size of the army by 40,000 and a doubling of the Special Forces.[38] In April 2005 Senate Democrats led by Senators Evan Bayh (D-IN) and Edward Kennedy (D-MA) proposed to increase funding levels to provide more armor for Humvees in Iraq.[39]

Even as Democrats became increasingly supportive of reducing or ending America's presence in Iraq, they did not generally link this stand to a broader critique of the defense establishment as Vietnam doves did 40 years ago. The leading Democratic contenders in 2008, Senators Hillary Clinton (D-NY) and Barack Obama (D-IL), agreed both that troops should be withdrawn from Iraq and that the military needed to be expanded.[40]

Thus there have been six party position changes on defense issues since 1930. First, Franklin Roosevelt reoriented the Democratic Party in the early 1930s away from their skepticism toward the military, which dated from the time the Union Army occupied the South. Then there was a brief shift by congressional Democrats toward attacking a Republican administration for excessive defense spending in 1957. After this episode the Democrats reverted to their long-standing position that the GOP was too stingy with the Pentagon. This traditional alignment ended in the mid-1960s, and the now familiar pattern of Democrats taking the "dovish" side on defense issues arose. This was disrupted in 2000–2001 when

---

[37] *Congressional Record*, April 4, 2001, S3402–3415.
[38] "GI John Marches In," *New York Daily News*, July 29, 2004, 7.
[39] "Senate OKs Extra Humvee Spending," *USA Today*, April 22, 2005, 4A.
[40] "'08 Hopefuls Would Grow the Military," *The Hill*, May 2, 2007, http:/thehill.com.

the parties briefly traded places before the issue largely subsided in the wake of the attacks of September 11th.

At the time of this writing the future positioning of the parties on the defense issue is difficult to predict. Yet the instability evident over time is notable. It is hard to imagine similar reversals in policies like abortion and race, where party-linked groups constrain the behavior of political elites. On a groupless issue like defense spending, by contrast, party elites enjoy much more room to maneuver.

### DEFENSE POLITICS AND INTERESTS

I have argued that the Democrats and Republicans were able to rapidly and repeatedly reverse positions on defense spending because this is a "groupless" issue in which party-linked constituencies are largely absent. This may not be an intuitive claim, however, so it requires some justification.

The first claim that requires some discussion is that liberals chose "butter" while conservatives chose "guns." This is certainly a widespread view, and at the time many politicians indeed framed the choice in this way. Accordingly, one might say that the Democrats' constituency, being more interested in nondefense spending than the Republicans', inclined them to make this choice. This is a problematic argument, however. First of all, framing the choice this way assumes both that no more revenue can be secured and that running a deficit is intolerable. Politicians and interest groups have certainly not always felt this way.

Beyond this, the timing of the parties' shifts on defense issues calls into question the guns vs. butter explanation. As Fordham (2007b) notes, military spending was a larger share of the budget and of the gross domestic product in the early 1950s, when Democrats were more supportive of Pentagon funding, than it was in the mid-1960s, when the parties traded places on the issue. Moreover, as Grassmuck (1951) showed, in the 1930s Democrats became the party of defense spending at precisely the same time that they were supporting a much larger federal role in the domestic sphere. None of this is to deny that many voters, activists, and even politicians have internalized the guns vs. butter frame. Yet it needs to be seen as a result of politics as much as a cause.

Beyond the guns vs. butter argument, there are two major claims for interests driving MCs' positions on defense. It has been argued that MCs vote the economic interest of their district and that they are swayed by campaign contributions. In the following section I show that the disagreement between the parties on defense spending is not a product of regional differences in their bases of support. I also demonstrate that contributions from defense contractors do not flow overwhelmingly to one party.

In fact, there is a regional aspect to conflict over defense policy, but it is mostly not over the macro-policy questions such as the size of the defense establishment or the fate of weapons systems built in many states and districts. Instead, the distributive aspect of defense policy is evident primarily where military installations are concerned. Legislators who vote consistently to cut defense spending nonetheless fight to retain and even expand bases in their states and districts. These facilities are often crucial to local economies, and an MC who did not fight to protect the communities she represents where bases are concerned would be considered derelict in her duty.

The politics of military bases has been quite distinct from the debate over military spending. Congress long ago institutionalized the difference between these policy areas. Expenditures to support troops and weapons development were reviewed by the Defense Subcommittees of the House and Senate Appropriations Committees. By contrast, jurisdiction over the funding of bases belonged to the Appropriations Subcommittees on Military Construction in both chambers.

Although there are typically substantial differences in defense policy that occur when one party replaces another in the White House, recent presidents, regardless of party, have supported the work of base-closing commissions. These commissions were established because military construction was widely understood to be a species of "pork-barrel" politics in which Congress, if left unchecked, would have a strong tendency to produce suboptimal policy by overspending in order to create a coalition that would preserve if not enhance facilities in most states or districts (Mayer 1995).

Relatedly, the politics of base closing was far less partisan than debate over weapons systems or the overall level of the defense budget. In those macro-policy areas, a Democratic senator typically votes differently from his Republican colleague in the states that send mixed delegations to the Senate. By contrast, on military construction matters both senators from a state are apt to agree, even if they are not co-partisans.

It is also the case that even MCs who are skeptical of Pentagon budget requests make exceptions for programs of great economic importance to their constituents. Senator Alan Cranston of California and his successor Barbara Boxer are cases in point. Both California Democrats were noted doves and Pentagon critics. Cranston was an early opponent of the

Vietnam War and a persistent advocate of arms control. The "nuclear freeze" was the signature issue of his failed presidential bid in 1984. Yet Cranston was an active supporter of the controversial B-1 bomber, produced primarily in California.[41]

Similarly, Boxer first won national visibility in 1984 as a critic of defense budgets by brandishing a "$7,622 coffee pot" the Pentagon was purchasing (Barone and Ujifusa 1989, 97). Nonetheless, from early in her career Boxer fought to defend military installations and programs in her district.[42] These examples illustrate the fact that politicians have been able to tend to parochial concerns in military matters in high-profile cases while still maintaining a generally critical view of the defense budget. As a result, regional variation in the presence of defense-related employment does not necessarily explain MCs' voting on defense issues.

Nonetheless, some scholars argue that local economic interests underlie parties' positioning on the question of military spending. Trubowitz (1998) sees defense politics as driven by regional economic interests. His claims are important for the current discussion for two reasons. By focusing on the regional realignment that has remade the bases of the two parties, he provides a potential interest-based explanation for the reversal of the parties on defense issues. In addition, this theory implies that elite replacement is driving the process, since modern MCs do not change states, let alone regions, during the course of their careers.

Yet the argument that constituency economic interests underlie MCs' disagreements on defense issues flies in the face of much research (Bernstein and Anthony 1974; Clotfelter 1970; Lindsay 1990; Mayer 1991; Moyer 1973) showing that party affiliation and "ideology" measured by ADA scores or other indices were the best predictors of senators' voting patterns on defense-related roll calls. Even in studies finding a role for constituency economic interests, such as Bartels (1991), the strength of defense-related industry in their states proved a factor of secondary importance at most.

However, these studies are very time-bound. All cover the period from the late 1960s to the 1980s. They do not offer a longitudinal perspective on these matters, and they do not explore the period in which Democrats were more supportive of defense spending than Republicans. Even though they call Trubowitz's claims into considerable question, we could have

---

[41] "Trying to Find the Pork in the Pentagon's Barrel," *Christian Science Monitor,* May 5, 1983, 13; "Dark Horse from California," *New York Times Magazine,* December 4, 1983, 58.

[42] "On Hill, Legislators Erect Home-District Defenses; Pursuit of Pentagon Money under Way," *Washington Post,* April 7, 1985, A10.

more confidence if the investigation of these dynamics were extended to the earlier period as well.

Table 5-2 shows the results of ordinary least squares regression models estimating the effect of party affiliation and two measures of local defense interests, contract awards as a share of the state economy and military and civilian defense payrolls, on senators' votes on defense issues in the 86th, 92nd, 97th, and 101st Congresses.

The table reveals that the variables measuring the size of defense contracts and payrolls of military and civilian defense personnel in states have a weak and inconsistent effect on senators' voting patterns on defense issues. In some years their effect is positive, in others it is negative. This is not true of party. Party affiliation is a consistently strong predictor of senators' votes on defense issues. In the early years Democrats are more supportive of defense spending, in later years Republicans are.

A glance at the $R^2$ statistic in the various models makes clear that the predictive power of local economic interests regarding senators' voting on defense issues has been very limited. The addition of variables measuring the strength of the defense sector in the local economy slightly improves the fit of the model in some cases. Yet these variables take the wrong sign in other instances, and they never meaningfully reduce the coefficient of the party dummy. Thus even an analysis extending farther back in time than most studies do supports the dominant view: congressional voting on defense issues is *not* explainable by local economic interests.

Trubowitz (1998, 221) rejects this view. He notes, "Many concluded that politicians' views on matters of national defense had very little to do with whether (or how much) their districts or states benefited from military spending." Yet he calls that conclusion "premature" and "based on a conception of interests that is far too narrow and a view of politicians that is far too simple." He holds that these studies are not dispositive because it is the net economic cost and benefit of defense spending that is at stake and that this varies by region in ways measures of defense-related employment fail to capture.

This rebuttal is unpersuasive for two reasons. First, Trubowitz fails to convincingly demonstrate that the opportunity costs of defense spending varied clearly by state or that this was known or understood by legislators at the time. Second, he cannot account for the wide gaps on defense issues that existed among MCs with constituency factors held constant.

For example, consider the states that sent one Democrat and one Republican to the Senate. Such mixed delegations constitute a sort of "natural experiment" allowing us to observe the effect of party affiliation on

TABLE 5-2. *Party and Local Interests as Predictors of Senators' Votes on Defense, Selected Congresses, 86th through 101st Congresses (1959–1990), OLS Models*

| 86th Congress 1959 | Party Model | Local Defense Interests | Combined Model |
|---|---|---|---|
| Republican | −.57 (.09)* | | −.61 (.09)* |
| DOD payroll | | −1.2 (1.4) | −2.7 (1.1)* |
| DOD contracts | | 2.4 (1.5) | 3.3 (1.2)* |
| Constant | 1.3 (.13)* | .4 (.1)* | 1.3 (.14)* |
| $R^2$ | .30 | .03 | .36 |
| N | 94 | 94 | 94 |

| 92nd Congress 1971–1972 | Party Model | Local Defense Interests | Combined Model |
|---|---|---|---|
| Republican | .38 (.06)* | | .39 (.06)* |
| DOD payroll | | 1.16 (1.25) | 1.51 (1.06) |
| DOD contracts | | −1.14 (1.67) | −.11 (1.43) |
| Constant | −.01 (.1) | .57 (.07)* | −.04 (.11) |
| $R^2$ | .28 | .01 | .30 |
| N | 100 | 100 | 100 |

| 97th Congress 1981–1982 | Party Model | Local Defense Interests | Combined Model |
|---|---|---|---|
| Republican | .41 (.06)* | | .41 (.06)* |
| DOD payroll | | 2.5 (1.7) | 2.43 (1.34) |
| DOD contracts | | −2.84 (1.74) | −2.86 (1.41)* |
| Constant | −.02 (.09) | .67 (.06)* | .04 (.1) |
| $R^2$ | .34 | .04 | .38 |
| N | 100 | 100 | 100 |

| 101st Congress 1989–1990 | Party Model | Local Defense Interests | Combined Model |
|---|---|---|---|
| Republican | .55 (.05) | | .56 (.04)* |
| DOD payroll | | 1.06 (.99) | 1.76 (.61)* |
| DOD contracts | | −.05 (1.21) | −.17 (.74) |
| Constant | −.24 (.07)* | .51 (.06)* | −.32 (.08)* |
| $R^2$ | .6 | .01 | .64 |
| N | 100 | 100 | 100 |

senators while controlling for all possible local interests. Significant differences in the voting patterns of Democratic and Republican senators representing the same state at the same time demonstrate that the parties' differences on defense issues are not reflections of sectional economic interests.

TABLE 5-3. *Comparison of Interparty Differences on Mean Support for Defense Spending, Selected Votes among All Senators and Democrats and Republicans from the Same States, 84th through 101st Congress (1955–1990)*

| Congress/Year | Democratic Mean | Republican Mean | Interparty Difference of Means for All Senators[a] | Interparty Difference of Means for Mixed Delegation Senators Only |
|---|---|---|---|---|
| 84th Congress (1955–1956) | .92 (N = 51) | .14 (N = 47) | .78 (N = 98) | .8 (N = 20) |
| 86th Congress (1959–1960) | .69 (N = 61) | .12 (N = 34) | .57 (N = 95) | .83 (N = 24) |
| 92nd Congress (1971–1972) | .40 (N = 55) | .78 (N = 46) | −.38 (N = 101) | −.57 (N = 36) |
| 97th Congress (1981–1982) | .43 (N = 47) | .84 (N = 54) | −.41 (N = 101) | −.36 (N =53) |
| 101st Congress (1989–1990) | .32 (N = 56) | .87 (N = 45) | −.55 (N = 101) | −.51 (N = 42) |

[a] In some Congresses results are reported for 101 senators because senators who served for only part of the Congress are included in the analysis.

In order to further explore this question, in Table 5-3 I report the mean defense support score for each party in the Senate in the 84th Congress (1955–1956), 86th Congress (1959–1960), 92nd Congress (1971–1972), 97th Congress (1981–1982), and 101st Congress (1989–1990). I report first the means for each party in the Senate. Then I show the mean for Democrats and Republicans from states with mixed delegations.

The results are clear. When we look at the difference in mean support for defense spending across the parties, large differences are evident, even among senators from mixed delegations. This is true both during the first two Congresses, when Democrats were more supportive of defense spending, and in the latter three, in which Republicans were more generous to the Pentagon. In the 97th and 101st Congresses the gap between the parties is slightly smaller in states with mixed delegations; in all the other cases it is actually larger. These results demonstrate that the gap between the parties on the defense issue is not chiefly a function of their geographical bases of support. Likewise, the reversal in the parties' positions on the question does not stem from the changes in their regional bases.

Yet regional bases are not the only ones that matter for parties. Campaign contributions are also important, and they travel easily across state and district lines. Trial lawyers, a numerically tiny group, are an important Democratic constituency, largely because of their campaign contributions (Burke 2002). If military contractors are likewise aligned with one party in their contribution pattern, they could greatly constrain the ability of party elites to shift their positions on defense issues.

However, studies of campaign contributions by defense contractors belie the stereotypical view that they are overwhelmingly Republican.[43] According to the Center for Responsive Politics, a group that codes Federal Election Commission data, the defense sector has been less partisan than most. As Table 5-4 shows, in the 1992 and 1994 elections, the last ones before the GOP gained control of Congress, a narrow majority of the contributions tied to the defense industry actually went to Democratic candidates. This was true even though Republican MCs had been generally more supportive of the defense budget than Democratic ones since the mid-1960s. Only in the 1990 cycle did Republicans enjoy a very slight edge in contributions from defense contractors. As late as the 2000 election the two biggest contractors, Boeing and Lockheed-Martin, were reported to be "hedging their bets, distributing 'soft money' contributions more or less equally between the two parties."[44]

For comparative perspective, Table 5-4 includes comparable totals for two GOP-leaning industries, oil and gas and forest and forestry products, as well as pro-life groups, a single-issue bloc known to be aligned with Republicans, and two Democratic-leaning sectors, organized labor and trial lawyers. Compared to the defense sector, all the other groups are more partisan in their giving patterns; the forestry and oil sectors are very Republican, while the unions and trial lawyers strongly favor the Democrats.

Another important fact illustrated by Table 5-4 is that the changes from Democratic to Republican control in 1994 and the Democrats'

---

[43] Peak business associations that are more partisan have not generally focused on defense issues. Soffer (2001) describes a turn toward support for expansive military budgets by the National Association of Manufacturers in the mid-1960s. Yet not only was this posture short-lived, but as Soffer notes (794), it truly emerged only "after 1964." Indeed, Soffer points to "broad conservative support for Barry Goldwater in 1964 when most conservative opinion united behind his calls for increased military spending" as a *cause* rather than an effect of the NAM's repositioning on defense issues.

[44] "Defense Industry Sees Gap in Both Candidates' Plans," *Washington Post*, October 19, 2000, A9.

TABLE 5-4. *Share of Campaign Contributions Given to Republican Congressional Candidates: The Defense Sector in Comparative Perspective*

| Election Cycle | Defense Contractors | Oil and Gas Sector | Forest and Forestry Products | Pro-Life Groups | Labor Unions | Trial Lawyers |
|---|---|---|---|---|---|---|
| 1990 | 54% | 63% | 75% | 79% | 8% | 16% |
| 1992 | 47 | 67 | 75 | 90 | 6 | 10 |
| 1994 | 41 | 63 | 72 | 88 | 4 | 8 |
| 1996 | 68 | 76 | 80 | 94 | 6 | 14 |
| 1998 | 67 | 77 | 80 | 97 | 8 | 14 |
| 2000 | 64 | 78 | 82 | 92 | 6 | 11 |
| 2002 | 65 | 80 | 76 | 99 | 7 | 8 |
| 2004 | 62 | 80 | 80 | 98 | 13 | 8 |
| 2006 | 60 | 82 | 78 | 98 | 12 | 7 |
| 2008 | 48 | 74 | 71 | 99 | 8 | 5 |

*Source:* Center for Responsive Politics, www.opensecrets.org.

return to power in 2006 coincided with large shifts in the giving pattern of defense sector contributors unmatched by other groups. Defense contractors were more balanced in their giving and favored the majority party consistently from 1992 to 2008. Thus they notably increased the share of their funds going to Republican candidates after 1994 and to Democrats after 2006. As of November 2008 it appeared that Democrats received a small majority of contributions from the defense sector in that year's elections.

By contrast to the defense sector, other industries were much more partisan in their contribution patterns. The forestry and oil sectors gave mostly to Republican candidates, even when the GOP was in the minority in the early 1990s and again in the 2008 cycle. Similarly, regardless of partisan control of Congress, the lion's share of contributions by unions and trial lawyers went to their Democratic allies. In this context the far more balanced distribution of funds by the defense sector stands out. It provides strong evidence that the defense industry has not been aligned with either political party.

These findings are temporally limited, since the Center for Responsive Politics does not collect data before the 1990 campaign. Yet earlier studies suggest that the basic pattern presented above is one of long standing. Mayer (1991, 83–85) found that from 1978 through 1988 Democrats received a majority of defense PAC contributions to candidates for the House in every cycle, except 1982. In no year, however, did either party receive more than 60 percent of the contributions.[45]

Gopoian (1984) and Burris (2001) reviewed evidence from various campaign cycles and concluded that the firms in the defense industry have pursued an "access strategy" rather than an "electoral strategy." Interests pursuing an access strategy tend to favor incumbents regardless of party, especially those ensconced in key committee positions. Although they may contribute more to MCs of one party at a given time, this is usually a result of that party being in power.

These scholars noted that defense contractors are in a special position. Although most firms in a typical industry seek to influence policy in broadly the same direction, typically toward less regulation or for a greater sectoral subsidy, defense contractors are often competing against one another. While all can agree that a larger defense budget would be welcome, this is a "public good" from the standpoint of individual firms, who are more likely to concentrate on winning a contract and then securing continued support for their projects, as opposed to those of other claimants on the Pentagon's funds.

By contrast, lobbies with little hope of winning over MCs to their cause tend to employ electoral strategies, intervening in campaigns in order to increase the odds that more friendly officials will be elected. These groups include those active on divisive issues such as gun control or abortion, or those in which lobbies on the other side are also mobilized, such as labor-management issues. In such cases contributions are less concentrated on incumbents, and groups' donating practices are more partisan.

If the defense industry has considerable resources, but lacks party ties, the opposite could be said about disarmament groups. The Center for Responsive Politics reported in 2003 that the major disarmament advocacy groups contributed just over $1.4 million in the last seven election cycles, overwhelmingly to Democrats. By comparison, the defense industry gave more than $72.5 million in individual, PAC, and soft money

---

[45] Mayer (1991, 85–86) also found that if one categorized MCs on the basis of voting records rather than party affiliation, "hawks" received more defense-related contributions than doves. Even so, doves got about one-third of the funding, and over 90 percent of incumbents received some defense PAC money. This distribution of support differs greatly from that of other groups. NARAL does not give one-third of its funds to pro-life MCs, and the NRA does not deliver one-third of its contributions to gun control advocates.

contributions in that time.[46] Even Democratic MCs received far more financial support from defense contractors than from disarmament groups. After the 2002 election the major vehicle for disarmament advocates seeking to support friendly candidates, the Council for a Livable World's PEACE PAC, actually disbanded.[47] So although disarmament groups and their supporters strongly favor the Democrats, they have usually lacked sufficient resources to have much leverage over that party's elected officials.

In the context of my argument that defense spending was generally a "groupless" issue on which party leaders were free to maneuver, it is important to discuss the role of the antiwar movement of the 1960s. The social movement hostile to U.S. involvement in Vietnam won far more support from Democrats than Republicans. It helped drive Lyndon Johnson from the presidency and fueled George McGovern's successful bid for the 1972 Democratic presidential nomination. So it is not unreasonable to look here for an explanation for the parties' repositioning on defense issues.

If the antiwar movement precipitated the parties' role reversal on support for Pentagon budgets, my claim that defense was a groupless issue would be undermined, much as Lee (2002) has used his study of the civil rights movement's effect on public opinion to challenge the top-down accounts of both Zaller (1992) and Carmines and Stimson (1989) regarding the parties' reversals on racial matters.

Yet in this case the chronology is clear, and the antiwar movement cannot be credited with more than a reinforcing role in this process. Whether we use the statements of leading politicians as a measure or the few recorded votes in Congress during this period, the parties' reversal on defense spending was already evident in early 1964, months before the Gulf of Tonkin Resolution, let alone the start of the sustained bombing campaign at the beginning of March 1965 that preceded the first campus "teach-ins" or the major commitment of troops during the summer of that year that sparked further protest.[48] The prominence of the antiwar movement in the Democratic Party in the late 1960s and early 1970s may have temporarily reinforced the parties' new alignment on defense issues, but the chronology shows that it could not have caused it.

---

[46] "Can't Buy Me Peace," *Capitol Eye*, Center for Responsive Politics, February 23, 2003, http://www.opensecrets.org/capital_eye/inside.php?ID=66.

[47] Ibid.

[48] The first major campus protest, a "teach-in" at the University of Michigan, occurred only in late March 1965 (Schuman 1972, 514).

The last possible constituency that might make some observers question the "grouplessness" of defense issues is the military itself. Yet while the uniformed military play an important role in policymaking, they are not a part of the party system. The Uniform Code of Military Justice restricts the political activity of military personnel on active duty. Perhaps as a result, survey data on the partisan affiliations of active duty personnel are scarce. Those that exist, however, indicate that at present the officer corps is largely Republican.

Yet, however prominent these leanings seem at present, it is important to note that they may postdate the parties' shift on the issue. Holsti (1998) found that from 1976 to 1996 the officer corps grew steadily more Republican and, because it was doing so at a far faster rate than the rest of society, it became increasingly distinctive. In 1976, 33 percent of officers considered themselves Republicans, as opposed to 25 percent of the overall population.

This comparison somewhat understates the civil-military gap already evident in the 1970s, because most of the non-Republicans in the officer corps survey were independents, not Democrats. By 1996 the gap between the officer corps and the public had widened considerably, with 67 percent of the former identifying as Republicans compared to only 34 percent of Americans generally. We cannot know what the figures were when the parties' began to trade places on defense issues in the mid-1960s, but it is likely that the civil-military gap in party identification was far smaller then.

Yet there was no sign that the military vote was at all organized or able to prevent the Bush administration from making tax cuts rather than military spending their priority before September 11th, despite the evident disappointment and surprise this decision produced in defense circles.[49] This may be due to the fact that the Uniform Code of Military Justice restricts the political activity of active duty personnel.

Given the absence of consequential party-linked groups focused on the size of the defense budget, we should expect to see less stability on this issue than others where party leaders are constrained by coalition allies. When shifts in party positioning occur, they should be relatively rapid because they do not depend on the gradual movements of voters transforming MCs' subconstituencies.

Survey data reveal that the parties' reversal did not come in response to attitudinal shifts among party loyalists in the electorate. Figure 5-3

---

[49] "Bush Actions Shock Defense Establishment," *Copley News Service*, February 9, 2001, via Nexis.

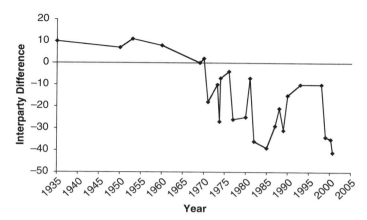

FIGURE 5-3. Interparty Difference on Defense Spending (Net Democratic Support – Net Republican Support), Gallup Polls, 1935–2000

depicts the interparty difference in net support for defense spending among respondents in a series of Gallup polls. Net support is the percentage of respondents within a party saying defense spending was too low minus the percentage saying it was too high.

Gallup polls taken from 1935 through 1960 showed Democratic voters more supportive of defense spending than Republicans, matching the parties' alignment in Congress on the issue. Unfortunately, neither Gallup nor the National Election Study asked voters about defense spending and broke their views down by party affiliation between 1960 and 1969, precisely the years in which party elites reoriented themselves on the issue. Yet in 1969 and 1970 Gallup found no significant difference between the parties in the electorate on defense spending, suggesting that when the party elites began to trade places on the issue in the mid-1960s Democratic voters were probably still slightly more supportive of military spending than Republicans. Only in 1971 did Democratic respondents become notably less supportive of defense spending than Republicans, finally matching the pattern that had existed among political elites since 1964. This chronology indicates that the parties' reversal was not a result of politicians catering to the sentiments of their voters.

These findings lend credence to the top-down issue evolution view as well as Zaller's (1992) model of elite leadership of public opinion. The public realigned more quickly on defense issues than it later would on abortion, but less rapidly than it had on racial issues. Elite conversion, not elite replacement, produced this issue evolution.

There is little evidence that group pressures, public opinion, or an ideological revolution among their respective cadres of policy and public intellectuals provoked the parties' repeated reversals on defense issues. Nor were MCs constrained by their voting records. Rather, this case reveals politicians proactively adjusting their program. Petrocik (1996) argues that "issue ownership" often stems from the social composition of party coalitions. Since the military was not part of either party's base, ownership of the defense issue was especially volatile. Defense policy is distinctive in its grouplessness, but not unique. A study of the politics of taxes and fiscal balance reveals similar dynamics.

COALITION EXPANSION: FISCAL POLICY

Fiscal policy has long been central to party competition. Republicans have generally been more supportive of tax reductions and opposed to tax increases than Democrats since the late 1970s. Two aspects of tax policy have long generated controversy: its incidence and the relation to expenditures. Democrats and liberals have been more supportive of the notion of progressive taxation. Yet on the other key aspect of tax policy, the question of fiscal balance, there have been sharp and repeated reversals in the parties' stands. If deficits and debt are the greatest problem, taxes can be cut only in conjunction with reductions in spending. Thus advocates of tax reductions have tended to minimize the dangers of deficits and debt, or claimed that lowering tax rates will increase revenue, perhaps in the long run. They have also argued that only spending reductions will reduce debts and deficits because surpluses will invariably be spent.

In line with the categories I have established, it is notable that until recently no important groups in either party have been organized around the question of "fiscal responsibility" or the need for tax cuts per se.[50] Thus parties have been comparatively free to adjust their positions on this issue and reinterpret the implications of their ideology. They can then reframe it to show their supporters that the new stand is indeed consistent with their values and designed to further their interests. In hopes of *coalition expansion* Republicans embraced a new strategy, unprompted by a preexisting constituency and independent of efforts to woo a particular single-issue group.

[50] The only visible group devoted to promoting "fiscal conservatism" in the old "Eisenhower Republican" balanced-budget, tax-acceptant sense is the Concord Coalition. This group prides itself on its bipartisanship and plays little effective role in campaigns.

In this way tax politics resembles the defense issue. It contrasts sharply with the cases of trade and civil rights in the North, where organized groups focused on the issue identified their interests and constrained parties and politicians, or abortion and gun control where parties gradually took in groups that subsequently constrained them.

The modern GOP is associated with tax cuts, even at the price of deficits. Yet the position of Republicans was once quite different. It could be summed up by the comment of Eisenhower's first treasury secretary, George Humphrey, that "deficits should be avoided like the plague" (Reichard 1975, 98). In 1953 Eisenhower himself told Congress, "As a matter of basic long-term policy, we must look forward to reducing tax revenues as Government expenditures are curtailed. But it is also wise under existing conditions not to reduce receipts any faster than we can cut back on expenditures."[51]

Eisenhower's stand, while eventually adopted by most GOP MCs, was initially controversial among them (Reichard 1975, 98), as until that time congressional Republicans had overwhelmingly favored tax cuts despite the deficits of the Truman administration. In fact, tax politics during the Truman years bore a great resemblance to that of the Carter or Clinton administrations. In all of these cases a Democratic president opposed Republican tax cut proposals and justified this in part by reference to the need to balance the budget and reduce the debt. In his 1947 budget message Truman reported, "I cannot recommend tax reduction. The responsibilities of the federal government cannot be fully met in the fiscal year 1948 at a lower cost than here indicated. Even if the cost were less, it would be desirable in our present economic situation to maintain revenues in order to make a start toward the repayment of the national debt."[52]

In turn, Truman era Republicans made arguments associated more recently with supply-siders. The argument that supply-side tax cuts would "starve the beast," that is, that deficits will be a long-term constraint on spending, a motive attributed to the Reagan administration by Senator Daniel Patrick Moynihan (D-NY) and later avowed openly by some supply-side advocates,[53] was foreshadowed by Republicans in

---

[51] "Special Message to the Congress Recommending Tax Legislation," May 20, 1953, *Public Papers of the President Dwight D. Eisenhower*, no. 84, at http://www.presidency.ucsb.edu.

[52] Congressional Quarterly, vol. III, 1947, 159.

[53] "The Deficit Dilemmas; Shortfalls Are Taxing the Ability of Government to Be Innovative," *Washington Post*, February 3, 1991, H1, "Cut Taxes, Starve the Beast," *Wall Street Journal*, September 30, 1996, 18.

the 1940s, who saw tax cuts as "a means of reversing the spending policies of the New Deal by forcing government retrenchment" (Hartmann
1971, 75). Like contemporary Republicans, midcentury GOP MCs
rejected the use of tax increases to redress fiscal imbalance. In 1951
House minority leader Joseph Martin (R-MA) rejected Truman's proposed tax increase by arguing "The Administration's contention that
this tax bill is needed to control inflation is economic voodoo talk. No
set of controls and no pyramid of taxes ever devised by man will stop
inflation in American when the root of the evil is government spending"
(Witte 1985, 141).[54]

Republicans' antitax positioning in the Truman years was more than
just talk. The 80th Congress, the first GOP-controlled Congress since the
1930s, overrode President Truman's veto to cut income taxes (Griffith
1989, 72). Even under a new Republican administration in 1953, Ways
and Means Committee Chairman Daniel Reed (R-NY) reportedly held,
much like supply-siders a generation later, that "tax reduction, far from
enlarging the deficit, would serve to increase federal revenues by stimulating economic growth."[55]

Yet after brief intraparty controversy in 1953 President Eisenhower
was able to overcome these objections and convert most congressional
Republicans to the view that budget balancing was more important than
tax cutting. His stand became Republican gospel for many years thereafter. In Eisenhower's second term it was liberal Democrats who pushed,
unsuccessfully, for stimulative tax cuts.[56] Republicans and more conservative Democrats defeated these proposals.

During the Kennedy and Johnson administrations Democrats and
liberals enacted a large tax reduction designed to create a deficit and
stimulate the economy. Republican and conservative MCs opposed this,
seeking to block any tax cut that was not linked to a commensurate
reduction in expenditures (Witte 1985, 162). Business groups eventually
endorsed the Kennedy administration's tax cut (Sundquist 1968, 47–48).
Perhaps as a result, "Republicans, unwilling or unable to oppose tax cuts
as such, centered their attack upon the failure of the administration to cut
spending" (49). Still, there did appear to be a brief and uncharacteristic

---

[54] Rep. Martin's invocation of "voodoo" in a debate on fiscal policy may remind readers of George H. W. Bush's 1980 description of Ronald Reagan's supply-side plans as
"voodoo economics." Yet Bush was making the opposite point from Martin's. He was
claiming that tax cuts would *not* balance budgets.

[55] Morgan (1990, 56).

[56] Sundquist (1968, 15–34).

gap between the GOP and its business allies on this particular proposal. Yet, unlike the unions that later punished some congressional Democrats for supporting trade agreements, there is no evidence that any business groups sanctioned Republican MCs who insisted that tax reductions be tied to spending limits.

Republican politicians seemed to enjoy autonomy on fiscal policy. Two possible explanations suggest themselves. First, it appears that fiscal balance was of limited concern to business groups compared to the narrow "private goods" agendas many firms and sectoral trade associations pursued. Additionally, it seemed that the difference between the corporate lobbies and GOP MCs was one of priorities and not principle: that is, they too would have preferred spending limits, although the tax cut under any circumstances was the highest priority. The fact that GOP opposition was ineffectual in this case may have made business groups more forgiving. This episode has to be considered something of an anomaly at present.

During this era, fiscal conservatism still generally meant balancing the budget at all costs. The view expressed by GOP congressional spokesman during the Truman years, that inflation could be defeated only on the spending side, was abandoned. In his book *The Conscience of a Conservative*, Barry Goldwater, while critical of Eisenhower's "modern Republicanism" in many ways, did not fundamentally differ with the president on fiscal policy. He argued:

> While there is something to be said for the proposition that spending will never be reduced so long as there is money in the federal treasury, I believe that as a practical matter spending cuts must come before tax cuts. If we reduce taxes before firm, principled decisions are made about expenditures, we will court deficit spending and the inflationary effects that follow. (Goldwater 2007 [1960], 58)

Goldwater maintained this position when he became the GOP's presidential nominee in 1964. An innovator in many other respects, Goldwater did not break with the then-prevailing GOP orthodoxy on taxes. In the 1964 campaign he denounced the Kennedy-Johnson tax cut, contrasting his proposal for more gradual tax reductions allowing for a balanced budget with the "impulsive, massive, politically-motivated tax cut gimmickry" of the "reckless" Democratic plan. Goldwater explicitly rejected the use of tax cuts to stimulate the economy.[57] Thus although the

---

[57] "Goldwater calls Tax Cut 'Cynical,'" *New York Times*, September 9, 1964, 27.

Goldwater campaign is often seen as the foundation of the modern conservative Republican Party, on tax policy the "conservatism" Goldwater
offered was not that of Reagan and later GOP leaders.

In 1968 and 1969 questions of taxation were again prominent in politics. The key issue concerned a surtax to pay for increased social and
military spending. The surtax was first enacted in 1968 at the end of the
Johnson administration. It was not a clearly partisan issue. Many liberal
Democrats were resistant to the surtax, which they linked to the administration's Vietnam policy.

Early in his administration Richard Nixon reiterated the position that
President Eisenhower had taken in the 1950s. He argued, "if taxes are to
be reduced, there must be corresponding reductions on the expenditure
side."[58] After having promised during the campaign to reduce or eliminate the surtax, Nixon came out in spring of 1969 for extending it. This
was a controversial proposal on Capitol Hill. Eventually the president
prevailed, but he did so chiefly with GOP backing.

As late as the Ford administration Democrats were more supportive
of tax reduction than Republicans. In late 1974 President Ford asked
the Democratic Congress to raise taxes, calling for a "one year temporary tax surcharge of 5 percent on corporate and upper-level individual
incomes."[59] Congress ignored this request. Ford proposed a larger tax
cut in response to Democratic tax cut plans in late 1975, but insisted
on making it conditional on a large reduction in spending. When this
approach was rejected, Ford vetoed a bill reducing taxes on the grounds
that it would be inflationary and fiscally irresponsible.

Like Nixon and Eisenhower before him, Ford generally found balanced
budgets a higher priority than tax cuts, welcome as the latter may have
been. He insisted, "I want any cut in federal tax revenues coupled with a
cut in the runaway growth in federal spending."[60] Later Ford agreed to
tax cuts, but only when linked with promises of restraint on spending.
During the 1976 campaign it was Carter who denounced the tax code as

---

[58] "Text of President Nixon's December 30, 1969 Statement on Signing of the Tax Reform
Act of 1969," *Congressional Quarterly Almanac 1969*, 649.

[59] "Address to a Joint Session of the Congress on the Economy," October 8, 1974, no. 121,
http://www.presidency.ucsb.edu/ws/index.php?pid=4434&st=&st1=.

[60] "Veto of a Tax Reduction Bill," December 17, 1975, *Public Papers of the Presidents,
Gerald Ford, Book II*, July 21 to December 31, 1975 (Washington, DC: U.S. GPO,
1977).

a "disgrace to the human race."[61] He was focused more on closing loopholes than tax rates, but it is still noteworthy that the Democrats were not on the defensive regarding taxes in this race.

All this was soon to change as the GOP leadership embraced a "supply-side" approach to fiscal policy. Republicans stopped insisting that tax cuts be linked to spending cuts. Instead they focused on rate reductions, despite the existence of budget deficits. In so doing, they were not shy about claiming to be following in Kennedy's footsteps.

There is some dispute about how comparable the Kennedy-Johnson tax cut was with the program of the Republican "supply-siders." In general, supply-side Republicans have claimed Kennedy as an ancestor while Democrats have, predictably, rejected such kinship claims. In both cases administrations sought to reduce income taxes to stimulate the economy. In both instances the top rate was reduced substantially, and a deficit was deliberately created.

Yet some observers, usually those more sympathetic to Kennedy than to Reagan, have emphasized differences between the cases. The 1964 tax cut was inspired by Keynesian theory and geared toward stimulating demand. By contrast, the Republicans' supply-side tax cuts were designed to increase investment (Greenberg 2004).

This may have been true as a distinction between the doctrine of Kennedy's economists and Reagan's. Certainly Kennedy's surviving advisors claimed as much. Walter Heller, Kennedy's chairman of the Council of Economic Advisors, noted that the earlier cut "was a demand-side response, exactly the opposite of … the implausible supply-side theory" (Collins 2000, 177).[62] Similarly, another Kennedy economic advisor, Arthur Okun, contended, "The Revenue Act of 1964 was aimed at the demand, rather than the supply side of the economy" (Greenberg 2004).

Yet in the realm of politics, matters were murkier. Not only were the policies similar in practice, but on at least one important occasion the rhetoric was as well. In an address to the Economic Club of New York on

---

[61] "Carter to Propose 'Substantial' Cuts in Tax Next Year," *Washington Post,* December 1, 1977, A1.

[62] On another occasion, however, Heller argued, "We were practicing supply-side economics in the early 1960s, without having the wit to call it that. We called it stimulating investment in plant and equipment in order to promote modernization and growth in capacity. But the notion that slashing taxes across the board will release such torrents of work effort that it will fuel tremendous growth and almost pay for itself – that is their point of departure. "The New Economics View: From the Supply-Side," *New York Times,* March 5, 1981, A1.

December 12, 1962, Kennedy spoke not only of boosting consumption, but made some arguments that foreshadowed those Reagan and others would later put forward. He argued that the tax system

> reduces the financial incentives for personal effort, investment, and risk taking. … It is a paradoxical truth that tax rates are too high today and tax revenues are too low and the soundest way to raise the revenues in the long run is to cut the rates now. The experiences of a number of European countries and Japan have borne this out. This country's own experience with tax reduction in 1954 has borne this out. And the reason is that only full employment can balance the budget, and tax reduction can pave the way to full employment. (Sundquist 1968, 44)

If Republicans adopted some of the rhetoric and policies of John F. Kennedy and Democrats retained their traditional view, the issue would not have been a divisive one in partisan politics. Yet, in the late 1970s, Democrats reacted to the Republican initiative on taxes much as GOP MCs had responded to Kennedy in 1963. A prominent Democratic response to the Kemp-Roth proposal in 1978 was the "Nunn Amendment." Senator Sam Nunn (D-GA) proposed that income taxes be cut 25 percent over five years *provided the budget was balanced*. This measure split Democrats, many of whom did not support tax cuts at that time. While viewing it as second best to the Kemp-Roth bill, which did *not* make tax cuts contingent on spending cuts, most Republicans were willing to support the Nunn plan if the alternative was no tax cut.[63] Eventually Democratic MCs voted to include only a symbolic version of the Nunn Amendment, which reporters termed "the Democratic version of the Roth-Kemp tax cut plan" in that year's tax bill.[64]

Beyond noting that the Republican's position on fiscal policy changed, it is useful to examine various explanations that have been put forward to account for this important development.

One possible explanation is public opinion. Some suggest that voters' decisions showed the Republicans that the tax issue was a useful one to engage. The most famous of these incidents was California's Proposition 13, a limitation on property taxes approved by the state's voters on June 6, 1978, often seen as evidence of a "tax revolt." An election on the other side of the country that same day reinforced the view that antitax sentiment was pervasive. Jeffrey Bell, a conservative and former Reagan aide, upset long-serving Senator Clifford Case (R-NJ), a

---

[63] "House Conferees Told to Accept Senate Tax Plan," *Washington Post*, October 13, 1978, A1.
[64] "Congress Quits after All-Night Session," *Washington Post*, October 16, 1978, A1.

liberal Republican, in the GOP Senate primary. Bell's surprise win was also seen as evidence of the appeal of an antitax message because he had made the Kemp-Roth plan the central theme of his campaign. These developments probably did encourage Republicans to highlight their new stand on taxes; Kemp-Roth became the centerpiece of the GOP's campaign in the midterm elections later that year.[65]

Yet while these events may have encouraged Republican leaders to emphasize an antitax message, they cannot explain the GOP's initial embrace of Kemp-Roth. Republican leaders had already endorsed the tax cut plan months before California and New Jersey voters signaled that the issue might be a fruitful one. In October 1977 the Republican congressional leaders, Senator Howard Baker (R-TN) and Rep. John Rhodes (R-AZ), publicly endorsed the plan. By December, 142 House Republicans (virtually the entire GOP conference) had cosponsored the Kemp-Roth plan.[66]

If we look at public opinion more broadly, we find little evidence that the parties in the electorate impelled the party elites to reverse course on fiscal policy. General Social Surveys taken in 1976 and 1977 found no significant differences between Democrats and Republican identifiers in the electorate regarding whether they thought their taxes were too high.

If voters and survey respondents do not provide evidence that masses led elites on the tax issue, party-linked interest groups are another logical place to look. Yet the Republicans' new position on taxes was *not* taken at the behest of any component of their coalition. Certainly business lobbies favored the concept of lower taxes and were generally supportive of the proposals first of congressional Republicans in the late 1970s and later those of the Reagan administration in 1981. Yet accounts suggest that there was ambivalence within business circles at the time (regarding the merits of supply-side economics and that the initiative for this move did *not* come from business lobbies) (Blumenthal 1981; Jacobs 1985).

Rather, the evidence suggests that Republican politicians adopted this policy and then convinced business interests to support it.[67] This was possible because corporate lobbies were less concerned with the broad

---

[65] "GOP Plans 'Blitz' to Push Tax Cut Bill," *Washington Post*, July 7, 1978, A4; "Bell's Victory: Tax Cut Idea Very Popular," *Washington Post*, June 8, 1978, A2.

[66] "G.O.P. Leaders Ask Carter to Support 30% Tax Cut," *New York Times*, October 6, 1977, 20; "New York Congressmen Help State Get $525 Million 'Extra' in U.S. Aid," *New York Times*, December 27, 1977, 30.

[67] Sinclair (2006, ch. 9) reports a similar pattern in the 2000s. Business lobbies focused on narrower concerns deferred to Republican leaders on major tax proposals.

issue of fiscal balance than with specific provisions dealing with corporate taxation. Once these lobbies "got on board," pressure on individual GOP MCs to toe the line increased, but the corporate groups were not the source of the innovation in party policy.

Recalling this sequencing is critical because it highlights the fact that although each party coalition includes constituencies with opinions on many topics, politicians retain a substantial degree of room to maneuver. When there are no groups focused on a particular policy, and even the constituents that do care are ambivalent or are interested only in narrow aspects of the issue in question, the autonomy of elected officials is enhanced. Schattschneider (1960, 43) recognized this dynamic long ago:

> The Republican party has played a major role in the political organization of the business community, a far greater role than many students of politics seem to have realized. ... The political education of business is a function of the Republican party that can never be done so well by anyone else. In the management of the political relations of the business community, the Republican Party is much more important than any combination of pressure groups ever could be. The success of special interests in Congress is due less to the "pressure" exerted by these groups than it is due to the fact that Republican members of Congress are committed in advance to a general probusiness attitude. The notion that business groups coerce Republican congressmen into voting for their bills underestimates the whole Republican posture in American politics.

### SHIFTS AMONG ELITES

As in other cases, it is important to assess the relative importance of conversion and replacement as mechanisms of party position change on fiscal policy among political elites. Berkman (1993) argues that the GOP's growth in the Sunbelt inspired the party's turn toward antitax stands. His claim that compositional shifts in the parties' congressional caucuses led to policy realignment is analogous to the assertions of other scholars on the cases of abortion and civil rights. Burns and Taylor (2000) cast doubt on Berkman's claims. They note the very modest increase in GOP congressional strength in the South and West in the mid-1970s and the nearly unanimous Republican support for tax cuts from 1978 on.

Yet these scholars do not study the changing positions of continuing MCs and longtime party leaders. The evidence suggests that replacement played little or no role in realigning the parties on fiscal policy. Consider the case of Gerald Ford, the last Republican president to veto a tax cut. He had rejected supply-side ideas while in office. Yet in 1978 when Republicans turned toward supply-side tax cuts Ford was very much on the team. At that time the former president was still considered a serious prospect for the 1980 GOP presidential nomination. Despite his own record, Ford endorsed Kemp-Roth in 1978.[68]

For Ronald Reagan too the embrace of Kemp-Roth's supply-side logic was a new position. Reagan is more associated than any other politician with reorienting the GOP on fiscal policy. Yet during his 1976 presidential campaign Reagan was still a traditional balance-the-budget Republican. His major fiscal initiative that year was a plan to substantially reduce federal spending. Reagan argued that expenditures needed to be cut $90 billion before a tax cut would be possible (Stein 1988, 255).

Yet by 1980, Reagan was singing a different tune. Reagan did not claim, as some supply-side advocates did, that deficits do not matter. Yet he rejected the contention that they should act as a break on tax reduction. In a debate with his rival for the GOP presidential nomination, George H. W. Bush, who had not yet fully accepted the new supply-side wisdom, Reagan defended it this way:

I've heard for a great many years that we can't possibly reduce taxes – this is Washington's cry – we can't reduce taxes until we reduce government spending and I have to point out that government does not tax to get the money it needs; government always needs the money it gets. Now your son can be extravagant with his allowance and you can lecture him day after day about saving money and not being extravagant, or you can solve the problem by cutting his allowance."[69]

The story is similar for other leading Republicans. Although Bush famously dubbed Reagan's fiscal plan "voodoo economics" in 1980, he later embraced the policy. Senators Howard Baker and Bob Dole also sought the GOP's presidential nomination, and they both were known to be skeptical of the merits of supply-side economics. Even when loyally supporting Reagan's program as Senate majority leader, Baker admitted that the tax and budget program was a "riverboat gamble."[70]

Typically, Dole was more caustic. In 1982 he joked about good and bad news. "The good news is that a bus filled with supply-siders went over a

---

[68] "GOP Starts Push for Tax Cut Bill," *Washington Post*, September 21, 1978, A3; "Stumping for Tax Cut; GOP Takes Kemp-Roth Plan to 7 States but Finds Crowds Aren't Turning Out," *Washington Post*, September 23, 1978, A2.

[69] League of Women Voters Presidential Forum, April 23, 1980 (Swerdlow 1987).

[70] "Reagan's Confidence Gap," *Newsweek*, September 26, 1981, 26.

cliff. The bad news is that there were three empty seats."[71] Yet Dole, who as a young representative had voted against the Kennedy tax cut in 1963, supported Kemp-Roth in 1978 and 1980, and as Senate Finance Committee chairman in 1981 he steered Reagan's tax cut proposal through the Senate.

Nonetheless, when Dole became the Republican presidential nominee in 1996 he still retained something of his reputation as a "deficit hawk" skeptical of tax cuts in the absence of spending restraint.[72] Yet Dole chose as his running mate Rep. Jack Kemp (R-NY), the politician most associated with supply-side economics. The Kansas senator also pledged to "finish the job that Ronald Reagan started so brilliantly," making a large tax cut the centerpiece of his presidential campaign despite the existence of a deficit.[73] All in all, with "enemies" like Dole among veteran Republicans, supply-side advocates hardly needed friends.

The residual doubts of these veteran GOP leaders were not wholly irrelevant. Many observers credit them with pushing Reagan to roll back some of the tax cut in 1982 in view of the enormous emerging deficit, and Bush famously ended up violating his famous pledge "Read my lips; no new taxes!" in 1990. Yet although their attachment to this new policy might have been weak, these leaders did support it at crucial moments. Had Baker, Bush, Dole, Ford, and other senior Republicans not gone along with the new program, the GOP could never have been so rapidly and decisively "rebranded" on the tax issue.

Senator Bill Roth (R-DE) and Jack Kemp were the two MCs most closely associated with the supply-side cause before Reagan. Both men had served several years in Congress embracing GOP fiscal orthodoxy before they became advocates of supply-side economics. Kemp explained: "I came in as a balance-the-budget, root canal, austere Republican. Then I looked around and realized that my career was going to be ended very quickly if I couldn't come up with something more hopeful" (Blumenthal 1986, 6). Kemp's ability to promote a new policy was enhanced by the absence of key constituencies providing contrary cues to legislators of his own party.

Leading Democrats sometimes ruefully acknowledged the parties' trading places where fiscal policy was concerned. In a meeting when his staff was debating priorities in economic policy and in which the fiscally

---

[71] "Dole Shows His Supply Side," *Washington Post*, March 5, 1982, D8.
[72] "Dole's Tax Choices All Pose Perils; Boldest Move Would Shift Long-Held Views," *Washington Post*, June 15, 1996, C1.
[73] "Dole Offers Economic Plan Calling for Broad Tax Cut Spurring Growth," *New York Times*, August 6, 1996, A1.

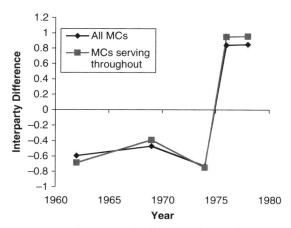

FIGURE 5-4. Interparty Difference of Mean Support for Income Tax Cuts among Representatives (Republican Mean – Democratic Mean), 88th through 96th Congresses (1963–1980)

orthodox faction, led by Robert Rubin, eventually prevailed, Bill Clinton reportedly complained, "I hope you're all aware we're all Eisenhower Republicans. We're Eisenhower Republicans here, and we are fighting the Reagan Republicans. We stand for lower deficits and free trade and the bond market. Isn't that great?" (Woodward 1994, 161).

Discussion of the behavior of leading figures must be accompanied by more systematic analysis to produce a fuller picture of party position change on fiscal policy. In Figure 5-4 I show the shifting interparty difference of means on votes in the House on income tax cuts from the 88th through the 96th Congresses (1963–1980), both among all representatives in each Congress as well as the 81 who served throughout the period. The period surveyed begins with the Congress in which the tax cut Kennedy proposed was voted on and ends with the first two Congresses to consider the "Kemp-Roth" proposals.

As this chart shows, the shift on tax issues in the 95th Congress (1977–1978) was a radical one. As in previous cases, the long-serving MCs' behavior does not differ appreciably from that of their colleagues. The surviving opponents of the Kennedy tax cut (which supply-siders claimed as an inspiration) overwhelmingly supported Kemp-Roth tax cut proposals in the late 1970s. By contrast, the MCs who supported across-the-board tax cuts in the early 1960s had much less enthusiasm for them 15 years later. These results cast further doubt on Berkman's (1993) findings and the applicability of the issue evolution model more

TABLE 5-5. *Percentage of Long-Serving Representatives (Stayers) and the Rest of the House Supporting Tax Cuts on Two Votes with Similar Cutpoints: 1963 and 1978*

| Congress | Type of Representative | Democrats | Republicans |
|---|---|---|---|
| 88th Congress (1963–1964)[a] | Stayers | 97.3% (N = 73) | 0% (N = 25) |
| 95th Congress (1977–1978)[b] | Stayers | 5.5% (N = 73) | 96% (N = 25) |
| 88th Congress (1963–1964)[a] | Rest of House | 86.7% (N = 180) | .7% (N = 151) |
| 95th Congress (1977–1978)[b] | Rest of House | 16.8% (N = 208) | 98.3% (N = 121) |

[a] 88th Congress (59.5% Democratic), Var. 78,. H.R. 8363, September 25, 1963: Motion to recommit the Revenue Act with instructions to amend it to prevent the tax reductions from taking effect unless the president specified that spending for fiscal 1964 was not expected to exceed $98 billion (53.1% voting pro–tax cut)
[b] 95th Congress (67.1% Democratic), Var. 1317, H.R. 13511, August 10, 1978: Motion to recommit to the Ways and Means Committee with instructions to report it back with an amendment that would provide for an across-the-board cut in individual income taxes of approximately 33% to be phased in over the next three years (42.6% voting pro–tax cut)

generally. Among veteran legislators the Republicans and Democrats changed sides on the question of tax cuts versus "fiscal responsibility."

Also noteworthy in Figure 5-3 is the great rapidity of the change depicted. The parties' reversals on taxes happened virtually overnight, in sharp contrast to the comparatively glacial shifts on gun control, abortion, and, to a lesser degree, race.

Table 5-5 reports the positions of individual MCs who were present and voting for the Kennedy tax cut in 1963 and the first time the Kemp-Roth proposal was the subject of a recorded vote in 1978 and compares these long-serving legislators to the rest of the House. Unfortunately, in contrast to the other cases I examine, it is not possible to find two votes for which both the party compositions of the House and the percentage voting on the same side of this issue are very similar. The roll calls I use in this table are as close as possible to that ideal. In any case, much like Figure 5-3 this test reveals that the reversal of the parties on the issue of fiscal balance between the first and second votes is nearly total, reducing concerns about cutpoints and the comparability of the two votes.

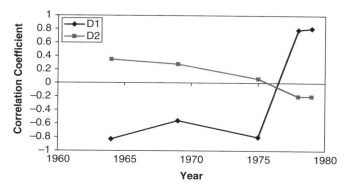

FIGURE 5-5. Correlation between Support for Income Tax Cuts and D1 and D2 NOMINATE Scores, House of Representatives, 88th through 96th Congresses (1963–1980)

Analysis using the Rapoport and Stone formula tells the same story as Figure 5-3. It shows that the overwhelming majority of the change in the parties' positioning on fiscal policy occurred rapidly, and 90.4 percent was a product of conversion by MCs. Breaking down the results by parties reveals that conversion accounts for 83 percent of change among Republicans and 102 percent for Democrats.

Unsurprisingly in view of the above findings, the NOMINATE scores also tell a story of radical transformation. As Figure 5-5 depicts, those with conservative scores, that is, high ones on the dominant D1 dimension, opposed tax cuts in the early 1960s on budget-balancing grounds while liberals supported them. But by the late 1970s the sign had reversed: it was liberals who resisted tax increases and conservatives who advocated them. Once again, ideological or spatial stability was accompanied by policy or substantive instability.

The Republicans' embrace of supply-side economics in the late 1970s required them to jettison their long-standing fiscal policy. The absence of organized groups in their party with a clear stake in this issue left GOP politicians comparatively free to reinterpret their ideology and argue that their new stands were consistent with their voters' interests. Similarly, the Democrats were free to abandon their Keynesian policies because they too were able to maintain their coalition while engaging in "Rubinomics."

Whether an issue is groupless is an empirical question, the answer to which may change over time. In the past business and labor groups have taken positions on tax policy, but the bulk of their lobbying concerned narrow provisions of the tax code and distributional questions. The parties may no longer enjoy the same room to maneuver on fiscal issues they once did. The rise of antitax lobbies including "The Club for Growth" and "Americans for Tax Reform" is one reason.

While dating back to the 1980s, the Club became a mass membership group only recently and did not play a significant role in elections until the 2000 campaign. Yet it has achieved great prominence in political circles in a relatively short period of time.

The Club's power stems both from its substantial resources and its narrow focus on fiscal issues. The group raises large sums via direct mail and the internet. It endorses candidates and directs individual contributions from its members to them. This intermediary role allows the Club to circumvent the contribution limits that constrain other lobbies. The group also runs independent advertising in campaigns. The Club supports like-minded candidates in Republican primaries, even when the GOP leadership has coalesced around another individual, usually an incumbent whom it sees as electable.

Unlike most lobbies concerned with economic issues, the Club is not focused on the needs of a firm, an industrial sector, or even business interests generally. Rather, the Club advocates cutting taxes and spending. The Club's definition of fiscal conservatism differs, however, from that of Eisenhower Republicans or the Concord Coalition. Although the group does seek reduced spending, it does not believe, as many traditional fiscal conservatives have, that tax increases should be employed to achieve fiscal balance. Instead the Club seeks to punish "RINOs" (Republicans in Name Only) who do not support tax cuts in all instances.[74] Unlike Republican politicians and the formal party structures they dominate, which support even legislators who often stray from the fold if they seem best positioned to hold a seat, the Club demands fealty from legislators on its key issue.

The 2004 Republican senatorial primary in Pennsylvania is a recent case in point. President Bush and the National Republican Senate Committee backed the longtime incumbent, Arlen Specter, although he had broken ranks more than most Republicans. GOP leaders viewed Specter as the candidate most likely to hold the seat for the GOP at a time when control

---

[74] "The Club That's Clubbing Republican Moderates," *Business Week*, April 1, 2002, 43; "Club for Growth," *Campaigns & Elections*, August 2002, 8; "Fight Club," *New York Times Magazine*, August 10, 2003, 24.

of the Senate was in question. (The NRA also supported Specter in the primary because he has consistently opposed gun control.)

Yet Specter's opponent, Rep. Patrick Toomey, won significant backing, not only from the National Right to Life Committee (Specter is generally pro-choice), but from the Club for Growth as well. The Club directed more than $2,000,000 in contributions to the Toomey campaign.[75] Specter narrowly prevailed in the primary with 51 percent of the vote and won the general election by a wider margin. (The Club later endorsed Specter against his Democratic opponent, Rep. Joseph Hoeffel.)

Specter and some other GOP moderates, including former representative Marge Roukema of New Jersey and former senator Lincoln Chafee of Rhode Island, had close calls in primaries due in part to Club backing for their challengers.[76] The group also backed winners in several recent contested primaries, including Senators Jim DeMint (R-SC) and Tom Coburn (R-OK).[77] Yet until recently the Club could not claim credit for the defeat of an incumbent in a Republican primary.

That changed in 2006. In that year the Club devoted over $1,000,000 in independent expenditures to a successful campaign to unseat freshman incumbent Joe Schwarz of Michigan. Schwarz was a moderate on social as well as economic issues and had won nomination with less than a third of the primary vote in 2004 against a large field of conservative candidates. Since he had antagonized many conservative factions, the extent to which the Club's expenditures contributed to Schwarz's defeat is unclear. Nevertheless, as one reporter noted, the race was important as a signal to Washington Republicans; "the Club had finally scalped its first incumbent."[78]

Schwarz's scalp was the first the Club claimed, but it was not the last. In 2008 Rep. Wayne Gilchrest of Maryland, another Club target, was defeated in the Republican primary. Gilchrest's loss was more striking than Schwarz's. While Schwarz was a freshman who had won his primary with 28 percent of the vote only because conservatives split their votes among several candidates, Gilchrest was more entrenched; he

[75] "Specter Survives Toomey Challenge: Four Term Senator Wins by Slim Margin," *Pittsburgh Post-Gazette*, April 28, 2004, A1.
[76] On Roukema and the Club see Hacker and Pierson (2005, 121–123). On Chafee and the Club see "Republican Group Attacks Chafee for Votes on Spending, Tax Bills," *Associated Press*, August 17, 2006.
[77] "A Senate Race in Oklahoma Lifts the Right," *New York Times*, September 19, 2004, 1.
[78] "Growing Pains," *The New Republic*, September 4, 2006, 8.

had served since 1990, sailing to renomination before first encountering choppy seas after 2000. The Club funded serious primary challenges to Gilchrest in 2002 and 2004, but he survived. Finally in 2008 they spent over $600,000 and contributed to Gilchrest's defeat at the hands of conservative State Senator Andy Harris.[79] Like Schwarz, Gilchrest had antagonized many Republicans on noneconomic issues well beyond the Club's purview; he was pro-choice and favored gun control. After initially backing the war in Iraq, Gilchrest was one of just two GOP representatives to support a timetable for withdrawal of U.S. forces from that country in 2007.[80] Several months after his loss in the Republican primary Gilchrest endorsed Frank Kratovil, the Democratic nominee, who went on to defeat Harris in November.[81]

Thus these cases do not show that the Club can defeat a Republican incumbent who irritates the antitax organization but is orthodox in other respects. Both of the organization's victims had antagonized many other conservatives as well. Still, the Club's prominent association with the defeat of two incumbents coupled with their support of winners in several competitive open-seat primaries must factor into the calculations of risk-averse Republican politicians on tax issues.

Between campaigns the Club remains active. The organization has run television ads critical of Republican MCs in their home states and districts when they take stands it dislikes. In 2003 the Club ran ads attacking Senators George Voinovich (R-OH) and Olympia Snowe (R-ME) as "Franco-Americans," comparing their attempts to reduce the size of President Bush's proposed tax cut with French president Jacques Chirac's opposition to U.S. policy in Iraq. In 2005 the Club took to the airwaves to denounce Senator Lindsey Graham (R-SC) in his home state when he proposed removing the "cap" on the amount of income subject to payroll tax as part of a broader Social Security reform plan.[82]

The Club is not the only Republican-leaning antitax organization. Americans for Tax Reform, headed by veteran GOP activist Grover Norquist, lobbies Republican candidates to sign a "taxpayer protection

---

[79] "Party Activists Bring Down Maryland Duo," *Politico,* February 13, 2008.
[80] "House, 218 to 212, Votes to Set Date for Iraq Pullout," *New York Times,* March 24, 2007, 1.
[81] "Gilchrest Breaks with the GOP in Md. 1st District Endorsement," *Washington Post,* September 3, 2008, B1.
[82] "Attacks on Fiscal Moderates Fuel Battles within GOP," *Boston Globe,* May 19, 2003, A3. "GOP Senator under Fire from the Right," *Human Events Online,* March 29, 2005.

pledge." The existence of lobbies like the ATR and the Club constrains politicians and makes it much harder for them to redefine the party line on taxes for voters. At least as far as Republicans are concerned, taxes are no longer a groupless issue. These lobbies may have only organized Republicans with antitax sentiments rather than bringing new voters into the party, but to the extent that they can mobilize formerly inchoate sentiment they can hold Republican politicians accountable and reduce their autonomy on the tax issue.

Government spending in the generic sense may still be a groupless issue, however. Norquist argues that "since each constituency in the Republican coalition has gotten what it wants on its 'vote-moving issues' (judges, assault weapons, tax cuts), they tolerate increased spending even if they don't like it. 'Thank you very much for my vote-moving issue and grumble, grumble, you spend too much,'" they say, according to Norquist. "But 'spend too much' doesn't make people walk out of the room, it doesn't make people throw heavy objects."[83] If a group arose that was focused on limiting spending with the intensity that the Club for Growth (or Americans for Tax Reform) bring to the tax issue, it might affect party positioning.

In this chapter I have explored the politics of two issues, defense spending and taxation/fiscal balance. I have argued that interest group activity does not explain shifts in party positioning in either of these policy areas. The lobbies most active historically on both tax and defense policy have had narrow "private goods" agendas and are not focused on the macrolevel policies parties use to define their images in hopes of winning broad-based support.

As a result, party elites have been freer to reinvent themselves in these areas than they are on issues such as abortion or gun control, policy areas in which party constituencies constrain the behavior of politicians. Thus we have seen repeated reversals in parties' positioning on groupless issues. The reorientation of elites that has occurred in these cases has stemmed overwhelmingly from conversion, not replacement, and has not been a function of the gradual movement of groups into party coalitions. The fact that conversion was the mechanism of elite adaptation on groupless issues has meant that party position change could be rapid in these cases.

---

[83] "Vote-Movers, Deficits and the Blue Dogs," Capitolism Blog, *The Nation*, May 15, 2008, http://www.thenation.com/blogs/jstreet.

The issues discussed above are not the only examples of topics on which party elites are generally unconstrained by coalitional concerns. Another contemporary example of a groupless issue is the space program. At its inception in the late 1950s, Democrats were the leading supporters of America's space program. Democrats prodded a reluctant Eisenhower to respond to the Soviets' launch of *Sputnik* in 1957 with the creation of a space program, a move the president considered an overreaction. Kennedy had criticized the Eisenhower administration for "letting us fall behind" (Mandelbaum 1969, 649). Later it was President Kennedy who made the famous commitment to go to the moon. By comparison congressional Republicans were relatively critical of the space program, citing fiscal concerns. GOP spokesmen also made the argument that the monies spent for NASA could be put to better use building weaponry, even at a time when they were generally less supportive than Democrats of Pentagon budgets. On May 10, 1963, the Senate Republican Policy Committee issued a statement concluding:

A decision must be made as to whether Project Apollo is vital to our national security or merely an excursion, however interesting, into space research. If our vital security is not at stake a less ambitious program may be logical and desirable. Greater emphasis might be placed on the multitude of human problems we face here on earth. Since our resources in dollars and manpower are not inexhaustible, the entire question becomes a matter of priority. ... To allow the Soviet Union to dominate the atmosphere 100 miles above the earth's surface while we seek to put a man on the moon could be a ... fatal error.[84]

Shortly thereafter former president Eisenhower declared that "Anybody who would spend $40 billion in a race to the moon for national prestige is nuts," and Barry Goldwater concluded that "while our eyes are fixed upon the moon we could lose the earth or be buried in it."[85]

This kind of rhetoric characterized the space debate from the launch of *Sputnik* in late 1957 to mid-1964. In a series of votes in 1963 and 1964 Republicans and conservatives generally attempted to reduce funding levels for NASA while liberals and Democrats rebuffed their attempts. (There were Democrats who were prominent in the fights against NASA, such as Senators Fulbright and Proxmire, but their stands were initially atypical of their party, and the amendments they offered at first won primarily GOP support.)

---

[84] "Moon Race Dispute," *Congressional Quarterly Almanac* 1963, 413.
[85] Ibid.

There followed a brief period from late 1964 to mid-1967 when liberals and conservatives as defined by Poole-Rosenthal scores were about equally divided on the question of NASA. This was a time when the parties had already traded places on the question of defense spending, but their reversal on the space program did not follow immediately.

After 1967 it was liberal Democrats who led the opposition to NASA budgets. A statement by Rep. Ed Koch (D-NY) – then considered an extreme liberal – is typical: "Rather than increase the NASA budget I would recommend that it be reduced. ... I cannot justify approving monies to find out whether or not there is some microbe on Mars when in fact I know there are rats in Harlem apartments."[86]

If liberal Democrats were becoming less enamored of the space program, conservative Republicans were finding new merit in it. By this time Barry Goldwater had offered an amendment to increase the amount of money granted NASA for research and development beyond what the agency had requested. The new senatorial scourge of the space shuttle was Walter Mondale (D-MN), an orthodox liberal. After 1973 congressional debate over spending for NASA became much less conflictual. There were no stand-alone votes on NASA in the Senate for 15 years. In the late 1980s the issue of the Space Station arose. In this case amendments to the HUD-VA appropriations bill were again offered cutting NASA funding. Once again, these efforts were supported largely by Democrats. Thus the space program was in turn, a Democratic priority, a Republican one, an uncontroversial program, and once again a target of Democratic attacks, all within a 30-year period.

The discussion of the politics of defense spending and fiscal policy in this chapter, along with the briefer review of the parties' positioning on NASA, illustrates a broader point. Public policy exists in many areas that are not the focus of important group lobbying and activism. In some cases activism and lobbying exists, but it is sufficiently parochial and "distributive" that it is not incorporated into party coalitions. In such cases party politicians have more leeway to take positions and to reevaluate them. The goals that motivate their behavior are the same ones that impel them to please existing party constituencies and seek out new ones, but they result in very different patterns of behavior over time.

---

[86] Congressional Quarterly Almanac 1970, 203.

# 6

# Conclusions

In this book I have sought to highlight major changes in the positioning of American political parties in the last 50 years and to identify an underlying logic that would enhance our understanding of parties. As a result, my emphasis has been on change. Yet it is worth recalling that amid all the change in the policies and coalitions of the Democrats and Republicans there is much stability as well. The essential nature of American political parties, election-oriented coalitions of groups with intense preferences on distinct policies managed by politicians, has remained constant. Important continuities in party coalitions are also visible. Republicans' alignment with the business community, evident already in Lincoln's day, is one example. The parallel alignment of organized labor with the Democrats is more recent, but still in its eighth decade. A host of relative party policy positions consistent with the stable preferences of these coalition components, such as on labor-management relations and the welfare state, have remained in place for generations.

Yet the policies and coalitions of the Democratic and Republican parties have changed radically since 1960. Many of the parties' defining policy stands are relatively recent, as are the affiliations of many of the component groups with the contemporary Democratic and Republican coalitions. Recognizing this puts a new perspective on two major findings widely discussed by students of American politics: that the parties have "polarized," and that this is a result of replacement because legislators' overall spatial positions are stable. This study demonstrates that the "poles" toward which the parties are moving are not themselves stable.

Moreover, although most legislators are party stalwarts or moderates throughout their careers, when it comes to parties' positions changing on particular issues, I demonstrate that conversion more than replacement is the important mechanism. Both of these findings cast a new light on claims that members of Congress have stable spatial or ideological positions. That observation is valid, but it masks much substantive change.

The best way, I have argued, to understand these changes is to view parties not as groups of like-minded citizens and not as candidate-centered organizations designed to serve politicians, but as coalitions of groups with intense preferences on issues who come together to win elections and further their individual policy agendas. In this conception, politicians play a managerial and coordinating role, but their autonomy and discretion vary systematically across issue areas depending on the nature of group involvement with the issue and the relationship between the groups in question and the party system.

I showed that there is important variation in the process of party position change across issues. The speed at which the process occurs, the relative importance of conversion as opposed to replacement among party elites, and the stability of the new position all vary across cases.

The models of party position change explain this variation. I have argued that while every issue is unique, there are a small number of identifiable mechanisms at work that can be captured in three major models of change, all of which are based on an understanding of parties as coalitions of groups with intense preferences managed by politicians. If my claims have validity, they will allow us to predict the speed of change, the stability of the new position, and the role of elite conversion versus replacement in other cases not examined in these pages.

This perspective emerges not least because this study is comparative, whereas previous work in this area has been dominated by single-case studies. I examined six cases of party position change on long-standing issues: trade, race, abortion, gun control, fiscal policy, and national defense. In all cases I observed the parties' positioning over a period of decades, focusing on the votes cast by MCs along with the positions taken by presidents and presidential nominees. Wherever possible, I employed multiple measures to gain confidence in basic findings. The thesis I present and my major conclusions are not based on a single case or a single test.

These cases differed in certain key respects. I have argued that shifts on these and other issues result from three distinct processes: coalition maintenance, coalition group incorporation, and coalition expansion. I show that these processes differ in the impetus for change at work, the speed of the parties' repositioning, and the degree to which elite replacement is the mechanism of party position change.

The parties' trade policy reversal was the purest case of coalition maintenance. Parties' constituencies changed little, but the preferences of their longtime allies in business and labor lobbies were altered by developments in the world economy. Politicians shifted positions on an issue in order to retain the supporters they already had.

By contrast, gun control and abortion were instances of coalition group incorporation. On these issues party positioning proceeded more slowly as Democrats and Republicans courted and won new constituencies. Elite replacement played a relatively greater role in these cases.

The politics of race was characterized by a mixture of coalition maintenance and group incorporation as the parties both responded to old constituencies and courted new ones. The shift on civil rights among Northern politicians was primarily one of coalition maintenance as Democrats and Republicans reacted to divergent signals from business and labor lobbies that had once evinced little concern about civil rights. In the South and – to a lesser degree – the North during the New Deal, coalition group incorporation was at work as African Americans entered the Democratic Party and racially conservative whites became a source of votes for Republicans.

Finally, the shifts on tax policy and defense spending are examples of coalition expansion in which parties' positions were the least stable. On these issues party elites experimented repeatedly in hopes of winning widespread support not limited to any lobby or discrete subgroup of voters.

Collectively, these changes have reshaped the identity of the two parties since 1960. While focusing on these six issues, I argued that the models I developed could illuminate the politics of several others I briefly discussed, including support for private schools, tort reform, the space program, immigration, and women's rights.

Although each case is unique, some threads run through several of them. In general, my findings reinforce the view that party politicians are ahead of their voters. The polarization among partisans in the electorate lagged that of politicians not only on race and abortion, as other scholars have noted, but on gun control and defense spending as well.

One other notable point is that shifts in party coalitions have long-term consequences unimagined by the groups and politicians involved. Repeatedly, a group entered a party for one reason, only to eventually influence its policy in an entirely different issue area. The preferences of an existing coalition component affected and sometimes impeded party elites' attempts to reach out to other constituencies.

Business groups that entered the new Republican Party in large part because of its tariff policies in the mid-nineteenth century later encouraged the GOP to adopt stands unfriendly to unions and later still discouraged that party from continuing its historic role as the champion of civil rights for blacks. Most African Americans entered the Democratic Party in the 1930s, not as a result of civil rights activism by Roosevelt (who was famously cautious on race), but because of their support for New Deal social programs.

Yet the Democrats' increasing dependence on black votes along with pressure from labor unions later led the party's politicians to embrace racial liberalism. This trend was evident first among Northern Democratic MCs, who did not have to weigh the wishes of blacks and other civil rights supporters against those of white Southerners, and only later among Democratic presidents who were more cross-pressured.

The entrance of unions into the Democratic Party in the 1930s stemmed from New Dealers' support for them in unions' struggles with employers. Trade policy had nothing to do with labor's decision to align with Roosevelt's party, and the incorporation of this new coalition component had no immediate ramifications for Democrats' traditional low-tariff stand. Yet 35 years later, when changes in the world economy prompted unions to seek protection from imports, labor's new protectionist stand led its Democratic congressional allies to abandon their traditional position on trade.

A related point is that groups' entry into party coalitions is often a reaction to earlier movements by other factions. The unions entered the Democratic Party because of the manufacturers' influence in the Republican Party. Manufacturers were initially drawn to the GOP, not because it defended them against unions, which barely existed when the Republican Party formed in 1854, but rather in reaction to Democrats' low-tariff agrarian backers. More recent cases also illustrate this dynamic. Both environmentalists and trial lawyers have found a better reception from Democrats than Republicans in part because of the preexisting ties between GOP officials and business lobbies that oppose environmental regulations and support tort reform.

## DIRECTIONS FOR FUTURE RESEARCH

This study has encompassed several cases that are both politically important in their own right and that, taken together, illustrate the logic of party position change. Other issues could also usefully be examined in

the framework I advance, establishing more conclusively the generalizability of my claims.

Beyond examining more cases, other related topics merit further
exploration. For party politicians a major task in coalition management
is balancing the concerns of distinct constituencies within the party.
Franklin Roosevelt's ability to retain Southern white support while
steadily increasing his vote among African Americans is perhaps the best-
known example, but to some degree politicians in a two-party system are
always dealing with similar potentially explosive conflicts, which they
must strive to keep latent. Other more contemporary examples include
the occasional conflicts between labor unions and environmentalists in
the Democratic Party (Obach 2004) and business interests and the religious right in the GOP (Karol 2005).

The generalizability of my claims, not only for contemporary issues
but across time as well, could be assessed by examination of cases drawn
from earlier eras. A look back earlier in U.S. history reveals other cases
of party position change on issues, such as monetary policy (the Banks of
the United States, free silver, etc.) and "internal improvements" or public
works. Examination of such issues in my framework would be useful
because my cases are centered in the twentieth century and especially in
the years since 1960.

One salient difference between nineteenth-century politics and our
own is the far greater turnover in Congress (Polsby 1968) and other
offices in the earlier era. An implication of this is that earlier in American
history party position change *could* have occurred rapidly even without
conversion among party politicians. Yet although the question remains
open pending further investigation, it seems likely that conversion
has always been an important mechanism producing party position
change.

There is also the question of whether the dynamics I revealed in postwar American politics will continue to operate in the same way in the
twenty-first century. Many of the basic factors important in this book
(electorally minded politicians, groups with intense preferences, an electoral system that encourages two-party competition) remain in place.

However, recent developments suggest that the autonomy of party
politicians may be waning. In Chapter 5 I demonstrated how elected
officials were able to execute radical shifts, repositioning their parties
on groupless issues, because there was no organized group that could
mobilize party supporters to constrain politicians on the policies in question. Yet the increasing connectedness of people and the greater ease in

mobilization via talk radio and the internet, shown by both the anti-Iraq war "netroots" in the Democratic Party and the anti-immigration activists in the GOP, suggest that it may be easier for activists to organize party supporters in a way that compels politicians to take notice.

These trends should not be overstated, however. Both of these recent cases of rapid emergence of grassroots activism suggest that such mobilization requires a galvanizing issue. Absent a cause that generates massive and intense public interest or an organized group within their coalition focused on an issue, politicians may still retain considerable autonomy to reshape their parties' positions. Even in the cases of immigration and Iraq it may also be argued that party activists have enjoyed only limited success in constraining politicians.

One area ripe for future study is a phenomenon I discussed in Chapter 2: the fact that some issues are marked by institutional as well as, or even to the exclusion of, partisan conflict. The postwar pattern of trade politics, in which the issue remains partisan in Congress but presidents all support freer trade, is not unique. Other issue areas are marked by persistent institutional conflict as well, including foreign aid, immigration, and farm subsidies. Moreover, some issues, such as gun control and support for veterans, have been highly partisan in one era and chiefly characterized by interbranch conflict in another. This area is ripe for exploration that would complement the findings I have presented here.

Future research could also move in a comparative direction, exploring cases of party position change outside the United States. Comparing American cases to the development of issues in countries with multiparty systems might be especially useful. Groups that need to work within the framework of the two-party system in the United States often have their own parties in other countries, especially those using proportional representation electoral systems.

## IMPLICATIONS

The implications of this study extend beyond the question of issue evolution and the replacement versus conversion debate familiar to students of Congress. It complements the theory of "issue ownership" developed by Petrocik (1996), Ansolabehere and Iyengar (1994), and Sellers (1998). These scholars assert that, given an imperfectly informed electorate, parties that "own" the more popular position on a given issue profit by raising the issue's salience in voters' minds. Their analysis is dynamic within the framework of the campaign, allowing candidates' choices of issue emphasis to affect voters' decisions. Yet, while recognizing its impermanence, these scholars take parties' ownership of most issues as fixed in the medium term.

I have shown that parties can gain or lose "ownership" of issues rapidly. Scholars have long accepted that this is so for "performance" or "valence" issues, such as peace, prosperity, and avoidance of scandal. Yet this book demonstrates this also to be the case for issues scholars have considered "owned," including defense and taxes.

My findings also have implications for the literature about the role of ideas and intellectuals in leading developments. Some thoughtful students of parties find intellectual elites to be the catalyst for party position change (Zaller 1992; Noel 2007). At least for the cases surveyed, I find little evidence consistent with this view. It is true that a politician who thinks about taking and promoting a new stand will often make use of experts or wordsmiths, but often he has his choice among advocates of various viewpoints.

This book also revises the conventional wisdom regarding the mechanism that reorients party elites on issues. Change in the parties' relative issue positions stems more from veteran politicians' reversals than from elite turnover. In every case at least one party changed primarily via conversion, and in some both did. Replacement supplements the effect of conversion, as there is some inertial quality to MCs' stands, but this is a secondary factor important primarily when an issue shift is linked to a new group's incorporation into a party coalition. Some aspects of the issue evolution model, such as the notion of elite leadership, are vindicated by this study, but others, such as its mechanism of change among elites, are not.

The neo-Darwinian view of politicians as tied to their earliest stands misrepresents the issue evolution process, making it seem more rare than it actually is. If a biologist can help us here, it is Lamarck rather than Darwin. The former held that individual organisms could evolve and pass on these changes to their offspring. In biology, Lamarck's work has been justly supplanted by neo-Darwinian approaches. Yet for politics a Lamarckian view allowing for "evolution" during politicians' careers is more realistic than a Darwinian one. As Steven Jay Gould (1997, 50) noted:

Cultural change manifestly operates on the radically different substrate of Lamarckian inheritance, or the passage of acquired characteristics to subsequent generations. Whatever we invent in our lifetimes we can pass on to our children by our writing and teaching. Evolutionists have long understood that Darwinism cannot operate effectively in systems of Lamarckian inheritance, for Lamarckian change has such a clear direction, and permits evolution to proceed so rapidly, that the much slower process of natural selection shrinks to insignificance before the Lamarckian juggernaut.

Ironically, Carmines and Stimson (1989, 18) cite Gould's neo-Darwinian punctuated equilibrium model –which predicts change via replacement – while Gould held that Lamarck better explains social change. Contrary to many scholars' assumptions that careerism requires politicians to be consistent, much evidence suggests that judicious reversals may further political careers. The abilities both to shape the position of one's party and to adapt to it are hallmarks of a successful politician.

Although flexibility is necessary in politics, politicians seem to believe that they will profit most if they can adjust their positions without being seen to have done so. In literature we see this tendency in extreme form. In Orwell's *1984* the states of Oceania, Eastasia, and Eurasia are always warring in an ever-changing series of two-against-one permutations. Yet in their internal propaganda the "allies" of the moment always claim eternal friendship with each other and permanent hostility toward their current foe.

Similarly, politicians are generally loath to admit to the many "evolutions" their views have undergone. Inconsistency might indeed make them seem unreliable to voters, as scholars suggest. Thus both Al Gore and George W. Bush initially denied (Bush more successfully) that their positions on abortion had changed, despite evidence to the contrary. Yet these politicians' desire to maintain reputations for constancy was not compelling enough to make them actually remain consistent!

In politics, the *appearance* of consistency is an asset. No one wants to be seen as a flip-flopper. Yet the ability to "evolve" when circumstances dictate is a necessity. It is unlikely that had George H. W. Bush remained pro-choice, pro-gun control, and a critic of what he called "voodoo economics" he could have been Reagan's vice president or successor. Similarly, had Al Gore remained friendlier with the NRA than the National Abortion Rights League it is doubtful that he could have become Bill Clinton's running mate or the Democrats' presidential nominee. The more recent selection of Joe Biden as Barack Obama's running mate would also have been much less likely had Biden persisted in his early opposition to *Roe v. Wade*. Beyond these high-profile figures many less celebrated politicians made less-well publicized retreats from one position or another, avoiding primary challengers and securing their positions by adapting to their party's new program.

The evidence suggests both that politicians often do not view themselves as "locked into" issue positions, and that their assessment is well founded. A "foolish consistency" may not only be the "hobgoblin of little minds," but an impediment to political advancement as well. Since individual politicians comprise party elites, the fact that they can modify their positions without suffering at the ballot box means that the parties to which they belong can do so as well.

# Appendix

## Data Sources and Procedures for Tables, Figures, and Rapoport and Stone Totals

I chose roll calls used to create scores on the various issues for members of Congress based on their policy content and validated by use of principal components factor analysis to insure that scales tapped into one dimension. I took votes from ICPSR Study no. 4, which includes all recorded votes in the House and Senate through the 104th Congress. I took more recent votes from the web sites www.senate.gov and www.house.gov.

I initially selected roll calls in the same substantive policy area based on ICPSR descriptions as well as the summaries in the *Congressional Quarterly Almanacs* and – in ambiguous cases – by consulting the *Congressional Record* itself. After this initial substantive selection I retained only those votes that remained in a factor analysis in which only one component had an eigenvalue with a value of one or greater, and in which each roll call loaded at 0.6 or more on the dominant factor.

This is a fairly stringent standard that resulted in discarding a fair number of votes, but I found that more liberal criteria for determining which roll calls to keep, such as using all those that loaded primarily on the factor that explained the greatest share of the variance, did not meaningfully alter results.

In creating the issue scores for MCs I used both roll calls that were "procedural" and "substantive": a vote on a rule, a relevant amendment, the motion to recommit, and the final passage vote might all be included in a given scale if I viewed them as linked and factor analyses confirmed that they hung together (similarly, the Senate scores include votes on cloture, amendments, and passage). I coded pairs and announcements of support or opposition as equivalent to yeas and nays for purposes of scale construction. I discarded votes with fewer than 10 percent of MCs on the losing side or those in which more than 25 percent failed to vote. Pairs and cases in which a legislator announced a position are coded. Scores ranged from 0 to 1 and represent positions on a cumulated rating scale.

I list and briefly describe all the roll calls I used below. These summaries are adapted from the ICPSR codebooks and the *Congressional Quarterly Almanacs*.

SOURCES FOR TABLES

**Table 2-1. Interparty Differences in Support for Freer Trade among All Senators and among Democrats and Republicans from the Same States: Key Votes, 79th through 109th Congresses (1945–2006)**

1945 H.R. 3240 June 19, 1945 Amendment to extension of recipro-cal trade striking a provision permitting increase or decrease by more than 50 percent of any rate of duty existing on January 1, 1945.

1949 H.R. 1211 September 15, 1949 Amendment extending the president's authority under the Trade Agreements Extension Act for two years and requiring that the tariff commission report show only those articles on which peril points have been exceeded.

1955 H.R. 1 May 4, 1955 Amendment to reciprocal trade exten-sion eliminating provisions requiring immediate publication of tariff commission findings, providing for the use of an "escape clause" if imports threatened domestic industry, and permitting one segment of an industry to seek protection against injury from imports.

1958 H.R. 12591 July 22, 1958 Amendment to Trade Agreements Act to delete section providing that a presidential veto of Tariff Commission escape-clause findings shall not take effect unless it is approved within 90 days by a majority vote in both houses of Congress.

1962 H.R. 11970 September 18, 1962 Amendment to Trade Expansion Act restoring "peril point" procedure of existing trade law.

1974 H.R. 10710 December 13, 1974 Cloture motion on Trade Reform Act giving president powers to negotiate agreements.

1985 H.R. 1562 November 13, 1985 Passage of bill limiting textile and apparel imports.

1987 H.R. 3 July 21, 1987 Passage of omnibus trade bill authorizing negotiations to reduce tariff and mandating retaliation against countries that maintain unfair trade practices.

1988 H.R. 3 June 8, 1988 Override of president's veto of omnibus Trade and Competitiveness Act.

1991 H.R. 2212 July 23, 1991 Passage of Conditional Most-Favored Nation status for China prohibiting the president from granting this status unless he certifies China has made improvements in human rights, in respecting intellectual property, and in removing trade barriers and limiting arms exports.

1993 H.R. 3450 November 20, 1993 Passage of North American Free Trade Agreement Implementation Act.

1994 H.R. 5110 December 1, 1994 Motion to waive budget act to circumvent point of order against bill implementing the Uruguay Round of the GATT creating the World Trade Organization.

1997 S. 1269 November 4, 1997 Cloture motion on bill granting president "fast-track authority" to negotiate trade agreements.

2002 H.R. 3009 May 23, 2002 Passage of bill to extend the Andean Trade Preference Act, which includes Trade Promotion Authority for the president.

2005 S. 1307 June 30, 2005 A bill to implement the Dominican Republic–Central America–United States Free Trade Agreement.

**Table 2-2. Percentage of Long-Serving Representatives (Stayers) and the Rest of the House Voting for Freer Trade on Two Trade Policy Votes with Similar Cutpoints: 1962 and 1973**

*87th Congress*

Var. 175 (ICPSR Study No. 4) H.R. 11970 June 28, 1962 Motion to recommit Trade Expansion Act.

*93rd Congress*

Var. 482 (ICPSR Study No. 4) H. Res. 657 December 10, 1973 Rule for consideration of H.R. 10710, Trade Reform Act of 1973.

Table 3-1 Percentage of Long-Serving Representatives (Stayers) and the Rest of the House Voting Pro-Choice on Two Abortion Votes with Similar Cutpoints: 1974 and 1994

*93rd Congress*

> Var. 793 (ICPSR Study No. 4) H.R. 15580 June 27, 1974 Amendment prohibiting use of funds for abortions, abortion referral services, or abortifacient drugs or devices.

*103rd Congress*

> Var. 118 (ICPSR Study No. 4) H.R. 670 March 25, 1993 Motion to kill motion to reconsider passage of bill funding family planning and removing restrictions on discussion of abortion (the gag rule) at federally funded clinics.

Table 3-2. OLS Regression Models: Support for Gun Control among Representatives: All MCs and Those Serving in Both the 90th and 103rd Congresses (1967–1968 and 1993–1994)

90th Congress

> Var. 405 H.R. 17735 July 24, 1968 Amendment to provide for a better control of interstate traffic in firearms by excluding rife shotgun and 22-caliber rim fire ammunition from the provisions of the bill.
> Var. 407 H.R. 17735 July 24, 1968 Amendment exempting people, organizations, and institutions engaged in competition and military training from provisions of the bill under certain circumstances.
> Var. 408 H.R. 17735 July 24, 1968 Passage of the State Firearms Control Assistance Act.
> Var. 483 H.R. 17735 October 10, 1968 Adoption of the conference report on the State Firearms Control Assistance Act.

*103rd Congress*

> Var. 567 H.R. 1025 November 10, 1993 Rule to provide for House floor consideration of the "Brady Bill" requiring a five-business-day waiting period before an individual could purchase a handgun to allow local officials to conduct a background check.

Var. 569 H.R. 1025 November 10, 1993 Amendment to sunset the five-day waiting period five years after enactment.

Var. 570 H.R. 1025 November 10, 1993 Amendment to preempt any state or local law requiring waiting periods for the purchase of handguns once a national instant check system is instituted.

Var. 572 H.R. 1025. November 10, 1993 Amendment to sunset the five-day waiting period five years after enactment.

Var. 573 H.R.1025 November 10, 1993 Motion to recommit the bill to the Judiciary Committee with instructions to report it back with an amendment to eliminate the unfunded mandates to the states in the bill by either authorizing additional funds for personal background checks or removing the mandate for personal background checks.

Var. 574 H.R. 1025 November 10, 1993 Passage of the Brady Bill.

Var. 616 H.R.1025 November 22, 1993 Agreeing to a conference with the Senate on the Brady Bill.

Var. 780 H.R. 4296 May 5, 1994 Rule to provide for House floor consideration of the bill to ban the manufacture and possession of 19 types of semiautomatic weapons and high-capacity ammunition clips.

Var. 781 H.R. 4296 May 5, 1994 Passage of the bill to ban the manufacture and possession of 19 types of semiautomatic weapons and high-capacity ammunition clips.

## Table 3-3. Percentage of Long-Serving Representatives (Stayers) and the Rest of the House on Supporting Gun Control on Two Gun Control Votes with Similar Cutpoints: 1968 and 1988

### 90th Congress

Var. 407 H.R. 17735 July 24, 1968 Amendment exempting people, organizations, and institutions engaged in competition and military training from provisions of the Gun Control Act under certain circumstances.

### *100th Congress*

Var. 807 H.R. 5210 September 15, 1988 Amendment to omnibus drug bill removing seven-day waiting period for handgun purchases (the Brady Bill).

**Table 4-1. Interparty Difference of Means on Civil Rights Measures
Opposed by Business and on Noneconomic Civil Rights Issues
Compared, House of Representatives, Selected Congresses, 1965–1992**

*89th Congress*

*Measures Opposed by Business:*

> Var. 302 H.R. 14765 August 9, 1966 Motion to recommit the Civil
> Rights Act of 1966 to the Judiciary Committee with instructions to
> delete Title IV, the open housing title.
> (Business supported this motion because it opposed open housing
> regulation.)

*Noneconomic Civil Rights Measures:*

> Var. 92 H.R. 14765 July 6, 1965 Rule providing for 10 hours of debate
> on H.R. 6400, the Voting Rights Act of 1965.
> Var. 96 H.R. 6400 July 9, 1965 Motion to recommit the Voting Right
> Act with instructions to substitute the text of H.R. 7896 prohibiting
> the denial to any person of the right to register or to vote because of
> his failure to pay a poll tax or any other such tax, for the language
> of the committee amendment.
> Var. 97 H.R. 6400 July 9, 1965 Passage of the Voting Rights
> Act.
> Var. 117 S. 1564 August 3, 1965 Motion Agreeing to the conference
> report S. 1564, the Voting Rights Act.
> Var. 185 H.R. 4644 September 29, 1965 Motion to recommit the D.C.
> Home Rule Bill.
> Var. 186 H.R. 4644 September 29, 1965 Passage of the D.C. Home
> Rule Bill.
> Var. 303 H.R. 14765 August 9, 1966 Passage of the Civil Rights Act
> of 1966.

*90th Congress*

*Measures Opposed by Business:*

> Var. 304 H. Res. 1100 April 10, 1968 Previous question motion on
> resolution adding Senate amendment banning discrimination in
> sale or rental of housing to Civil Rights/Anti-Riot bill.
> Var. 305 H. Res. 1100 April 10, 1968 Adding Senate amendment ban-
> ning discrimination in housing to Civil Rights/Anti-Riot Bill.

*Noneconomic Civil Rights Issues:*

Var. 22 H. Res. 278 March 1, 1967 Previous question motion seating Adam Clayton Powell. Resolution recommends that Powell be seated, censured, and made to pay back $40,000 of the money he improperly expended and that his seniority commence from the date of his seating in the 90th Congress.

Var. 23. H. Res. 278 March 1, 1967 Previous question motion on H. Res. 278 together with the Curtis Amendment, which excludes Powell from the 90th Congress and declares his seat vacant.

Var. 24 H. Res. 278 March 1, 1967 Amendment excluding Powell from the 90th Congress and declaring his seat vacant.

Var. 123 H.R. 2516 August 16, 1967 Passage of a bill establishing penalties for interference with civil rights.

Var. 467 H.R. 18037 October 3, 1968 Motion to concur with Senate amendment limiting antibusing provisions to elementary schools.

Var. 469 H.R. 18037 October 3, 1968 Motion that the House agree with Senate amendment modifying antibusing provisions in the bill.

### 92nd Congress

*Measures Opposed by Business:*

Var. 183 H.R. 1746 September 16, 1971 Amendment providing court enforcement powers for the EEOC in lieu of "cease and desist authority."

Var. 184 H.R. 1746 September 16, 1971 Motion to agree to previous amendment.

*Noneconomic Civil Rights Measures:*

Var. 41 H.R. 7016 April 7, 1971 Amendment striking out section banning forced busing.

Var. 368 S. 659 March 8, 1972 Tabling motion to instruct conferees to insist on antibusing amendments to omnibus education amendments of 1972.

Var. 369 S. 659 March 8, 1972 Motion to instruct conferees to insist on the House antibusing amendments.

Var. 423 S. 659 May 11, 1972 Motion to table motion to instruct House conferees to insist on antibusing provisions.

Var. 569 H.R. 13915 August 17, 1972 Amendment increasing authorization by $1.5 billion annually for Title I, assistance for educationally deprived students attending schools enrolling high concentrations of students from low-income families.

Var. 570 H.R. 13915 August 17, 1972 Amendment striking out language of the subsequent amendment (Var. 571) that authorizes busing other than busing to the school.

Var. 571 H.R. 13915 August 17, 1972 Amendment forbidding busing and allowing court orders and school segregation plans already in effect under Title VI of the Civil Rights Act to be reopened and modified to comply with the provisions of this bill.

Var. 572 H.R. 13915 August 17, 1972 Amendment specifying that provisions of the bill comply with Amendment XIV of the Constitution.

Var. 574 H.R. 13915 August 17, 1972 Amendment specifying that "nothing in this act is intended to be inconsistent with, or violative of any provision of the Constitution."

Var. 586 H.R. 13915 August 17, 1972 Amendment qualifying the neighborhood as the appropriate bases for determining school assignments.

### 96th Congress

*Measures Opposed by Business:*

Var. 963 H.R. 5200 June 11, 1980 Motion to agree to a substitute for an amendment to the Fair Housing bill that permits appraisers to take into consideration factors other than race, color, religion, national origin, sex, or handicap. The original amendment permitted appraisers to consider all factors shown by documentation to be relevant.

Var. 964 H.R. 5200 June 11, 1980 Amendment modifying an amendment in order to provide for adjudication of fair housing cases by Justice Department–appointed administrative law judges to require the secretary of housing and urban development to certify that conciliation has been attempted and failed prior to such hearing and directing the secretary to refer all land use control cases to the attorney general.

Var. 967 H.R. 5200 June 12, 1980 Motion to recommit the Fair Housing bill to the Judiciary Committee with instructions to transfer the adjudication of fair housing cases from HUD administrative law judges to the district court system.

*Noneconomic Civil Rights Issues:*

Var. 190 H.R. 2641 June 8, 1979 Amendment to the Civil Rights Commission authorization reducing the ceiling from $14,000,000 to $11,372,000.

Var. 212 H.R. 2444 June 12, 1979 Amendment deleting the additional authority given the assistant secretary for civil rights to collect data required to ensure compliance with civil rights laws, to hire and supervise employees, and to contract out for services pursuant to compliance and enforcement functions.

Var. 325 S. 210 July 17, 1979 Motion instructing House conferees to insist on language in stating that no individual should be denied educational opportunities by rules that utilize any ratio or other numerical requirement related to race, creed, color, national origin, or sex.

Var. 349 H.J. Res. 74 July 24, 1979 To discharge the Judiciary Committee from further consideration of an antibusing constitutional amendment.

Var. 350 H.J. Res. 74 July 24, 1979 Motion to order previous question on antibusing constitutional amendment.

Var. 371 H. Res. 391 July 30, 1979 Motion tabling resolution expelling Rep. Charles Diggs, Jr.

Var. 588 H.R. 5461 November 13, 1979 Motion to suspend the rules and pass the bill designating Martin Luther King, Jr.'s birthday a legal public holiday.

Var. 634 H.R. 5461 December 5, 1979 Amendment to Martin Luther King, Jr. Holiday Bill designating the third Monday in January rather than January 15 as the legal holiday.

Var. 635 H.R. 5461 December 5, 1979 Motion to agree to a substitute that designates the third Sunday in January each year as the holiday to celebrate Martin Luther King, Jr.'s birthday.

Var. 636 December 5, 1979. Motion to have the Committee of the Whole rise during debate on the Martin Luther King Jr. holiday.

Var. 1092 H.R. 7583 August 19, 1980 To sustain ruling of the chair regarding the Ashbrook Amendment as legislation on an appropriation bill.

## *101st Congress*

*Measures Opposed by Business:*

Var. 93 H.R. 1278 June 15, 1989 Amendment to Savings and Loan Restructuring to require federal regulatory agencies to disclose ratings and evaluations given to banks and thrifts and to disclose the number of applications received and approved by categories of race, income, and gender.

Var. 665 H.R. 4000 August 2, 1990 Previous question motion on rule for the Civil Rights Act of 1990.

Var. 666 August 2, 1990 Adoption of the rule to provide for consideration of H.R. 4000, the Civil Rights Act of 1990.

Var. 670 H.R. 4000 August 3, 1990 Amendment to provide a different definition of the proof of "business necessity" required from an employer to justify employment practices having a disparate impact on women and minorities.

Var. 671 H.R. 4000 August 3, 1990 Passage of the Civil Rights Act of 1990.

Var. 831 S. 2104 October 17, 1990 Adoption of conference report on Civil Rights Act.

*Noneconomic Civil Rights Measures:*

Var. 35 H.R. 1385 April 17, 1989 Passage of the bill making permanent the Martin Luther King, Jr. Federal Holiday Commission and authorizing annual funds for activities to honor Dr. King on the anniversary of his birth.

Var. 354 H.R. 3532 November 15, 1989 Passage of bill extending the life of the Civil Rights Commission.

Var. 780 H.R. 5269 October 5, 1990 Amendment to Comprehensive Crime Control Act to modify provisions relating to racially discriminatory death penalty sentences.

Var. 781 H.R. 5269 October 5, 1990 Amendment to strike provisions that bar execution of prisoners who show that racial discrimination was a factor in their sentence.

### *102nd Congress*

Var. 135 H.R. 1 June 4, 1991 Motion to order the previous question on the rule for consideration on the rule for the Civil Rights Act of 1991.

Var. 136 H.R. 1 June 4, 1991 Adoption of the rule to provide for House floor consideration of Civil Rights Act of 1991.

Var. 138 H.R. 1 June 4, 1991 Substitute for administration's civil rights bill. The substitute would remove compensatory and punitive damages for job discrimination based on sex, religion, or disability but allow up to $150,000 for cases involving harassment; define business necessity as a practice that has a manifest relationship to the employment or that serves a legitimate employment goal; allow intentional discrimination when it is only a contributing factor; allow challenges to consent decrees; ban the use of race-based adjustments to hiring-test scores; and make other changes.

Var. 140 H.R. 1 June 5, 1991 Amendment to cap punitive damages at $150,000 for victims of intentional job discrimination or the amount of compensatory damages, whichever is greater; define "business necessity" as a practice that must bear a significant manifest relationship to the requirements for effective job performance; ban the use of race-based adjustments to hiring-test scores; include a provision explicitly prohibiting the use of quotas; and for other purposes.

Var. 141 H.R. 1 June 5, 1991 Passage of the bill to reverse or modify a series of Supreme Court rulings that narrowed the reach and remedies of job discrimination laws and to authorize compensatory and punitive damages for victims of discrimination.

*Noneconomic Civil Rights Measures:*

Var. 193 H.R. 2508 June 20, 1991 Amendment to the Foreign Aid Authorization prohibiting aid to the South African Communist Party and to any organization affiliated with a communist party and requiring the president to ensure that aid recipients have democratic processes in place for selecting leaders and do not have a record of human rights abuses.

Var. 332 H.R. 3371 October 22, 1991 Amendment to omnibus crime bill that prohibits the consideration of race in determining a defendant's sentence and the use of statistics to invalidate a sentence.

Var. 334 H.R. 3371 October 22, 1991 Amendment to Crime Bill to strike the provisions that allow death row prisoners to raise certain race-bias claims in habeas corpus appeals.

Var. 488 H.R. 3844 February 27, 1992 Passage of the bill to suspend for six months the repatriation of Haitians who were in the custody of the United States before February 5, 1992; require the administration to report on the fate of repatriated Haitians; provide 2,000 refugee admission slots to Haitians; and prohibit the admission to the United States of any person involved in the September 1991 coup in Haiti.

Var. 515 H.R. 3553 March 26, 1992 Amendment to Higher Education Act to express the sense of Congress that institutions of higher learning should not discriminate based on race in admissions, particularly with regard to Asian Americans.

**Table 4-2. Comparison of the Positions of Long-Serving Representatives (Stayers) and the Rest of the House on Two Civil Rights Votes with Similar Cutpoints: 1964 and 1970**

*88th Congress*

Var. 138 (ICPSR Study No. 4) H.R. 7152 February 10, 1964 Passage of the Civil Rights Act.

*91st Congress*

Var. 284 (ICPSR Study No. 4) H.R. 4249 June 17, 1970 Agreeing to Senate amendments to Voting Rights Act Extension.

**Table 5-1 Percentage of Long-Serving Senators (Stayers) and the Rest of the Senate Supporting Defense Spending on Two Votes with Similar Cutpoints: 1959 and 1968**

*86th Congress*

Var. 32 (ICPSR Study No. 4) H.R. 7454 July 13, 1959 Amendment to Defense Department appropriation to increase army procurement funds and designate $453 million of the total for modernizing army combat equipment.

*90th Congress*

Var. 405 (ICPSR Study No. 4) S. 3293 April 18, 1968 Amendment to Military Procurement Authorization limiting aggregate authorizations for research and development to $7.366 billion.

**Table 5-2. Party and Local Interests as Predictors of Senators' Votes on Defense, Selected Congresses, 86th through 101st Congresses (1959–1990), OLS Models**

*86th Congress*

Var. 32 H.R. 7454 July 13, 1959 Amendment to Defense Department Appropriation to increase army procurement funds and designate $453 million of the total for modernizing army combat equipment.

## *92nd Congress*

Var. 92 H.R. 6531 June 16, 1971 Amendment barring use of funds to support U.S. forces in Indochina after June 1, 1972, if all American POWs are released at least 60 days prior to that date.

Var. 93 H.R. 6531 June 16, 1971 Amendment barring use of funds to support U.S. troops in Indochina after December 31, 1971.

Var. 148 H.R. 9388 July 20, 1971 Amendment to Authorization for the Atomic Energy Commission canceling the planned Cannikin underground nuclear test to be conducted at Amchitka, Alaska.

Var. 149 H.R. 9388 July 20, 1971 Amendment providing that the detonation of the Cannikin underground nuclear test in Alaska be delayed until the end of fiscal 1972, or until the completion of the SALT talks.

Var. 216 H.R. 8687 September 22, 1971 Amendment to Military Procurement Authorizations, barring use of funds for Navy communication project until an environmental impact statement has been made.

Var. 218 H.R. 8687 September 23, 1971 Amendment providing for the president's submittal of an alternative Defense Department budget of not to exceed $60 billion for fiscal 1973.

Var. 219 H.R. 8687 September 24, 1971 Amendment calling for placement in a special Treasury Department account of funds for MIRV to be used only on the joint decision of the president and Congress that U.S. testing and deployment is necessary.

Var. 220 H.R. 8687 September 28, 1971 Amendment calling for a study by the Senate and House Committees on Armed Services of the Defense Department budget for the next five fiscal years.

Var. 222 H.R. 8687 September 29, 1971 Amendment reducing authorizations for research and development on the Navy's communications system, Project Sanguine.

Var. 223 H.R. 8687 September 29, 1971 Amendment deleting authorization for F-14 aircraft program.

Var. 225 H.R. 8687 September 30, 1971 Amendment reducing funds for research and development of a prototype of the Army XM-803 tank.

Var. 235 H.R. 8687 October 5, 1971 Amendment providing for the cessation of bombing and other air attacks in Indochina.

Var. 237 H.R. 8687 October 5, 1971 Amendment authorizing funds for research and development to improve the *Poseidon* submarine-launched ballistic missile system.

Var. 255 H.R. 9910 October 28, 1971 Motion to table motion to reconsider amendment striking call for withdrawal of all U.S. military forces from Indochina.

Var. 256 H.R. 9910 October 28, 1971 Motion to reconsider amendment striking call for withdrawal of all U.S. military forces from Indochina.

Var. 373 H.R. 11731 November 23, 1971 Amendment setting ceiling on expenses of the CIA, NSA, DIA, and military intelligence activities.

Var. 724 H.R. 15495 July 26, 1972 Amendment to military procurement authorization striking $299 million for procurement of CVN-70 nuclear attack aircraft carrier.

Var. 728 H.R. 15495 July 27, 1972 Amendment deleting approximately $500 million for acceleration of development and procurement of Navy Trident Missile–firing submarine.

Var. 732 H.R. 15495 August 1, 1972 Amendment limiting to $77,630,000.000 funds for new obligational authority for DOD.

Var. 89 H.R. October 2, 1972 Amendment barring use of funds for bombing of Vietnam, Laos, and Cambodia and reducing by $2 billion appropriations as a result.

Var. 893 H.R. 16593 October 2, 1972 Amendment reducing by $98.3 million funds for Air Force testing and evaluation of aircraft.

Var. 894 H.R. 16593 October 2, 1972 Amendment reducing defense spending by 5 percent.

## 97th Congress

Var. 89 S. 694 April, 7, 1981 Motion to table amendment to supplemental defense authorizations prohibiting use of funds for reactivation of the *U.S.S. New Jersey*.

Var. 118 S. Con. Res. 19 May 12, 1981 Amendment to budget resolution to reduce defense spending and to increase funding for education and income security progress.

Var. 123 S. 815 May 13, 1981 Motion to table amendment requiring approval by both houses of Congress with regard to the basing mode for the MX missile

Var. 127 S. 815 May 14, 1981 Motion to table amendment reducing the amount of funds that may be expended for operations and maintenance.

Var. 138 H.R. 3512 May 21, 1981 Amendment adding $20 million for a binary chemical munitions production facility and to reduce the operation and maintenance appropriation for the Army by $20 million.

Var. 455 H.R. 4995 December 3, 1981 Amendment deleting all funding for any interim program for the basing or deployment of the MX missile.

Var. 457 H.R. 4995 December 3, 1981 Motion to table amendment providing that it is the sense of the Congress that the United States should not take any action in connection with its defense programs that would undercut existing strategic arms limitation agreements, unless the president determines (1) that the USSR is no longer exercising the same restraint, or (2) that such action would be vital to the national security interest of the United States.

Var. 458 H.R. 4995 December 3, 1981 Amendment deleting funding for the B1-B bomber aircraft program and to increase funding for other programs.

Var. 618 S. 2248 May 13, 1982 Motion to table amendment that deletes authorization of funds for one *Nimitz*-class aircraft carrier and add funds for two light aircraft carriers of the Type 45 class.

Var. 619 S. 2248 May 13, 1982 Motion to table amendment that deletes authorization of funds for one *Nimitz*-class aircraft carrier and add funds for two light aircraft carriers of the Type 45 class.

Var. 620 S. 2248 May 13, 1982 Motion to table amendment to set aside $565 million for research, development, test, and evaluation of a new intercontinental ballistic missile system in lieu of research, development, test, and evaluation of the MX missile system or on basing of the MX missile system.

Var. 632 S. Con. Res. 92 May 19, 1982 Motion to table amendment to budget resolution to reduce defense budget authority by $7.4 billion and new outlays by $1.3 billion and by similar additional reductions in the next two years.

Var. 711 S. 2586 June 30, 1982 Motion to table amendment to military construction authorization prohibiting airfield construction and improvement projects in Honduras.

Var. 877 H.J. Res. 599 September 29, 1982 Motion to table amendment limiting funds for production of MX missiles for which Congress has not approved a basing mode.

Var. 931 H.J. Res. 631 December 16, 1982 Amendment requiring a comprehensive comparative analysis of strategic modernization programs by the secretary of defense.

Var. 947 H.J. Res. 631 December 16, 1982 Motion to table amendment increasing funds for naval operations and maintenance and aircraft depot maintenance activities by eliminating funds for building a nuclear-powered aircraft carrier.

Var. 949 H.J. Res. 631 December 16, 1982 Motion to table amendment to defense appropriations deleting funds for procurement of the Maverick missile.

### *101st Congress*

Var. 158 S. 1352 July 27, 1989 Motion to table amendment to National Defense Authorization Act to limit funds for SDI.

Var. 222 H.R. 3072 September 28, 1989 Amendment to committee amendment to defense appropriations to increase Department of Defense share for funding SDI.

Var. 530 S. 2884 August 2, 1990 Amendment to National Defense Authorization Act to terminate funding for production of the B-2 aircraft.

Var. 531 S. 2884 August 2, 1990 Amendment to National Defense Authorization Act to limit use of funds for the B-2 aircraft.

Var. 541 S. 2884 August 3, 1990 Motion to table amendment to limit amount of 1991 fiscal year funds that may be obligated for the Kinetic Energy ASAT Program.

Var. 547 S. 2884 August 4, 1990 Motion to table amendment reducing funding for SDI.

Var. 548 S. 2884 August 4, 1990 Motion to table amendment to authorize the transfer of $400 million of funds appropriated for SDI to be appropriated for drug treatment, pregnant women, and veterans health programs.

Var. 594 S. 3189 October 15, 1990 Amendment to Department of Defense appropriations to limit use of funds for the B-2 bomber program.

For defense spending by state see

1960: Table No. 319 *1961 Statistical Abstract of the United States,* p. 238

1970: Table No. 407 *1972 Statistical Abstract of the United States,* p. 254

1982: Table No. 582 *1982 Statistical Abstract of the United States,* p. 354

1990: Table No. 531 1992 *Statistical Abstract of the United States*, p. 338

**Table 5-3. Comparison of Interparty Differences on Mean Support for Defense Spending, Selected Votes among All Senators and Democrats and Republicans from the Same States, 84th through 101st Congresses (1955–1990)**

*84th Congress*

> Var. 68 H.R. 6042 June 20, 1955 Amendment to increase Marine Corps funds by $46 million.
> Var. 182 H.R. 10986 June 26, 1956 Amendment to defense appropriations reducing funds for aircraft and air force operations.
> Var. 183 H.R. 10986 June 26, 1956 Amendment to defense appropriations increasing funds for aircraft and related procurement.
> Other votes same as in Table 5-2

**Table 5-4. Share of Campaign Contributions Given to Republican Congressional Candidates: The Defense Sector in Comparative Perspective**

See www.opensecrets.org.

**Table 5-5. Percentage of Long-Serving Representatives (Stayers) and the Rest of the House Supporting Tax Cuts on Two Votes with Similar Cutpoints: 1963 and 1978**

*88th Congress*

> Var. 78. (ICPSR Study No. 4) H.R. 8363 September 25, 1963 Motion to recommit the Revenue Act with instructions to amend it to prevent the tax reductions from taking effect unless the president specified that spending for fiscal 1964 was not expected to exceed $98 billion.

*95th Congress*

> Var. 1317 (ICPSR Study No. 4) H.R. 13511 August 10, 1978 Motion to recommit to the Ways and Means Committee with instructions to report it back with an amendment that would provide for an

across-the-board cut in individual income taxes of approximately 33 percent to be phased in over the next three years.

SOURCES FOR FIGURES

**Figure 2-1. Interparty Difference in Support for Freer Trade on Key Votes: House of Representatives (Democratic Support – Republican Support), 79th through 109th Congresses (1945–2006)**

All votes taken from CQ Key Votes Series in *Congressional Quarterly Almanacs* for various years. These are all the House votes in the series focused on trade issues. Descriptions are condensed from this source.

H.R. 3240 May 26, 1945 Passage of bill to extend Trade Agreements Act of 1934. (Bill grants president authority for four years to reach agreements with other countries.)

H.R. 1211 February 9, 1949 Trade Agreements Extension Act of 1949: Motion to recommit with instructions to insert "peril points " provision. (The peril point is a level of imports determined by the Tariff Commission to "threaten serious injury" to an industry. The president would have to justify tariff reductions that lead to imports triggering peril point provisions.)

H.R. 1612 February 7, 1951 Trade Agreements Extension Act of 1951. Amendment to restore peril points provision.

H.R. 5894 July 23, 1953 Trade Agreements Act providing for import quotas on petroleum products and for a sliding tariff rate on lead and zinc. Motion to recommit.

H.R. 1 February 18, 1955 Reciprocal Trade Extension. Motion to recommit with instructions to amend bill to require the president to comply with recommendations of the Tariff Commission, except when national security is involved.

H.R. 12591 June 11, 1958 Trade Agreements Extension Act of 1958. Motion to recommit the bill without instructions, i.e., killing the bill.

H.R. 11970 June 28, 1962 Trade Expansion Act of 1962. Motion to recommit the bill with instructions to substitute a one-year extension of the expiring Trade Agreements Act. (The bill extends presidential authority for five years.)

H.R. 18970 November 18, 1970 Trade Act of 1970. Amendment to the rule permitting amendments deleting provisions from the bill. (This was an attempt to prevent protectionist amendments supported by textile and other lobbies.)

H.R. 10710 December 10, 1973 Trade Reform Act. Rule allowing only three amendments, one on an amendment penalizing communist countries restricting immigration, another to delete the section on trade with communist countries, and one deleting the section providing trade preferences to developing nations.

H.R. 5133 December 15, 1982 Auto Domestic Content Requirements. Passage of bill requiring auto companies to use set percentages of U.S. labor and parties in autos they sell in the United States.

H.R. 6023 October 3, 1984 Generalized System of Preferences Renewal Act. Amendment to remove Taiwan, Hong Kong, and South Korea from the list of countries and territories eligible for duty-free treatment under the generalized system of preferences.

H.R. 1562 October 10, 1985 Textile Import Quotas. Passage of bill to establish new quota restrictions on textile imports.

H.R. 1562 August 6, 1986 Textile Import Quotas. Veto override attempt.

H.R. 3 April 29, 1987 Omnibus trade bill. Amendment to require identification of countries with excess trade surpluses with the United States and quantify the extent to which unfair trade practices contribute to that surplus, to mandate negotiations to eliminate those unfair trade practices, and, if negotiations fail or an agreement is not fully implemented, to mandate imposition of tariffs or quotas to yield annual 10 percent reductions in that country's trade surplus.

H.R. 4328 October 10, 1990 Textile Trade Act. Veto override of bill restricting textile and footwear imports.

H. Res. 101 May 23, 1991 Disapproval of Fast-Track Procedures. Adoption of resolution to disapprove the president's request to extend for two more years fast-track procedures that would require legislation implementing trade agreements to be considered within 60 days of introduction under limited debate and with no amendments permitted.

H.R. 3450 November 17, 1993 NAFTA Implementation Act. Passage of the North American Free Trade Agreement.

H.R. 2644 November 4, 1997 Caribbean and Central American Trade. Passage of bill providing Caribbean and Central American countries duty-free trade benefits on certain products similar to those accorded to Mexico under NAFA.

H.R. 975 March 17, 1999 Steel Imports bill. Passage of bill directing the president to take necessary steps, including imposition of quotas, tariff surcharges, or negotiated enforceable voluntary export restraints to ensure that the volume of steel products imported into the United States during any month does not exceed the average of monthly import volumes during the three years preceding July 1997.

H.R. 4444 May 24, 2000 China Trade Resolution. Passage of bill making permanent normal trade relations with China.

H.R. 3005 December 6, 2001 Bipartisan Trade Promotion Authority Act. Passage of the bill to allow expedited negotiation and implementation of trade agreements between the executive branch and foreign countries.

H.R. 3009 July 27, 2002 Trade Promotion Authority. Adoption of the conference report.

H.R. 3045 July 28, 2005 CAFTA. Passage of a bill implementing free trade agreements with Costa Rica, El Salvador, Honduras, Nicaragua, and the Dominican Republic.

**Figure 2-2. Correlation between Representatives' Positions on Key Trade Votes and D1 and D2 NOMINATE Scores, House of Representatives, 79th through 109th Congresses (1945–2006)**

For votes see Figure 2-1. NOMINATE scores are from voteview.com.

**Figure 2-3. Difference of Means between Republican and Democratic Support for Trade Liberalization among Representatives (Republican Mean – Democratic Mean), 87th through 93rd Congresses (1961–1974)**

*87th Congress*

Var. 175 H.R. 11970 June 28, 1962 Motion to recommit Trade Expansion Act.

Var. 176 H.R. 11970 June 28, 1962 Passage of Trade Expansion Act.

Var. 235 H.R. 11970 October 4, 1962 Adoption of conference report for the Trade Expansion Act.

*89th Congress*

Var. 139 H.R. 9042 August 31, 1965 Passage of a bill implementing U.S.-Canada Automotive Products Agreement.

## 91st Congress

Var. 388 H. Res. 1225 November 18, 1970 Previous question motion on Trade Act H.R. 18970.

Var. 389 H. Res. 1225 November 18, 1970 Amendment to rule, by opening the bill for any amendment in the form of a strikeout.

Var. 390 H. Res. 1225 November 18, 1970 Rule for H.R. 18970 Trade Act of 1970.

Var. 391 H.R. 18970 November 19, 1970 Motion to recommit.

Var. 392 H.R. 18970 November 19, 1970 Passage of the Trade Act of 1970.

## 93rd Congress

Var. 482 H. Res. 657 December 10, 1973 Rule for consideration of H.R. 10710, Trade Reform Act of 1973.

Var. 485 H.R. 10710 December 11, 1973 Passage of Trade Act.

**Figure 3-1. Interparty Difference in Support for Abortion Rights (Democratic Support – Republican Support), General Social Survey, 1972–2006**

Data available at http://sda.berkeley.edu/archive.htm.

**Figure 3-2. Difference of Means between Democratic and Republican Support for Abortion Rights among Representatives (Democratic Mean – Republican Mean), 93rd through 103rd Congresses (1973–1994)**

## 93rd Congress

Var. 193 H.R. 7824 June 21, 1973 Amendment to prohibit legal assistance in litigation to compel nontherapeutic abortions contrary to religious beliefs.

Var. 194 H.R. 7824 June 21, 1973 Amendment prohibiting legal assistance in litigation regarding abortion.

Var. 717 H.R. 14449 May 29, 1974 Amendment prohibiting the use of family planning funds for paying medical expenses in abortion cases.

*94th Congress*

> Var. 958 H.R. 14232 June 24, 1976 Amendment prohibiting funds under Title II to be used to pay for abortions or promote or encourage abortions.
>
> Var. 962 H.R. 14232 June 24, 1976 Amendment prohibiting the use of funds in the bill to pay for or promote abortions.
>
> Var. 1102 H.R. 14232 August 10, 1976 Receding from its disagreement from a Senate amendment striking a section that forbids the use of federal funds to pay for, promote, or encourage abortions.

*95th Congress*

> Var. 336 H.R. 7555 June 17, 1977 Amendment to Departments of Labor/HEW appropriations prohibiting the use of funds to perform, encourage, or promote abortions.
>
> Var. 476 H.R. 7555 August 2, 1977 Amendment restricting federal funding for abortions to cases in which pregnancy endangers the mother's life. The original bill also permitted funding when abortion was "medically necessary" or in cases of rape and incest.
>
> Var. 560 H. Res. 780 September 27, 1977 Motion to suspend the rules and instruct conferees to agree to Senate amendment to Departments of Labor/HEW appropriations that prohibit the use of federal funds for abortion except when pregnancy endangers the mother's life, when medically necessary, or in cases of rape or incest.
>
> Var. 605 H.R. 7555 October 12, 1977 Motion that the House recede from amendment to Senate amendment to the Departments of Labor/HEW appropriation limiting use of funds for abortions.
>
> Var. 613 H.R. 7555 October 13, 1977 Motion to concur in Senate amendment allowing the use of funds for abortion in cases of rape or incest or when the pregnancy would endanger the mother's life or could cause "serious health damage" to her or the fetus.
>
> Var. 685 H.R. 7555 November 3, 1977 Motion to concur in Senate amendment on conditions for use of federal funds for abortion.
>
> Var. 691 H.R. 7555 November 29, 1977 Motion to concur in the Senate amendment that authorizes the use of federal funds for abortion when the mother's life would be endangered by the pregnancy or would cause severe and long-lasting physical health damage to the mother, or when the mother is a victim of rape or incest.

Var. 700 H.J. Res. 662 December 6, 1977 Amendment including a clause prohibiting use of funds for abortions except for certain medical procedures for victims of rape or incest that have reported the incident promptly, or when severe and long-lasting physical health damage would result to the mother if the fetus were carried to term.

Var. 706 H.J. Res. 622 December 7, 1977 Concurring in Senate amendment prohibiting the use of the supplemental funds for abortion except when the mother's life would be endangered if the fetus were carried to term, when severe and long-lasting physical health damage would result to mother, and for certain medical procedures for the treatment of victims of rape and incest that have reported the incident promptly.

Var. 711 H.J. Res. 622. December 7, 1977 Concurring in Senate amendment prohibiting the use of the supplemental HEW funds for abortion except when the pregnancy would endangered the mother's life, when severe and long-lasting physical health damage would result to the mother "as determined by two physicians," and for certain medical procedures to treat victims of rape or incest who have reported the incident promptly to a law enforcement agency or a health service agency.

Var. 1097 H.R. 12929 June 13, 1978 Amendment striking language that prohibits use of the authorized funds for abortions, except where the life of the mother would be endangered if the fetus were carried to term.

Var. 1098 H.R. 12929 June 13, 1978 Amendment striking the bill's changes to existing law regarding federal funding of abortions.

Var. 1300 H.R. 13635 August 9, 1978 Amendment prohibiting use of funds to pay for abortions except when the pregnancy would endanger the life of the mother.

Var. 1354 H.R. 12432 September 6, 1978 Amendment to authorization for Civil Rights Commission prohibiting the commission from studying and appraising abortion policies and abortion laws of the federal government or of any other governmental authority.

Var. 1506 H.R. 12929 October 12, 1978 Motion to concur with Senate amendment to Departments of Labor/HHS appropriation that prohibits the use of these funds for abortions except when the pregnancy endangers the life of the mother, or when severe and long-lasting physical health damage would occur to the mother, or when the mother is the victim of rape or incest and has reported the incident promptly to a law enforcement agency.

Var. 1526 H.R. 12370 October 13, 1978 Motion to recommit bill with instructions to report it back with an amendment prohibiting the use of these funds for any program providing abortions, abortion counseling, or abortion referral services.

Var. 1531 H.R. 12929 October 14, 1978 Concurring with a Senate amendment prohibiting the use of funds for abortion except when the life of the other would be otherwise endangered, or when severe and long-lasting physical health damage would occur if pregnancy was completed, or when the mother is a victim of rape or incest and has promptly reported the incident to a law enforcement agency.

## 96th Congress

Var. 280 H.R. 4389 June 27, 1979 Amendment substituting anti-abortion language in current law for the language in the bill.

Var. 298 H.R. 2444 July 11, 1979 Amendment prohibiting the use of facilities under the control of the proposed Department of Education by any institution of higher education that uses mandatory student fees to pay for the performance of abortions except where the life of the mother would be endangered if the fetus were carried to term.

Var. 321 H.R. 4580 July 17, 1979 Amendment to D.C. appropriations prohibiting the denial of funds appropriated in the bill for the medical expenses necessary to save the life of a pregnant woman entitled to receive medical benefits.

Var. 322. H.R. 4580 July 17, 1979 Amendment prohibiting the use of funds provided by the federal payment to perform abortions.

Var. 497 H.J. Res. 413 October 9, 1979 Amendment to Departments of Labor/HEW continuing appropriations prohibiting use of federal funds for abortions except where the mother's life is endangered or in cases of rape or incest.

Var. 560 H.R. 4389 October 30, 1979 Motion to concur with Senate amendment prohibiting federal funding of abortion except where medically necessary or in cases of rape or incest.

Var. 639 H.R. 4962 December 6, 1979 Amendment permitting medical assistance to terminate a pregnancy resulting from rape or incest.

Var. 640 H.R. 4962 December 6, 1979 Amendment prohibiting funding for medical assistance for abortions except when the life of the mother is endangered.

Var. 643 H.R. 4962 December 11, 1979 Amendment prohibiting the use of funds to perform abortions except where the life of the mother would be endangered if the fetus were carried to term.

Var. 1099 H.R. 7583 August 20, 1980 Amendment prohibiting use of funds to pay for abortions or administrative expenses of any health plan under the Federal Employees Health Benefit Program that provides benefits for abortions under the expiration of existing contracts.

Var. 1134 H.R. 8061 September 3, 1980 Amendment to D.C. appropriations prohibiting use of any of these funds to pay for abortions.

## 97th Congress

Var. 47 H.R. 3512 May 13, 1981 Amendment prohibiting the use of funds to pay for an abortion or the administrative expenses in connection with any federal employee health plan that provides any benefits or coverage for abortions under such negotiated plan after the last day of contracts currently in force.

Var. 88 H.R. 3480 June 18, 1981 Amendment prohibiting the provision of legal advice respecting a client's rights and responsibilities regarding abortion.

Var. 181 H.R. 4121 July 30, 1981 Amendment to Treasury and Postal Service appropriations prohibiting the use of funds, except where the life of the mother is endangered, to pay for an abortion or the administrative expenses connected with any health plan under the Federal Employees Health Benefits Program that covers abortion.

Var. 721 H.R. 6457 September 30, 1982 Amendment to Public Health Service Act restricting fetal and infant research by NIH before or after an induced abortion.

## 98th Congress

Var. 178 H. Res. 222. June 8, 1983 Rule for consideration of H.R. 3191, the appropriation for the Treasury Department, U.S. Postal Service, the Executive Office of the President, and certain independent agencies.

Var. 180 H.R. 3191 June 8, 1983 Amendment prohibiting the use of health benefit funds to pay for abortions unless the life of the mother is endangered.

Var. 344 H.R. 3913 September 22, 1983 Amendment to the Departments of Labor, HHS, and Education and related agencies appropriation prohibiting use of funds to perform abortions.

Var. 406 H.R. 4139 October 27, 1983 Motion that the Committee of the Whole Rise and report the bill back to the House with sundry amendments, with the recommendation that the amendments be agreed to and that the bill as amended to pass.

Var. 755 H.R. 5798 June 27, 1984 Amendment to the appropriations bill for the Treasury Department, U.S. Postal Service, Executive Office of the President, and certain independent agencies, for the fiscal year ending September 30, 1985, striking language prohibiting the use of federal health plan benefits to pay for abortions.

### 99th Congress

Var. 207 H.R. 1555 July 10, 1985 Amendment restricting use of funds by foreign nongovernmental organizations that perform or promote abortion.

Var. 226 H.R. 2965 July 17, 1985 Motion to rise and report the bill back to House blocking consideration of amendment that prohibits any Legal Services Corporation funds to be used for litigation with respect to abortion.

Var. 257 H.R. 3067 July 30, 1986 Amendment to D.C. appropriations eliminating the use of federal or local funds for abortions in the District of Columbia except in cases of rape, incest, or danger to the mother.

Var. 658 H.R. 5161 July 17, 1986 Motion to rise from the Committee of the Whole and report bill, the failure of which allowed for consideration of an amendment to the Justice Department Appropriations prohibiting the use of funds to pay for an abortion or to provide facilities for the performance of an abortion, except where the life of the mother would be endangered if the foetus were carried to term.

### 100th Congress

Var. 220 H.R. 2713 June 26, 1987 D.C. Appropriations prohibiting use of funds to pay for any abortions.

Var. 694 H.R. 4776 June 28, 1988 Amending D.C. appropriations to bar the use of funds to perform abortions under any circumstances.

Var. 795 H.R. 4783 September 9, 1988 Vote to persist in disagreement with Senate amendment to Departments of Labor/HHS appropriation permitting the use of Medicaid funds for abortions when pregnancy results from cases of rape or incest.

Var. 845 H.R. 4776 September 28, 1988 Motion to recommit D.C. appropriations demanding language to ban the use of funds for abortions except in cases where the life of the mother would be at risk.

## *101st Congress*

Var. 106 H.R. 2655 June 22, 1989 Amendment to foreign aid authorization permitting the prohibition concerning abortion to the extent that it is consistent with U.S. law.

Var. 205 H.R. 3026 August 2, 1989 Amendment to D.C. appropriations prohibiting the use of any of the district's funds toward providing abortions.

Var. 277 H.R. 2990 October 11, 1989 Amendment to Departments of Labor/HHS appropriations concurring with Senate amendments to permit funds to pay for abortion in cases of rape or incest.

Var. 278 H.R. 2990 October 11, 1989 Amendment.

Var. 568 H.R. 5114 June 27, 1990 Amendment to foreign operations appropriations retaining $1.5 million for family planning in Romania, but striking from the bill language that earmarks funds for the International Planned Parenthood Federation of London and the UN Population Fund.

Var. 637 H.R. 5311 July 26, 1990 Passage of D.C. appropriations.

Var. 702 H.R. 4739 September 18, 1990 Amendment of defense authorization to provide servicemen and their dependents stationed overseas with reproductive health services.

Var. 847 H.R. 5311 October 20, 1990 Adoption of conference report on D.C. appropriations.

Var. 876 H.R. 5311 October 25, 1990 Adoption of conference report on D.C. appropriations.

## *102nd Congress*

Var. 119 H.R. 2100 May 22, 1991 Amendment to defense authorization to provide servicemen and their dependents stationed overseas with reproductive health services including privately paid abortions at military hospitals.

Var. 158 H.R. 2508 June 12, 1991 Amendment to foreign aid authorization to preserve the $20 million in funding for the United Nations Population Fund (UNFPA), which supports family-planning programs in many countries. The previous version would have removed the funding on the grounds that the UNFPA operates in China, which uses forced abortions and involuntary sterilization as means of family planning.

Var. 159 H.R. 2508 June 12, 1991 Amendment to overturn the administration's Mexico City policy, which prohibits the Agency for International Development from funding foreign nongovernmental organizations that provide abortions or abortion counseling.

Var. 569 H.R. 2039 May 12, 1992 Amendment to Legal Services reauthorization to prohibit agencies that receive funds from the LSC from engaging in litigation or lobbying regarding abortion.

Var. 617 H.R. 5006 June 4, 1992 Amendment to defense authorization to allow military personnel stationed outside the United States to obtain abortions in military hospitals, provided they pay the cost.

Var. 912 S. 3144 October 3, 1992 Passage of the bill to allow military personnel and their dependents to receive abortions at overseas military facilities at their own expense.

### *103rd Congress*

Var. 70 H.R. 4 March 10, 1993 National Institutes of Health reauthorization amendment to add to the safeguards against women having abortions for the purpose of providing tissue for research by requiring that the abortion be performed in accordance with state law and requiring annual reports to Congress on the ethical safeguards for fetal tissue research. The amendment would add several other requirements, including that a woman provide consent for the abortion before the issue of tissue donation is raised and the woman be aware of any interest in tissue research by the doctor or medical risks.

Var. 71 H.R. 4 March 10, 1993 Amendment to add to the safeguards against women having abortions for the purpose of providing tissue for research by requiring that the abortions were performed in accordance with state law and requiring annual reports to Congress on the ethical safeguards for fetal tissue research.

Var. 74 H.R. 4 March 11, 1993 Amendment adopted to add to the safeguards against women having abortions for the purpose of providing tissue for research by requiring that abortions be performed in accordance with state law and requiring annual reports to Congress on the ethical safeguards for fetal tissue research.

Var. 105 H.R. 670 March 24, 1993 Amendment to add to the list of people allowed to advise patients at federally funded family planning facilities those who meet the criteria the secretary of Health and Human Services and those allowed under state law by requiring people giving advice to have a professional degree.

Var. 107 H.R. 670 March 24, 1993 Amendment clarifying that a counselor who objects to abortions would not be required to provide information but that the clinic would arrange for another person or clinic to give counseling.

Var. 114 H.R. 670 March 25, 1993 Amendment clarifying that a counselor who objects to abortions would not be required to provide information but that the clinic would arrange for another person or clinic to give counseling.

Var. 116 H.R. 670. March 25, 1993 Motion to recommit to the House Energy and Commerce Committee the bill with instructions to report it back with an amendment to federally funded Title X clinics to give parents 48 hours' notice before performing an abortion on a minor.

Var. 117 H.R. 670. March 25, 1993 Passage of the bill to authorize $238 million in fiscal 1994 and $270.5 million in fiscal 1995 for Title X family planning programs at clinics. The bill would codify the Clinton administration's lifting of the gag rule that prohibited staff at federally funded clinics from discussing abortion.

Var. 118 HR 670 March 25, 1993 Motion to table the motion to reconsider the vote by which the House passed the bill to authorize $238 million in fiscal 1994 and $270.5 million in fiscal 1995 for Title X family planning programs, codifying lifting the gag rule.

Var. 317 H.R. 2518 June 30, 1993 Amendment to prohibit funds in the Labor, HHS, and Education appropriations from being spent for an abortion except when it is made known that it is a case of rape, incest, or necessity to save the life of the mother.

Var. 319 H.R. 2518 June 30, 1993 Amendment to prohibit funds in the bill from being spent for an abortion except when it is made known that it is a case of rape, incest, or necessity to save the life of the mother.

Var. 588 H.R. 796 November 18, 1993 Rule to provide for House
floor consideration of the bill to establish federal criminal and civil
penalties for persons who use force, the threat of force, or physical
obstruction to block access to abortion clinics.

Var. 590 H.R. 796 November 18, 1993 Amendment to provide that
physical obstruction must be accompanied by force or threats of
force to be a crime, eliminate the punitive damages in the bill, establish standards for a court injunction, and prohibit state attorneys
general from bringing suits under the bill.

Var. 592 H.R. 796 November 18, 1993 Motion to recommit the bill to
the House Judiciary Committee with instructions to report it back
with an amendment eliminating the provisions providing a civil
cause of action by individuals and state attorneys general.

Var. 692 H. Res. 374 March 17, 1994 Adoption of the rule requesting a
conference with the Senate on the amendment to establish criminal
and civil penalties for people who use force, the threat of force, or
physical obstruction to block access to abortion clinics.

Var. 693 H.R. 796 March 17, 1994 Motion to table the House amendment to the Senate bill to establish federal criminal and civil penalties
for people who use force, the threat of force, or physical obstruction
to block access to abortion clinics.

Var. 694 S. 636 March 17, 1994 Motion to commit to the Judiciary
Committee the bill to establish federal criminal and civil penalties
for people who use force, the threat of force, or physical obstruction
to block access to abortion clinics.

Var. 695 S. 636 March 17, 1994 Passage of the bill to establish federal
criminal and civil penalties for people who use force, the threat of
force, or physical obstruction to block access to abortion clinics.

Var. 696 S. 636 March 17, 1994 Motion to insist on the House
amendments and ask for a conference on the bill to establish federal criminal and civil penalties for people who use force, the
threat of force, or physical obstruction to block access to abortion clinics.

Var. 782 H. Res. 417 May 5, 1994 Adoption of the rule to provide for
consideration of the conference report to establish federal criminal
and civil penalties for persons who use force, the threat of force, or
physical obstruction to block access to abortion clinics.

Var. 783 S. 636 May 5, 1994 Motion to recommit the bill to conference with instructions to report the bill back with an amendment
that allows the awarding of reasonable attorneys' fees whether the

prevailing party is the plaintiff or the defendant. The conference report only allows plaintiffs to recoup fees.

Var. 784 S. 636 May 5, 1994 Adoption of the conference report to establish federal criminal and civil penalties for persons who use force, the threat of force, or physical obstruction to block access to abortion clinics.

## Figure 3-3. Effects of Party- and State-Level Public Opinion on Senators' Votes on Abortion, 93rd through 106th Congresses (1973–2000)

For Votes from 93rd to 103rd Congresses see Adams (1997, 736)

### *104th Congress*

Var. 379 H.R. 2020 August 5, 1995 Amendment to Treasury–Post Office appropriations striking provisions to prohibit federal employees or their families from receiving abortion services through federal health insurance policies except when the life of the woman would be endangered.

Var. 380 H.R. 2020 August 7, 1995 Amendment to Treasury–Post Office appropriations to prohibit federal employees or their families from receiving abortion services through their federal health insurance policies except when the life of the mother would be endangered or in cases of rape or incest.

Var. 381 H.R. 2020 August 7, 1995 Amendment to prohibit federal employees or their families from receiving abortion services through their federal health insurance policies except when the life of the woman would be endangered or in cases of rape or incest or where abortion is determined to be medically necessary.

Var. 488 H.R. 2076 September 29, 1995 Motion to table amendment to Departments of Commerce, Justice, and State appropriations to strike provisions in the bill that prohibit the federal funding of abortions for women in prison except for cases of rape or when the life of the mother is endangered.

Var. 549 S. 1357 October 27, 1995 Motion to waive the Budget Act with respect to the point of order against the provisions of the bill applying the Hyde language on abortion to all federal programs. The Hyde language prohibits the federal funding of abortion except in cases of rape or incest or if the woman's life is endangered.

Var. 552 S. 1357 October 27, 1995 Motion to instruct the Senate conferees to retain the ban on the federal funding of abortions except in cases of rape or incest, or if the woman's life is endangered.

Var. 571 H.R. 1868. November 1, 1995 Motion to recede and concur with the House amendment with an amendment to the foreign operations appropriations to strike the House language reinstating the Mexico City Policy, which prohibits family planning assistance to foreign nongovernmental organizations that provide abortion or abortion counseling.

Var. 585 H.R. 1868 November 15, 1995 Motion to table amendment prohibiting family planning assistance to foreign nongovernmental organizations that provide abortion or abortion counseling and ban aide for the UN Population Fund unless it shut down its operations in China.

Var. 603 H.R. 1833 December 7, 1995 Amendment to give doctors greater legal protection for late-term abortions they perform in order to preserve the life of the woman or to avert serious adverse health consequences for the woman.

Var. 605 H.R. 1833 December 7, 1995 Substitute amendment to replace the provisions of the bill with provisions expressing the sense of the Senate that Congress should not criminalize a specific medical procedure and state that nothing in federal law prohibits states from regulating postviability abortions to the extent permitted by the Constitution.

Var. 606 H.R. 1833 December 7, 1995 Passage of the bill to impose penalties on doctors who perform certain late-term abortions, in which the person performing the abortion partially delivers the fetus before completing the abortion.

Var. 658 H.R. 3019 March 14, 1996 Amendment to omnibus appropriations to strike the provisions in the bill that would authorize the president to restore funding for international family planning agencies if he finds that continued denial of the funds would result in more pregnancies leading to a "significant increase in abortions."

Var. 661 H.R. 3019 March 19, 1996 Amendment to District of Columbia appropriations allow the district to use locally raised funds to help poor women obtain abortions.

Var. 662 H.R. 3019 March 19, 1996 Amendment that makes it possible for hospitals that lose their medical accreditation because they refuse to provide abortions or provide training in abortion services to get federal financial assistance.

Var. 906 H.R. 3756 September 11, 1996 Motion to waive Budget Act regarding point of order against amendment prohibiting managed care organizations from prohibiting physicians from informing physicians of all of their health care options.

Var. 907 H.R. 3756 September 11, 1996 Motion to table amendment to permit federal employee health insurance plans to offer abortion services.

Var. 924 H.R. 1833. September 26, 1996 Override of veto of bill banning late-term abortion procedure.

## 105th Congress

Vote 13 H.J. 36 February 25, 1997 Resolution supporting aid to overseas family planning without anti-abortion restrictions.

Vote 69 H.R. 1122 May 15, 1997 Amendment to partial birth abortion ban creating exemption for cases involving the health of the mother.

Vote 70 H.R. 1122 May 15, 1997 Amendment to partial birth abortion ban limiting it to cases of fetal viability.

Vote 71 H.R. 1122 May 20, 1997 Final passage of partial birth abortion ban.

Vote 129 S. 947 June 25, 1997 Amendment to Senate budget reconciliation removing ban on federal funding for abortions.

Vote 167 S. 936 July 10, 1997 Amendment to defense authorization bill allowing for privately funded abortions at overseas U.S. military hospitals.

Vote 190 S. 1023 July 22, 1997 Amendment to Treasury and General Government appropriations restricting the use of federal employee health plan funds to pay for abortions.

Vote 215 S. 1061 September 4, 1997 Amendment to Departments of Labor, HHS, and Education appropriations restricting research using fetal tissue.

Vote 176 S. 2057 June 25, 1998 Amendment to defense authorization bill allowing for privately funded abortions at overseas U.S. military hospitals.

Vote 277 H.R. 1122 September 18, 1998 Veto override of partial birth abortion ban.

Vote 282 S. 1645 September 22, 1998 Cloture motion on Child Custody Protection Act restriction transportation of minors across state lines for abortions if this circumvents state laws requiring parental or judicial involvement in the abortion decision.

### 106th Congress

Vote 148 S. 1059 May 26, 1999 Amendment to defense authorization allowing privately funded abortions in U.S. military hospitals.

Vote 197 S. 1282 July 1, 1999 Treasury Department and independent agencies appropriation banning funding for abortions in federal employee health plans.

Vote 336 S. 1692 October 21, 1999 Move to table amendment to Partial-Birth Abortion Act endorsing *Roe v. Wade*.

Vote 337 S. 1692 October 21, 1999 Amendment endorsing *Roe v.Wade*.

Vote 338 S. 1692 October 21, 1999 Amendment requiring detailed reporting on fetal tissue sales from abortions to medical researchers.

Vote 340 S. 1692 October 21, 1999 Passage of Partial-Birth Abortion Ban Act.

Vote 134 S. 2549 June 20, 2000 Amendment to defense authorization allowing privately funded abortions in U.S. military hospitals.

**Figure 3-4. Correlation between Senators' Positions on Abortion and D1 and D2 NOMINATE Scores, 93rd through 106th Congresses (1973–2000)**

For votes see Figure 3-3. For NOMINATE Scores see voteview.com.

**Figure 3-5. Support for Gun Control in the House of Representatives, 90th Congress (1967–1968) and 103rd Congress (1993–1994)**

See Table 3-2.

**Figure 3-6. Difference of Means between Democratic and Republican Support for Gun Control among Representatives (Democratic Mean – Republican Mean), 90th through 106th Congresses (1967–2000)**

### 90th Congress

Var. 405 H.R. 17735 July 24, 1968 Amendment to provide for a better control of interstate traffic in firearms, by excluding rife shotgun and 22-caliber rim fire ammunition from the provisions of the bill.

Var. 407 H.R. 17735 July 24, 1968 Amendment exempting people, organizations, and institutions engaged in competition and military training from provisions of the bill under certain circumstances.

Var. 408 H.R. 17735 July 24, 1968 Passage of the State Firearms Control Assistance Act.

Var. 483 H.R. 17735 October 10, 1968 Adoption of the conference report on the State Firearms Control Assistance Act.

### 91st Congress

Var. 435 H.R. 14233 December 21, 1970 Passage of a bill to modify ammunition record-keeping requirements.

### 95th Congress

Var. 1081 H.R. 12930 June 7, 1978 Amendment restoring a $4.2 million authorization for law enforcement and investigative activities of the Bureau of Alcohol, Tobacco, and Firearms, and by striking language barring the use of funds for implementation of computerized firearm regulation.

### 97th Congress

Var. 170 H.R. 4121 July 28, 1981 Amendment to Treasury Department and Postal Service appropriation reducing by $5 million funding for salaries and expenses of the Bureau of Alcohol, Tobacco, and Firearms.

### 99th Congress

Var. 513 H.R. 4332 April 9, 1986 Amendment to bill prohibiting interstate handgun sales removing provisions that preempt state and local laws to allow interstate transportation of handguns, to eliminate language that changes the existing law regarding dealer licensing, to keep current record-keeping requirements, and to prohibit silencers.

Var. 514 H.R. 4332 April 9, 1986 Amendment removing provisions that preempt state and local laws to allow transportation of handguns between states.

Var. 515 H.R. 4332 April 10, 1986 Amendment to the bill banning the interstate sale of handguns.

Var. 516 H.R. 4332 April 10, 1986 Move that the Committee of the Whole rise in order to end debate on the bill.

Var. 517 H.R. 4332 April 10, 1986 Amendment permitting interstate sales of rifles and shotguns and interstate transportation of all firearms, lessening record-keeping requirements for firearms transactions, restricting federal agents to one unannounced inspection of a gun dealer's business each year, deregulating ammunition sales, restricting forfeiture of firearms in certain cases, and permitting pardoned convicted felons to own firearms.

Var. 518 H.R. 4332 April 10, 1986 Passage of bill amending the 1968 Gun Control Act.

### 100th Congress

Var. 807 H.R. 5210 September 15, 1988 Amendment to omnibus drug bill removing the provisions that would set up a seven-day waiting period for handgun purchases and directing the Justice Department to develop a proposal for a system to identify people ineligible for handgun ownership, that is, the Brady Bill.

### 102nd Congress

Var. 91 H.R. 7 May 8, 1991 Amendment requiring the Justice Department to establish a national telephone hotline that licensed dealers must contact to determine if the prospective buyer is prohibited by law from purchasing a handgun.

Var. 92 H.R. 7 May 8, 1991 Motion to recommit to the House Judiciary Committee the bill to require a seven-day waiting period for handgun purchases, with instruction not to report the bill back until it has conducted a thorough and complete study, including hearings, of the provisions and merits of the bill in the overall context of violent crime problem confronting the nation and the president's message on violent crime of March 12, 1991.

Var. 93 H.R. 7 May 8, 1991 Passage of the bill to require a seven-day waiting period for handgun purchases, allowing local law enforcement authorities to check the background of prospective buyers to see if they have a criminal record or mental illness. The seven-day waiting period would be dispensed with when a national computer system for instant checks becomes operational.

Var. 328 H.R. 3371 October 17, 1991 Amendment to strike the provisions that prohibit the ownership or sale of 13 types of semiautomatic assault weapons and delete provisions that make it illegal to own or sell ammunition clips of more than seven rounds.

### 103rd Congress

Var. 567 H.R. 1025 November 10, 1993 Rule to provide for House floor consideration of the Brady Bill requiring a five-business-day waiting period before an individual could purchase a handgun to allow local officials to conduct a background check.

Var. 569 H.R. 1025 November 10, 1993 Amendment to sunset the five-day waiting period five years after enactment.

Var. 570 H.R. 1025 November 10, 1993 Amendment to preempt any state or local law requiring waiting periods for the purchase of handguns once a national instant check system is instituted.

Var. 572 H.R. 1025 November 10, 1993 Amendment to sunset the five-day waiting period five years after enactment.

Var. 573 H.R.1025 November 10, 1993 Motion to recommit the bill to the Judiciary Committee with instructions to report it back with an amendment to eliminate the unfunded mandates to the states in the bill by either authorizing additional funds for personal background checks or removing the mandate for personal background checks.

Var. 574 H.R. 1025 November 10, 1993 Passage of the Brady Bill.

Var. 616 H.R.1025 November 22, 1993 Agreeing to a conference with the Senate on the Brady Bill.

Var. 780 H.R. 4296 May 5, 1994 Rule to provide for House floor consideration of the bill to ban the manufacture and possession of 19 types of semiautomatic weapons and high-capacity ammunition clips.

Var. 781 H.R. 4296 May 5, 1994 Passage of the bill to ban the manufacture and possession of 19 types of semiautomatic weapons and high-capacity ammunition clips.

### 104th Congress

Var. 542 H.R. 2020 July 19, 1995 Amendment to Treasury Department and Postal Service appropriations prohibiting bonuses or merit-based raises for employees of the Bureau of Alcohol, Tobacco, and Firearms.

Var. 986 H.R.125 March 22, 1996 Rule to provide for House floor consideration of the bill to repeal the current ban on certain semi-automatic assault-style weapons and eliminate the prohibition on selling or manufacturing such guns.

Var. 987 H.R. 125 March 22, 1996 Passage of the bill to repeal the current ban on certain semiautomatic assault-style weapons and eliminate the prohibition on selling or manufacturing such guns.

Var. 1053 H.R. 2406 May 9, 1996 Amendment to add additional penalties for illegally possessing or discharging a firearm in a public housing zone.

Var. 1197 H.R. 3755 July 11, 1996 Amendment providing an additional $2.6 million for the Centers for Disease Control and Prevention in order to fund research at the National Center for Injury Prevention and Control on issues related to firearms use and to reduce by an equal amount the $3.1 billion in funding for health resources and services.

## 106th Congress

216 H.R. 1501 June 16, 1999 Amendment supporting Project Exile, an NRA-backed program transferring jurisdiction for some gun permit offenses from state to federal courts.

234 H.R. 2122 June 18, 1999 Mandatory Gun Show Background Check Act amendment easing proposed restrictions on purchases at gun shows.

235 H.R. 2122 June 18, 1999 Amendment requiring three-day waiting period for purchases at gun shows.

236 H.R. 2122 June 18, 1999 Amendment mandates the transfer of a secure gun storage or safety device with the transfer of any handgun and establishes liability criteria for damages resulting from the criminal or unlawful misuse of a handgun by a third party.

239 H.R. 2122 June 18, 1999 Amendment requires a background check on a person whose gun is returned to him by a pawnshop if that gun has been stored at the pawnshop for more than one year.

240 H.R. 2122 June 18, 1999 Amendment sought to repeal a District of Columbia law that prohibits residents from possessing a firearm.

241 H.R. 2122 June 18, 1999 Amendment allows law-abiding residents of the District of Columbia to keep a registered handgun in their home.

243 H.R. 2122 June 18, 1999 Amendment in the nature of a substitute to extend Brady Bill background checks to gun shows and regulate firearms transfers at gun shows.

306 H.R. 4635 June 21, 2000 Departments of Veterans Affairs and HUD and independent agencies appropriation. Amendment prohibits HUD from using funds in the bill to administer HUD's Community for Safer Guns Coalition.

308 H.R. 4635 June 21, 2000 Amendment sought to prohibit HUD from using funds in the bill to enforce, implement, or administer the provisions of the March 17, 2000, settlement between Smith & Wesson and HUD.

**Figure 3-7. Correlation between Senators' Positions on Gun Issues and D1 and D2 NOMINATE Scores, 90th through 106th Congresses (1967–2000)**

All votes as in Table 3-4. NOMINATE scores from voteview.com.

**Figure 3-8. Effects of Party Affiliation and State Public Opinion on Senators' Positions on Gun Control, 90th through 108th Congresses (1967–2004)**

Public opinion from GSS Cumulative Survey 1972–2002. The results exclude Hawaii, Idaho, Maine, Nebraska, Nevada, and New Mexico, as the GSS includes no respondents from those states.

**Figure 3-9. Interparty Difference in Support for a Handgun Ban (Democratic Support – Republican Support), Gallup Polls, 1975–1999**

Poll Dates: March 7–10, 1975, April 3–6, 1981, June 19–22, 1981, September 17–20, 1982, April 12–15, 1985, July 1–7, 1988, September 10–11, 1990.

**Figure 4-1. Interparty Difference of Means (Republican Mean – Democratic Mean) on Support for Racial**

**Liberalism, All MCs and Northern MCs Compared,
House of Representatives, 60th through 102nd Congresses
(1906–1992)**

*60th Congress*

> Var. 317 S. 5729 February 27, 1909 Passage of a bill relating to the
> "affray" at Brownsville, Texas, concerning the discharge of black
> soldiers following disturbances.

*61st Congress*

> Var. 135 H.J. Res. 88 June 20, 1910 Passage of the resolution
> creating Negro Freedom Joint Resolution creating a commission to
> investigate and report on the advisability of holding an exposition
> commemorating the semicentennial of Negro freedom.

*62nd Congress*

> Var. 139 H.R. 24016 May 10, 1912 Motion to recommit a bill grant-
> ing pensions and increase of pensions to certain soldiers and sailors
> of the Civil War and certain widows and dependent children, to the
> committee on invalid pensioners, with instructions to amend same
> by changing residence requirements for Negro soldiers in veteran
> homes.

*63rd Congress*

> Var. 243 H.R. 6060 January 7, 1915 Motion to concur in Senate
> amendment to a bill regulating the immigration of aliens and their
> residence in the United States excluding all members of African
> descent or blacks from immigration in the United States.
> Var. 244 H.R. 1710 January 11, 1915 Previous question motion on bill
> prohibiting and punishing miscegenation in the District of Columbia
> and voiding such intermarriage.
> Var. 245 H.R. 1710 January 11, 1915 Motion to recommit H.R. 1710
> to the Committee on the District of Columbia.
> Var. 246 H.R. 1710 January 11, 1915 Passage of bill prohibiting and
> punishing miscegenation in the District of Columbia and voiding
> such intermarriage.

## 64th Congress

Var. 54 H.R. 8348 April 24, 1916 Amendment to bill creating a juvenile court for the District of Columbia mandating racial segregation in the system.

Var. 55 H.R. 13048 April 24, 1916 Passage of a bill creating a juvenile court for the District of Columbia.

## 67th Congress

Var. 153. H. Res. 253. December 19, 1921 Motion to adjourn during debate on rule for antilynching bill.

Var. 154 H. Res. 253 December 19, 1921 Motion to adjourn during debate on rule for antilynching bill.

Var. 156 H. Res. 253 December 19, 1921 Previous question motion on rule for antilynching bill.

Var. 157 H.R. 253 December 19, 1921 Passage of H. Res. 253 rule allowing consideration of antilynching bill.

Var. 159 H.R. 13 December 20, 1921 Motion to adjourn rather than discuss the antilynching bill.

Var. 161 H.R. 13 December 20, 1921 Motion to resolve into the Committee of the Whole to consider the antilynching bill.

Var. 162 H.R. 13 January 4, 1922 Motion to dispense with all proceedings under the calendar Wednesday rule in order to discuss the antilynching bill.

Var. 164 H.R. 13 January 4, 1922 Motion to adjourn rather than discuss antilynching bill.

Var. 165 H.R. 13 January 4, 1922 Motion to dispense with further proceedings under the Call of the House in order to discuss the antilynching bill.

Var. 166 H.R. 13 January 4, 1922 Motion to resolve into the Committee of the Whole to consider the antilynching bill.

Var. 167 H.R. 13 January 10, 1922 Motion to dispense with further proceedings under the Call of the House in order to discuss the antilynching bill.

Var. 168 H.R. 13 January 10, 1922 Motion to resolve into the Committee of the Whole to consider the antilynching bill.

Var. 170 H.R. 13 January 17, 1922 Motion to resolve into the Committee of the Whole to consider the antilynching bill.

Var. 171 H.R. 13 January 18, 1922 Motion to dispense with the business in order under the Calendar Wednesday rule in order to discuss the antilynching bill.

Var. 172 H.R. 13 January 18, 1922 Motion to resolve into the Committee of the Whole to consider the antilynching bill.

Var. 175 H.R. 13 January 25, 1922 Motion to dispense with the business in order under the Calendar Wednesday rule in order to discuss the antilynching bill.

Var. 176 H.R. 13 January 26, 1922 Motion to resolve into the Committee on the Whole to consider the antilynching bill.

Var. 177 H.R. 13 January 26, 1922 Motion to resolve into the Committee on the Whole to consider the antilynching bill.

Var. 178 H.R. 13 January 26, 1922 Motion to recommit the antilynching bill to the Judiciary Committee.

Var. 179 H.R. 13 January 26, 1922 Passage of the antilynching bill.

Var. 224 H.J. Res. 270 May 10, 1922 Motion to recommit bill establishing credit with the United States for Liberia with instructions to amend by providing that no part of the money loaned to Liberia should be used to pay debts of Liberia that existed prior to August 1.

Var. 225 H.J. Res. 270 May 10, 1922 Authorizing the secretary of the treasury to establish a credit with the U.S. government for the government of Liberia.

## 68th Congress

Var. 185 H.R. 10020 February 28, 1925 Motion that the House recede from its disagreement to the Senate amendment to the Interior Dept. appropriation so as to appropriate funds for Howard University.

## 69th Congress

Var. 57 H.R. 9694 April 28, 1926 Motion to adjourn rather than consider bill authorizing the erection of a monument to commemorate the service of African American infantry regiments attached to the French army in World War One.

Var. 58 H.R. 9694 April 28, 1926 Motion to consider a bill authorizing the erection of a monument commemorating the service of African American infantry regiments attached to the French army.

Var. 59 H.R. 9694 April 28, 1926 Passage of a bill authorizing the erection of a monument commemorating the service of African American infantry regiments attached to the French army.

## 70th Congress

Var. 36 H.R. 9136 February 28, 1928 Concurring in Senate amendment to Interior Department appropriations that appropriated $390,000 for Howard University.

Var. 44 H.R. 149 March 29, 1928 Rule for consideration of H.R. 279 a bill to amend an act of 1867, which incorporated Howard University in the District of Columbia.

Var. 45 H.R. 279 March 29, 1928 Passage of a bill to amend an act of 1867 to incorporate Howard University in the District of Columbia.

Var. 81 S.J. Res. 132 March 2, 1929 Passage of a bill to create a commission to erect a memorial building for the National Memorial Association Inc., in the city of Washington as a tribute to the Negroes' contribution to the achievements of America.

## 72nd Congress

Var. 101 H.R. 13710 December 22, 1932 Motion to recommit to the Committee on Appropriations making appropriations for the Department of the Interior for fiscal 1934 with instructions to report an amendment appropriating $460,000 for construction of a power plant at Howard University.

Var. 102 H.R. 13710 December 27, 1932 Motion to recommit Interior Department Appropriations with instructions to report an amendment appropriating $460,000 for construction of a power plant at Howard University.

## 73rd Congress

Var. 108 H. Res. 236 April 25, 1934 Resolution preventing discrimination in the House of Representatives.

### 75th Congress

Var. 33 H. Res. 125 April 12, 1937 Motion to discharge Rules Committee from consideration of the rule for debate on H.R. 1507, an antilynching bill.

Var. 36 H.R. 1507 April 15, 1937 Amendment striking out sections 5 and 6 imposing fines on the counties in which lynching occurs.

Var. 37 H.R. 1507 April 15, 1937 Passage of an antilynching bill.

### 76th Congress

Var. 105 H. Res. 103 January 8, 1940 Motion to discharge the Rules Committee from further consideration of rule for consideration of H.R. 801, an antilynching bill.

Var. 106 H.R. 801 January 10, 1940 Passage of a bill making lynching a federal crime.

### 77th Congress

Var. 152 H. Res. 528 July 23, 1942 Passage of the rule for consideration of H.R. 7416, a bill for voting by members of the armed forces.

Var. 153 H.R. 7416 July 23, 1942 Motion that the House resolve itself into Committee of the Whole on the State of the Union to consider the bill for voting by members of the armed forces.

Var. 154 H.R. 7416 September 9, 1942 Motion to recommit conference report on armed forces voting bill without instructions, i.e., to kill the bill.

Var. 155 H.R. 7416 September 9, 1942 Motion to agree the conference report on the armed forces voting bill.

Var. 158 H. Res. 10 October 12, 1942 Motion to discharge Rules Committee from further consideration of rule for H.R. 1024, an anti–poll tax bill.

Var. 159 H. Res. 110 October 12, 1942 Rule for consideration of the anti–poll tax bill.

Var. 160 H.R. 1024 October 13, 1942 Passage of anti–poll tax bill.

### 78th Congress

Var. 50 H. Res. 131 May 24, 1943 to discharge the Rules Committee from further consideration of the rule for considering H.R. 7 the anti–poll tax bill.

Var. 51 H. Res. 131 May 24, 1943 Rule for considering the anti–poll tax bill.

Var. 52 H.R. 7 May 25, 1943 Passage of the bill banning poll taxes in elections for national office.

### 79th Congress

Var. 61 H. Res. 139 June 11, 1945 Motion to discharge Rules Committee from further consideration of rule for H.R. 7, the anti–poll tax bill.

Var. 62 H. Res. 139 June 11, 1945 Rule for consideration of anti–poll tax bill.

Var. 63 H.R. 7 June 12, 1945 Passage of anti–poll tax bill.

Var. 124 H.R. 3370 February 21, 1946 Amendment to School Lunch Bill requiring that any school making discrimination because of race creed, color, or national origin of children should not receive funds.

### 80th Congress

Var. 84 H.R. 29 July 21, 1947 Passage of the anti–poll tax bill.

Var. 138 H. Res. 603 May 24, 1948 Rule for consideration of the D.C. Home Rule bill.

Var. 139 H.R. 6227 May 25, 1948 Motion to strike the enacting clause, i.e., kill the D.C. Home Rule Bill.

### 81st Congress

Var. 79 H.J. 134 July 25, 1949 Motion to adjourn rather than consider rule for anti–poll tax bill.

Var. 80 July 25, 1949 Motion to approve previous question on approval of the Journal, a move designed to bring up the rule for the anti–poll tax bill.

Var. 81 July 25, 1949 Approval of the Journal, a move designed to bring up the rule for the anti–poll tax bill.

Var. 82 July 25, 1949 Motion to adjourn.

Var. 83 H. Res. 276 July 25, 1949 Previous question motion for rule permitting consideration of the anti–poll tax bill.

Var. 84 July 25, 1949 Motion to adjourn rather than consider anti–poll tax bill.

Var. 85 H. Res. 276 July 25, 1949 Rule for consideration of anti–poll tax bill.

Var. 86 H.R. 3199 July 26, 1949 Motion to recommit anti–poll tax bill.

Var. 87 H.R. 3199 July 26, 1949 Passage of ban on poll taxes in federal elections.

Var. 142 H.R. 4453 February 15, 1950 Motion that further proceedings under the call be dispensed with in order to debate the proposed Fair Employment Practices Commission (FEPC).

Var. 143 H.R. 4453 February 15, 1950 Motion to adjourn to prevent consideration of FEPC bill.

Var. 144 H.R. 4453 February 15, 1950 Motion to dispense with Calendar Wednesday, an attempt to prevent consideration of FEPC bill.

Var. 145 H.R. 4453 February 15, 1950 Motion to adjourn, an attempt to prevent consideration of FEPC bill.

Var. 146 H.R. 4453 February 15, 1950 Motion to adjourn, an attempt to prevent consideration of FEPC bill.

Var. 147 H.R. 4453 February 15, 1950 Motion that further proceedings under the call be dispensed with, an attempt to bring up the FEPC bill.

Var. 149 H.R. 4453 February 22, 1950 Motion to adjourn, an attempt to prevent consideration of FEPC bill.

Var. 150 H.R. 4453 February 22, 1950 Motion to dispense with Calendar Wednesday, an attempt to prevent consideration of FEPC bill.

Var. 151 H.R. 4453 February 22, 1950 Motion that further proceedings under the call be dispensed with, an attempt to bring up the FEPC bill.

Var. 152 H.R. 4453 February 22, 1950 Motion to adjourn and to defer discussion of FEPC.

Var. 153 H.R. 4453 February 22, 1950 Motion to consider FEPC bill.

Var. 154 H.R. 4453 February 22, 1950 Motion to adjourn during FEPC debate, an attempt to preempt discussion of the bill.

Var. 155 H.R. 4453 February 22, 1950 On question of consideration.

Var. 156 H.R. 4453 February 22, 1950 Amendment removing enforcement powers for the proposed FEPC.

Var. 157 H.R. 4453 February 23, 1950 Motion to recommit.

Var. 158 H.R. 4453 February 23, 1950 Passage of FEPC bill.

## 82nd Congress

Var. 46 H.R. 314 June 6, 1951 Motion to strike enacting clause on bill providing for the establishment of a veterans' hospital for Negro veterans at the birthplace of Booker T. Washington.

## 84th Congress

> Var. 132 H.R. 7535 July 5, 1956 Amendment to School Construction Aid Bill denying federal funds to any state that fails to comply with the decisions of the Supreme Court.
>
> Var. 144 H.R. 627 July 19, 1956 Motion to table a motion to dispense with routine proceedings, an attempt to delay consideration of the civil rights bill.
>
> Var. 145 H.R. 627 July 23, 1956 Motion to recommit providing means of further securing and protecting the civil rights of those within U.S. jurisdiction.
>
> Var. 146 H.R. 627 July 23, 1956 Passage of the Civil Rights Bill.

For later votes see Table 4-1.

**Figure 4-2. Racial Liberalism in the House of Representatives by Party, 81st (1949–1950), 86th (1959–1960), and 92nd Congresses (1971–1972)**

81st Congress: See Figure 4-1.
86th and 92nd Congresses: See Table 4-1.

**Figure 4-3. Interparty Difference between Republican and Democratic Means on Racial Liberalism (Republican Mean – Democratic Mean), All Representatives and Those Serving throughout the Period, House of Representatives, 85th through 89th Congresses (1957–1966)**

For Votes see Table 4-1.

**Figure 4-4. Party and Public Opinion as Predictors of Senators' Positions on Racial Issues, 90th through 102nd Congresses (1967–1992)**

## 90th Congress

> Var. 11 S. Res. 6 January 18, 1967 Motion to table point of order objecting to closing of debate on proposed rule change making it easier to end filibusters.
>
> Var. 12 S. Res. 6 January 18, 1967 Vote on point of order objecting to closing of debate on proposed rule change making it easier to end filibusters.
>
> Var. 13 S. Res. 6 January 24, 1967 Cloture motion on proposed rule change making it easier to end filibusters.

Var. 303 H.R. 7819 December 4, 1967 Amendment to Elementary and Secondary Education Amendments Act making certain exceptions to the barring of federal funds from use in busing students to achieve a better racial balance in schools.

Var. 304 H.R. 7819 December 4, 1967 Motion to table motion to reconsider antibusing amendment.

Var. 305 H.R. 7819 December 4, 1967 Motion to reconsider antibusing amendment.

Var. 327 H.R. 2516 February 6, 1968 Motion to table amendment restricting the civil rights bill's coverage to rights extended under the commerce clause of the Constitution and programs involving federal funds and would make it unlawful to interfere with the performance of these rights, no matter whether interference was racially motivated or not.

Var. 328 H.R. 2516 February 21, 1968 Cloture motion on Civil Rights Act.

Var. 329 H.R. 2516 February 21, 1968 Motion to table amendment adding a new title to provide for implementing a policy of open housing.

Var. 330 H.R. 2516 February 26, 1968 Cloture motion on Civil Rights Act.

Var. 332 H.R. 2516 March 1, 1968 Cloture motion on amendment consisting of Title I on interference with federally protected activities, and Title II on fair housing.

Var. 333 H.R. 2516 March 4, 1968 Cloture motion on amendment concerning interference with federally protected activities and fair housing.

Var. 334 H.R. 2516 March 4, 1968 Amendment exempting from fair housing provisions any single-dwelling private home owner in sale or rental of same.

Var. 335 H.R. 2516 March 4, 1968 Amendment barring court action that would impair any title to real property required under state registration or recording statutes.

Var. 337 H.R. 2516 March 5, 1968 Amendment providing that exemption given to individual home owners under Title II shall not be impaired by employment of a real estate agent, so long as he does not instruct the agent to discriminate in sale or rental.

Var. 338 H.R. 2516 March 5, 1968 Amendment extending protection of Title I relating to interference with federally protected activities of owners of shops or stores, so that they are protected from damage or injury during riot or civil disorder.

Var. 346 H.R. 2516 March 7, 1968 Amendment providing that single-family houses sold or rented in certain circumstances by an owner of not more than three such type houses be exempt from the provisions of the bill.

Var. 351 H.R. 2516 March 8, 1968 Amendment requiring that any prosecution of offense against a federally protected activity shall be only on formal, written authorization of attorney general or deputy attorney general and only then if a state or local law enforcement official has failed to act promptly against alleged offense.

## 91st Congress

Var. 14 S. Res. 11 January 16, 1969 Cloture motion on amendment to Senate rules making it possible to end filibusters with 3/5 rather than 2/3 vote in some cases.

Var. 15 S. Res. 11 January 16, 1969 Vote to sustain the decision of the vice president that cloture was adopted.

Var. 18 S. Res. 11 January 28, 1969 Cloture motion on proposal to allow a 3/5 rather a 2/3 vote to end filibusters.

Var. 129 H.R. 12964 November 5, 1969 Amendment increasing by $500,000 funds available for grants to state equal employment practices commissions and increasing from $11.5 to $15.9 million funds for fiscal 1970 budget for the EEOC.

Var. 230 H.R. 13111 December 17, 1969 Amendment to Departments of Labor/HEW appropriation adding the words "except as required by the Constitution" to sections involving the barring of funds to force school integration by busing or pupil transfer.

Var. 293 H.R. 514 February 18, 1970 Amendment providing for uniform application of federal guidelines in dealing with school segregation and prohibiting forced busing.

Var. 294 H.R. 514 February 18, 1970 Amendment to amendment deleting the words "without regard to the origin or cause of such segregation."

Var. 296 S. Res. 359 February 19, 1970 Motion to table a bill to establish a Select Committee on Equal Educational Opportunity.

Var. 298 H.R. 514 February 19, 1970 Amendment adding new section to bar courts and federal departments from requiring busing of students to alter the racial composition of a public school.

Var. 320 H.R. 15931 February 28, 1970 Amendment barring funds from use to force a school district to take action involving busing of students.

Var. 321 H.R. 15931 February 28, 1970 Amendment barring funds from any such uses as a condition precedent to obtaining federal funds otherwise available to any state, school district, or school.

Var. 322 H.R. 15931 February 28, 1970 Amendment deleting section of the bill that bars funds for use in any plan to deny a student, because of race, the right to attend a public school of his choice.

Var. 330 H.R. 4249 March 5, 1970 Motion to table amendment to extension of the Voting Rights Act.

Var. 332 H.R. 4249 March 6, 1970 Amendment excluding certain nonresidents, convicted felons, and mentally ill from the count of adult persons in a state in determining the percentage of citizens voting in the 1964 presidential election.

Var. 333 H.R. 4249 March 9, 1970 Amendment to authorize violations of the Voting Rights Act to be heard in U.S. District Court for District of Columbia, as in present law.

Var. 334 H.R. 4249 March 9, 1970 Amendment permitting a state that repealed literacy requirement to be exempt from coverage of Voting Rights Act.

Var. 335 H.R. 4249 March 9, 1970 Amendment changing method of enforcement in Section 5.

Var. 336 H.R. 4249 March 10, 1970 Amendment changing from 1964 to 1968 the time for "triggering" the suspension of literacy tests.

Var. 343 H.R. 4249 March 11, 1970 Amendment deleting certain language.

Var. 349 H.R. 4249 March 12, 1970 Amendment repealing sections of 1965 Voting Rights Act providing formula for suspension of literary tests.

Var. 350 H.R. 4249 March 13, 1970 Amendment providing that Sections 4 and 5 shall expire August 7, 1975.

Var. 351 H.R. 4249 March 13, 1970 Substitute Amendment.

Var. 404 H.R. 17399 June 22, 1970 Amendment to amendment inserting, after the word "services," the phrase "supported by federal funds."

Var. 410 H.R. 16916 June 24, 1970 Amendment to appropriations for the Office of Education striking section barring use of federal funds to implement any plan denying any student, because of his race, the right to attend any public school of his choice.

Var. 412 HR. 16916 June 24, 1970 Amendment striking sections 209 and 210 barring use of federal funds to force school districts that are desegregated to take any action to force the busing of students.

Var. 414 H.R. 16916 June 25, 1970 Amendment striking from a previous amendment the proviso that barred used of federal funds to assist a local education agency that engages or has unlawfully engaged in the gift, lease, or sale of property or services to a non-public school practicing racial discrimination.

Var. 569 S. 2453 September 30, 1970 Amendment providing for enforcement of equal employment opportunity in federal district courts.

Var. 570 S. 2453 September 30, 1970 Amendment prohibiting employees, officers, and members of the EEOC from filing charges.

Var. 571 S. 2453 October 1, 1970 Amendment excluding state and local employees from coverage by the act.

## 92nd Congress

Var. 48 S. 1557 April 22, 1971 Amending the Emergency School and Quality Integrated Education Act of 1971 by establishing uniform guidelines in all regions of the United States in dealing with conditions of school segregation practices.

Var. 52 S. 1557 April 26, 1971 Amendment allowing parents the right to choose the public school that their children will attend.

Var. 53 S. 1557 April 26, 1971 Amendment to prohibit the busing of children to effect the racial composition of schools.

Var. 54 S. 1557 April 26, 1971 Amendment allowing all school children the right to attend the public school nearest their home.

Var. 162 H.R. 8866 July 28, 1971 Amendment suspending sugar quotas for Republic of South Africa pending determination by the president of the United States that the South African government does not discriminate against certain of its citizens.

Var. 217 H.R. 8687 September 23, 1971 Amendment striking section that lifts restriction on importation of chrome ore from Rhodesia.

Var. 227 H.R. 8687 September 30, 1971 Amendment deleting provision on importation of chrome ore from Rhodesia.

Var. 228 H.R. 8687 September, 30, 1971 Table motion to reconsider amendment deleting provisions removing restrictions on importation of chrome ore form Rhodesia.

Var. 229 H.R. 8687 September, 30, 1971 Motion to reconsider amendment deleting provisions removing restrictions on importation of chrome ore from Rhodesia.

Var. 239 H.R. 8687 October 6, 1971 Amendment giving the president discretionary power in removing restriction on importation of chrome ore from Rhodesia.

Var. 436 S. 2515 January 24, 1972 Amendment allowing the EEOC to take certain unlawful employment practice disputes which they cannot conciliate to federal district courts for resolution.

Var. 437 S. 2515 January 24, 1972 Motion to table reconsideration of Var. 436.

Var. 438 S. 2515 January 24 1972 Reconsideration of Var. 436.

Var. 439 S. 2515 January 24, 1972 Amendment providing that all antidiscrimination litigations in the U.S. Court of Appeals system be conducted by the EEOC instead of by the attorney general.

Var. 441 S. 2515 January 26, 1972 Reconsideration of Var. 436.

Var. 442 S. 2515 January 26, 1972 Motion to table motion to reconsider rejection of Var. 436.

Var. 468 S. 2515 February 9, 1972 Amendment providing that with certain exceptions a charge filed with the EEOC shall be the exclusive remedy of any person claiming to be aggrieved by an unlawful employment practice.

Var. 471 S. 2515 February 15, 1972 Motion to reconsider previous amendment.

Var. 474 S. 2515 February 16, 1972 Amendment striking from the bill provisions transferring attorney general's "pattern and practice" authority to the Equal Employment Opportunity Commission.

Var. 487 S. 659 February 25, 1972 Amendment barring federal courts from issuing orders to require busing of schoolchildren on basis of race, religion, or national origin.

Var. 488 S. 659 February 25, 1972 Motion to reconsider previous amendment.

Var. 491 S. 659 February 29, 1972 Amendment stating that antibusing amendment was not intended to violate the Constitution.

Var. 492 S. 659 February 29, 1972 Amendment to bill blocking court-ordered busing providing that no provision of this or any other act shall be construed to require assignment or transportation of students or teachers for purpose of changing the racial composition of any school.

Var. 497 S. 659 February 29, 1972 Amendment postponing effectiveness of U.S. District Court busing orders until all appeals or time therefore have been exhausted.

Var. 505 S. 659 March 1, 1972 Amendment barring federal courts from issuing orders to require busing of schoolchildren on account of race, and postponing effectiveness of any such orders until all appeals in connection therewith have been exhausted.

Var. 607 S. 3526 May 31, 1972 Amendment providing that the president may not prohibit importation of a strategic material (Rhodesian chrome ore) from a noncommunist country if such strategic material is being imported from a communist country.

## 93rd Congress

Var. 274 S. 1435 July 10, 1973 Passage of a bill providing an elected mayor and city council for the District of Columbia.

Var. 487 S. 2589 November 19, 1973 Motion to table amendment limiting public transportation of schoolchildren to the school nearest their home in order to save fuel.

Var. 524 H.R. 3153 November 29, 1973 Motion to table amendment that would promote conservation of gasoline through reduction in busing of schoolchildren.

Var. 558 S. 2176 December 10, 1973 Motion to table amendment calling for the HEW secretary to encourage limitations on the busing of schoolchildren.

Var. 560 S. 1868 December 11, 1973 Cloture on a bill to ban importation of Rhodesian chrome ore.

Var. 794 S. 1539 May 15, 1974 Amendment prohibiting forced busing of students beyond the school next closest to his home.

Var. 795 S. 1539 May 15, 1974 Amendment providing freedom of choice in attending public schools.

Var. 798 S. 1539 May 16, 1974 Motion to table antibusing amendment.

Var. 799 S. 1539 May 16, 1974 Motion to table amendment to antibusing amendment clarifying that the Senate does not intend to violate the Constitution.

Var. 800 S. 1539 May 16, 1974 Amendment to antibusing amendment clarifying that the Senate does not intend to violate the Constitution.

Var. 801 S. 1539 May 16, 1974 Motion to table antibusing amendment.

Var. 802 S. 1539 May 16, 1974 Motion to table amendment denying U.S. courts jurisdiction to order school busing by state or local education agencies to alter the racial composition of the student body, with the exception of the Supreme Court when acting within its original jurisdiction.

Var. 803 S. 1539 May 16, 1974 Amendment substituting parental consent for the consent of local authorities as a condition for federal funding of busing.

Var. 804 S. 1539 May 16, 1974 Amendment prohibiting the withholding of funds for a state or local education agency based on determination that such agency is operating a discriminatory program if it is operating under a court-ordered desegregation plan.

Var. 983 H.R. 15580 September 17, 1974 Amendment barring use of funds to transport school students in order to overcome racial imbalance in public school.

Var. 984 H.R. 15580 September 17, 1974 Motion to reconsider previous amendment.

Var. 1065 H.R. 16900 November 19, 1974 Motion to table amendment providing that no funds may be used to compel any school system, as a condition for receiving grants, to classify teachers or students to schools for reasons of race or sex.

Var. 1067 H.R. 16900 November 19, 1974 Motion to table amendment providing that no funds shall be used to compel school systems, as a condition for receiving grants, to participate in any pilot investigation of discrimination in disciplinary action.

Var. 1106 H.R. 16900 December 11, 1974 Amendment requiring a determination by a U.S. court that discrimination exists before HEW may enforce these acts.

### 94th Congress

Var. 201 H.R. 5899 May 20, 1975 Amendment to supplemental appropriations agreeing to less restrictive language than the House had passed concerning administration of civil rights provisions by HEW.

Var. 313 H.R. 6219 July 21, 1975 Motion to proceed to the consideration of the extension of the Voting Rights Act.

Var. 314 S. Res. 166 July 21, 1975 Sustaining judgment of the chair that a motion to impose cloture is in order.

Var. 319 H.R. 6219 July 22, 1975 Motion to table amendment making provisions of the bill applicable to all of the states of the nation.

Var. 325 H.R. 6219 July 24, 1975 Motion to table amendment repealing the triggering mechanism (Section 4) of the Voting Rights Act.

Var. 326 H.R. 6219 July 24, 1975 Motion to table amendment changing the triggering date from November 1, 1964, until November 1, 1972.

Var. 328 H.R. 6219 July 24, 1975 Motion to table amendment repealing Section 5 of the act, which requires states covered by the act to get prior approval by the attorney general before any changes may be made in their election laws.

Var. 329 H.R. 6219 July 24, 1975 Motion to table amendment changing the triggering date from November 1, 1964, until November 2, 1976.

Var. 330 H.R. 6219 July 24, 1975 Motion to table amendment allowing a state or political subdivision to seek a declaratory court judgment with a presumption of nondiscrimination under certain conditions.

Var. 335 H.R. 6219 July 24, 1975 Motion to table amendment making Sections 4 and 5 inapplicable after November 1, 1976, to any state or political subdivision that has not maintained any test or device, and in which more than 50 percent of voting age were registered on that date or voted in the 1976 presidential election.

Var. 336 H.R. 6219 July 24, 1975 Motion to table amendment providing that no inference or presumption may be drawn from the past history of de facto segregation occurring prior to November 1, 1964, in state or political subdivision.

Var. 338 H.R. 6219 July 24, 1975 Motion to table amendment providing that any annexation of land which occurred prior to August 6, 1965, not be subject to prior approval provisions of the act.

Var. 339 6219 H.R. 6219 July 24, 1975 Passage of Voting Rights Act extension.

Var. 976 H.R. 14232 June 29, 1976 Amendment barring the use of funds to require that school systems bus students to attain racial balance in schools.

Var. 1239 S. 2278 September 21, 1976 Motion to table amendment to bill allowing a court to award attorneys' fees to a prevailing party in suits brought to enforce certain civil rights acts.

Var. 1242 S. 2278 September 21, 1976 Motion to table amendment which would allow for further amendments.

Var. 1248 S. 2278 September 22, 1976 Motion to table amendment which would exempt state and local governments from the provisions of the bill.

## 95th Congress

Var. 60 S. 174 March 14, 1977 Motion tabling an amendment to the bill amending the U.N. Participation Act and halting the importation of Rhodesian chrome ore. The amendment would delay the effective date of the bill for 30 days, thereby awaiting the president's advice on relations and negotiations with Rhodesia.

Var. 61 S. 174 March 14, 1977 Amendment prohibiting the importation of chromium in any form from the USSR.

Var. 62 S. 174 March 14, 1977 Amendment prohibiting chrome imports during the year prior to enactment of the bill.

Var. 66 S. 174 March 15, 1977 Amendment nullifying the bill if the president were to discover a significant interruption in the supply of any commodity essential to the security of the United States.

Var. 67 S. 174 March 15, 1977 Amendment establishing a U.S. liaison office in Rhodesia.

Var. 68 S. 174 March 15, 1977 Amendment making the bill's provisions inapplicable if it is discovered that the price of chromium has increased by 100 percent since the day of the bill's enactment.

Var. 69 H.R. 1746 March 15, 1977 Passage of bill amending United Nations Participation Act of 1945 to halt the importation of Rhodesian chromium.

Var. 258 H.R. 7555 June 28, 1977 Ruling on germaneness of amendments dealing with the manipulation of student assistance funds to higher educational institutions as a way of forcing compliance with affirmative action requirements.

Var. 259 H.R. 7555 June 28, 1977 Amendment prohibiting the use of HEW funds for the enforcement of affirmative action programs in college admissions, hiring, and promotions.

Var. 260 H.R. 7555 June 28, 1977 Amendment prohibiting the use of HEW funds to require any school, school system, or educational institution to classify their teachers or students by race or national origin in order to receive federal funds.

Var. 570 S. 1303 October 12, 1977 Motion to table amendment prohibiting the Legal Services Corporation from representing cases that deal with affirmative action quota systems used by institutions of higher education.

Var. 571 H.R. 6666 October 12, 1977 Passage of bill after striking all after the enacting clause and inserting in lieu thereof the text of S. 1303.

Var. 989 H.J. Res.554 August 22, 1978 Motion to table amendment providing for representation of the District of Columbia only in the House of Representatives.

Var. 999 S. 1753 August 23, 1978 Motion to table motion to reconsider tabling of amendment establishing guidelines that limit use of busing as a remedy in desegregation cases.

## 96th Congress

Var. 102 H.R. 3363 May 15, 1979 Amendment expressing the sense of Congress that Zimbabwe Rhodesia has complied with the provisions of the International Security Assistance Act of 1978 and that sanctions should be lifted within 10 days after the installation of a black majority government.

Var. 124 S. 1157 June 4, 1979 Amendment to the Justice Department authorization striking $2 million for the Civil Rights Division.

Var. 127 S. 1030 June 5, 1979 Motion to table amendment prohibiting busing of schoolchildren under voluntary desegregation programs when there is a national energy emergency.

Var. 133 S. 721 June 7, 1979 Motion to table amendment to the Civil Rights Commission authorization that restricts busing of schoolchildren under voluntary desegregation plans when in the previous year oil imports equal or exceed 40 percent of total U.S. oil consumption.

Var. 136 S. 428 June 12, 1979 Motion to table amendment to Department of Defense authorization to delete a provision in the bill to discontinue U.S. economic sanctions against Rhodesia,

Var. 206 H.R. 4389 July 20, 1979 Motion to table busing amendment.

Var. 224 H.R. 4392 July 24, 1979 Amendment to the State, Justice, Commerce, and the Judiciary Appropriation prohibiting the use of Justice Department funds to bring legal action to require the forced busing of students.

Var. 266 H.R. 4393 September 5, 1979 Amendment striking Section 614, which prohibits the IRS from carrying out proposed revenue procedures regarding the tax-exempt status of private schools.

Var. 267 H.R. 4393 September 6, 1979, amendment placing a one-year moratorium on the ability of the IRS to establish new procedures regarding the termination of the tax-exempt status of private schools.

Var. 268 H.R. 4393 September 6, 1979 Motion to table motion to reconsider previous amendment.

Var. 983 H.R. 7584 November 13, 1980 Amendment to Departments of State and Justice appropriations prohibiting the Justice Department from promoting for busing as a remedy to school desegregation.

Var. 1015 H.R. 7584 December 3, 1980 Motion to table amendment that provided that nothing in the act shall be interpreted to limit in any manner the Department of Justice in enforcing the Constitution nor shall anything in the act be interpreted to modify or diminish the authority of the courts to enforce fully the Constitution.

Var. 1016 H.R. 7584 December 3, 1980 Amendment to State Department and Justice Department Appropriation providing that none of the language in Section 607 shall be interpreted to modify the intent of the Congress as expressed in this section.

Var. 1018 H.R. 5200 December 3, 1980 Cloture on Fair Housing Bill.

Var. 1029 H.R. 5200 December 9, 1980 Cloture on Fair Housing Bill.

### 97th Congress

Var. 682 S. 1992 June 17, 1982 Amendment to Voting Rights Act striking Section 3 from the bill, which allows some violations of voting rights to be proven solely by showing that a particular election procedure results in discrimination.

Var. 683 S. 1992 June 17, 1982 Amendment limiting the power of the courts to require proportional representation or quotas in the election of members of a protected class.

Var. 685 S. 1992 June 17, 1982 Amendment providing that, after August 6, 1982, any legal action brought under either Section 4 or 5 of the Voting Rights Act would be brought in the U.S. district court ordinarily having venue over such cases.

Var. 686 S. 1992 June 17, 1982 Amendment easing provisions relating to "bailout" of covered jurisdictions.

Var. 687 S. 1992 June 17, 1982 Amendment easing bailout provisions.

Var. 688 S. 1992 June 17, 1982 Amendment to change bailout provisions so as to permit a state to bail out even if some of its counties have not qualified for a bailout under the listed criteria.

Var. 690 H.R. 3112 June 18, 1982 Amendment to House version of Voting Rights Act extension providing for the application of pre-clearance provisions to all states and political subdivisions.

Var. 691 H.R. 3112 June 18, 1982 Amendment reducing the time allowed for the Justice Department to object to an election law change.

Var. 692 H.R. 3112 June 18, 1982 Amendment easing requirements for jurisdictions to bail out of preclearance requirements.

Var. 693 H.R. 3112 June 18, 1982 Amendment clarifying the phrases "anywhere in the territory" and "all governmental units within its territory" under the bailout provision of the Voting Rights Act of 1965, making it easier for Alaska to bail out.

Var. 694 H.R. 3112 June 18, 1982 Amendment modifying the expiration date of Section 4 of the act from 25 to 15 years.

Var. 696 H.R. 3112 June 18, 1982 Amendment providing that any state in which black voter registration was less than 43.7 percent of those eligible shall be subject to the preclearance requirements and that any state with greater than 60 percent black voter registration shall not be subject to such requirements

Var. 961 H.J. Res. 631 December 18, 1982 Motion to table amendment providing that no funds under the joint resolution may be used by the IRS to deny tax-exempt status to private, religious schools.

## 98th Congress

Var. 301 H.R. 3706. October 18, 1983 Motion to recommit Martin Luther King, Jr. holiday bill to the Judiciary Committee.

Var. 302 H.R. 3706 October 18, 1983 Amendment making National Civil Rights Day on March 16 of each year a national holiday.

Var. 303 H.R. 3706 October 18, 1983 Amendment providing that instead of a paid holiday commemorating the birthday of Martin Luther King, Jr., there be a nonpaid holiday, called National Civil Rights Day, to be observed on the day of James Madison's birthday, which is March 16.

Var. 305 H.R. 3706 October 18, 1983 Amendment providing that January 15 be designated as "Martin Luther King's Birthday" and the president is authorized and requested to issue a proclamation each year calling on the people of the United States to observe the day with appropriate programs, ceremonies, and activities.

Var. 307 H.R. 3706 October 19, 1983 Amendment designating the third Sunday in January in honor of Martin Luther King, Jr.

Var. 308 H.R. 3706 October 19, 1983 Amendment making Lincoln's birthday a legal holiday to be observed on the second Sunday in February of each year.

Var. 309 H.R. 3706 October 19, 1983 Amendment establishing a public holiday for Thomas Jefferson and providing that the number of federal holidays not exceed nine.

Var. 313 H.R. 3706 October 19, 1983 Passage of the bill creating Martin Luther King Day as a federal holiday.

### 99th Congress

Var. 154 S. 995 July 11, 1985 Motion to table amendment requiring sanctions to be imposed on the signatories of the 1975 Helsinki Agreements if the president finds significant noncompliance among signatory nations.

Var. 155 S. 995 July 11, 1985 Motion to table amendment providing that no sanction may be imposed against South Africa if the imposition of such sanction would increase black unemployment in South Africa as determined by presidential certification or a resolution passed by either house of Congress.

Var. 156 S. 995 July 11, 1985 Amendment to extend sanctions to the Soviet Union, Poland, Afghanistan, Mozambique, Angola, Ethiopia, East Germany, Libya, Syria, Iran, Cuba, China, and any other country that the president certifies has a record of violations of human rights equal to or worse than that of South Africa or any country that has facilitated acts of terrorism against U.S. persons.

Var. 157 S. 995 July 11, 1985 Motion to table amendment expressing the sense of the Senate as to the terroristic nature of the African National Congress and to impose certain sanctions against it until such time as it renounces the use of violence.

Var. 159 H.R. 1460 July 11, 1985 Passage of bill imposing sanctions on South Africa.

Var. 181 H.R. 1460 September 9, 1985 Cloture motion on the conference report on a bill invoking economic sanctions on South Africa.

Var. 627 S. 2701 August 16, 1986 Motion to table amendment to the Comprehensive Anti-Apartheid Act that would require an affirmative vote for the Congress to terminate or suspend sanctions against South Africa.

Var. 630 S. 2701 August 15, 1986 Amendment providing that the provisions applicable to South Africa shall be equally applicable to the Soviet Union.

Var. 634 S. 2701 August 15, 1986 Amendment prohibiting takeoff and landing rights in the United States for Aeroflot, the Soviet airline.

Var. 702 H.R. 4868 October 2, 1986 To adopt, over the president's veto, the Anti-Apartheid Act, which would prohibit loans and investments in South Africa, ban the import of South African iron, steel, uranium, coal, textiles, sugar, and other agricultural products, and the export of petroleum products to that country.

## 100th Congress

Var. 129 H.R. 1827 May 21, 1987 Motion to table amendment to supplemental appropriations that would require that financial assistance be denied to countries that have not renounced "necklacing," a practice in which those suspected of having government ties are killed by placing articles around their necks and igniting them.

Var. 129 H.R. 1827 May 21, 1987 Amendment to supplemental appropriations requiring that financial assistance be denied to countries that have not renounced "necklacing."

Var. 799 H.R. 5210 October 13, 1988 Amendment to the omnibus drug bill restricting the use of the death penalty in the case of racially disproportionate capital sentencing.

## 101st Congress

Var. 62 S. 431 May 2, 1989 Amendment to eliminate all funding for the Martin Luther King, Jr. Federal Holiday Commission.

Var. 64 S. 431 May 2, 1989 Amendment prohibiting lobbying by the Martin Luther King, Jr. Federal Holiday Commission.

Var. 89 H.R. 2072 June 6, 1989 Tabling amendment to Dire Emergency Supplemental Appropriations to make it illegal for municipalities and states to have policies concerning South Africa.

Var. 460 S. 1970 June 28, 1990 Amendment to omnibus crime bill to limit required studies on the role of race in state criminal justice systems to instances where constitutional violations have been found or suspected.

Var. 480 S. 2104 July 17, 1990 Cloture motion on amendment to Civil Rights Act of 1990 restoring and strengthening civil rights law that bans discrimination in employment and for other purposes.

Var. 481 S. 2104 July 17, 1990 Amendment to prohibit the denial to any person of the due process of law required by the Constitution.

Var. 482 S. 2104. July 18, 1990 Amendment including language stating that nothing in the amendments made by this act shall be construed to require an employer to adopt hiring or promotional quotas or to affect court-ordered remedies, conciliation agreements, or otherwise in accordance with the law.

Var. 483 S. 2104 July 18, 1990 Passage of Civil Rights Act of 1990.

Var. 597 S. 2104 October 16, 1990 To recommit the conference report of the Civil Rights Act of 1990 to the conference committee with instructions that the conferees consider an amendment to specifically prohibit employers from using quotas.

Var. 598 S. 2104 October 16, 1990 To adopt the conference report on the Civil Rights Act of 1990.

Var. 626 S. 2104 October 24, 1990 Overriding veto of the Civil Rights Act of 1990.

### 102nd Congress

Var. 112 S. 1241 June 20, 1991 Amendment to the Crime Bill to strike the Racial Justice Act provisions allowing minorities to challenge a death sentence as discriminatory if statistics show a disproportionate number of their race being condemned to die.

Var. 120 S. 1241 June 26, 1991 Motion to table amendment to the Crime Bill to prohibit federal agencies and courts from interpreting Title VII of the Civil Rights Act of 1964 to permit an employer to grant preferential treatment in employment to any group or individual on account of race, religion, sex, or national origin.

Var. 230 October 15, 1991 Confirmation of Clarence Thomas to be an associate justice of the Supreme Court.

Var. 243 S. 1745 October 29, 1991 Motion to table amendment to Civil Rights Act of 1991 to limit attorney contingency fees to 20 percent of civil rights cases, require prior disclosure of all likely legal costs in civil rights cases, provide plaintiffs with a private right of action against their lawyers for not complying, and provide the plaintiff with the option of paying for legal services on an hourly rate basis or a contingency fee basis.

Var. 482 September 9, 1992 Cloture motion on nomination of Edward
E. Carnes, Jr., of Alabama to the 11th Circuit Court of Appeals.
Var. 483 September 9, 1992 Confirmation of Edward E. Carnes, Jr., of
Alabama to the 11th Circuit Court of Appeals.

State Public Opinion on Race from GSS Cumulative Survey
1972–2000.

### Figure 5-1. Interparty Difference of Means on Defense Spending (Democratic Mean – Republican Mean), Senate, 86th through 93rd Congresses (1959–1974)

See Table 5-4 for votes.

### Figure 5-2. Correlation between Defense Spending Scores and D1 and D2 NOMINATE Scores, Senate, 86th through 100th Congresses (1959–1988)

See Table 5-1 for votes. See voteview.com for NOMINATE scores.

### Figure 5-3. Interparty Difference on Defense Spending (Net Democratic Support – Net Republican Support), Gallup Polls, 1935–2000

Poll Dates: December 1–6, 1935, March 26–31, 1950, August 15–20, 1953, March 2–7, 1960, July 10–15, 1969, March 11–14, 1971, February 16–19, 1973, September 21–24, 1973, September 6–9, 1974, January 30–February 2, 1976, July 8–11, 1977, January 25–28, 1980, April 3–6, 1981, March 12–15, 1982, January 25–28, 1985, April 10–13, 1987, June 24–26, 1988, July 6–9, 1989, August 9–12, 1990, March 29–31, 1993, November 20–22, 1998, May 7–9, 1999, May 18–21, 2000, August 24–27, 2000.

### Figure 5-4. Interparty Difference of Mean Support for Income Tax Cuts among Representatives (Republican Mean – Democratic Mean), 88th through 96th Congresses (1963–1980)

*88th Congress*

Var. 77 H. Res. 527 September 24, 1963 A closed rule for H.R. 8363, the Revenue Act of 1963.

Var. 78. H.R. 8363 September 25, 1963 Motion to recommit the Revenue Act with instructions to amend it to prevent the tax reductions from taking effect unless the president specified that spending for fiscal 1964 was not expected to exceed $98 billion.

Var. 79. H.R. 8363 September 25, 1963 Passage of the Revenue Act of 1964.

Var. 141 H.R. 8363 February 25, 1964 Adoption of the conference report on the Revenue Act of 1964.

### 91st Congress

Var. 54 H.R. 12290 June 30, 1969 To continue the income tax surcharge and the excise taxes on automobiles and communication services for temporary periods, to terminate the investment credit, and to provide a low-income allowance for individuals.

Var. 72 H.R. 13080 July 30, 1969 To pass a bill to continue for an additional 15 days the existing rates of income tax withheld at source.

Var. 76 H. Res. 509 August 4, 1969 To concur with the Senate amendment to H.R. 9951, which extends the 10 percent surtax through December 31.

### 94th Congress

Var. 607 H.R. 5559 December 18, 1975 Passage of the Revenue Adjustment Act extending the provisions of the Tax Reduction Act for six months, the objections of the president notwithstanding.

### 95th Congress

Var. 1317 H.R. 13511 August 10, 1978 Motion to recommit to the Ways and Means Committee with instructions to report it back with an amendment that would provide for an across-the-board cut in individual income taxes of approximately 33 percent to be phased in over the next three years.

### 96th Congress

Var. 136 H. Con. Res. 107 May 10, 1979 Amendment providing for an adjustment of personal income tax rates for inflation in fiscal 1979 and a 10 percent reduction in tax rates in 1980.

**Figure 5-5. Correlation between Support for Income Tax Cuts and D1 and D2 NOMINATE Scores, House of Representatives, 88th through 96th Congresses, 1963–1980**

Same roll calls as used in Figure 5-4.

VOTES USED TO CALCULATE RAPOPORT-STONE SCORES

**Chapter 2: Votes Used to Calculate The Effect of Conversion on Change in Party Mean Scores on Trade Policy: House, 87th through 93rd Congresses (1961–1974)**

These are the same votes as used in Figure 2-3.

**Chapter 3: Votes Used to Calculate the Effect of Conversion on Change in Party Mean Scores on Abortion Rights: House of Representatives, 93rd through 104th Congresses**

*104th Congress*

For votes for the 93rd to the 103rd Congress see Figure 3-2.

*Votes from the 104th Congress:*

Var. 359 H.R. 1561 May 24, 1995 Amendment to codify the Mexico City Policy, which prohibits U.S. funding of any public or private foreign entity that directly or indirectly performs abortions except in cases of rape or incest, or when a woman's life is endangered.

Var. 360 H.R. 1561 May 24, 1995 Amendment codifying the Mexico City Policy.

Var. 392 H.R. 1530 June 15, 1995 Amendment to defense authorization to allow military personnel and their dependents to obtain abortions at overseas military bases as long as the woman pays for the procedure. The bill would prohibit the practice, and the amendment would strike the restriction and restore current law.

Var. 442 H.R. 1868 June 28, 1995 Amendment to eliminate the provisions that codify the Mexico City Policy, and to eliminate provisions that require foreign organizations receiving U.S aid to certify that they do not violate or lobby to change abortion laws.

Var. 443 H.R. 1868 June 28, 1995 Amendment to require foreign organizations receiving U.S. aid to certify that they do not violate or lobby to change abortion laws, and to withhold money from the

UNPFA unless the president certifies that the fund has terminated all activities in China or that for the past year there have been no coercive abortions in China.

Var. 536 H.R. 2020 July 9, 1995 Amendment to Treasury Postal Service Appropriation deleting a provision that would prohibit federal employees or their families from receiving abortion services through their federal health insurance policies except when the life of the woman would be endangered.

Var. 584 H.R. 2076 July 26, 1995 Amendment to strike from the bill provisions that prevent funds in Title I from being used in performing abortions in the federal prison system except in cases of rape or when the woman's life is endangered.

Var. 624 H.R. 2127 August 2, 1995 Amendment to Departments of Labor, HHS, and Education appropriations to terminate the Title X family planning program and transfer $193 million to block grant programs, $116 million to the Maternal and Child Health program, and $77 million to the Community and Migrant Health Centers program.

Var. 625 H.R. 2127 August 2, 1995 Amendment to provide $193 million for family planning projects under Title X of the Public Health Service Act and to prohibit funding under Title X for abortions, directed pregnancy counseling, lobbying, or political activity.

Var. 629 H.R. 2127 August 3, 1995 Amendment to strike provisions allowing states to withhold Medicaid funding for abortions except in cases where the life of the woman would be endangered if the fetus were carried to term.

Var. 630 H.R. 2127 August 3, 1995 Amendment to strike provisions to prohibit federal programs or states from withholding funds or accreditation from medical training programs that do not offer training in abortion procedures.

Var. 651 H.R. 2126 September 7, 1995 Substitute amendment to defense appropriations to prohibit abortions at overseas military facilities unless the life of the woman is endangered or the government is reimbursed with private money for any costs associated with the abortion.

Var. 652 H.R. 2126 September 7, 1995 Amendment to prohibit abortions at overseas military facilities unless the life of the woman is endangered.

Var. 761 H.R. 1868 October 31, 1995 Motion to recommit foreign
   operations appropriations bill to the conference committee with
   instructions to report it back with an amendment to prohibit the use
   of money in the bill from being used to lobby for or against abortion
   and to cut off funding for the UNFPA unless the president certifies
   that all UNFPA operations in China have ceased by May 1, 1996, or
   coercive abortions in China have stopped.
Var. 763 H.R. 1868 October 31, 1995 Motion that the House recede
   from its disagreement with the Senate with an amendment prohibiting funds in the bill from being used to lobby for or against abortion
   and requiring that foreign nongovernmental organizations seeking
   assistance from the Agency for International Development be subject
   to eligibility requirements no more stringent than those applied to
   foreign governments, prohibiting funds in the bill from being used to
   lobby for or against abortion, reinstating the so-called Mexico City
   Policy, and cutting off money for the UNFPA unless the president
   certifies that all UNFPA operations in China have ceased by March
   1, 1996, or coercive abortions in China have stopped for at least 12
   months.
Var. 764 H.R. 1833 November 1, 1995 Adoption of rule providing for
   consideration of the bill to ban partial birth abortions, a procedure
   used in some late-term abortions.
Var. 765 H.R. 1833 November 1, 1995 Motion to permit exhibits to
   be used on the House floor during debate on the bill to ban "partial
   birth" abortions.
Var. 766 H.R. 1833 November 1, 1995 Passage of the bill to ban partial birth abortions.
Var. 804 H.R. 1868 November 15, 1995 Motion to insist on language in
   the foreign operations appropriations bill that reinstates the Mexico
   City Policy and cuts off funding for the UNFPA unless the president
   certifies that all UNFPA operations in China have ceased by March
   1, 1996, or coercive abortions in China have stopped for at least a
   year.
Var. 859 H. Res. 296 December 13, 1995 Adoption of the rule to provide for consideration of motion to dispose of the remaining Senate
   amendments concerning international family planning funds to the
   foreign operations appropriations bill. The motion would require
   that appropriations for private, nongovernmental, or multilateral
   organizations (including the UNPFA) involved with population

planning not be released until separate authorizing language is enacted.

Var. 860 H.R. 1868 December 13, 1995 Motion to recede from the House amendment to the Senate amendment with a further amendment to require that appropriations for private, nongovernmental, or multilateral organizations (including the UNPFA) involved with population planning not be released until separate authorizing language is enacted.

Var. 946 H.R. 3019 March 7, 1996 Amendment to strike from the bill a provision allowing states not to permit Medicaid to finance abortions in cases of rape or incest.

Var. 988 H.R. 1833 March 27, 1996 Adoption of the rule to provide for consideration of the Senate amendments to the bill that would impose penalties in the case of certain late-term abortions, in which the person performing the abortion partially delivers the fetus before completing the abortion.

Var. 989 H.R. 1833 March 27, 1996 Motion to agree to the Senate amendments to shift the burden of proof from the defendant to the prosecution to show beyond a reasonable doubt that the abortion procedure was not necessary to save the woman's life, to clarify who can be held liable for performing the procedure, and to allow a prospective father to sue for civil damages only if he was married to the woman at the time of the abortion.

Var. 1215 H.R. 3756 July 17, 1996 Amendment to Treasury Department and Postal Service appropriations striking the bill's provisions that restrict women who receive health care under the Federal Employee Health Plan from receiving abortions through those plans.

Var. 1227 H.R. 3845 July 22, 1996 Amendment to District of Columbia appropriations to restrict only the use of federal funds for abortions in the district.

Var. 1316 H.R. 1833 September 19, 1996 Motion to discharge from the Judiciary Committee the bill that would ban certain late-term abortion procedures.

Var. 1317 H.R. 1833 September 19, 1996 Passage, over the president's veto, of the bill banning a late-term abortion procedure, where the physician partially delivers the fetus before completing the abortion.

Votes Used to Calculate the Effect of Conversion on Change in Party Mean Scores on Gun Control: House, 90th through 106th Congresses (1967–2000)

See Figure 3-6.

## Chapter 4: Votes Used to Calculate the Effect of Conversion on Change in Party Mean Scores on Racial Issues: House of Representatives, 85th through 102nd Congresses (1957–1992)

### *85th Congress*

Var. 50 H. Res. 259 June 5, 1957 Open rule for Civil Rights Bill HR 6127.

Var. 51 H.R. 6127 June 18, 1957 Motion to Recommit civil rights bill with instructions to insert provision for jury trial in any criminal contempt case.

Var. 52 H.R. 6127 June 18, 1957 Passage of the Civil Rights Act.

Var. 105 H. Res. 410 August 27, 1957 Motion to end debate on whether to take H.R. 6127, the Civil Rights Act, from the speaker's desk and concur in Senate jury trial amendment with House-Senate compromise amendment.

Var. 106 H. Res. 410 August 27, 1957 Take H.R. 6127, the Civil Rights Act, from the speaker's desk and concur in Senate jury trial amendment with House-Senate compromise amendment.

Var. 132 H.R. 10589 April 1, 1958 Executive offices appropriation bill. Amendment to appropriate $750,000 for Civil Rights Commission.

### *86th Congress*

Var. 97 H.R. 8385 September 15, 1959 Motion that House concur in Senate amendment to extend life of Civil Rights Commission for two years and appropriate $0.5 million in funds.

Var. 108 H. Res. 359 March 10, 1960 Open rule providing 15 hours of House debate on H.R. 8601, the Civil Rights Act.

Var. 110 H.R. 8601 Civil Rights Act of 1960 March 23, 1960 Amendment embodying administration proposal for court-appointed referees to help Negroes register and vote when the court has found that a "pattern of practice" of discrimination existed.

Var. 111 H.R. 8601 March 24, 1960 Motion to recommit with instructions to delete the words making it a crime to obstruct court orders for school desegregation "by any threatening letter or communication."

Var. 112 H.R. 9801 March 24, 1960 Passage of the Civil Rights Act of 1960.

Var. 116 H.R. 8601 April 21, 1960 Approval by the House of the Senate's amendments to the Civil Rights Act.

Var. 146 H.R. 10128 May 26, 1960 School Construction Assistance Act. Powell Amendment to require that school facilities built with help of money available under the act be open to all students without regard to race, color, creed, national origin, or religion.

Civil Rights Discharge Petition (*Congressional Quarterly 1960 Almanac*, p. 203). I include this petition because it was – atypically for the time – publicized, and signatures on it functioned as position taking, much as recorded votes did.

### 87th Congress

Var. 104 H.R. 7371 September 13, 1961 Fiscal 1962 Appropriations bill for Justice and State Departments. Amendment to agree to Senate amendment extending Civil Rights Commission for two years.

Var. 190 H.R. 12580 July 20, 1962 Departments of State, Justice, and Commerce and related agencies appropriation, including funds for the Civil Rights Commission.

Var. 201 August 27, 1962 Motion to dispense with further proceedings under the quorum call before roll call delaying House consideration of S.J. Res. 29, a constitutional amendment banning the poll tax in federal elections.

Var. 202 August 27, 1962 Motion to dispense with further proceedings and take up S.J. Res. 29, anti–poll tax amendment.

Var. 203 S.J. Res. 29 August. 27, 1962 Constitutional amendment to ban the use of the poll tax as a requirement in federal elections.

### 88th Congress

Var. 43 June 4, 1963 Motion to adjourn in order to stop discussion of civil rights legislation under special orders for House speeches.

Var. 48 H.R. 7063 June 18, 1963 Appropriations for the Departments of State, Justice, and Commerce, the Judiciary and related agencies including the Civil Rights Commission.

Var. 82 H.R. 3369 October 7, 1963 Private relief bill including Senate amendment extending the life of the Civil Rights Commission for one year.

Var. 138 H.R. 7152 February 10, 1964 Passage of the Civil Rights Act.

Var. 192 H.R. 7152 July 2, 1964 Adoption of resolution approving Senate version of the Civil Rights Act.

## 89th Congress

Var. 92. H. Res. 440 July 6, 1965 Rule providing for the consideration of and 10 hours of debate on H.R. 6400, the Voting Rights Act of 1965.

Var. 96 H.R. 6400 July 9, 1965 Motion to recommit the Voting Rights Act with instructions to substitute the text of H.R. 7896 prohibiting the denial to any person of the right to register or to vote because of his failure to pay a poll tax or any other such tax, for the language of the committee amendment.

Var. 97 H.R. 6400 July 9, 1965 Passage of the Voting Rights Act.

Var. 117 August 3, 1965. Motion agreeing to the conference report on S. 1564, the Voting Rights Act.

Var. 155 H. Res. 506 September 13, 1965 Open rule for the consideration of H.R. 10065, the Equal Employment Opportunity Act.

Var. 185 H.R. 4644 September 29, 1965 Motion to recommit the D.C. Home Rule Bill.

Var. 186 H.R. 4644 September 29, 1965 Passage of the D.C. Home Rule Bill.

Var. 253 H.R. 10065 April 27, 1966 Passage of the Equal Employment Opportunity Act of 1966.

Var. 302 H.R. 14765 August 9, 1966 Motion to recommit the Civil Rights Act of 1966 to the Judiciary Committee with instructions to delete Title IV, the open housing title.

Var. 303 H.R. 14765 August 9, 1966 To pass the Civil Rights Act of 1966.

## 90th Congress

Var. 22 H. Res. 278 March 1, 1967 Previous question motion on seating Adam Clayton Powell. Resolution recommends that Powell be seated, censured, and made to pay back $40,000 of the money he improperly expended and that his seniority commence from the date of his seating in the 90th Congress.

Var. 23 H. Res. 278 March 1, 1967 To order the previous question on H. Res. 278 together with the Curtis Amendment, which excludes Powell from the 90th Congress and declares his seat vacant.

Var. 24 H. Res. 278 March 1, 1967 Amendment excluding Powell from the 90th Congress and declaring his seat vacant.

Var. 123 H.R. 2516 August 16, 1967 To pass a bill to establish penalties for interference with civil rights. Interference with a person engaged in one of the eight activities protected under this bill must be racially motivated to incur the bill's penalties.

Var. 304 H. Res. 1100 April 10, 1968 To order the previous question on a resolution.

Adding Senate amendment banning discrimination in sale or rental of housing to Civil Rights/Anti-Riot bill.

Var. 305 H. Res. 1100 April 10, 1968 Adding Senate amendment banning discrimination in housing to Civil Rights/Anti-Riot bill.

Var. 467 H.R. 18037 October 3, 1968 To concur with Senate amendment limiting antibusing provisions to elementary schools

Var. 469 H.R. 18037 October 3, 1968 Motion that the House agree with Senate amendment modifying antibusing provisions in the bill.

### 91st Congress

Var. 160 H.R. 4249 December, 11, 1969 Amendment to the Voting Rights Act Extension concerning discriminating use of tests and devices.

Var. 161 H.R. 4249 December 11, 1969 Passage of the Voting Rights Act Extension.

Var. 283 H. Res. 914 June 17, 1970 Previous question motion providing for agreement to the Senate amendments to H.R. 424, extension of the Voting Rights Act.

Var. 284 H. Res. 914 June 17, 1970 Agreeing to Senate amendments to Voting Rights Act.

Var. 383 S. 2455 November 16, 1970 Passage of authorization for Civil Rights Commission.

Var. 439 H.R. 19446 December 21, 1970 Move that the House resolve itself into the Committee of the Whole for the further consideration of bill assisting school districts with special problems incident to desegregation.

Var. 440 H.R. 19446 December 21, 1970 Motion that Committee of the Whole Ruse and report back bill with the recommendation that the enacting clause by stricken out, i.e., killing the bill.

Var. 441 H.R. 19446 December 21, 1970 Passage of extension of the Voting Rights Act.

### 92nd Congress

Var. 41 H.R. 7016 April 07, 1971 Amendment striking out section banning forced busing.

Var. 183 H.R. 1746 September 16, 1971 Amendment providing court enforcement powers for the EEOC in lieu of "cease and desist authority."

Var. 184 H.R. 1746 September 16, 1971 Motion to agree to previous amendment.

Var. 265 H.R. 8687 November 10, 1971 Agreeing to language designed to remove the embargo on the importation of chrome ore from Rhodesia in the conference report.

Var. 368 S. 659 March 8, 1972 Tabling motion to instruct conferees to insist on antibusing amendments to omnibus education amendments of 1972

Var. 369 S. 659 March 8, 1972 Motion to instruct conferees to insist on the House antibusing amendments.

Var. 423 S. 659 May 11, 1972 Table motion to instruct House conferees to insist on antibusing provisions.

Var. 586 H.R. 13915 August 17, 1972 Amendment qualifying the neighborhood as the appropriate bases for determining school assignments.

Var. 569 H.R. 13915 August 17, 1972 Amendment increasing authorization by $1.5 billion annually for Title I, assistance for educationally deprived students attending schools enrolling high concentrations of students from low-income families.

Var. 570 H.R. 13915 August 17, 1972 Amendment striking out language of the subsequent amendment (Var. 571) that authorizes busing other than busing to the school nearest to the student's residence.

Var. 571 H.R. 13915 August 17, 1972 Amendment forbidding busing and allowing court orders and school desegregation plans already in effect under Title VI of the Civil Rights Act to be reopened and modified to comply with the provisions of this bill.

Var. 572 H.R. 13915 August 17, 1972 Amendment specifying that provisions of the blll comply with Amendment XIV of the Constitution.

Var. 574 H. R. 13915 August 17, 1972 Amendment specifying that "nothing in this act is intended to be inconsistent with, or violative of any provision of the Constitution."

### 93rd Congress

Var. 171 H.R. 8152 June 18, 1973 Amendment stating that nothing in the bill shall be construed to require the adoption by a grantee of a quota system or discontinue a grant because of the refusal of a grantee to adopt such a quota system.

Var. 190 H.R. 7824 June 21, 1973 Amendment prohibiting legal services with respect to any proceeding or litigation relating to the desegregation of schools.

Var. 496 H.R. 1145 December 13, 1973 Amendment to ban the allocation of petroleum for busing of students to a school farther than the school nearest to their homes.

Var. 502 H.R. 11450 December 14, 1973 Amendment allowing for the allocation of petroleum for school busing where a busing plan has been ordered by the appropriate school board.

Var. 623 H.R. 69 March 26, 1974 Amendment aimed at prohibiting busing for the purpose of achieving racial balance in amendments to the Elementary and Secondary Education Act.

Var. 626 H.R. 69 March 27, 1974 Amendment prohibiting the use of any funds to implement busing plans.

Var. 739 H.R. 69 June 5, 1974 Motion to instruct House conferees to insist on provisions relating to busing of students.

Var. 784 H.R. 69 June 27, 1974 Motion to instruct House conferees to insist on House-passed provisions on busing.

Var. 829 H.R. 69 July 22, 1974 Motion to instruct conferees to insist on antibusing provisions.

Var. 908 H.R. 12859 August 15, 1974 Amendment prohibiting the use of any funds to implement busing plans in order to overcome racial imbalances in any school or school system.

Var. 1033 H.R. 16900 December 4, 1974 Concurring with Senate amendments providing that no funds shall be used to compel any school system to classify students or teachers by race, religion, sex, or national origin.

## 94th Congress

Var. 192 H.R. 6219 June 3, 1975 Amendment to extension of Voting Rights Act approving coverage when less than 50 percent of Spanish or black citizens have voted in the previous federal election, in districts in which 5 percent of the population is black or Spanish and would require the federal presence for 10 years after such election, instead of until the next election in which 50 percent of such minorities vote.

Var. 193 H.R. 6219 June 3, 1975 Amendment making it easier for states to "bail out" of coverage of the act.

Var. 194 H.R. 6219 June 3, 1975 Amendment adding a section repealing the preclearance procedures for voting law changes including redistricting contained in Section 5.

Var. 195 H.R. 6219 June 3, 1975 Amendment changing the provision of the bill which bans forever all voter qualification tests and devices to one which extends said ban for 10 years.

Var. 202 H.R. 6219 June 4, 1975 Passage of extension of the Voting Rights Act

Var. 304 H.R. 8597 July 16, 1975 Amendment to Department of the Treasury, Postal Service, Executive Office of the President, and certain independent agencies appropriation deleting language prohibiting the use of IRS funds to require private colleges and other organizations to prove they have adopted racially nondiscriminatory policies.

Var. 710 H.J. Res. 280 March 23, 1976 Amendment limiting representation of Washington, DC, in the House to one member with a mechanism allowing Congress to increase the number to full representation.

Var. 712 H.J. Res 280 March 23, 1976 Passage of resolution regarding representation of the District of Columbia in Congress.

Var. 1278 H. Res. 1591 October 1, 1976 Rule for consideration of S. 2278, the Civil Rights Attorneys' Fees Awards Act of 1976.

Var. 1279 S. 2278 October 1, 1976 Motion to recommit S. 2278 to the Judiciary Committee with an amendment excluding cases filed prior to the effective date of the act.

Var. 1280 S. 2278 October 1, 1976 Passage of the Civil Rights Attorneys' Fees Awards Act.

*95th Congress*

Var. 66 H.R. 1746 March 14, 1977 Amendment to bill banning Rhodesian chrome imports prohibiting chrome imports from any country that has not complied with the human rights provisions of the United Nations Charter.

Var. 68 H.R. 1746 March 14, 1977 Passage of bill banning importation of Rhodesian chrome.

Var. 265 H.R. 6884 May 24, 1977 Amendment deleting the provision that would have established a Southern Africa Special Requirements Fund and $100 million security assistance for that fund.

Var. 347 H.R. 7797 June 22, 1977 Amendment deleting the appropriation of $100 million for the Southern Africa Special Requirements Fund that aids the nations bordering Rhodesia.

Var. 364 H.R. 6666 June 27, 1977 Amendment prohibiting the use of Legal Services funds for legal assistance in any case relating to school desegregation.

Var. 631 H.R. 6666 October 20, 1977 Motion to instruct conferees to insist on language in Legal Services Corporation appropriation prohibiting that authorized funds be used to fund legal assistance in cases dealing with desegregation in any elementary or secondary school or school system.

Var. 672 H.Con. Res. 388 October 31, 1977 Resolution expressing the concern of the Congress about recent acts of repression performed by the government of South Africa against its people.

Var. 794 H.J. Res. 554 March 2, 1978 Passage of a resolution amending the Constitution to provide for full voting representation of the District of Columbia.

Var. 926 H. Res. 1049 April 25, 1978 Resolution stating that the House does not approve of Reorganization Plan 1, which consolidates various equal employment programs into one program to be administered by an Equal Employment Opportunity Commission.

Var. 1060 H.R. 12157 June 2, 1978 Amendment striking language that prohibits the Export-Import Bank from participating in transactions with the Republic of South Africa.

Var. 1099 H.R. 12989 June 13, 1978 Amendment prohibiting use of funds to issue or enforce any ratio, quota, or other admissions or hiring formula related to race, creed, color, national origin, or sex.

Var. 1185 H. Res. 1267 July 13, 1978 Motion to table resolution calling for the impeachment of UN ambassador Andrew Young.

Var. 1256 H.R. 12432 July 28, 1978 Amendment prohibiting members of the Civil Rights Commission or its staff from lobbying for any legislation.

Var. 1271 H.R. 12514 August 2, 1978 Amendment immediately lifting U.S. economic sanctions against Rhodesia unless the president determines that the government of Rhodesia has "refused" to participate and negotiate in good faith at an All-Parties Conference to discuss relevant issues, or if the president determines that the Rhodesian government failed to schedule free elections.

Var. 1272 H.R. 12514 August 2, 1978 Amendment banning U.S. sanctions against Rhodesia after December 31, 1978, unless the president determines that a new Rhodesian government has not been installed nor elected by free elections in which all political groups have been free to participate.

Var. 1413 H.R. 10792 September 18, 1978 Passage of the bill authorizing the Smithsonian Institution to acquire the Museum of African Art.

Var. 1454 H.R. 12005 September 26, 1978 Amendment to Justice Department appropriations prohibiting the use of funds to enforce busing of students to schools other than those nearest to their homes, except for cases involving busing of mentally or physically handicapped children.

Var. 1503 H.R. 12929 October 12, 1978 Motion to recommit the conference report on the Departments of Labor and HEW appropriation with instructions to accept Senate amendment prohibiting the use of these funds to implement affirmative action admission policies at institutions of higher education.

## 96th Congress

Var. 83 H.R. 3324 April 9, 1979 Amendment deleting language providing for impartial observers at elections in southern Africa and a $20 million grant in aid for the United States to Rhodesia after the April 1979 elections in that country.

Var. 84 H.R. 3324 April 9, 1979 Amendment reinstating language providing for impartial observers at elections in southern Africa, and $20 million, which could be made available to Rhodesia and is not required.

Var. 85 H.R. 3324 April 9, 1979 Amendment authorizing $68 million in economic assistance to southern Africa, providing election observers and earmarking $20 million in aid to Rhodesia that could be made available after its April elections.

Var. 190 H.R. 2641 June 8, 1979 Amendment to the Civil Rights Commission authorization reducing the ceiling from $14,000,000 to $11,372,000.

Var. 212 H.R. 2444 June 12, 1979 Amendment deleting the additional authority given the assistant secretary for civil rights to collect data required to ensure compliance with civil rights laws, to hire and supervise employees, and to contract out for services pursuant to compliance and enforcement functions.

Var. 292 H.R. 4439 June 28, 1979 Amendment to Zimbabwe Rhodesia sanctions extending the date for sanctions to December 1, 1989, and requiring the president to recommend appropriate legislation to Congress to extend such sanctions further if he determined it to be in our national interest to do so.

Var. 301 H.R. 3363 July 11, 1979 Motion to instruct House conferees to agree to language in Senate amendment to State Department authorization expressing the sense of Congress on the nonenforcement of sanctions against Zimbabwe Rhodesia.

Var. 325 S. 210 July 17, 1979 Motion instructing House conferees to insist on language in stating that no individual should be denied educational opportunities by rules that utilize any ratio or other numerical requirement related to race, creed, color, national origin, or sex.

Var. 349 H.J. Res. 74 July 24, 1979 To discharge the Judiciary Committee from further consideration of an antibusing constitutional amendment.

Var. 350 H.J. Res. 74 July 24, 1979 Motion to order previous question on antibusing constitutional amendment.

Var. 371 H. Res. 391 July 30, 1979 Motion tabling resolution expelling Rep. Charles Diggs, Jr.

Var. 588 H.R. 5461 November 13, 1979 Motion to suspend the rules and pass the bill designating Martin Luther King, Jr.'s birthday a legal public holiday.

Var. 634 H.R. 5461 December 5, 1979 Amendment to Martin Luther King Holiday Bill designating the third Monday in January rather than January 15 as the legal holiday.

Var. 635 H.R. 5461 December 5, 1979 Motion to agree to a substitute that designates the third Sunday in January each year as the holiday to celebrate Martin Luther King, Jr.'s birthday.

Var. 636 December 5, 1979 Motion to have the Committee of the Whole Rise during debate on the Martin Luther King Holiday.

Var. 963 H.R. 5200 June 11, 1980 Motion to agree to a substitute for an amendment to the Fair Housing Bill that permits appraisers to take into consideration factors other than race, color, religion, national origin, sex, or handicap. The original amendment permitted appraisers to consider all factors shown by documentation to be relevant.

Var. 964 H.R. 5200 June 11, 1980 Amendment modifying an amendment in order to provide for adjudication of fair housing cases by Justice Department appointed administrative law judges to require the Secretary of Housing and Urban Development to certify that conciliation has been attempted and failed prior to such hearing and directing the secretary to refer all land use control cases to the attorney general.

Var. 967 H.R. 5200 June 12, 1980 Motion to recommit the Fair Housing Bill to the Judiciary Committee with instructions to transfer the adjudication of fair housing cases from HUD administrative law judges to the District Court system.

Var. 1092 H.R. 7583 August 19, 1980 To sustain ruling of the chair regarding the Ashbrook Amendment as legislation on an appropriation bill.

## 97th Congress

Var. 190 H.R. 4169 September 9, 1981 Amendment to the Departments of Commerce, Justice, and State, the Judiciary, and related agencies appropriations preventing the use of Justice Department funds to require, request, or recommend, in connection with any cause of action that is or may be brought for violation of the Fair Housing Act of 1968.

Var. 211 H.C.R. 183 September 22, 1981 Resolution expressing the sense of the Congress that the National Rugby Team of South Africa should not play in the United States.

Var. 233 H.R. 3112 October 5, 1981 Amendment eliminating a provision that made the signing of a consent decree in a voting rights lawsuit a bar to bailing out from coverage of the act if the decree were signed within 10 years of a jurisdiction's petition to bail out.

Var. 234 H.R. 3112 October 5, 1981 Amendment permitting bailout cases to be heard in an appropriate federal district court in the jurisdiction seeking bailout rather than in the District of Columbia.

Var. 235 H.R. 3112 October 5, 1981 Amendment allowing a state covered by the Voting Rights Act to bail out from coverage if two-thirds of its counties are eligible to bail out.

Var. 765 H.R. 6957 December 10, 1982 Amendment to Departments of Commerce, Justice, and State, the Judiciary and related agencies prohibiting the use of Department of Justice funds to require the transportation of students to schools other than those in their neighborhoods, with the exception of students requiring specialized education.

## 98th Congress

Var. 2999 H.R. 3706 August 2, 1983 Passage of a bill making the birthday of Martin Luther King, Jr. a legal public holiday.

Var. 317 H.R. 2230 August 4, 1983 Amendment to bill extending the life of the Civil Rights Commission providing that the president can remove a member only for neglect of duty or malfeasance in office.

Var. 457 H.R. 3222 November 8, 1983 Motion to recede from disagreement and concur in a Senate amendment providing $11.89 million for the Civil Rights Commission.

## 99th Congress

Var. 120 H.R. 1460 May 21, 1985 Amendment to sanctions on South Africa bill to permit U.S. businesses to make new investments in South Africa if they implement fair employment practices, also known as the "Sullivan Principles."

Var. 133 H.R. 1460 June 4, 1985 Amendment to make the prohibition on krugerrand imports effective only if the ban is not inconsistent with the obligations of the United States under the General Agreement on Tariffs and Trade.

Var. 136 H.R. 1460 June 5, 1985 Amendment establishing a Commission on South Africa to examine South Africa's progress toward the elimination of apartheid, requires American businesses to comply with the Sullivan Principles, and authorizes funds to support black and other nonwhite concerns and development.

Var. 137 H.R. 1460 June 5, 1985 Amendment in the nature of a substitute establishing the Sullivan Principles, with penalties for noncompliance, imposes sanctions within two years of enactment if certifiable progress toward ending apartheid has not been made, authorizes $15 million in funds for education and teaching training and $1.5 million in funds for human rights, and establishes a United States–South Africa Commission.

Var. 139 H.R. 1460 June 5, 1985 Motion to recommit sanctions bill with instructions that it be reported back containing an amendment that prohibits the provisions of the act from taking effect for one year, or from taking effect if the president certifies to the Congress that the African National Congress has not renounced the use of violence.

Var. 140 H.R. 1460 June 5, 1985 Passage of sanctions on South Africa.

Var. 213 H.R. 1555 July 11, 1985 Amendment to allow the Overseas Private Investment Corporation to be eligible for certain joint ventures between businesses owned or controlled by South African blacks or nonwhites.

Var. 271 H.R. 1460 August 1, 1985 Adoption of resolution waiving certain points of order against the conference report imposing sanctions against the government of South Africa until laws and policies enforcing apartheid and segregation are eliminated.

Var. 608 H. Res. 478 Rule for H.R. 4868, the South Africa sanctions bill.

Var. 610 H.R. 4868 June 18, 1986 Amendment to exempt companies located in South Africa that implement the Sullivan Principles from the bill's sanctions.

Var. 772 H.R. 4428 August 14, 1986 Amendment increasing the set-aside for minority business concerns from 5 percent to 10 percent of all defense contracts and to include the operation and maintenance spending in the set-aside.

Var. 839 H.R. 4868 September 29, 1986 Override of veto on sanctions of South Africa.

### *101st Congress*

Var. 35 H.R. 1385 April 17, 1989 Passage of the bill making permanent the Martin Luther King, Jr. Federal Holiday Commission and authorizing annual funds for activities to honor Dr. King on the anniversary of his birth.

Var. 93 H.R. 1278 June 15, 1989 Amendment to Savings and Loan Restructuring to require federal regulatory agencies to disclose ratings and evaluations given to banks and thrifts and to disclose the number of applications received and approved by categories of race, income, and gender.

Var. 354 H.R. 3532 November 15, 1989 Passage of bill extending the life of the Civil Rights Commission.

Var. 665 H.R. 4000 August 2, 1990 Previous question motion on rule for Civil Rights Act of 1990.

Var. 666 August 2, 1990 Adoption of the rule to provide for consideration of H.R. 4000, the Civil Rights Act of 1990.

Var. 670 H.R. 4000 August 3, 1990 Amendment to provide a different definition of the proof of "business necessity" required from an employer to justify employment practices having a disparate impact on women and minorities.

Var. 671 H.R. 4000 August 3, 1990 Passage of the Civil Rights Act of 1990.

Var. 780 H.R. 5269 October 5, 1990 Amendment to Comprehensive Crime Control Act to modify provisions relating to racially discriminatory death penalty sentences.

Var. 781 H.R. 5269 October 5, 1990 Amendment to strike provisions that bar execution of prisoners who show that racial discrimination was a factor in their sentence.

Var. 831 S. 2104 October 17, 1990 Adoption of conference report on Civil Rights Act.

### 102nd Congress

Var. 135 H.R. 1 June 4, 1991 Motion to order the previous question on the rule for the Civil Rights Act of 1991.

Var. 136 H.R. 1 June 4, 1991 Adoption of the rule to provide for House floor consideration of Civil Rights Act of 1991.

Var. 138 H.R. 1 June 4, 1991 Substitute for administration's civil rights bill. The substitute would remove compensatory and punitive damages for job discrimination based on sex, religion, or disability but allow up to $150,000 for cases involving harassment; define business necessity as a practice that has a manifest relationship to the employment or that serves a legitimate employment goal; allow intentional discrimination when it is only a contributing factor; allow challenges to consent decrees; ban the use of race-based adjustments to hiring-test scores; and make other changes.

Var. 140 H.R. 1 June 5, 1991 Amendment to cap punitive damages at $150,000 for victims of intentional job discrimination or the amount of compensatory damages, whichever is greater, define "business necessity" as a practice that must bear a significant manifest relationship to the requirements for effective job performance, ban the use of race-based adjustments to hiring-test scores, include a provision explicitly prohibiting the use of quotas, and for other purposes.

Var. 141 H.R. 1 June 5, 1991 Passage of the bill to reverse or modify a series of Supreme Court rulings that narrowed the reach and remedies of job discrimination laws and to authorize compensatory and punitive damages for victims of discrimination.

Var. 193 H.R. 2508 June 20, 1991 Amendment to the foreign aid authorization prohibiting aid to the South African Communist Party and to any organization affiliated with a communist party and requiring the president to ensure that aid recipients have democratic processes in place for selecting leaders and do not have a record of human rights abuses.

Var. 332 H.R. 3371 October 22, 1991 Amendment to omnibus crime bill that prohibits the consideration of race in determining a defendant's sentence and the use of statistics to invalidate a sentence.

Var. 334 H.R. 3371 October 22, 1991 Amendment to crime bill to strike the provisions that allow death row prisoners to raise certain race-bias claims in habeas corpus appeals.

Var. 488 H.R. 3844 February 27, 1992 Passage of the bill to suspend for six months the repatriation of Haitians who were in the custody of the United States before February 5, 1992, require the administration to report on the fate of repatriated Haitians, provide 2,000 refugee admission slots to Haitians, and prohibit the admission to the United States of any person involved in the September 1991 coup in Haiti.

Var. 515 H.R. 3553 March 26, 1992 Amendment to Higher Education Act to express the sense of Congress that institutions of higher learning should not discriminate based on race in admissions, particularly with regard to Asian Americans.

## Chapter 5: Votes Used to Calculate the Effect of Conversion on Change in Party Mean Scores on Defense Issues: Senate, 86th through 100th Congresses (1959–1988)

86th, 92nd, 97th, and 101st Congress votes as in Tables 5-2 and 5-3.

### 87th Congress

Var. 287 H.R. 11289 June 13, 1962 Amendment to defense appropriation providing $171 million for development of RS-70, but permitting transfer of additional funds for RS-70 bomber if secretary of defense so decided.

Var. 288 H.R. 11289 June 13, 1962 Amendment to limit funds for RS-70 to $171 million.

### 88th Congress (First Session):

Var. 144 H.R. 7179 September 24, 1963 Amendment to defense appropriations cutting procurement appropriation by 1 percent.

### 88th Congress (Second Session):

Var. 279 H.R. 9637 February 27, 1964 Amendment to defense authorization deleting $52 million authorized for development of an advanced bomber to replace current bombers in the 1970s.

Var. 476 H.R. 10939 July 29, 1964 Amendment to defense appropriations reducing each amendment by 2 percent.

Var. 539 H.R. 9124 September 28, 1964 Amendment to Reserve Officers' Training Corps Vitalization Act of 1964 deleting junior ROTC provisions setting a 300 unit ceiling on the existing ROTC program.

### 89th Congress

Var. 190 H.R. 9070 August 11, 1965 Amendment to bill on the increase in basic pay for uniformed services increasing pay of enlisted men with under two years of service by an average of 32.4 percent over existing rates instead of 17.3 percent as in the bill.

Var. 212 H.R. 9221 August 25, 1965 Amendment to defense appropriations adding funds for Army Special Training Enlistment Program.

Var. 428 H.R. 15491 August 18, 1965 Amendment to defense appropriations reducing funds in procurement and research and development by 2.2 percent or $522.5 million.

Var. 430 H.R. 15941 August 18, 1965 Amendment striking $153.5 million for army procurement of the Nike X antiballistic missile system (ABM).

### 90th Congress

Var. 96 S. 1432 May 11, 1967 Amendment extending the present Universal Military Training and Service Act for two rather than four years.

Var. 102 S. 1432 May 11, 1967 Passage of the Selective Service Act of 1967.

Var. 405 S. 3293 April 18, 1968 Amendment to military procurement authorization limiting aggregate authorizations for research and development to $7.366 billion.

Var. 406 S. 3293 April 18, 1968 Amendment reducing the authorization for missiles.

Var. 407 S. 3293 April 18, 1968 Amendment barring use of authorized funds for deployment of ABM system until the system is practicable and that its cost can be determined with reasonable accuracy.

Var. 409 S. 3293 April 19, 1968 Amendment reducing by individual category the authorizations to the amount appropriated in fiscal 1968.

Var. 479 H.R. 16703 June 24, 1968 Amendment to military construction authorization barring use of any authorized funds for an ABM system prior to fiscal year beginning July 1, 1969.

Var. 486 H.R. 16703 June 25, 1968 Amendment authorizing $280,000 for operational facilities for Charleston, SC, Air Force base.

Var. 488 H.R. 17734 June 26, 1968 Amendment to supplemental appropriations reducing funds for B-52 bombing operations in Vietnam.

Var. 547 H.R. 18785 August 1, 1968 Amendment to military construction appropriation reducing funds by $227 million.

Var. 582 H.R. 18707 October 2, 1968 Amendment to defense appropriations to bar use of funds during balance of fiscal 1969 for production and deployment of the Sentinel ABM system.

Var. 583 H.R. 18707 October 2, 1968 Amendment eliminating funds for the Sage bomber defense system.

Var. 587 H.R. 18707 October 3, 1968 Amendment limiting to $7,108,600,000 funds for research development test and evaluation.

Var. 590 H.R. 18707 October 3, 1968 Amendment opening to competitive bidding repair contracts for any Navy vessel if work is to be in a place other than its home port.

## 91st Congress

Var. 64 S. 2546 August 6, 1969 Amendment to defense authorization providing that funds for research, development, testing, and evaluation of components and related procurement of any other ABM system or other weapons system shall not be affected.

Var. 65 S. 2546 August 6, 1969 Amendment providing that funds authorized by this or any other legislation for acquisition of an antiballistic missile system may be used for research and development at sites other than for a proposed ABM system and barring funds for development of such a system or acquisition or preparation of any site therefor.

Var. 84 S. 2546 September 16, 1969 Amendment reducing from $95 million to $20 million funds for research and development, test and evaluation for the Advanced Manned Strategic Aircraft (AMSA).

Var. 218 H.R. 15090 December 15, 1969 Motion to table amendment to defense appropriation prohibiting use of funds to support local forces in Laos and Thailand.

Var. 221 H.R. 15090 December 15, 1969 Amendment striking from the bill all funds for Safeguard ABM system with the exception of funds for military personnel that may be used elsewhere.

Var. 393 H.R. 15628 June 3, 1970 Amendment to bill establishing ceilings on foreign military sales to make inoperative provisions that limit U.S. military involvement in Cambodia during any period in which the president determined that U.S. citizens were held prisoners of war in Cambodia by North Vietnam or the National Liberation Front.

Var. 394 H.R. 15628 June 11, 1970 Amendment providing that nothing in the proposed amendment shall preclude the president from taking such actions as may be necessary to protect U.S. forces in South Vietnam or facilitate their withdrawal.

Var. 430 H.R. 15628 June 30, 1970 Amendment making clear that the United States will not be barred by the proposed Cooper-Church Amendment from assisting noncommunist nations in Asia that cooperate in lending support to a neighboring country.

Var. 431 H.R. 15628 June 30, 1970 Motion to table motion to reconsider Var. 430.

Var. 432 H.R. 15628 June 39, 1970 Motion to reconsider Var. 430.

Var. 433 H.R. 15628 June 30, 1970 New vote on Var. 430.

Var. 435 H.R. 15628 June 30, 1970 Amendment including modified Church-Cooper Amendment barring funds for U.S. involvement in Cambodia after June 30, 1970, unless specifically authorized by law.

Var. 493 H.R. 17123 August 12, 1970 Amendment striking from the bill $322.2 million for proposed development of additional Safeguard ABM sites.

Var. 494 H.R. 17123 August 13, 1970 Amendment to defense authorization requiring Defense Department to comply with provisions of National Environmental Policy Act in development and use of weapons systems affecting quality of the human environment.

Var. 497 H.R. 17123 August 19, 1970 Amendment limiting expenditure of funds for ABM defenses to present sites.

Var. 509 H.R. 17123 August 27, 1970 Amendment prohibiting use of herbicides for purposes of crop destruction warfare.

Var. 513 H.R. 17123 September 1, 1970 Amendment to limit to 280,000 the maximum number of U.S. troops in Vietnam after April 30, 1971, and providing for complete troop withdrawal of such forces by December 31, 1971.

Var. 638 H.R. 19590 December 8, 1970 Defense appropriations that would have reduced from $30 million to $20 million the limitations on funds that may be expended for defense public information, public affairs, and public relations activities.

## 93rd Congress

Var. 405 H.R. 9286 September 21, 1973 Amendment to military procurement authorization authorizing funds for a comprehensive study by the defense secretary of alternatives to the B-1 bomber program.

Var. 407 H.R. 9286 September 21, 1973 Amendment giving Congress procedures for establishing ceilings on number of military personnel stationed overseas in peacetime.

Var. 414 H.R. 9286 September 24, 1973 Amendment calling for the army secretary to keep the XM-1 battle tank within strict cost parameters.

Var. 420 H.R. 9286 September 26, 1973 Amendment reducing by $40 percent over a three-year period the number of U.S. ground troops stationed overseas.

Var. 422 H.R. 9286 September 26, 1973 Amendment placing a $73 billion ceiling on Defense spending for military functions instead of proposed $78 billion.

Var. 423 H.R. 9286 September 27, 1973 Amendment reducing by $85 billion authorizations for development and procurement of *Trident* submarines.

Var. 428 H.R. 9286 September 27, 1973 Amendment barring the use of any funds for research, development, test, or evaluation of the Sam-D missile program.

Var. 435 H.R. 9286 September 28, 1973 Amendment deleting funds for procurement or construction of the CVN-70 nuclear attack aircraft carrier.

Var. 820 S. 3000 June 4, 1974 Amendment to military procurement authorization requiring the CIA to submit annual report to the Congress disclosing the amount of funds requested for its activities in the next succeeding year.

Var. 823 S. 3000 June 5, 1974 Amendment reducing funding for development of the B-1 bomber program.

Var. 824 S. 3000 June 5, 1974 Amendment barring expenditure of funds until the president notifies Congress that he has received formal assurances that the South Vietnamese government will release by December 31, 1974, all persons imprisoned without the benefit of court trial.

Var. 833 S. 3000 June 7, 1974 Amendment requiring quarterly Defense Department reports to justify contracts above $2,500 let without competitive bidding, and authorizing a GAO study and report on defense procurement with a view to determine how competitive bidding through formal advertising can be increased.

Var. 835 S. 3000 June 10, 1974 Amendment halting funding of counterforce research and development until SALT talks fail to reach arms control agreements.

Var. 842 S. 3000 June 11, 1974 Amendment setting authorization ceiling at $21.6 billion.

Var. 961 H.R. 16243 August 21, 1974 Amendment reducing by approximately $1 billion total appropriations in the bill.

### 94th Congress

Var. 209 S. 920 June 4, 1975 Amendment to military procurement authorization barring the use of funds for research and development for five systems designed to improve accuracy of U.S. strategic missiles.

Var. 214 S. 920 June 5, 1975 Amendment barring funds to produce additional airborne warning and control system planes until NATO agrees to purchase such type equipment.

Var. 215 S. 920 June 5, 1975 Amendment barring the use of funds for development of Site Defense Program.

Var. 216 S. 920 June 5, 1975 Amendment deleting funds for continued development or procurement of the B-1 bomber aircraft program.

Var. 217 S. 920 June 5, 1975 Amendment deleting funds for the procurement of 50 Minuteman III operational test missiles.

Var. 223 S. 920 June 6, 1975 Amendment deferring funds for flight testing maneuvering reentry vehicle until the president certified to the Congress that the USSR is flight testing its own "MARV" system.

Var. 350 S. Res. 160 July 28, 1975 Passage of resolution expressing Senate disapproval of U.S. military construction on the island of Diego Garcia in the Indian Ocean.

Var. 483 H.R. 10029 November 26, 1975 Amendment to defense appropriation barring use of funds prior to July 1, 1976, for military construction on the island of Diego Garcia.

Var. 494 H.R. 9861, November 13, 1975 Amendment delaying for six months flight testing on the long-range cruise missile.

Var. 495 H.R. 9861 November 13, 1975 Amendment that would permit the Air Force to build only two additional airborne warning and control systems.

Var. 500 H.R. 9861 November 14, 1975 Amendment providing for dismantling the Safeguard ABM site at Grand Forks, ND.

Var. 501 H.R. 9861 November 14, 1975 Motion to table motion to reconsider previous amendment.

Var. 504 H.R. 9861 November 14, 1975 Reconsideration of Var. 500.

Var. 805 H.R. 12438 May 20, 1976 Amendment to military procurement authorization barring the use of any funding for purposes of procurement in connection with the B-1 bomber program.

Var. 806 H.R. 12438 May 20, 1976 Amendment barring funds to be obligated for the B-1 bomber program prior to February 1, 1977.

Var. 1073 H.R. 14262 August 2, 1976 Amendment to defense appropriation deferring until February 1, 1977, expenditure of $274.5 million for Minuteman III missile procurement.

Var. 1130 H.R. 14262 August 9, 1976 Amendment deleting $350 million for the navy's new nuclear-powered aircraft carrier.

## 95th Congress

Var. 281 H.R. 7553 July 1, 1977 Amendment to public works appropriation requiring that an arms control impact statement be filed with Congress along with a presidential statement on the national need for the weapons before the production of neutron bombs can commence.

Var. 283 H.R. 7553 July 1, 1977 Motion to table amendment allowing Congress to bar the production of neutron bombs by means of a concurrent resolution that is passed within 60 days of a proposal for weapons production.

Var. 290 H.R. 7553 July 13, 1977 Amendment unconditionally prohibiting the production of the neutron bomb.

Var. 291 H.R. 7553 July 13, 1977 Amendment barring the production
of the neutron bomb until the president formally approves its production. Either house of the Congress could then by simple resolution veto the presidential decision.

Var. 292 H.R. 7553 July 13, 1977 Amendment tabling previous
amendment.

Var. 293 H.R. 7553 July 13, 1977 Amendment barring production of
the neutron bomb until the president certifies to Congress that the
production of these weapons is in the national need. Congress shall
further have the power to veto the presidential decision by means of
a concurrent resolution that must be submitted within 45 days of the
date of presidential certification.

Var. 672 H.R. 9375 February 1, 1978 Amendment to supplemental
appropriations rescinding $462 million for the production of addi-
tional B-1 bombers and halts production of several of the aircraft.

Var. 777 S. Con. Res. 80 April 25, 1978 Amendment decreasing budget authority for defense by $1.4 billion and decrease outlays by
$900 million.

Var. 784 S. Con. Res. 80 April 26, 1978 Amendment increasing budget authority for defense by $1.6 billion and the outlays for defense
by $400 million.

### 96th Congress

Var. 89 S. 429 May 3, 1979 Amendment to military procurement
authorization permitting the Service Life Extension program to be
conducted not on the basis of least cost if the president determines
that the national interest requires other considerations.

Var. 304 S. Con. Res. 36 September 18, 1979 Amendment to increase
defense spending to provide for 5 percent real growth in budget
authority in fiscal 1981 and 1982

Var. 803 H.R. 6974 July 1, 1980 Amendment prohibiting use of funds
for reactivation of the battleship *New Jersey*.

Var. 804 H.R. 6974 July 1, 1980 Motion to table amendment increasing funds for design and development of space-based laser anti-
ballistic missile defense system.

Var. 808 H.R. 6974 July 1, 1980 Motion to table amendment that
deleted $25 million in air force aircraft procurement and $66 million

in air force research development, test, and evaluation for the FB-III program and to add $91 million in air force research, development, test, and evaluation for an advanced technology strategic bomber

Var. 809 H.R. 6974 July 1, 1980 Motion to table substitute to amendment that widens the options with regard to the B-1 bomber.

Var. 810 H.R. 6974 July 1, 1980 Motion to table substitute to amendment that widens the options with regard to the B-1 bomber.

Var. 811 H.R. 6974 July 1, 1980 Motion to table substitute to amendment that changes the date to 1986.

## 98th Congress

Var. 90 S. Con. Res. 27 May 10, 1983 Amendment to budget resolution providing additional funding for defense.

Var. 91 S. Con. Res. 27 May 10, 1983 Motion to table amendment cutting funds for nuclear warhead production.

Var. 123 S. Con. Res. 26 May 24, 1983 Motion to table motion to postpone consideration of resolution approving the obligation and expenditure of funds for MX missile procurement and full-scale engineering development of a basing mode.

Var. 124 S. Con. Res. 26 May 25, 1983 Approval of budget resolution obligating expenditure of funds for MX missile procurement and full-scale engineering development of a basing mode.

Var. 224 S. 675 July 21, 1983 Cloture motion on defense authorization.

Var. 227 S. 675 July 25, 1983 Motion to table amendment transferring sufficient funds from recruiting activities to provide a 4 percent cost of living increase for military personnel of Grade E-1 with less than four months active duty.

Var. 228 S. 675 July 26, 1983 Amendment providing that no funds are authorized under the act for the production, procurement, or deployment of the MX missile.

Var. 229 S. 675 July 26, 1983 Amendment providing that amendment providing that no funds are authorized under the act for the deployment of the MX missile.

Var. 347 H.R. 4185 November 7, 1983 Amendment deleting funds for the MX missile.

Var. 350 H.R. 4185 November 7, 1983 Motion to table amendment extending anticipated 4 percent cost of living increase to all military personnel in the grade E-1.

Var. 351 H.R. 4185 November 11, 1983 Motion to table amendment to add back $124 million in funds for binary weapons.

Var. 352 H.R. 4185 November 8, 1983 Amendment to add back into the bill $124.4 million in funds for binary weapons.

Var. 518 S. 2723 June 13, 1984 Motion to table amendment limiting funds for SDI.

Var. 521 S. 2723 June 14, 1984 Motion to table motion to recommit defense authorization.

Var. 522 S. 2723 June 14, 1984 Motion to table amendment deleting funds for 21 MX missiles and adding a comparable amount for conventional weapons systems and readiness.

Var. 523 S. 2723 June 14, 1984 Motion to table amendment prohibiting the deployment of the MX missile in favor of a system of small, single-warhead ICBMS.

Var. 542 S. 2723 June 20, 1984 Motion to table amendment limiting the obligation of funds for the high mobility multipurpose wheeled vehicle pending the completion of follow-up evaluation testing.

### 99th Congress

Var. 29 S.J. Res. 71 March 19, 1985 Passage of a measure approving the obligation of $1.5 billion in funds available for the procurement of MX missiles.

Var. 30 S.J. Res. 75 March 20, 1985 Passage of resolution further approving the obligation of $1.5 billion in funds available for the procurement of MX missiles.

Var. 46 S. Con. Res. 32 May 2, 1985 Amendment to budget resolution to limit the growth in fiscal year 1986 budget authority for defense to an inflation adjustment.

Var. 95 S. 1160 May 21, 1985 Amendment deleting funds for production of the MX missiles.

Var. 100 S. 1160 May 22, 1985 Amendment to promote an international ban on the production and stockpiling of lethal, binary, and chemical weapons.

Var. 105 S. 1160 May 24, 1985 Amendment establishing a moratorium during fiscal years 1985 and 1986 on the testing of antisatellite weapons against objects in space.

Var. 110 S. 1160 June 4, 1985 Amendment reducing funds authorized for SDI and increasing funds for certain programs by an amount equal to the reduction,

Var. 111 S. 1160 June 4, 1985 Amendment reducing funds authorized for SDI and imposing certain limitations on such programs.

Var. 112 S. 1160 June 4, 1985 Amendment reducing the funds authorized for research, development, test, and evaluation under SDI.

Var. 113 S. 1160 June 4, 1985 Amendment providing that of the funds authorized for SDI $800 million is available only for research and development of non-nuclear ballistic missile defense systems to be deployed within five to seven years.

Var. 187 S. 1200 September 12, 1985 Motion to table amendment delaying testing of an antisatellite weapon until the conclusion of the summit conference between the United States and USSR.

Var. 375 H.J. Res. 465 December 10, 1985 Motion to table amendment prohibiting the use of nuclear devices in research for the SDI program.

Var. 513 H.R. 4515 June 6, 1986 Ruling on germaneness motion to amendment to Urgent Supplemental Appropriations transferring $62 million from Defense Department SDI program to nutrition programs.

Var. 567 S. 2638 August 5, 1986 Motion to table amendment to defense authorization reducing funding for the SDI to $3.24 billion.

Var. 568 S. 2638 August 5, 1986 Amendment reducing funding for SDI to $3.56 billion.

Var. 571 S. 2638 August 6, 1986 Cloture motion.

Var. 573 S. 2638 August 7, 1986 Amendment prohibiting the use of funds for binary chemical munitions until certain conditions are met.

Var. 574 S. 2368 August 7, 1986 Motion to table amendment restricting procurement in connection with the Bigeye binary chemical bomb program.

Var. 575 S. 2638 August 7, 1986 Amendment restricting procurement in connection with the Bigeye binary chemical bomb program.

Var. 583 S. 2638 August 8, 1986 Motion to table amendment barring testing of an antisatellite weapon against an object in space until the USSR had conducted such a test.

Var. 587 S. 2638 August 8, 1986 Motion to table amendment to defense authorization that would prohibit in connection with the strategic defense program, the test of a warhead, bomb, or other explosive device which used fissionable material until the Soviet Union has conducted a test of any nuclear weapon.

### 100th Congress

Var. 124 S. 1174 May 19, 1987 Cloture motion on motion to proceed to defense authorization.

Var. 126 S. 1147 May 20, 1987 Cloture motion on motion to proceed to defense authorizations.

Var. 145 H.R. 1827 May 28, 1987 Motion to table amendment to supplemental appropriations that would provide $5 million for the insertion of Minuteman III ICBMs into Minuteman II ICBM silos.

Var. 258 S. 1174 September 17, 1987 Motion to table amendment to defense authorization which would remove restrictions prohibiting the testing of space-based or other anti-ballistic missile systems.

Var. 267 S. 1174 September 18, 1987 Motion to table amendment that would authorize the Air Force to replace aging Minutemen II missiles with stockpiled Minuteman III missiles.

Var. 307 S. 1174 October 1, 1987 Cloture motion on the defense authorization.

Var. 309 S. 1174 October 2, 1987 Amendment to defense authorization to prohibit the deployment of certain strategic offensive nuclear weapons.

Var. 310 H.R. 1748 October 2, 1987 Passage of defense authorization allocating $303 billion for defense programs.

Var. 555 S. 2355 May 11, 1988 Motion to table amendment to defense authorization requesting that some of the authorized funds for SDI be used to reimburse NASA for partial space shuttle operating costs.

Var. 556 S. 2355 May 11, 1988 Motion to table motion to reconsider the vote by which the motion to table an amendment to authorize NASA to receive $700 million reimbursement from the SDI funds to bring the Space Shuttle up to operating level.

Var. 558 S. 2355 May 11, 1988 Reconsideration of the vote by which the motion to table the amendment to authorize NASA to receive $700 million reimbursement from the SDI for restoring operation of the space shuttle.

Var. 681 H.R. 4264 July 14, 1988 Motion to recommit the conference report of the defense authorization back to conferees with instructions to adopt more favorable positions toward intercontinental

ballistic missile modernization, SDI development, and other programs in addition to striking authorizations not requested by the
president.

Var. 726 H.R. 4781 August 5, 1988 Motion to table amendment providing an additional $500 million in funding for SDI.

## Votes Used to Calculate Effect of Conversion on Change in Party Mean Scores on Tax Policy:

Same votes as used in Figure 5-4.

# Bibliography

Abramowitz, Alan I. 1994. "Issue Evolution Reconsidered: Racial Attitudes and Partisanship in the U.S. Electorate" *American Journal of Political Science* 38(1): 1–24.

——— 1995. "It's Abortion, Stupid: Policy Voting in the 1992 Presidential Election." *Journal of Politics* 42(1): 176–186.

Adams, Greg D. 1997. "Abortion: Evidence of an Issue Evolution." *American Journal of Political Science* 41(3): 718–737.

Adorno, Theodor W., Else Frenkel-Brunswik, Daniel Levinson, and R. N. Sanford. 1950. *The Authoritarian Personality.* New York: Harper Brothers.

Aldrich, John. 1995. *Why Parties? The Origins and Transformation of Political Parties in America.* Chicago: University of Chicago Press.

Alford, John R., Cary L. Funk, and John R. Hibbing. 2005. "Are Political Orientations Genetically Transmitted?" *American Political Science Review.* 99(2): 153–168.

Ambrose, Stephen E. 1984. *Eisenhower: The President.* New York: Simon and Schuster.

——— 1987. *Nixon: Volume 1 The Education of a Politician 1913–1962.* New York: Simon and Schuster.

Andersen, Kristi. 1979. *The Creation of a Democratic Majority 1928–1936.* Chicago: University of Chicago Press.

Ansolabehere, Stephen, and Shanto Iyengar, 1994. "Riding the Wave and Claiming Ownership over Issues – The Joint Effects of Advertising and News Coverage in Campaigns." *Public Opinion Quarterly* 22(fall): 335–357.

Barone, Michael, and Grant Ujifusa. 1989. *The Almanac of American Politics.* Washington, DC: National Journal.

Barone, Michael, Grant Ujifusa, and Douglas Matthews. 1972. *The Almanac of American Politics.* Boston: Gambit.

Bartels, Larry M. 1991. "Constituency Opinion and Congressional Policy Making: The Reagan Defense Buildup." *American Political Science Review* 85(2): 457–474.

1998. "Electoral Continuity and Change: 1868–1996." *Electoral Studies* 17(3): 301–326.

2002. "Beyond the Running Tally: Partisan Bias in Political Perceptions." *Political Behavior* 24(2): 117–150.

Bauer, Raymond A., Ithiel De Sola Pool, and Lewis Anthony Dexter. 1972. *American Business & Public Policy: The Politics of Foreign Trade.* Chicago: Aldine-Atherton.

Bawn, Kathleen, Marty Cohen, David Karol, Seth Masket, Hans Noel, and John Zaller. 2006. "A Theory of Parties." Paper presented at the 2006 Annual Meeting of the American Political Science Association, Philadelphia.

Beck, Paul Allen. 1974. "A Socialization Theory of Partisan Realignment." In *The Politics of Future Citizens,* ed. Richard G. Niemi. San Francisco: Jossey-Bass.

1977. "Partisan Dealignment in the Postwar South." *American Political Science Review* 71(2): 477–496.

Bensel, Richard Franklin. 1984. *Sectionalism in American Political Development, 1880–1980.* Madison: University of Wisconsin Press.

Berkman, Michael B. 1993. *The State Roots of National Politics: Congress and the Tax Agenda, 1978–1986.* Pittsburgh: University of Pittsburgh Press.

Berman, William C. 1970. *The Politics of Civil Rights in the Truman Administration.* Columbus: Ohio State University Press.

Bernhardt, Michael D., and Daniel E. Ingberman. 1985. "Candidate Reputations and the Incumbency Effect." *Journal of Public Economics* 27:47–67.

Bernstein, Robert A., and William A. Anthony. 1974. "The ABM Issue in the Senate, 1968–1970: The Importance of Ideology." *American Political Science Review* 68:1196–1206.

Black, Earl, and Merle Black. 2002. *The Rise of Southern Republicans.* Cambridge, MA: Harvard University Press.

Blumenthal, Sidney. 1981. "Whose Side Is Business on Anyway?" *New York Times Magazine,* October 25, p. 29.

1986. *The Rise of the Counter-Establishment: From Conservative Ideology to Political Power.* New York: Times Books.

Boyarsky, Bill. 1981. *Ronald Reagan: His Life and Rise to the Presidency.* New York: Random House.

Brace, Paul, Kellie-Sims Butler, Kevin Arceneaux, and Martin Johnson. 2002. "Public Opinion in the American States: New Perspectives Using National Survey Data." *American Journal of Political Science* 46(1): 173–189.

Brady, David W. 1988. *Critical Elections and Congressional Policy-Making.* Stanford, CA: Stanford University Press.

Brady, David W., Kara Buckley, and Douglas Rivers. 1999. "The Roots of Careerism in the U.S. House of Representatives." *Legislative Studies Quarterly* 24(4): 489–510.

Branch, Taylor. 1989. *Parting the Waters: America in the King Years.* New York: Touchstone Books.

Bruce, John M., and Clyde Wilcox (eds.). 1998. *The Changing Politics of Gun Control.* Lanham, MD: Rowman and Littlefield.

Burelli, David F. 2002. "Abortion Services and Federal Military Facilities." *Report for Congress*. Washington, DC: Congressional Research Service Library of Congress.

Burke, Thomas F. 2002. *Lawyers, Lawsuits and Legal Rights: The Battle over Litigation in American Society*. Berkeley: University of California Press.

Burnham, Walter Dean. 1970. *Critical Elections and the Mainsprings of American Politics*. New York: W. W. Norton.

Burns, John W. 1997. "Party Policy Change: The Case of the Democrats and Taxes 1956–1968." *Party Politics* 3:513–532.

Burns, John W., and Andrew J. Taylor. 2000. "The Mythical Causes of the Republican Supply-Side Revolution." *Party Politics* 6:419–440.

Burris, Val. 2001. "The Two Faces of Capital: Corporations and Individual Capitalists as Political Actors." *American Sociological Review* 66(June): 361–381.

Burstein, Paul. 1985. *Discrimination, Jobs and Politics: The Struggle for Equal Opportunity in the United States since the New Deal*. Chicago: University of Chicago Press.

Campbell, Angus, Philip E. Converse, Warren E. Miller, and Donald E Stokes. 1960. *The American Voter*. New York: Wiley.

Cannon, Lou. 1991. *President Reagan: The Role of a Lifetime*. New York: Simon and Schuster.

Carmines, Edward G., and James A. Stimson. 1980. "The Two Faces of Issue Voting." *American Political Science Review* 74(1): 78–91.

1989. *Issue Evolution: Race and the Transformation of American Politics*. Princeton, NJ: Princeton University Press.

Caro, Robert A. 2002. *Master of the Senate: The Years of Lyndon Johnson*. New York: Knopf.

Carter, Dan T. 1995. *The Politics of Rage: George Wallace, the Origins of the New Conservatism and the Transformation of American Politics*. New York: Simon and Schuster.

Carter, Gregg Lee. 1997. *The Gun Control Movement*. New York: Twayne.

Casstevens, Thomas W. 1967. *Politics, Housing and Race Relations: California's Rumford Act and Proposition 14*. Berkeley, CA: Institute for Governmental Studies.

Chen, Anthony S. 2006. "'The Hitlerian Rule of Quotas': Racial Conservatism and the Politics of Fair Employment Legislation in New York State, 1941–1945." *Journal of American History* 92(4): 1238–1264.

Chen, Anthony S., Robert W. Mickey, and Robert P. Van Houweling. 2008. "Explaining the Contemporary Alignment of Race and Party: Evidence from California's 1946 Ballot Initiative on Fair Employment," *Studies in American Political Development* 22(2): 204–228.

Clausen, Aage. 1973. *How Congressmen Decide: A Policy Focus*. New York: St. Martin's Press.

Clotfelter, James. 1970. "Senate Voting and Constituency Stake in Defense Spending." *Journal of Politics* 32:979–983.

Clubb, Jerome M., William H. Flanigan, and Nancy H. Zingale. 1980. *Partisan Realignment: Voters, Parties and Government in American History.* Beverly Hills, CA: Sage.

Clymer, Adam. 1999. *Edward M. Kennedy: A Biography.* New York: William Morrow.

Cohen, Martin G. 2005. "Moral Victories: Cultural Conservatism and the Creation of a New Republican Congressional Majority." Unpublished dissertation, UCLA.

Coleman, John J. 1996. *Party Decline in America: Policy, Politics and the Fiscal State.* Princeton, NJ: Princeton University Press.

Collins, Robert M. 2000. *More: The Politics of Economic Growth in Postwar America.* New York: Oxford University Press.

*Congressional Quarterly Almanac.* Various years. Washington, DC: CQ Press.

Conover, Pamela Johnston, and Stanley Feldman. 1983. "Candidates, Issues and Voters: The Role of Inference in Political Perception." *Journal of Politics* 45(4): 810–839.

Converse, Phillip E. 1964. "The Nature of Belief Systems in Mass Publics." In *Ideology and Discontent,* ed. David E. Apter. New York: Free Press.

Cook, Elizabeth Adell, Ted G. Jelen, and Clyde Wilcox. 1998. "Abortion and Realignment: Itemizing the Deductions from the Party Coalition." Paper given at the Annual Meeting of the Western Political Science Association, March 19–21, Los Angeles.

Cooper, Joseph, and William West. 1981. "Voluntary Retirement, Incumbency, and the Modern House." *Political Science Quarterly* 96(2): 279–300.

Cowden, Jonathan A. 2001. "Southernization of the Nation and Nationalization of the South: Racial Conservatism, Social Welfare and White Partisans in the United States, 1956–1992." *British Journal of Political Science* 31(April): 277–301.

Cronin, Patrick, and Benjamin O. Fordham. 1999. "Timeless Principles or Today's Fashion? Testing the Stability of the Linkage between Ideology and Foreign Policy in the Senate." *Journal of Politics* 61(4): 967–998.

Dallek, Robert. 1981. *Franklin D. Roosevelt and American Foreign Policy 1932–1945.* New York: Oxford University Press.

1998. *Flawed Giant: Lyndon Johnson and His Times, 1961–1973.* New York: Oxford University Press.

Dark, Taylor E. 2001. *The Unions and the Democrats: An Enduring Alliance.* Ithaca, NY: Cornell University Press.

Day, Christine L., and Charles D. Hadley. 2001. "Feminist Diversity: The Policy Preferences of Women's PAC Contributors." *Political Research Quarterly* 54(3): 673–686.

Dean, John. 2001. *The Rehnquist Choice: The Untold Story of the Nixon Appointment That Redefined the Supreme Court.* New York: Free Press.

Destler, I.M. 1995. *American Trade Politics.* Washington, DC: Institute for International Economics.

De Vries, Walter, and Jack Bass. 1978. "Cross-Pressures in the White South." In *Emerging Coalitions in American Politics,* ed. Seymour Martin Lipset. San Francisco: Institute for Contemporary Studies.

Dougan, William R., and Michael C. Munger. 1989. "The Rationality of Ideology." *Journal of Law and Economics* 32:119–142.

Downs, Anthony. 1957. *An Economic Theory of Democracy.* New York: Harper Collins.

Enelow, James M., and Michael C. Munger. 1993. "The Elements of Candidate Reputation: The Effect of Record and Credibility on Optimal Spatial Location." *Public Choice* 77(December): 757–772.

Engel, Steven T., and David J. Jackson. 1998. "Wielding the Stick Instead of the Carrot: Labor PAC Punishment of Pro-NAFTA Democrats." *Political Research Quarterly* 51(3): 813–828.

Epstein, Lee, and Joseph F. Kobylka. 1992. *The Supreme Court and Legal Change: Abortion and the Death Penalty.* Chapel Hill: University of North Carolina Press.

Erikson, Robert S. 1971. "The Relationship between Party Control and Civil Rights Legislation in the American States." *Western Political Quarterly* 24:178–182.

Farrell, James A. 2001. *Tip O'Neill and the Democratic Century.* New York: Little, Brown.

Feinstein, Brian, and Eric Schickler. 2008. "Platforms and Partners: The Civil Rights Realignment Reconsidered." *Studies in American Political Development* 22(1): 1–31.

Fenno, Richard F., Jr. 1978. *Home Style: House Members in Their Districts.* Boston: Little, Brown.

Fleisher, Richard. 1993. "PAC Contributions and Congressional Voting on National Defense." *Legislative Studies Quarterly* 18(3): 391–409.

Flint, Andrew R., and Joy Porter. 2005. "Jimmy Carter: The Re-emergence of Faith-Based Politics and the Abortion Rights Issue." *Presidential Studies Quarterly* 35(1): 28–51.

Fordham, Benjamin O. 1998. *Building the Cold War Consensus: The Political Economy of U.S. National Security Policy, 1949–1951.* Ann Arbor: University of Michigan Press.

2007a. "The Evolution of Republican and Democratic Positions on Cold War Military Spending." *Social Science History* 31(4): 603–636.

2007b. "Paying for Global Power: Assessing the Costs and Benefits of Postwar American Military Spending." In *The Long War: A New History of U.S. National Security Policy since World War Two,* ed. Andrew J. Bacevich. New York: Columbia University Press.

Francia, Peter L. 2001. "The Effect of the North American Free-Trade Agreement on Corporate and Labor PAC Contributions." *American Politics Research* 29(1): 198–209.

Freeman, Gary P., and Bob Birrell. 2001. "Divergent Paths of Immigration Politics in the United States and Australia." *Population and Development Review* 27(3): 525–551.

Freeman, Jo. 1986. "The Political Culture of the Democrats and the Republicans." *Political Science Quarterly* 101(3): 327–356.

1988. "Women at the 1988 Democratic Convention." *PS: Political Science and Politics* 21(4): 875–881.

Frymer, Paul. 2007. *Black and Blue: African Americans, The Labor Movement, and the Decline of the Democratic Party.* Princeton, NJ: Princeton University Press.

Frymer, Paul, and John David Skrentny. 1998. "Coalition-Building and the Politics of Electoral Capture during the Nixon Administration: African Americans, Labor, Latinos." *Studies in American Political Development* 12:131–161.

Gamm, Gerald. 1989. *The Making of New Deal Democrats: Voting Behavior and Realignment in Boston, 1920–1940.* Chicago: University of Chicago Press.

Geer, John G. 1996. *From Tea Leaves to Opinion Polls.* New York: Columbia University Press.

Gellman, Irwin F. 1999. *The Contender: Richard Nixon, the Congress Years, 1946–1952.* New York: Free Press.

Gerring, John. 1998. *Party Ideologies in America 1828–1996.* New York: Cambridge University Press.

Goldberg, Robert Alan. 1995. *Barry Goldwater.* New Haven, CT: Yale University Press.

Goldwater, Barry M. 1962. *Why Not Victory? A Fresh Look at American Foreign Policy.* New York: McGraw Hill.

2007 (1960). *The Conscience of a Conservative.* Princeton, NJ: Princeton University Press.

Gopoian, J. David. 1984. "What Makes PACS Tick? An Analysis of the Allocation Patterns of Economic Interest Groups." *American Journal of Political Science* 28:259–281.

Gordon, Rita Werner. 1969. "The Change in the Political Alignment of Chicago's Negroes during the New Deal." *Journal of American History* 56(3): 584–603.

Goren, Paul. 2005. "Party Identification and Core Political Values." *American Journal of Political Science* 49(4): 881–896.

Gottschalk, Marie. 2000. *The Shadow Welfare State: Labor, Business and the Politics of Health Care in the United States.* Ithaca, NY: Cornell University Press.

Gould, Stephen Jay. 1997. "The Pleasures of Pluralism." *New York Review of Books* 44(11): 47–52.

Grassmuck, George L. 1951. *Sectional Biases in Congress on Foreign Policy.* Baltimore: Johns Hopkins University Press.

Green, Steven K. 1992. "The Blaine Amendment Reconsidered." *American Journal of Legal History* 36(1): 38–69.

Greenberg, David. 2004. "Tax Cuts in Camelot?" *Slate,* January 16.

Greene, Julie. 1998. *Pure and Simple Politics: The American Federation of Labor and Political Activism, 1881–1917.* New York: Oxford University Press.

Griffith, Robert. 1989. "Forging America's Postwar Order; Domestic Politics and Political Economy in the Age of Truman." In *The Truman Presidency,* ed. Michael J. Lacey. New York: Cambridge University Press.

Grofman, Bernard. 2004. "Downs and Two-Party Convergence." *Annual Review of Political Science* 7: 25–46.

Groseclose, Tim, Steven D. Levitt, and James M. Snyder, Jr. 1999. "Comparing Interest Group Scores across Time and Chambers: Adjusted ADA Scores for the U.S. Congress." *American Political Science Review* 93(1): 33–50.

Hacker, Jacob S. 1997. *The Road to Nowhere: The Genesis of President Clinton's Plan for Health Security.* Princeton, NJ: Princeton University Press.

Hacker, Jacob S., and Paul Pierson. 2005. *Off Center: The Republican Revolution & the Erosion of American Democracy.* New Haven, CT: Yale University Press.

Halperin, Morton H. 1972. "The Decision to Deploy the ABM: Bureaucratic and Domestic Politics in the Johnson Administration." *World Politics* 25(October): 62–95.

Hamby, Alonzo L. 2004. "World War II: Conservatism and Constituency Politics." In *The American Congress: The Building of Democracy,* ed. Julian E. Zelizer. New York: Houghton Mifflin.

Hansen, John Mark. 1991. *Gaining Access: Congress and the Farm Lobby, 1919–1981.* Chicago: University of Chicago Press.

Harding, Sandra Friend. 2000. *The Book of Jerry Falwell: Fundamentalist Language and Politics.* Princeton, NJ: Princeton University Press.

Hartmann, Susan M. 1971. *Truman and the 80th Congress.* Columbia: University of Missouri Press.

Hartnett, Stephen John. 2002. *Democratic Dissent and the Cultural Fictions of Antebellum America.* Urbana: University of Illinois Press.

Herrera, Richard. 1995. "The Crosswinds of Change: Sources of Change in the Democratic and Republican Parties." *Political Research Quarterly* 48(2): 291–312.

Hershey, Marjorie Randon. 1992. "The Constructed Explanation: Interpreting Election Results in the 1984 Presidential Race." *Journal of Politics* 54(4): 943–976.

1993. "Citizens' Groups and Political Parties in the United States." *Annals of the American Academy of Political and Social Science* 528: 142–156.

Hibbing, John R. 1982. "Voluntary Retirements from the House in the Twentieth Century." *Journal of Politics* 44(4): 1020–1034.

Hinich, Melvin J., and Michael C. Munger. 1994. *Ideology and the Theory of Political Choice.* Ann Arbor: University of Michigan Press.

Hixson, William B., Jr. 1969. "Moorfield Storey and the Defense of the Dyer Anti-Lynching Bill." *New England Quarterly* 42(1): 65–81.

Hoff, Joan. 1994. *Nixon Reconsidered.* New York: Basic Books.

Holian, David B. 2004. "He's Stealing My Issues! Clinton's Crime Rhetoric and the Dynamics of Issue Ownership." *Political Behavior* 26(2): 95–124.

Holsti, Ole R. 1998. "A Widening Gap between the U.S. Military and Civilian Society? Some Evidence, 1976–1996." *International Security* 23 (3) 5–42.

Hood, M. V. Quentin Kidd, and Irwin L. Morris. 1999. "Of Byrd(s) and Bumpers: Using Democratic Senators to Analyze Political Change in the South, 1960–1985." *American Journal of Political Science* 43(2): 465–487.

Hughes, Kent Higgon. 1979. *Trade, Taxes and Transnationals: International Decisionmaking in Congress.* New York: Praeger.

Irwin, Douglas, and Randall S. Kroszner. 1999. "Interests, Institutions and Ideology in Securing Policy Change: The Republican Conversion to Trade Liberalization after Smoot-Hawley." *Journal of Law and Economics* 42(2): 643–673.

Jackson, David J., and Steven T. Engel. 2003. "Don't Bite the PAC That Feeds You – Business PAC Punishment over the China Vote." *American Politics Research* 31(2): 138–154.

Jacobs, Charles E. 1985. "Reaganomics: The Revolution in American Political Economy." *Law and Contemporary Problems* 48(4): 7–30.

Jacobson, Gary C. 2004. *The Politics of Congressional Elections.* San Francisco: Pearson-Longman.

Jacobson, Gary C., and Samuel Kernell. 1981. *Strategy and Choice in Congressional Elections.* New Haven, CT: Yale University Press.

Jain, Sagar C., and Laurel F. Gooch. 1972. *Georgia Abortion Act 1968: A Study in Legislative Process.* Chapel Hill: Department of Health Administration, School of Public Health and Carolina Population Center.

Johnson, Donald Bruce. 1978. *National Party Platforms.* Urbana: University of Illinois Press.

Johnston, Richard, Andre Blais, Henry E. Brady, and Jean Crete. 1992. *Letting the People Decide: Dynamics of a Canadian Election.* Stanford, CA: Stanford University Press.

Johnson, Walter (ed.). 1972. *The Papers of Adlai E. Stevenson. Volume VI: Toward a New America 1955–1957 & Volume VII: Continuing Education and the Unfinished Business of American Society, 1957–1961.* Boston: Little, Brown.

Kalt, Joseph A., and Mark A. Zupan. 1984. "Capture and Ideology in the Economic Theory of Politics." *American Economic Review* 74(3): 279–300.

Karol, David. 1999. "Protecting the Public Interest against 'The Interests': Presidents, Congresses and Interbranch Differences in Historical Perspective." Paper presented at the Annual Meeting of the American Political Science Association, Atlanta.

2000. "Divided Government and U.S. Trade Policy: Much Ado about Nothing?" *International Organization* 54(autumn): 825–844.

2005. "Party Coalitions, Interest Groups and the Limits of Unidimensionality in Congress." Paper presented at the 2005 Annual Meeting of the American Political Science Association, Washington, DC, September 2.

2007a. "Does Constituency Size Affect Trade Policy Preferences?" *Journal of Politics* 69(2): 483–494.

2007b. "Polling and Representation: Evidence from the Literary Digest Issue Polls." *Studies in American Political Development* 21(spring): 16–29.

Kaufman, Robert G. 2000. *Henry M. Jackson: A Life in Politics.* Seattle: University of Washington Press.

Kaufmann, Karen. 2004. "Reexamining and Disaggregating Issue Ownership and Voter Choice." *Polity* 36(2): 283–299.

Keech, William, and K. Pak. 1995. "Partisanship, Institutions and Change in American Trade Policy." *Journal of Politics* 57(November): 1130–1142.

Kesselman, Louis Coleridge. 1948. *The Social Politics of FEPC: A Study in Reform Pressure Movements*. Chapel Hill: University of North Carolina Press.

Key, V.O., Jr. 1955. "A Theory of Critical Elections." *Journal of Politics* 17:3–18.

1958. *Politics, Parties and Pressure Groups*. New York: Crowell.

1959. "Secular Realignment and the Party System." *Journal of Politics* 21:198–210.

1961. *Public Opinion and American Democracy*. New York: Alfred Knopf.

Koch, Jeffrey W. 2001. "When Parties and Candidates Collide." *Public Opinion Quarterly* 65(1): 1–21.

Ladd, Everett Carl. 1981. "The Brittle Mandate: Electoral Dealignment and the 1980 Presidential Election." *Political Science Quarterly* 96(1): 1–25.

1990. "Like Waiting for Godot: The Uselessness of 'Realignment' for Understanding Change in American Politics." *Polity* 22(spring): 311–325.

Laird, Melvin R. 1962. *A House Divided: The Strategy Gap*. Chicago: Henry Regnery.

Layman, Geoffrey C. 2001. *The Great Divide: Religious and Cultural Conflict in American Party Politics*. New York: Columbia University Press.

Layman, Geoffrey C., and Thomas M. Carsey. 1998. "Why Do Party Activists Convert? An Analysis of Individual-Level Change in the Abortion Issue." *Political Research Quarterly* 51(September): 723–750.

2002. "Party Polarization and Conflict Extension in the American Electorate." *American Journal of Political Science* 46(4): 786–802.

Lee, Taeku. 2002. *Mobilizing Public Opinion: Black Insurgency and Racial Attitudes in the Civil Rights Era*. Chicago: University of Chicago Press.

Leiter, Robert D. 1961. "Organized Labor and the Tariff." *Southern Economic Journal* 28(1): 55–65.

Leonard, Kevin Allen. 1990. "Is That What We Fought For? Japanese Americans and Racism in California, the Impact of World War II." *Western Historical Quarterly* 21(4): 463–482.

Licklider, Roy E. 1970. "The Missile Gap Controversy." *Political Science Quarterly* 85(fall): 600–615.

Lieberman, Myron. 2000. *The Teacher Unions: How They Sabotage Educational Reform and Why*. San Francisco: Encounter Books.

Lindsay, James M. 1990. "Parochialism, Policy, and Constituency Constraints: Congressional Voting on Strategic Weapons Systems." *American Journal of Political Science* 34(4): 934–960.

Long, Norton. 1951. "Party Government and the United States." *Journal of Politics* 13(2): 187–214.

Lublin, David. 2004. *The Republican South: Democratization and Partisan Change*. Princeton, NJ: Princeton University Press.

Luker, Kristin. 1984. *Abortion and the Politics of Motherhood*. Los Angeles: University of California Press.

Lytle, Clifford M. 1966. "The History of the Civil Rights Bill of 1964." *Journal of Negro History* 77(1): 275–296.

Mandelbaum, Leonard. 1969. "Apollo: How the United States Decided to Go to the Moon." *Science*, New Series, 163(3868): 649–654.

Mansbridge, Jane J. 1986. *Why We Lost the ERA*. Chicago: University of Chicago Press.

Martin, Charles H. 1971. "Negro Leaders, the Republican Party and the Election of 1932." *Phylon* 32(1): 85–93.

Matusow, Allen J. 1998. *Nixon's Economy: Booms, Busts Dollars and Votes*. Lawrence: University Press of Kansas.

Mayer, Jeremy D. 2002. *Running on Race: Racial Politics in Presidential Campaigns 1960–2000*. New York: Random House.

Mayer, Kenneth R. 1991. *The Political Economy of Defense Contracting*. New Haven, CT: Yale University Press.

  1995. "Closing Military Bases (Finally): Solving Collective Dilemmas through Delegation." *Legislative Studies Quarterly* 20(3): 393–413.

Mayer, William G. 1993. *The Changing American Mind: How and Why American Public Opinion Changed between 1960 and 1988*. Ann Arbor: University of Michigan Press.

Mayhew, David R. 1966. *Party Loyalty among Congressmen: The Difference between Democrats and Republicans, 1947–1962*. Cambridge, MA: Harvard University Press.

  1974. *Congress: The Electoral Connection*. New Haven, CT: Yale University Press.

  2002. *Electoral Realignments: A Critique of an American Genre*. New Haven, CT: Yale University Press.

McCoy, Donald R. 1960. "The Good Neighbor League and the Presidential Campaign of 1936." *Western Political Quarterly* 13(4): 1011–1021.

Midford, Paul. 1993. "International Trade and Domestic Politics: Improving on Rogowski's Model of Political Alignments." *International Organization* 47(4): 535–564.

Miller, Gary, and Norman Schofield. 2003. "Activists and Partisan Realignment in the United States." *American Political Science Review* 97(2): 245–259.

Miller, James. 1994. *Democracy Is in the Streets: From Port Huron to the Siege of Chicago*. Cambridge, MA: Harvard University Press.

Miller, Warren E., and J. Merrill Shanks. 1996. *The New American Voter*. Cambridge, MA: Harvard University Press.

Mitchell, Franklin D. 1968. *Embattled Democracy: Missouri Democratic Politics, 1919–1932*. Columbia: University of Missouri Press.

Mooney, Christopher Z., and Mei-Hsien Lee. 1995. "Legislative Morality in the American States: The Case of Pre-Roe Abortion Regulation Reform." *American Journal of Political Science* 39(August): 599–627.

Morgan, Iwan W. 1990. *Eisenhower versus "the Spenders": The Eisenhower Administration, the Democrats and the Budget, 1953–60*. London: Pinter.

Moyer, H. Wayne. 1973. "House Voting on Defense: An Ideological Explanation." In *Military Force and American Society*, ed. Bruce M. Russett and Alfred Stepan. New York: Harper and Row.

Murphy, Marjorie. 1990. *Blackboard Unions: The AFT and the NEA, 1900–1980*. Ithaca, NY: Cornell University Press.

Murphy, Walter, and Joseph Tanenhaus. 1968. "Public Opinion and the Supreme Court: The Goldwater Campaign." *Public Opinion Quarterly* 32(1): 31–50.

Nixon, Richard M. 1968. *Major Speeches and Statements by Richard M. Nixon in the Presidential Campaign of 1968.* New York: Nixon-Agnew Campaign Committee.

Noel, Hans. 2007. "Listening to the Coalition Merchants: Measuring the Intellectual Influence of Academic Scribblers." *The Forum* 5(3): Article 7.

Nordin, Dennis. 1997. *The New Deal's Black Congressman: A Life of Arthur Wergs Mitchell.* Columbia: University of Missouri Press.

Norpoth, Helmut, and Bruce Buchanan. 1992. "Wanted: The Education President: Issue Trespassing by Political Candidates." *Public Opinion Quarterly* 56:87–99.

Novak, Robert D. 2007. *The Prince of Darkness: 50 Years of Reporting in Washington.* New York: Crown Forum.

Obach, Brian K. 2004. *Labor and the Environmental Movement: The Quest for Common Ground.* Cambridge, MA: MIT Press.

Olien, Roger M. 1981. *From Token to Triumph: The Texas Republicans since 1920.* Dallas: Southern Methodist University Press.

Orren, Karen, and Stephen Skowronek. 2004. *The Search for American Political Development.* New York: Cambridge University Press.

Parmet, Herbert S. 1997. *George Bush: The Life of a Lone Star Yankee.* New York: Scribner's.

Pastor, Robert. 1984. "The Cry and Sigh Syndrome." In *Making Economic Policy in Congress,* ed. Allen Shick. Washington, DC: AEI.

Patterson, James T. 1972. *Mr. Republican: A Biography of Robert A. Taft.* Boston: Hougton-Mifflin.

Petrocik, John R. 1981. *Party Coalitions: Realignments and the Decline of the New Deal Party System.* Chicago: University of Chicago Press.

   1996. "Issue Ownership in Presidential Elections with a 1980 Case Study." *American Journal of Political Science* 40(August): 825–851.

Piper, J. Richard. 1997. *Ideologies and Institutions: American Conservative and Liberal Governance Prescriptions since 1933.* Lanham, MD: Rowman and Littlefield.

Plotke, David. 1996. *Building a Democratic Political Order: Reshaping American Liberalism in the 1930s and 1940s.* New York: Cambridge University Press.

Polsby, Nelson W. 1968. "The Institutionalization of the U.S. House of Representatives." *American Political Science Review* 62(March): 144–168.

   2005. *How Congress Evolves: Social Bases of Institutional Change.* New York: Oxford University Press.

Pomeroy, Richard, and Lynn C. Landman. 1972. "Public Opinion Trends: Elective Abortion and Birth Control Services to Teenagers." *Family Planning Perspectives* 4(4): 44–55.

Pomper, Gerald. 1967. "Classification of Presidential Elections." *Journal of Politics* 29(3): 535–566.

Poole, Keith T. 2007. "Changing Minds? Not in Congress!" *Public Choice* 131(3–4): 435–451.

Poole, Keith T., and Howard Rosenthal. 1997. *Congress: A Political-Economic History of Roll Call Voting.* New York: Oxford University Press.

Popkin, Samuel L. 1991. *The Reasoning Voter: Communication and Persuasion in Presidential Campaigns.* Chicago: University of Chicago Press.

Prechel, Harlan. 1990. "Steel and the State: Industry Politics and Business Policy Formation, 1940–1989." *American Sociological Review* 55(October): 648–668.

Quirk, Paul J., and Joseph Hinchliffe. 1998. "The Rising Hegemony of Mass Opinion." *Journal of Policy History* 10(1): 19–50.

Rahn, Wendy M. 1993. "The Role of Partisan Stereotypes in Information-Processing about Political Candidates." *American Journal of Political Science* 37(2): 472–496.

Rapoport, Ronald B., and Walter J. Stone. 1994. "A Model for Disaggregating Political Change." *Political Behavior* 16(4): 505–532.

Reed, Merl E. 1991. *Seedtime for the Modern Civil Rights Movement: The President's Committee on Fair Employment Practice, 1941–1947.* Baton Rouge: Louisiana State University Press.

Reichard, Gary W. 1975. *The Reaffirmation of Republicanism.* Knoxville: University of Tennessee Press.

Remini, Robert V. 1984. *Andrew Jackson and the Course of American Democracy, 1833–1845.* New York: Harper & Row.

Riker, William. 1982. *Liberalism against Populism: A Confrontation between the Theory of Democracy and the Theory of Social Choice.* San Francisco: W. H. Freeman.

Robertson, David Brian. 1999. "Voluntarism against the Open Shop: Labor and Business Strategies in the Battle for American Labor Markets." *Studies in American Political Development* 13(spring): 146–185.

Rochon, Thomas R. 1998. *Culture Moves: Ideas, Actions and Changing Values.* Princeton, NJ: Princeton University Press.

Rogowski, Ronald. 1989. *Commerce and Coalitions: How Trade Affects Domestic Political Alignments.* Princeton, NJ: Princeton University Press.

Rohde, David W. 1991. *Parties and Leaders in the Postreform House.* Chicago: University of Chicago Press.

Roman, Peter. 1995. *Eisenhower and the Missile Gap.* Ithaca, NY: Cornell University Press.

Rose, Melody. 2006. *Safe, Legal and Unavailable? Abortion Politics in the United States.* Washington, DC: CQ Press.

Rosenberg, Gerald N. 1991. *The Hollow Hope: Can Courts Bring about Social Change?* Chicago: University of Chicago Press.

Rubin, Eva R. 1982. *Abortion, Politics and the Courts: Roe v. Wade and Its Aftermath.* Westport, CT: Greenwood Press.

Russett, Bruce M. 1975. "The Americans Retreat from World Power." *Political Science Quarterly* 90(spring): 1–21.

Sanbonmatsu, Kira. 2002. *Democrats, Republicans and the Politics of Women's Place.* Ann Arbor: University of Michigan Press.

Schattschneider, E. E. 1942. *Party Government.* New York: Holt and Rinehart.

1960. *The Semi-Sovereign People*. New York: Holt, Rinehart and Winston.

Schlesinger, Arthur M., Jr. 1965. *A Thousand Days: J.F.K. in the White House*. Boston: Houghton Mifflin.

Schlesinger, Joseph A. 1984. "On the Theory of Party Organization." *Journal of Politics* 46(2): 369–400.

1991. *Political Parties and the Winning of Office*. Ann Arbor: University of Michigan Press.

Schnietz, Karen E. 2000. "The Institutional Foundation of U.S. Trade Policy: Revisiting Explanations for the 1934 Reciprocal Trade Agreements Act." *Journal of Policy History* 12(4): 417–444.

Schuman, Howard. 1972. "Two Sources of Antiwar Sentiment in America." *American Journal of Sociology* 78(3): 513–536.

Self, Robert O. 2003. *American Babylon: Race and the Struggle for Postwar Oakland*. Princeton, NJ: Princeton University Press.

Sellers, Patrick J. 1998. "Strategy and Background in Congressional Campaigns." *American Political Science Review* 92(March): 159–172.

Shafer, Byron E. 2003. *The Two Majorities and the Puzzle of Modern American Politics*. Lawrence: University Press of Kansas.

Shafer, Byron E., and Richard Johnston. 2006. *The End of Southern Exceptionalism: Class, Race and Partisan Change in the Postwar South*. Cambridge, MA: Harvard University Press.

Shefter, Martin. 1994. *Political Parties and the State: The American Historical Experience*. Princeton, NJ: Princeton University Press.

Shoch, James. 2001. *Trading Blows: Party Competition and U.S. Trade Policy in a Globalizing Era*. Chapel Hill: University of North Carolina Press.

Sigelman, Lee, and Emmett H. Buell, Jr. 2004. "Avoidance or Engagement? Issue Convergence in U.S. Presidential Campaigns 1960–2000." *American Journal of Political Science* 48(4): 650–661.

Silbey, Joel H. 1991. "Beyond Realignment and Realignment Theory: American Critical Eras 1789–1989." In *The End of Realignment?* ed. Byron Shafer. Madison: University of Wisconsin Press.

Simon, Adam F. 2002. *The Winning Message: Candidate Behavior, Campaign Discourse, and Democracy*. New York: Cambridge University Press.

Sinclair, Barbara. 1982. *Congressional Realignment 1925–1978*. Austin: University of Texas Press.

2006. *Party Wars: Polarization and the Politics of National Policymaking*. Norman: University of Oklahoma Press.

Sitkoff, Harvard. 1984. Review of *Farewell to the Party of Lincoln* by Nancy Weiss. *American Historical Review* 89(5): 1404–1405.

Skinner, Richard M. 2007. *More than Money: Interest Group Action in Congressional Elections*. Lanham, MD: Rowman and Littlefield.

Skowronek, Stephen. 1993. *The Politics Presidents Make: Leadership from John Adams to George Bush*. Cambridge, MA: Belknap Press.

Soffer, Jonathan. 2001. "The National Association of Manufacturers and the Militarization of American Conservatism." *Business History Review* 75(4): 775–805.

Spencer, Thomas T. 1978. "The Good Neighbor League Colored Committee and
    the 1936 Democratic Presidential Campaign." *Journal of Negro History*
    63(4): 307–316.
Spitzer, Robert J. 1995. *The Politics of Gun Control*. Chatham, NJ: Chatham
    House.
Stanwood, Edward. 1903. *American Tariff Controversies in the Nineteenth
    Century*. New York: Houghton Mifflin.
Stein, Herbert. 1988. *Presidential Economics: The Making of Economic Policy
    from Roosevelt to Reagan and Beyond*. Washington, DC: AEI.
Stewart, Charles, III, and Barry R. Weingast. 1992. "Stacking the Senate,
    Changing the Nation." *Studies in American Political Development*
    6:223–271.
Stimson, James A. 2004. *Tides of Consent: How Public Opinion Shapes
    American Politics*. New York: Cambridge University Press.
Sundquist, James L. 1968. *Politics and Policy: The Eisenhower, Kennedy and
    Johnson Years*. Washington, DC: Brookings Institution.
    1983. *Dynamics of the Party System: Alignment and Realignment of Political
    Parties in the U.S.* Washington, DC: Brookings Institution.
Swerdlow, Joel L. 1987. *Presidential Debates: 1998 and Beyond*. Washington,
    DC: Congressional Quarterly.
Taussig, Frank W. 1931. *A Tariff History of the United States*. New York: G. P.
    Putnam's Sons.
Tichenor, Daniel. J. 2002. *Dividing Lines: The Politics of Immigration Control
    in America*. Princeton, NJ: Princeton University Press.
Trubowitz, Peter. 1998. *Defining the National Interest: Conflict and Change in
    American Foreign Policy*. Chicago: University of Chicago Press.
Ware, Alan. 2006. *The Democratic Party Heads North, 1877–1962*. New York:
    Cambridge University Press.
Weiss, Nancy J. 1983. *Farewell to the Party of Lincoln: Black Politics in the Age
    of FDR*. Princeton, NJ: Princeton University Press.
Whalen, Charles, and Barbara Whalen. 1985. *The Longest Debate: A Legislative
    History of the 1964 Civil Rights Act*. Cabin John, Md.: Seven Locks Press.
Wildavsky, Aaron. 1965. "'The Goldwater Phenomenon': Purists, Politicians
    and the Two-Party System." *Review of Politics* 27(July): 386–413.
Williams, Phil. 1985. *The Senate and US Troops in Europe*. London:
    Macmillan.
Wilson, James Q. 1962. *The Amateur Democrat: Club Politics in Three Cities*.
    Chicago: University of Chicago Press.
Witte, John F. 1985. *The Politics and Development of the Federal Income Tax*.
    Madison: University of Wisconsin Press.
Wolbrecht, Christina. 2000. *The Politics of Women's Rights: Parties, Positions
    and Change*. Princeton, NJ: Princeton University Press.
    2002. "Explaining Women's Rights Realignment: Convention Delegates
    1972–1992." *Political Behavior* 24(3): 237–282.
Wolfinger, Raymond E., and David B. Filvaroff. 2000. "The Origin and Enactment
    of the Civil Rights Act of 1964." In *Legacies of the 1964 Civil Rights Act*,
    ed. Bernard Grofman. Charlottesville: University Press of Virginia.

Woodward, Bob. 1994. *The Agenda: Inside the Clinton White House.* New York: Simon and Schuster.

Wunderlein, Clarence E. (ed.). 2003. *The Papers of Robert A. Taft: Volume 3.* Kent, OH: Kent State University Press.

Zaller, John. 1992. *The Nature and Origins of Mass Opinion.* New York: Cambridge University Press.

2003. "Coming to Grips with V. O. Key's Concept of Latent Opinion." In *Electoral Democracy*, ed. Michael MacKuen and George Rabinowitz. Ann Arbor: University of Michigan Press.

Zangrando, Robert L. 1965. "The NAACP and a Federal Antilynching Bill, 1934–1940." *Journal of Negro History* 50(2): 106–117.

# Index